To hell w/ this book.
(says Kelly) — Don't
agree w/ it just in
case someone I love
finds it on my
bookshelf after I'm
gone.
Kari

HELL YES / HELL NO

What really is the extent of
God's grace . . . and wrath ?

JOHN NOĒ, Ph.D.

Hell Yes / Hell No

By John Noë, Ph.D.

Unless otherwise noted, all Scripture quotations are from the Holy Bible, *New International Version* © 1973, 1978, 1984 International Bible Society. Used by permission of Zondervan Bible Publishers.

Published by:

East2West Press
Publishing arm of the Prophecy Reformation Institute

5236 East 72nd Street
Indianapolis, IN 46250 USA
(317)-842-3411

Cover: Tom Haulter

ISBN: 978-0-9834303-1-5

Library of Congress Control Number: 2011931744

Bible. New Testament Revelation. Prophecy.

Dedication

To my Thursday morning Bible study group,
whose insistence, assistance, and perseverance
made this book possible.

To the many writers, past and present,
whom I quote extensively throughout this book.
I have drawn on your wisdom,
been blessed by your insights,
and gained from your disagreements.
I am standing on your shoulders.

To my wife, Cindy,
for her many and invaluable contributions
and her supportive posture for my endeavors,
especially this one.

To those over the years
who have read my books, listened to my teachings,
participated in my various Bible study groups,
and questioned, challenged, and encouraged me.

And to my pastor, Dave Rodriguez,
for his ear and encouragement as well.

I send forth this book with the hope and prayer that
its pro-and-con, argumentative interactions
and synthesis resolution
will advance "this conversation—very, very much."

(see p-25)

Contact Us:

EAST2WEST PRESS

Pioneering the next reformation

www.east2westpress.org

Publishing arm of . . .

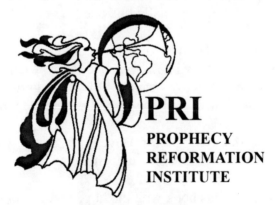

PRI

**PROPHECY
REFORMATION
INSTITUTE**

**5236 East 72nd Street
Indianapolis, IN 46250**
www.prophecyrefi.org
jnoe@prophecyrefi.org
Ph. # 317-842-3411

Contents

PART II: THE GREATER ISSUE CONTESTED

PART III: ANALYSIS OF CONFLICTING ARGUMENTS

Introduction

You've Gotta Be Kidding...
Right?

*H*ell *yes*!" What better way to kick off a serious book about a sobering subject, and as the cover suggests, a vast gray area of theology and controversy, than with a bit of light-hearted, hellacious humor?

Pickles by Brian Crane · · · · · · · · · · · · · · September 04, 2009

(*The Indianapolis Star*, 9/4/09)

But, "*hell no*," I'm not kidding; by *gosh*, hell is a *heck* of a problem. What images race through your mind when this subject comes up? How have those images influenced your life, positively or negatively? Have they affected the lives of others you know or love? Have those images and beliefs changed during your life? If so, how so? Has the idea of an eternal hell troubled, comforted, confused, worried, or delighted you? How have you grappled with it?

All joking aside, hell is a huge problem for a lot of people. Its terrifying and haunting concept has thoroughly permeated and embedded itself in almost all areas and aspects of our society. Nobody is immune. In her book, *Razing Hell*, author Sharon L. Baker characterized our modern-day obsession with hell this way: "Hell intrigues us, plagues us, causes us fearful discomfort, and begs us to think critically and honestly through its implications."[1] Furthermore, this attraction to and obsession for hell has been going on for centuries.

Fact is, every week in churches all around the world multiple millions sit snug in their pews believing that when they die they will go up a proverbial "fire escape" to heaven to spend an eternity of bliss with God because they are born again and saved. Meanwhile, the vast majority of humankind—untold billions of others—will go down the proverbial "stairs" from the "platform of life" into the flames of hell after they die because they have not believed in Jesus, repented and been forgiven for their sins, and are not Christians. There they will suffer awful, painful, and conscious punishment and torment, forever and ever, with no hope or chance of escape. Christians are further told and taught that this eternal punishment and torment glorifies God because "it serves divine justice."[2]

Baker cautions that "if you think these heinous representations of hell are horrific, take a look at these equally ghastly portraits of God, the mastermind behind this abysmal abyss." She quotes the famous Christian preacher, Jonathan Edwards (1741) as he rants and raves about "the God that holds you over the pit of hell, much as one holds a spider, or some loathsome insect over the fire, abhors you, and is dreadfully provoked: his wrath towards you burns like fire; he looks upon you as worthy of nothing else, but to be cast into the fire."[3]

Continually, Christians have been and are assured by their leadership of the certainty of these two opposite and other-worldly destinies. Hence, for most Christians, hell is an established fact, a core belief, and a foundational doctrine that's taken very seriously—or so it seems. It is, as Baker sarcastically points out, "part and parcel of the good news! . . . But when is anyone's eternal torment good news?"[4] For other Christians, hell is not so taken, but is considered to be a soul-sickening subject, whether it's a figurative "hell-on-earth" situation or going to a literal "hell" after this life is over.

Ironically, Muslims are taught exactly the opposite. It's Christians and all non-Muslims (the "infidels") and any Muslim who does not rigidly follow Islam who are going to burn in hell forever—no matter how pious and God-fearing they may have been during their earthly lives. In the Qur'an, the holy book of Islam, which was written five to six hundred years after the last book of the Bible, and draws from the Bible, one passage reads as follows, "The unbelievers among the People of the Book and the pagan shall burn forever in the fire of Hell. They are the vilest of all creatures" (Qur'an 98:1-8). The phrase "the People of the Book" refers specifically to Jews and Christians.

Several other world religions subscribe to a general belief in a hell-like "place or state inhabited by demons, where wicked people are punished after death."[5] For instance, "in Hinduism and Buddhism, a soul may descend into one of many hells as a result of wicked *karma* (thoughts, words, and deeds). The stay in hell is not eternal, however. It lasts only until the effects of the evil karma have been removed."[6]

Hell also has been graphically depicted in literature and art. The Roman Catholic Italian poet, Dante Alighieri's *Dante's Divine Comedy* is the most famous. Set in the year A.D. 1300, the figure of Virgil guides Dante through *The Inferno* and its "three divisions of Hell." These stand for "the three categories of . . . all the sins of the world"[7] Thus, the first part of Dante's *Comedy* "is a painful descent into Hell."[8] Details are elaborately described as Virgil and Dante descend deeper and deeper down into the earth through nine concentric rings or levels. The deeper they descend, the worse the punishments—where sinners are bitten by snakes, tormented by wild beasts, coated with icy rain, submerged in rivers of blood, trapped in flaming tombs—until they reach the center and find Satan himself trapped in a frozen lake. (Catch the irony—a frozen lake at the center of fiery hell?). Below are two excerpts to give you an introductory flavor for this famous piece of literature, which has significantly contributed to our traditional concepts of hell and its horrific nature:

> Therefore, for your own good, I think it well you follow me and I will be your guide and lead you forth through an eternal place. There you shall see the ancient spirits tried in endless pain, and hear their lamentation as each bemoans the second death of souls.[9]

(Sign on the gate to hell) – ABANDON ALL HOPE YE WHO ENTER
HERE. These mysteries I read cut into stone above a gate. And turning
I said: "Master, what is the meaning of this harsh inscription?"[10]

In 1855, European artist Gustave Doré illustrated the three afterlife
regions of Dante's *Divine Comedy* in 135 plates—"from the depths of
hell onto the mountain of purgatory and up to the empyrean realms of
paradise, Doré's illustrations depict the passion and grandeur of Dante's
masterpiece."[11] Doré's grotesque visual images of suffering and anguish
have horrified and haunted humankind ever since. In the 17th century,
controversial English poet John Milton set forth a similar presentation of
the eternal punishments of hell in his highly acclaimed epic, *Paradise
Lost*.

Exactly where hell is located, however, has not proven easy to pin
down. Whether this infernal region, or regions, reside deep down in the
middle of the earth as the ancients believed, on another planet
somewhere, between planets, in no particular place, or everywhere
heaven and/or God is not, neither our religious or heathen brethren are
quite sure. Nor is there agreement about who goes there, for how long,
what happens, and if there is any chance of escape. For instance, the
question of what happens to children dying without having been baptized
has plagued Catholics and Protestants for centuries. The irony of ironies,
however, is that many people who have real and severe problems with
afterlife beliefs about hell, as well as those who do not believe in hell at
all, readily and frequently use this word in everyday speech—usually in a
denigrating manner.

Hell Cursing and Slang

If we've heard it once, we've heard it a thousand times . . .

"YOU'RE GOIN' TO HELL!" "THE HELL I WILL! "GO TO
HELL!" "DAMN IT TO HELL!" "COME HELL OR HIGH
WATER!" "FOR THE HELL OF IT!" "ONE HELL OF A MESS!"
"ONE HELL OF A GAL/GUY!" "GOIN' TO HELL IN A
HANDBASKET!" "NOT UNTIL HELL FREEZES OVER!"
"YOU'RE GONNA CATCH HELL FOR THAT!" "TO HELL WITH
IT!" "IT'S HOTTER THAN HELL!" "IT'S COLDER THAN

HELL!" "LET'S GET THE HELL OUT OF HERE!" "WHAT THE HELL IS GOING ON?" "SHE'S MAD AS HELL!" "HELL YES!" "HELL NO!"

And on and on it goes as "hell has had a surprisingly prominent place in the popular imagination of cultures and religions around the world."[12]

Nowadays, the Bible is considered the primary source of "hell" proclamations, denunciations, and slang phrases. Another irony is the strong impression that hell (or the avoidance of) is the main tenet of Christianity, and Christians find a perverse pleasure in believing that all others get punished forever in that afterlife and permanent region of the lost. This traditional belief and afterlife curse is so ingrained in the collective consciousness of society that it is now variously and negatively termed:

- "One of Christianity's most offensive doctrines."[13]
- "The ultimately intolerant doctrine."[14]
- "Invented by church leaders to 'keep the people in line.'"[15]
- "Theology's H-word, a subject too trite for serious scholarship."[16]
- "It's like capital punishment for a traffic violation."[17]
- "There is no good news if there is no bad news."[18]

A recent article in *U.S. News & World Report* magazine titled "Hell Hath No Fury" highlighted the benefits that hell supposedly has provided the Church. "The threat of hell has served as a potent incentive to refrain from evil and cling to faith . . . . There was a hell to shun and a heaven to gain." It further acknowledged that hell has been "a potent theological weapon in the church's struggle against evil" and its "roots run deep in Judeo-Christian teaching." Professor Stephen J. Patterson of the Eden Theological Seminary in St. Louis, on the other hand, was quoted in dissent, "[A literal hell is] part of an understanding of the cosmos that just doesn't exist anymore."[19] Even evangelical traditionalists recognize that "Christianity's historic teaching on hell . . . . is now routinely dismissed as an embarrassing artifact from an ancient age—a reminder of Christianity's outdated worldview."[20]

Not surprisingly, while many TV and church evangelists, as well as stereotyped fire-and-brimstone preachers, pound on the pulpit, harp on the heaven-or-hell message, and threaten churchgoers with burning in an eternal hell if they don't come to Jesus, "many theologians and preachers . . . have downplayed or dropped the idea of hell."[21] Most non-Christians today scoff at the notion of hell and take a sarcastic "you've-gotta-be-kidding . . . right?" attitude. Nevertheless, the vast majority of today's proclamations of hell come from Christians reading their Bibles. In this book we are going to take a fresh but honest, objective, fair, and balanced new look at the totality of this belief system. We will do so from the biblical point of view.

Admittedly, we will be entering some new territory where few have trodden or mapped. We will be re-questioning and re-challenging issues and topics that have not been resolved for over 2,000 years. I, however, am not the first to undertake such an effort. Several Christian leaders and theologians throughout the church age (1st century A.D. to the present) have questioned whether a just and loving God would have created such a hell. Others have ambiguously claimed that "hell is not a real place but a symbol of the anguish caused by the loss of God or goodness."[22] Most Christians, however and rightfully, warn that "God has appointed us to faithfully deliver his message, not to compose and edit it."[23] So please be assured, this is exactly what we will do.

The vast majority of today's proclamations of hell come from Christians reading their Bibles.

As we proceed, I implore you to examine and weigh the evidence—both pro and con—on the various positions and arguments presented. Also, per the title of this book, I will be frequently asking you to decide, "hell yes" or "hell no." To facilitate your participation, I have tried to assemble the material covered herein in a logical and easy-to-follow manner. My sincere desire and motivation has been solely to seek truth and not to defend one position against all others. Hence, my bottom line for you is the same as it has been for me, and as Michael E. Wittmer well puts it, "whichever positions you eventually take, you'll at least be making informed decisions. . . . Our beliefs about heaven and hell are extremely important."[24]

WARNING: For some of you, this re-exploration may be unsettling. In his recent book, *Erasing Hell*, Francis Chan readily admits that "coming face-to-face with these passages on hell and asking these tough questions is a heart-wrenching process. . . . [because] this is not about doctrines; it's about destinies."[25] For others, however, this process will be exciting, rewarding, and a breath-of-fresh-air, as it has been for me. So, if you have been frustrated or disturbed with how hell and the greater issue of the eternal afterlife destiny of non-believers in Christ have been handled, not handled, or mishandled by the church, TV media (like documentaries on A&E or the History Channel), in news magazines and/or in books, this book is for you. I promise you, this will be an adventure of re-discovery.

Purpose and Scope

This book is written for intelligent readers without a formal theological education. It is not written for scholars, *per se*, although some contents may be pushing the boundary into academia. These portions I have included because they are necessary to particular arguments and issues.

The purpose of this book is to be a fair-and-balanced, scholarly re-exploration. Therefore, we will be asking tough questions and raising challenging arguments, pro and con and from all sides of the debate. To this author's knowledge, this type, degree, and breadth of approach has not been done before in the arena of this subject matter. Anyone, however, who thinks he or she already has the corner on truth on the topics we will be re-evaluating, is likely to become upset somewhere along this process. On the other hand, those of you who are open to an honest and sincere test of Scripture (per 1 Thessalonians 5:21, "Test everything. Hold on to the good" – also see Acts 17:11) have nothing to fear and should only be encouraged by my *modus operandi*.

My hopes are to clearly communicate and motivate you, as well as religious leaders, to better think through what you believe about these important subjects; to equip you with the biblical facts and historical perspectives you need to defuse fallacious beliefs; to encourage you to lead more effective and rewarding lives, here and now, and to prepare you for the then-and-there in the afterlife. My further hope is to break through into some new ground of understanding and consensus.

To make this presentation livelier, we will be interacting, throughout, with critical comments I have compiled over the years from both proponents and opponents of the different positions herein presented. Hence, this book's scope and format is as follows:

- **Part I** – We will re-examine what the Bible actually says about hell, reassess its scriptural viability, and expose the paucity of biblical support for this traditional belief and modern-day doctrine.

- **Part II** – We will go beyond hell and introduce the controversy over the related but greater issue of the extent of God's plan of salvation and condemnation—i.e., his love, grace, mercy, justice, and wrath—regarding who and how many people will be saved and go to heaven eventually vs. those condemned eternally. Then, we shall lay out the scriptural landscape of verses and logic employed by each side, as well as opposing objections, in this stand-off and stalemated dispute.

- **Part III** – We will re-evaluate, re-analyze, weigh, and score the strengths and weaknesses of the seven major areas of argumentation used in this debate over the afterlife and eternal destiny of nonbelievers. As we shall see, nonbelievers encompass two groups: 1) The un-evangelized—those who never heard of Jesus or the gospel during their earthly lives, or died as unborns, infants, young children, mentally disabled (or "cognitively challenged" – I'm told is the p.c. term), heathens, before or after Christ, and thus never had the gospel shared with them. 2) The evangelized—those who heard but rejected.

- **Part IV** – We will offer a solution of synthesis—one that meets with and reconciles the twelve demands of Scripture, as collectively used by each side, and explains how God *could, may* and *might* accomplish his stated will, desire, and purpose to bring all to salvation, eventually.

Once again, to my knowledge, no author, theologian, scholar, or other book has ever attempted anything of this scope of inquiry. No doubt, some critics will take a "you've-gotta-be-kidding . . . right?"

attitude and/or try to discredit me. They may dismiss me and this book outright without ever reading or wrestling with its contents or engaging the substance of my comparative presentations and arguments. Others will attack me more personally by calling into question or declaring outright that I am not or could not be a Christian. Sadly, as I have learned over the years, some people can be vicious toward anyone who does not conform to their version of orthodoxy. That's how they operate—no questioning, no testing, no dissent allowed.

Practically speaking, we are all capable of believing things that may not be true. Then when confronted by facts that prove us wrong, our first line of defense usually is to protect our position by ignoring, twisting, discrediting, and/or dismissing those facts. This common tendency relieves the pressure of a troubling cognitive dissonance. But the higher the stakes, the more consequences this denial-avoidance process produces. It does, however, prop up our sense of self-righteousness and allows us to sleep at night.

Another sad reality is, most churches won't allow the issues re-explored in this book to be discussed from the pulpit, in a Sunday school class, or even in a home Bible study group. The classic methodology employed for perpetuating their traditional beliefs in this regard has been to assert them, use one or two supportive verses, and move on. Everyone is expected to toe the line, believe it, and pass it along as is. In my opinion, this methodology is not only a form of censorship but also a display of arrogance. It's similar to the way most churches deal with end-time beliefs that do not match their own.[26]

Practically speaking, we are all capable of believing things that may not be true.

Consequently, whatever dialogue has existed in Christian circles about hell and the afterlife eternal destiny of all people has degenerated over time into "proof-text" debates. Each side gravitates to its batch of scriptures and ignores or tries to explain away the batch used by the other side. So, who's right? If you think you already know and are firmly convinced, you may be in for a few surprises in the pages ahead. You just may discover that God is more mysterious and wonderful than you've been led to believe or could have imagined.

But I believe that by utilizing the approach presented in this book we can make significant progress toward a better and more biblical understanding. You be the judge.

Two Simple Ground Rules

Please be assured, I am a conservative, evangelical, heaven-bound, saved, born-again, Bible-believing Christian who has spent most of my life in the church. I am not and have never been a liberal Christian. I hold to a very high view of Scripture and to the deity of Christ and the Trinity. I mention this specifically because some have jumped in the past, and no doubt will in the future, to a premature and false assumption about me even before reading a word of this book.

This tendency is so prevalent in Christian circles that whenever I begin a teaching series or Bible study with a new group, I always insist up-front that we agree on and commit to follow two simple ground rules or guidelines. I would ask that you and I do the same. They are appropriate here as well.

1). *Sola Scriptura* **("Only the Scriptures")** – I define *Sola Scriptura* to simply mean: what does the Bible say and not say (period). Not, how do you interpret this or that? Or, what do you think something means or have been told it means? Nor can we allow condescending nonsense like "what Jesus, Paul, or Peter *really* meant was . . . ."

As we "test everything" and "hold on to the good" (1 Thess. 5:21)— and this book's subject matter is certainly a part of "everything"— another aspect of *Sola Scriptura* we will employ is the basic hermeneutical (interpretive) tool or principle of "Letting Scripture interpret Scripture"—and not basing interpretation on today's newspaper, what your pastor believes, your church says, or what you've been told all your life.

Again, please be assured that while I'm completely committed to the authority of Scripture and the truth revealed in it, I admit that I'm skeptical (perhaps jaded) by what some church leaders and traditions have told us about a number of issues that will simply not stand up to an honest and sincere test of Scripture. Indeed, I've seen example after example of how the traditions of men can "nullify the word of God" and make it of little or "none effect" (Mark 7:13; Matt. 15:6 *KJV*). This is why, in my opinion, many have erred on other significant aspects of our faith—diluting, devaluing, diminishing, and depreciating it in the process. These other troubled traditions will have to remain topics for future books (see Future Books at the end of this book). Meanwhile, the issues we will be re-exploring in this book are too important to mishandle or misrepresent.

2). In Love – Discussions or debates (when allowed) on topics pertaining to the issues presented herein tend to be driven more by emotion than by Scripture (on all sides). And, we all tend to defend, repeat, and "Poly-parrot" what we've been told, taught, and have believed over the years, usually without ever critically thinking about it or checking it out thoroughly. Therefore, we must agree to treat each other in a civil manner with love and respect. Sadly, once again, my experience has been that some Christians cannot or will not do this. They treat those who disagree with them in an unkind, unloving, and un-Christ-like manner.

That's it. These are the only two ground rules or guidelines I insist on. They are simple, straightforward, and non-burdensome. But, as you will see, they are also profound. I suggest they will serve us well in the journey ahead. But again, you be the judge.

Into the Afterlife

For more than twenty years, I have been reading, researching, thinking, and collecting material and opinions about this issue of hell and the greater issue of the eternal afterlife destiny of non-believers and believers. During this time the one passage of Scripture I keep coming back to and to which I am still compelled to submit is Romans 11:33-36:

> *Oh, the depth of the riches of the*
> *wisdom and knowledge of God!*
> *How unsearchable his judgments,*
> *and his paths beyond tracing out!*
> *"Who has known the mind of the Lord?*
> *Or who has been his counselor?"*
> *"Who has ever given to God that God should repay him?"*
> *For from him and through him and to him are all things.*
> *To him be glory forever! Amen.*

And "*hell yes*," I'm perfectly willing and content to leave the issues we will be re-exploring—which I believe are part of "his unsearchable judgments"—fully and finally up to God and his sovereignty as Christ "works out everything in conformity with the purpose of his will" (Eph. 1:11b).

And, "*hell no*," or *heck* . . . by *gosh*, I'm not kidding about this. In the meantime, much that has been revealed can better inform us in these important areas of the Christian faith and theology. Unfortunately, much that has been revealed has also been covered back up again by centuries of man-made traditions and translation problems. Therefore, unlearning will be a necessary part of our learning process. And unlearning is the hardest part of learning.

But I like the dual perspective my longtime friend and radio talk show host of the *Voice of Reason*, the late John Anderson, always used to put on this relearning process . . .

"You've got to be willing to be wrong to be right."
(and)
"God doesn't fall off his throne because someone asks questions."

So if you are ready to re-open and stretch your mind, perhaps warm your heart, and honestly and sincerely re-consider some significant things, let us begin our adventure of re-discovery by re-exploring why "clearly, something is wrong."

PART I: DOES HELL REALLY EXIST?

Chapter 1

Clearly, Something Is Wrong

You're going to Hell!" heralds the unfurled, 5' x 7' banner atop a ten-foot high pole waving above the heads of the crowd. "Heaven or Hell?" queries a second banner. "Turn or Burn!" asserts a third.

Like most people most of the time, I try not to think or talk about hell. But on this day, my son and I and five of my grandchildren (ages 6-12 at the time) are side-by-side, hand-in-hand, trying to stay together in the midst of a slow-moving mass of humanity. Tightly compressed together, shoulder-to-shoulder, our feet shuffle along as the crowd funnels down toward a small gate two or three football fields away in the distance.

Were we really headed to hell as one of the banners proclaimed?

Hell no! We were among approximately 300,000 people and pressing our way down Georgetown Road, through one of the narrow gates, onto the grounds, and up into the stands, and into our seats for the Indianapolis 500-Mile Race that year.

For years, I have taken members of my family to the race. And nowadays I'm taking some of my thirteen grandchildren. They love it and look forward to it every year. And for several years, signs like these have been paraded high aloft by activist Christians and street preachers who really believe this (God bless them). They also pass out tracks explaining how to escape this disastrous fate and ultimate doom by turning to Jesus and believing in Him. Of course, we can question their effectiveness, but certainly not their sincerity.

But for centuries, the prospect and doctrine of going to hell has been a mainstay of the historic Christian church and faith. As Dinesh D'Souza succinctly put it in his book, *What's So Great about Christianity*, hell is considered "an essential part of the Christian scheme."[1] And these Bible-believing demonstrators are dedicated. They must be because they do suffer persecution from the verbal abuses and even a few tossed beer cans hurled at them by some in the slow-moving crowd of sometimes rowdy and/or semi-intoxicated race fans.

But let's picture and think about a different experience for a moment. Have you ever been burned by fire or touched something hot? How did it feel? Can you possibly imagine yourself (or anyone else) being burned over your/their whole body like this for an hour, a month, a year, or for millions of centuries and without any hope of relief—and all because God either predestined you/them for this destiny long before you/they were born and long before you/they had done anything good or bad, or because you/they were turned off by some Christian or church somewhere at some time and decided you/they wanted nothing to do with them or their religion?

For most of us, punishment in this *way* for this *long* is almost if not impossible to humanly imagine. Then there are the questions of: 1) How does this magnitude and duration of punishment fit the crime—i.e., infinite punishment for a finite offense? 2) What kind of a God creates and maintains an eternal hell? 3) Can you lose your salvation and end up in hell? More and more today, the answers to these questions, and others like them, seem to depend on who you ask.

Yet the "good news" of this type of an afterlife scenario in a "Godless hell" is what is being preached and presented in many churches (not all) and on most evangelical TV shows (not all) as "divine justice" from an all wise, all knowing, all loving, all merciful, and just God. Perhaps, you have observed congregations or program audiences laughing and enthusiastically applauding the notion that many not sitting there in the pews with them are going to burn forever in this afterlife place called "hell" and with no hope of escape. Tragically and incredulously, the vast majority of those sitting snug in their pews will never warn or even mention this soul-sickening destiny to anyone they think might be headed there. Clearly, something is wrong.

X Has no clue about the seriousness of sin & the offense to God.

An Almost Sacrilegious Question

No doubt, you too have heard some of the above proclamations and denunciations. Or, perhaps you've been exposed to or heard it said positively about some screaming preacher, "he's a strong hell-fire-and-brimstone preacher." And given most of our religious backgrounds, it seems almost sacrilegious to question if there really is such a place as "hell" with its awful and eternal horrors.

Some people, of course, think they have or are experiencing a literal (actually it would be figurative) "hell on earth" in their daily life. And factually speaking, there are all kinds of "hells" created by cruelty and injustices as part of this world's reality. But we are not talking about those kinds of "hells." We are talking about why God would predestine some people to an afterlife place of eternal conscious punishment or allow them to go there by their own freewill choice (another theological debate and conundrum within Christian circles). *Why does God allow suffering here?*

An additional modern-day fact is, this hell-centered message is at the forefront of evangelism methods and missions efforts. Some preachers preach on it, regularly—literally scaring the "hell" out of the people in the pews with thoughts of people screaming and suffering in a fiery lake and demons tormenting them with no relief or hope of escape.

A tragic consequence of this type of preaching occurred in Texas in 2001. Do you remember the name Andrea Yates? She became well known, internationally, for having drowned her five young children in the family bathtub (Noah 7, John 6, Paul 3, Luke 2, and Mary 6 months). During her trial she pleaded insanity and was found not guilty. The news media reported that a few years prior to these murders and after many years of counseling, her minister had chastised her and her husband contending that they were still "headed for hell." Then, after a nervous breakdown and two suicide attempts, Yates began to believe she was a "bad mother" who was damaging her children and it would be better to kill both herself and her children than to raise them to go to hell. She told her jail psychiatrist, "It was the seventh deadly sin. My children weren't righteous. They stumbled because I was evil. The way I was raising them, they could never be saved. They were doomed to perish in the fires of hell."[2] So she killed them before they reached the supposed age of accountability in an attempt to save them from this eternal fate.

This can't be attributed solely to preaching re: hell!

Other preachers, on the other hand, only occasionally mention hell, and not nearly as much as they used to. Some never mention it at all, anymore. Seems hell is just too terrible, embarrassing, or politically incorrect. But evangelicals argue that hell cannot be repudiated "without altogether repudiating Christ." And though "hell is dreadful . . . it is not evil." It "is moral because a good God must punish evil."[3] Another meekly volunteers that "all I know is that from my best understanding of Scripture, hell is a real place for those who choose to reject God."[4]

So, how is this message of heaven-or-hell working out here in America? According to pollster George Barna:

- "76 percent of Americans believe in heaven, and 71 percent believe in hell.
- Only 32 percent believe that hell is 'an actual place of torment and suffering.'
- 40 percent believe it is 'a state of eternal separation from God's presence.'
- 64 percent believe that they will go to heaven,
- Only 0.005 percent believe that they will be sent to the flames."

U.S. News and World Report (31 Jan. 2000) generally agreed. Their survey showed that:

- "64 percent of Americans think there is a hell.
- 25 percent don't.
- And 9 percent don't know.
- More believed in hell in 2000 than did in 1990 or in the 1950s."[5]

A 2008 Pew Forum on Religion and Public Life survey "showed that 59 percent of Americans believe in hell as a place of eternal punishment for all those who did not repent of their sin. . . . Although this number has decreased from 71 to 59 percent over the last decade."[6]

Regardless of which survey is more accurate, these results show how deeply entrenched traditional views of hell still are. And given the 0.005 percent figure above, one must wonder how effective of a deterrent the threat of an eternal hell really is? Another paradoxical fact is, hell is one of the main reasons most Christians are so lackadaisical about their

Fact ? ^

biblical responsibility and disinclined to share their faith with other people. One would think the opposite would be true—that if they really believed in hell, you couldn't stop them from constantly warning their family, friends, relatives, everyone about it and explaining how to avoid being burned in the flames. Then why don't most Christians do this?

What If?

When I was growing up in the church and for many years in adult life, it never occurred to me to question the widespread belief in hell, or in heaven, or in anything I was being told and taught. But consider this scenario. *What if* you suddenly woke up some morning and discovered there is no such place as our presently conceived and traditionally understood afterlife concept of "hell?"

- How would that affect you, your faith, and your relationship with God?
- How would that affect your relationship with other Christians and with non-believers?
- How do you think this would affect the Church and the world?
- Might you be really ticked off, or what?

These questions, most likely, would precipitate other questions like:

- Then why am I a Christian?
- Why attend church?
- Why bother with Jesus?
- Why share our faith with others?
- What is Christianity all about?
- Have we been scared into becoming Christians?
- Are we being intimidated with threats of hell and promises of heaven to keep us in line?
- If there is no hell, what happens to Christian morality?
- Why not just live it up?—after all, "what the hell!"
- Does anything make any sense any more?

Another fact today is, many people don't want to think about hell let alone talk about it or study it. The reason is, they have family or friends who have died and didn't believe in Christ. Or, they know others who are still alive, and don't so believe, and who will be going there someday. It's a real problem. They cannot imagine enjoying the pleasures of heaven knowing that their mother, father, brother, sister, children, or best friend will be suffering everlasting and unimaginable tortures in hell. So they ignore and avoid the subject. Others, like Andrea Yates, develop obsessive fears of being damned to hell and experience mental health problems in trying to cope with their fears.

Conservative theologian, Wayne Grudem, attempts to elaborate on this defensive-behavioral tendency thusly:

> The reason it is hard for us to think of the doctrine of hell is because God has put in our hearts a portion of his own love for people created in his image, even his love for sinners who rebel against him . . . . it should cause us great distress and agony of spirit to think about eternal punishment. Yet we must also realize that whatever God in his wisdom has ordained and taught in Scripture is *right*.[7]

Edwin Lutzer, senior pastor of the Moody Church in Chicago, has developed an interesting response to the question of how can we "be happy in heaven if one or more of our relatives is in hell?" Before answering, he notes that this question has "vexed the minds of theologians." Then he suggests that "in heaven God will blank out a part of our memory. The child will not know that his parents are lost in hell; the mother will not remember that she had a son."[8] I don't know about you, but I do not find Lutzer's bit of non-scriptural speculation consoling. Rather, I find it quite dissatisfying.

But Brian Jones in his recent evangelistic book, *Hell Is Real (But I Hate to Admit It)*, not only believes that "hell is real," he also contends that this "changes everything." He's convinced "that if we were to truly believe in hell, there would be no cost too high, no sacrifice too great, no pain too unbearable to keep us from doing everything in our power to convince people of this reality and show them the way out." He concludes that "to live any other way would be unthinkable. . . . immoral. . . . heinous."[9] He laments, however, that "most Christians I meet either don't believe that their non-Christian friends are going to hell, or worse, don't care."[10]

Fifteen or so years ago, when I started asking these "what if" questions, several Christian leaders cautioned me that it was poison to do this. If I pursued this train-of-thought, they warned, I'd be banned from teaching in the church, shunned, and dis-fellowshipped by most evangelical Christians. Since I didn't want that to happen, I mostly kept these questions to myself for years. But I did continue to read, research, and collect material on the subject.

Then, in 2001, I made my first exception. During my doctoral program, I wrote a paper for my course in Romans and titled it "The 'All' Controversy." Only two people saw this paper—my wife, who proof-read all my papers, and my professor. He gave me an "A" and a perfect "100 out of 100" points. He also notified me of his stance on this topic with this short handwritten note, "Though I may not agree with your conclusion, I find your research and reasoning to be thorough and engaging. And that's my ultimate basis for the high mark." Such is the positive nature of academic freedom to search out and question even sacrosanct, controversial ideas. And I was encouraged by my grade and his comments. But, sad to say, this type of freedom and latitude does not exist in most churches.

So I did nothing more with this material, until 2009. That's when a weekly Bible study and discussion group I was leading insisted I take them through it. After much repeated persistence on their part, I relented. But I insisted on two conditions. One, we close the group (no new attendees). Two, no recordings or handouts, and everything would be strictly confidential. They also agreed that they would not divulge where or from whom they were getting this information. So, and for the first time, I pulled all my fifteens years or more of collected materials and research together, organized it, and went through it with them. Subsequently, and based on their affirming response and encouragement, I decided to turn that 13-week series into this book. Some of you will be pleased I did. Others of you may not be so pleased.

But please be assured, I am acutely aware that the contents of this book will be met with resistance from some, perhaps many, in the Christian community. No doubt, I will be castigated, perhaps demonized. Such is the nature of theological discourse and reform on controversial and provocative issues. Church history is full of this tumult.

A Bit of Hard-core Reality

If you are a Bible-reading and -believing Christian like me, you may be a little shocked by this bit of hard-core reality. I was the first time I discovered it. Here's how I introduced this dose of hard-core reality to my aforementioned weekly Bible study and discussion group.

I showed them one of Reverend Billy Graham's recent, nationally syndicated newspaper columns in which a reader inquired of the much-revered evangelist, "After we die will God give us a second chance to believe in Jesus and go to heaven?" In his response, Dr. Graham first assured the reader that "not one word in the Bible suggests that there will be a second chance after death . . . ." He then affirmed that "once this life is over, you will go into eternity – either to that place of eternal joy the Bible calls heaven, or that place of eternal sorrow and separation from God that the Bible calls hell."[11]

Next, I gave them this short numerical exercise. I asked each one to write down this series of numbers on a piece of paper: 570, 54, 32, 14, 13, and 0. Then I asked two questions:

1) Does the Bible ever "call" or literally mention "heaven?"

Correct answer: YES! There are **570 matches** in the original King James Version for original language words translated as "heaven."[12] And Scripture takes us to heaven—describing it in Isaiah 6, Daniel 7, and Revelation 4, 5, 6, for instance. The Apostle Paul also talks about a man he knew who was caught up to the "third heaven." There is no disagreement about any of this.

2) Do you know what the Bible "calls," says, or literally mentions about "hell"?

Correct answer: **NOTHING! ZERO!** And Scripture never takes us to hell by describing it to us. My group stared at me like a tree full of owls. Moreover, not everyone agreed. After all, many scholars confidently assure us that "Hell is vividly described in the pages of the New Testament."[13]

Next, I shared this tidbit and explained this absence with my group, this way. The Italians have a saying, "traduttore, traditore." It literally means, "translator, traitor." Or more freely, "all translators are traitors." In this vein, I showed them a revealing statistic in the form of a graphic illustration regarding translation matches for the word "hell" throughout both the Old and New Testaments in a few notable translations, along with their original publication dates:

54 matches in the original King James Version (1611)
32 matches in the New King James Version (1982)
14 matches in the New International Version (1978)
13 matches in the New American Standard Bible (1971) and American Standard Version (1901)
0 matches in Young's Literal Translation (1862)—i.e., the word "hell" is not found once.

What's going on? I asked. Why such great discrepancy among Bible translations? Do you see a trend here or sense a problem? Clearly, in my opinion, these differences indicate something is wrong, or at least changing. So, are any of these translators traitors, as the Italian saying goes?

As we will soon see, the reason for this variance from 54 to zero is . . . there are no equivalent Hebrew words in the Old Testament or Greek words in the New Testament for the present-day term, concept, and eternal place of damnation variously and differently translated (or perhaps mistranslated) as "hell."

One hell critic explains this disparity this way:

> If 150 scholars swear to a statement of faith that there is a Hell of everlasting punishment before they are allowed to work on a translation which they will be paid to produce, what are the odds that the translation will contain a Hell of everlasting punishment? (That is the case with the NIV, and most other Bible translations produced by committees.)[14]

Yes, this major inconsistency is a huge and troubling problem. It is ignored or denied by most scholars. Clearly, however, something is wrong—very wrong. And I certainly want to be cautious and careful here. Jones' admonition in this regard is well worth consideration: "there's something even worse than that. . . . We can influence another Christian to stop believing in hell."[15]

Hell under Fire!

Today, the message of hell is under fire, so-to-speak, as never before, and mostly from within Christianity's own ranks. Respected Anglican theologian N.T. Wright in his recent book, *Surprised by Hope*, acknowledges this present-day phenomenon: "In today's church is, I think, a confused combination of several things. For one, the old heaven-and-hell view has been under attack." [16]

Leading the attack are liberal-leaning Christian authors who cannot fathom how a loving God would send multibillions of people to an eternal destiny of doom and damnation. Many of them deny that hell even exits at all.

- **Timothy Keller**, for instance, in his plain-talk, popular 2008 book, *The Reason for God*, and in a chapter appropriately titled, "How Can a Loving God Send People to Hell?" simply concludes in this chapter's subheads that "a God of Judgment simply can't exist . . . . can't be a God of love . . . . a loving God would not allow hell . . . . [and] I believe in a God of Love."[17] But in another book in 2011, and as one of several contributors and in a seemingly contradictory manner, he "provides suggestions for talking about hell amidst a tolerance loving culture"[18] and advises that "to preach the good news, we must also preach the bad."[19]

- Well-known, emergent-church spokesman **Brian McLaren** is another example. On the back cover of his book titled, *The Last Word and the Word After That*, an endorser explains McLaren's encrypted title. "The last word . . .is hell. . . . after that word, there is still the word of divine grace and forgiveness that overrides all the threat." Inside, McLaren volunteers that "perhaps intuitively, we have known that something is wrong and so we've backed off until we figure out the problem—or until some foolhardy person ventures to do so for us." That "foolhardy person" would be yours truly.

Next, he raises these searching but tradition-troubling questions:

> "Is there a better alternative?
>
> Could our views of hell . . . be the symptoms of a deeper set of problems?
>
> [Such as]—misunderstandings about what God's justice is, misunderstandings about God's purposes in creating the world, deep misunderstandings about what kind of person God is?"

McLaren surmises that "a great many people do, in fact, need this conversation—very, very much."[20] And I agree. Hopefully, the book you now hold in your hands does and will advance "this conversation—very, very much."

- **Sharon L. Baker** chimes in with her provocatively titled book, *Razing Hell: Rethinking Everything You've Been Taught about God's Wrath and Judgment*. Baker offers readers "an alternative and biblical view of hell" in an attempt to help those "who just couldn't harmonize the knowledge of the love of God through Jesus with the image of God as a merciless judge who sends billions of people to hell."[21] Her alternative view is simply "different ways of thinking about hell that are consistent with a God of love, justice, mercy, and compassion, who desires the salvation of all creation (1 Tim. 2:4)." But she also acknowledges upfront that she has "no intention of doing away with hell," simply saying, "I can't."[22] So, she offers a view of hell that is not eternal but temporal for every unbeliever as they go through varying durations of time and amounts of "restorative" or "reconciling justice" before they all eventually go to heaven. This is contrasted with the traditional view of an eternity of "retributive justice" (i.e., punishment and vengeance).[23] It is during this time, "when a person is brought face-to-face with his or her sins and experiences the unexpected grace of forgiveness rather than the expected retributive punishment," that she suggests, "real repentance may occur."[24] She bases her alternative view upon the claim that "reconciling rather than retributive justice is also a major theme in the New Testament."[25] Baker terms this solution "a view of hell that conquers evil with love, that wins the battle with sin by winning over the heart of the sinner, solves the problem of evil and suffering in the face of a loving, powerful God." Thus, "no one ever finds oneself beyond God's grace."[26] She concludes, "With our alternative view of hell, we maximize the powerful effectiveness of the cross. Jesus wins the final and absolute victory over evil and death. He breaks the power of sin. He fully, completely, absolutely accomplishes God's mission to reconcile the world to himself. Glory to God—truly!"[27] In essence, Baker's book offers "a more hospitable view of hell."[28]

• This next book is the proverbial "800-pound gorilla in the room." It is titled, *Love Wins: A Book About Heaven, Hell, and the Fate of Every Person Who Ever Lived* (HarperOne, 2011) and is authored by mega-church, "evangelical" pastor **Rob Bell**. Its significance lies not in its content, which is rather light, but in the massive amount of controversy it has stirred up in evangelical Christian circles and the feeding frenzy it has created in the media.

One prominent blogger characterizes Bell's book this way: It "addresses one of the most controversial issues of faith—the afterlife—arguing that a loving God would never sentence human souls to eternal suffering." In other words, "Bell puts hell on trial."[29] But like McLaren's and Baker's books above, Bell also assumes the validity of hell. He just provides a rather weak theological treatment of this topic. In his Preface, he even admits that "nothing in this book hasn't been taught, suggested, or celebrated by many before me" and "said an untold number of times."[30] And Bell is correct about that—his book adds nothing. It only stirs the pot, but it has done so quite effectively, having ignited a firestorm of controversy. Below is a small sampling of heated anti-Bell responses:

One **theological reviewer** charges Bell with "cherry-picking certain Scriptures and ignoring others . . . hoodwinking people into believing half-truths which are all the more dangerous because they sound so reasonable."[31]

The Washington Times claims that "controversial author Rob Bell wants to change what it means to be Christian. . . . with the implication that there is no hell. Thus . . . he throws out the doctrine of salvation and the necessity for Christ's death on the cross for our sins. . . . Such views are not Christian, nor are they evangelical. . . . Mr. Bell's new packaging has fooled many readers who do not recognize that his theology follows mainline liberalism."[32]

Christianity Today reports that Bell's book "set Twitter on fire with both speculation and condemnation," such as . . . "Bell is no longer evangelical, or orthodox, or maybe even Christian." It cites "eternal, conscious punishment" as being "the nearly unquestioned doctrine of the church from the beginning" and dismisses "alternatives to the standard view" as only having "cropped up here and there, and not more so in the last couple of centuries . . . . a decidedly minority view in church history and contemporary evangelicalism." And yet, somewhat amazingly, *CT* recommends "that frank, honest, theological exchange should . . . take place."[33]

World magazine calls Bell's book "A MARKETING COUP" and notes that his publisher, HarperCollins "dubs Bell 'the most vibrant, central religious leader of the millennial generation'" and that *Time* magazine pictures him "a singular rock star in the church world." Others, however, argue that Bell "is moving farther and farther away from anything resembling biblical Christianity. . . . promotes 'universalism'" and "so dilutes Christian teachings on salvation and the afterlife that what remains is no longer Christian at all." Not surprisingly, "many

secular publications, including *The New York Times* and CNN,
gave Bell's book favorable publicity." But despite the clamor,
Bell continues to insist he is "not a universalist" and "Christ
alone is the means of redemption." *World* summarizes Bell's
tome as "just a reissue of the powerless message of theological
liberalism."[34]

Time magazine's front cover, April, 25, 2011 issue, headlined:
"WHAT IF THERE'S NO HELL? – A popular pastor's best-
selling book has stirred fierce debate about sin, salvation and
judgment." In the six-page, inside article titled, "Is Hell Dead?"
writer, Jon Meacham, believes the reason Bell's book "has been
especially controversial among Evangelical Christians" is
"because it comes from one of their own." R. Albert Mohler, Jr.,
president of the Southern Baptist Theological Seminary is quoted
as terming Bell's book "theologically disastrous" and elaborating
that "when you adopt universalism . . . then you don't need the
church, and you don't need Christ, and you don't need the cross.
This is the tragedy of non-judgmental mainline liberalism, and
it's Rob Bell's tragedy in this book too." Bell is next quoted as
saying, "I have long wondered if there is a massive shift coming
in what it means to be a Christian . . . . Something new is in the
air." Meacham astutely concludes that "this is what has many
traditional Evangelicals worried" and that "the ferocity of the
reaction suggests that he [Bell] is a force to be reckoned with."[35]

In a short, follow-up article in the next weekly issue of *Time*,
Meacham terms Bell's book, "interesting stuff . . . but hardly
notable in the world of theology" even though "Bell's questions
cut to the heart of a faith." He concludes, "lots of us be watching
to see how Bell's story unfolds."[36]

The practical reality is, the unprecedented controversy and strong
reactions surrounding this book from fellow evangelicals has propelled
Love Wins to best-seller-list status.[37] And yet its content is theologically
lightweight and at best a stream-of-consciousness rambling with no
coherent arguments, objective points, or solutions presented. But the
burr-under-the saddle, so to speak and as charged by evangelical author,

radio talk-show host, and head of the Christian Research Institute, Hank Hanegraff, is Bell has "opened the door to Universalism"[38]

What's next? A rash of Bell-blasting, counter-attacking-response books from major Christian publishers and bestselling evangelical authors are underway and scheduled for release this summer (see below). No doubt, they will accuse Bell of becoming a theological liberal and of betraying his evangelical position.

Next in the heat-of-attack action are conservative but lesser-known Christian authors who claim that hell will not prevail because God will eventually annihilate all unbelievers—i.e., at some point in time in the afterlife they will cease to exist in any form—spirit, soul, or body. Two notable books from this perspective are:

- *The Fire That Consumes: A Biblical and Historical Study of the Doctrine of Final Punishment* by Edward W. Fudge (Houston, TX.: Providential, 1982; Backinprint.com, Nov. 2000).
- *Two Views of Hell: A Biblical and Theological Dialogue* by Edward Fudge and Robert Peterson (Downers Grove, IL.: InterVarsity Press, 2000) – a side by side presentation and critique of the annihilationist view and the traditional view. We'll evaluate the annihilationist view in Chapter 12.

Third in the attack-on-hell scenario are the unabashed Universalists—a renegade, heresy-labeled group that believes everyone will be saved and go to heaven, eventually. Although the Internet offers a few websites dedicated to this view, little has been trade-published. Four minor exceptions are:

- *A Wilderness in God's Mercy: The Finality of Jesus Christ in a World of Religions* by Clark H. Pinnock (Grand Rapids, MI.: Zondervan, 1992).
- *Flame of Love* by Clark H. Pinnock (Downers Grove, IL.: InterVarsity Press, 1996).
- *Universal Salvation? The Current Debate* edited by Robin A. Parry & Christopher H. Partridge (Grand Rapids, MI.: Eerdmans, 2003).

- *The Evangelical Universalist: The biblical hope that God's love will save us all* by Gregory MacDonald (Great Britain, Society for Promoting Christian Knowledge, 2008).

On the other side and fiercely fighting back are tradition-upholding, conservative, evangelical, Christian scholars with dogmatic and defensive tomes like:

- *Hell Under Fire* by Christopher W. Morgan and Robert A. Peterson, (Grand Rapids, MI.: Zondervan, 2004), is a collection of essays from nine Christian scholars. Its back cover starts off by asking, "Whatever happened to hell?" and admitting that "the historic doctrine of hell has been contested since the Enlightenment. [But] the past fifty years have witnessed a new and unsettling development. Attacks that used to come from outside the church are now coming from within."[39] Hence, this book sets out to staunchly defend the traditional view that hell does exist and is a place of eternal conscious punishment. Additionally, it counterattacks the challenges of "two aberrations: universalism and annihilationism"[40] insisting that there is no second chance to "escape the consequences of sin." Escape "is possible only in this life" and "people who die in their sin will never leave hell."[41]

- *Sense & Nonsense About Heaven & Hell* by Kenneth D. Boa and Robert M. Bowman Jr. (Grand Rapids, MI.: Zondervan, 2007) unintentionally but rightly proclaims another truism about this attack and ongoing debate in its title. That is, each side claims its position is the "sense" side and labels anything that opposes its position as "nonsense." Yet these authors admit that "what some Christians think about the fate of the un-evangelized is bound to be inaccurate, since there is a diversity of views on the subject among Christians"[42] and "many people today find the very idea of Hell offensive and assume it was invented by church leaders to 'keep the people in line.'"[43] To top things off, they "admit that we don't know with certainty the answers to all of the questions people ask on this subject."[44] As we shall see, this is a major admission.

- ***One Minute After You Die*** by Erwin W. Lutzer (Chicago, IL.: Moody Press, 1997). This senior pastor of the Moody Church in Chicago also begins his defense of the traditional view by admitting that "hell is an unpleasant topic. Unbelievers disbelieve in it; most Christians ignore it. Even the staunchly biblical diehards are often silent out of embarrassment. Hell, more than any doctrine of the Bible, seems to be out of step with our times . . . . it is difficult to reconcile hell with the love of God . . . . The doctrine of hell has driven many people away from Christianity."[45] He further concedes, "to us the punishment of hell does not fit the crime . . . nothing that anyone has ever done can justify eternal torment."[46] But then, and somewhat inconsistently, he proceeds to defend the traditional view.

Next, is a batch of "Rob-Bell-response and countering" books that have just been released:

- ***God Wins: Heaven, Hell, and Why the Good News Is Better than Love Wins*** by *Christianity Today's* senior managing editor, Mark Galli (Tyndale, July 2011). With a title obviously playing off of Rob Bell's title, Galli presents a "penetrating critique."[47] He attempts to show "how the *Love Wins* version of the Good News is actually bad news" by offering a "biblical and historical . . . . foundation" to Bell's "attractive book heavy on feelings but light on biblical and historical reasoning." He criticizes *Love Wins* for asking "hundreds of questions" but offering "few answers."[48] He concedes, however, that "*Love Wins* is definitely a provocative book"[49] and the questions it raises "get at the heart of some of the most theologically troubling issues in the Christian faith."[50] Unfortunately, its "answers are difficult to grasp."[51] He proposes that "the Bible is much clearer than *Love Wins* lets on" and that Bell's book "does not do justice to the Bible's grand narrative; it is simply not an adequate reflection of the historic Christian faith . . . ."[52] What *Love Wins* is, is a book that "uses arguments favored by liberals" and "is so anxious to show that love wins, it fails to appreciate how important it is that justice also wins"[53] Furthermore, its "arguments . . . on hell" are "the most incoherent in the book."[54] Therefore, "the so-called

Christian story that *Love Wins* sets up is a distortion"[55] and is "most aligned" with "universalism: the teaching that all people will eventually be saved."[56] But on the positive side, Galli is "glad for the conversation that *Love Wins* has started."[57]

- ***Erasing Hell: What God Said about Eternity and the Things We Make Up*** by bestselling author and former pastor of the mega-church, Cornerstone Church in Simi Valley, California, Francis Chan and Preston Sprinkle (David C. Cook, July 2011). This is a big-time book, by a big-name pastor, and with a first printing run of 250,000 and a six-figure marketing budget. It's written in Chan's voice and is billed as "a model of careful biblical scholarship" that "accurately and clearly" reflects "the biblical teaching on heaven, hell, and eternal destiny."[58] Disappointingly, however, Chan begs off doing a thorough job citing that "we don't have time or space to cover every passage used to support Christian Universalism, so we'll take a look at a few of the big ones."[59] He cites only four. When explaining why "'all' doesn't mean every single person," he merely maintains that "you've got to figure out from the context what 'all' means."[60] Likewise and adamantly, he asserts that the only way to avoid hell is "through the blood of Jesus in *this life*." He sums his book up by acknowledging that "there are some passages in the New Testament that seem to say everyone will be saved. But after looking at the context, we see that these passages probably don't mean this" because "this would contradict many other passages . . . ."[61] He reinforces his position by assuring his readers that "the Bible does not say that there will be a second chance after death."[62] To be fair, he notes that "in his book *Love Wins*, Bell never actually comes out and says that this is what he believes." But "he [Bell] implies the view that all people will eventually be saved is actually much better news."[63] Chan concludes that "hell is for real." Then introspectively asks, "*Am I?*"[64]

- ***Christ Alone: An Evangelical Response to Rob Bell's Love Wins*** by Grand Rapids Theological Seminary professor, Michael E. Wittmer (Edenridge Press, April 2011). This third response book is characterized by one endorser as "a gracious, respectful biblical and theological engagement with *Love Wins*" that should "help readers discern the strengths and weaknesses of Rob Bell's positions."[65] Michael S. Horton in this book's Preface terms Bell's book "a wake-up call" as he recognizes that it "has sparked remarkable controversy" but also that "he's not the first evangelical to have challenged traditional Christian teaching on hell."[66] *Christ Alone* is then pitched as the "corrective."[67] In a similar manner, Wittmer starts off by claiming "I respect Rob Bell" and acknowledging that "he wrote *Love Wins* to start a dialogue about the most important issues of our faith, and this book is my attempt as an evangelical to join that conversation."[68] His *modus operandi* is "to reassess the subject of hell," which he insists is "impossible . . . without also reevaluating our beliefs about Scripture, God, sin, Jesus, the cross, and salvation."[69] Consequently, the vast majority of his book is taken up with a rehash of the orthodox and traditional Christian view on these subjects as Wittmer hopes "to persuade" his readers "to side with what the Scriptures and the church have historically said about these issues."[70] He concludes, in an accusatory fashion however, that "Bell's wishful words may unwittingly lead more people to hell" since Bell "assures them that they will have numerous chances to be 'saved' after they die . . . [and] even be able to leave hell if they want."[71] Hence, Wittmer warns that "its easy for readers to become so excited over the promise of postmortem salvation (a second chance after death) that they might not ask some basic questions" . . . [like] Is it true?"[72] He charges that "Bell offers no biblical passages which promise postmortem salvation, and his arguments from what universalistic texts supposedly imply isn't persuasive either."[73] When all this is combined with "Bell's diminished view of hell" what you end up with is "the start of a slippery slope" toward liberalism and the dismissal of "a high view of Scripture." Obviously, this position presents major "implications for one's view of God" Himself.[74] Thus, according to Wittmer, Bell is advocating a "weak-kneed version of Christianity."[75] Eventually, he asks, "Is Rob Bell a universalist?" He doesn't answer but points out that "this question has sparked most of the controversy over *Love Wins*."[76]

And yet, "Bell is careful not to unequivocally endorse universalism, but he clearly admires its belief . . . ."[77] But, Wittmer charges that "I also think it's fair to call Bell a 'functional universalist.'. . . And . . . there is no practical difference between full-on universalism and Bell's 'functional' or 'incipient' kind."[78] Hence, he summarizes that *"Love Wins* aims to open the door to salvation as wide as possible."[79]

- ***Hell Is Real (But I Hate to Admit It)*** by Brian Jones (David C. Cook, August 2011). This is the only response book that does not specifically mention Rob Bell or *Love Wins*. Its theme is simply: "hell is real" and "it is within your power to help people avoid going there."[80] Its content is basically an evangelistic guide that is filled with practical ways to show non-believing friends and family how to avoid hell and get to heaven—verses "simply telling someone they're going to hell," which Jones claims "isn't evangelism."[81] This book's endorsers note that while "many are trying to do away with hell [like Bell], Jones accepts its reality without compromise." They also bill it as "a welcome antidote to this heresy" and proclaim it is "sound biblical teaching" and an "often humorous account of why there is a hell."[82] Interestingly, this author confesses that he was once a Christian who was not a believer in hell. But he saw the light when he "discovered . . . the New Testament's teaching about hell is not an ambiguous topic supported by a few hard-to-understand passages." But rather, "it is inescapable" and "virtually every book in the New Testament underscores some aspect of the reality of hell." Additionally, he admits that he could no longer "discount what Jesus taught about hell."[83] Hence, the title for this book, *"Hell is real."*[84] But he also concedes, "I still have doubts about hell from time to time."[85] His prayer and ultimate purpose for his book "is for God to so disturb you by what you read in the following pages that it will be impossible for your life to go back to the way you live it before."[86]

• ***Is Hell for Real? Or Does Everyone Go To Heaven?***
(Zondervan, July 2011), is a short 83-page compilation of essays
from "several trusted pastors and theologians" [i.e., prominent
evangelicals]. It begins by noting that "traditional Christian
teaching on hell is under fire,"[87] "unpopular" and viewed as
"narrow-minded and intolerant."[88] As evidence, it cites the *Time*
magazine cover story, "What if there's no hell?" which was
sparked by Rob Bell's book "questioning hell." So this book's
stated purpose is to answer the question, "Would our public
witness and our faithfulness to the God of love be better off
without hell?" Not surprisingly, "the contributors conclude that
the church's historic teaching on hell must be maintained,"
because it is "central to a right understanding of God, the gospel,
humanity, and the purpose of life." Thus, the publisher hopes
"this book will provide readers with a simple, brief, and biblical
explanation and defense of hell."[89] In its chapter on
Universalism, and especially Christian Universalism, it
pejoratively characterizes this belief as "a speculative
hypothesis" and an attempt "to be wiser than the Word of God."
It further claims that this view will "not stand up to biblical
examination" and "wholly misses the tragic quality of human
sin, human unbelief, and human death set forth in the Bible."
Likewise, it inevitably weakens "the motive for evangelism" and
"is subversive of the church's mission." Hence, Christian
Universalism, which "reinvents" and "distorts, biblical teaching
about God and salvation, . . . needs to be actively opposed."[90]
Instead, what needs to be share "around the world" is "the whole
counsel of God—including hell—with Christians and non-
Christians alike."[91]

Lastly, are people who attest to having had a vision or mystical
experience of heaven or hell, or claim they died and actually went to one
of these places for a short stay and came back. These so-called personal
experiences are a dime a dozen. Some have capitalized on their so-called
experience and written major *New York Times* best-selling books.
Recently, these include:

90 Minutes in Heaven by Don Piper with Cecil Murphy (Revel, 2004)
My Time in Heaven by Richard Sigmund (Whitaker House, 2009)
Nine Days in Heaven by Dennis & Nolene Prince (Charisma House, 2011)
The Boy Who Came Back from Heaven (ThomasNelson, 2011)
23 Minutes in Hell by Bill Wiese (Charisma House, 2006)
A Divine Revelation of Hell by Mary K. Baker (Whitaker House, 1997)

But basing our theology or beliefs about the afterlife on these kinds of experiences is not a good idea. First, we have no way of knowing who is credible and who is not. Secondly, there are natural, as opposed to supernatural, explanations for this phenomenon (also called NDEs – near-death experiences), such as: a vivid dream, an overactive imagination, drug-induced hallucinations, or clinically dead psychosomatic physiology (i.e., a chemical by-product of a dying brain). Interestingly, only a small percentage of these reports are of the hellish nature. In most, people report having gone to a place of light and peace rather than to a place of torment and suffering.

If, on the other hand, the cases in which people reportedly went to hell are real and genuine experiences, why would God have allowed them to come back and tell their story if there is no second chance as we have been repeatedly told? Is it possible that God does and will let some people out of hell? Is it possible that He might do so in response to prayers for lost souls as many in the early Church believed? One Christian Universalist (we will cover this position in Chapter 5), Eric Stetson, suggests, "Why else would the dead man on the operating table suddenly, miraculously come back to life and return with a story of going to hell, if not because God was merciful and allowed him another chance?" Stetson also recognizes and wisely advises that "NDEs seem to be tailored to each person's spiritual understanding and needs, rather than a uniform presentation of absolute truth . . . . We cannot draw general theological conclusions from them."[92]

What Can We Conclude So Far?

The place and concept of hell is a vast gray area, a highly contested issue, and an emotionally charged debate from all sides. One embarrassing question we must raise again at this point is, if Christians really believe in hell, why aren't they more active in sharing their faith with non- or unbelievers so they won't end up going there, forever? This common omission is a major reason critics charge that most Christians are uncaring hypocrites. Yes, this charge sounds harsh. But think about it.

Bottom line is, the battle lines are drawn. The sides are fixed. And the arguments have been essentially exhausted. Still, the majority of Christians continue to defend the *status quo* proclaiming, "Hell yes!" Yet growing numbers are protesting, "Hell no!" Arguably, for nineteen centuries of church history and tumult no resolution or reconciliatory effort for ending this stalemate has been presented.

So, hell remains "one of Christianity's most offensive doctrines."[93] But is "hell" real and really part of God's plan? Or is it a doctrine of tradition and one of the greatest lies ever told? *Time* magazine insightfully reports that the reality or non-reality of hell "is a question that has vexed the Christian church for two millennia."[94]

Bottom line is, the battle lines are drawn. The sides are fixed. And the arguments have been essentially exhausted. Still, the majority of Christians continue to defend the *status quo* proclaiming, "Hell yes!" Yet growing numbers are protesting, "Hell no!"

One thing all the above-cited books have in common, with the possible exception of McLaren's, is, they all:

1) Assume the existence and viability of an afterlife placed called "hell."
2) Ignore or side-step significant arguments to the contrary.
3) Do an inadequate job of presenting and defending the view of Christian Universalism—i.e., that eventually everyone will be saved through Christ (see Part II).
4) Mostly ridicule opposition views, make assertions, and move on.

The end result is, not one of these books, including McLaren's, addresses and analyzes the numerous problems and inconsistencies that exist on all sides of this afterlife debate. This book, the one you hold in your hands, will not make this "hell" assumption or succumb to these deficiencies. Instead, we will test this traditional assumption about hell and weigh the various arguments on all sides of this debate to see what will and what won't stand up to an honest and sincere test of Scripture and history.

Lastly, let's return to the "800-pound gorilla in the room." Is it possible that Rob Bell and his highly controversial book, *Love Wins*, are onto something? Or is he a left-leaning liberal heretic who has left and is betraying his so-called orthodox, traditional, and evangelical Christian roots? Or, perhaps, is he a scripturally savvy sage who is opening wide the door for the further reformation of Christianity?

Whichever it is, clearly, something is wrong! And I take no pleasure in being disliked, resented, or maligned for pointing this out. But the reality is, there are roughly six to seven billion people alive in our world today. It is estimated that "no more than two billion" are Christians.[95] This, of course, does not count those who have lived and died previously or those yet to be born. Therefore, I affirm with Wittmer that "ultimately it doesn't matter how we or anyone else *feels* about hell, but only what God says about it."[96] In our next chapter, we will begin the re-discover process of what this something wrong might be as we unveil and re-explore two recent photographs of "hell."

Chapter 2

Two Recent Photos of Hell

A number of mistaken comments about hell commonly circulate and are perpetuated in Christian circles, such as:

- "Jesus believed in hell."
- "The person in the Bible who spoke the most about hell's reality was Jesus."
- "Jesus said more about hell than about heaven."
- "The biggest proportion of what the Bible has to say about hell is found in the Gospels."

Daniel Poole, the lead character in McLaren's fictional-account book, *The Last Word and the Word After That*, voices these misstatements thusly, "hell was not 'revealed' in the Old Testament . . . . the idea appears suddenly—to us anyway—in the Gospels, on the lips of Jesus. That's why it's such a thorny issue for Christians. Jesus is the first in all biblical literature to talk about hell, and he talks the most about it."[1]

A recent article in the Christian nonfiction magazine, *Charisma*, poignantly titled, "Don't Get Brainwashed" by Editor J. Lee Grady similarly assures us that "Hell is not a metaphor—it is a real place of dreadful separation from God that sinners choose when they reject Him."[2] And of course, none of us wants to "get brainwashed" by Grady, by me, or by anyone else.

Therefore, in this chapter we want to seriously start re-considering, re-questioning, and re-testing this mainstay and traditional belief of the Christian faith by addressing these questions:

- Is the doctrine of "hell" in and true to Scripture?
- Is there really an other-worldly, afterlife place called "hell?"
- Or, was "hell" an invention of the Roman Catholic Church to scare people into submission and obedience?
- Are there any major problems and inconsistencies with this traditional belief?

And, "*hell yes*," I am well aware of the fear most evangelical Christians harbor and their charge, as even *Time* magazine reminds us in its six-page cover story article about Rob Bell and his hell-questioning book, *Love Wins*, that "from a traditionalist perspective . . . to take away hell is to leave the church without its most powerful sanction."[3] But in light of the above, legitimate questions, and the scriptural injunction to "Test everything. Hold on to the good" (1 Thess. 5:21), would you like to see two recent photographs of what Jesus' "hell" looks like today? See below and on the next page, and welcome to hell—Jesus' "hell!"

Photo of the Valley of the Son of Hinnom (*Gehenna*) that surrounds today's old Jerusalem on the southwest.

Another recent photograph of this valley.

Does this look like "hell" to you? Is this the way you picture this afterlife place of eternal conscious punishment of departed un- or non-believers?

The first photograph appeared on the first page of an article titled, "Valley of Haunted History" in *The Holy Land Magazine* "Christian Tourism to Israel, 2008." The article invites readers and future tourists to "a walk through the green and tranquil Valley of Hinnom, below Jerusalem's Old City walls, [which] reveals beautiful views and some dark tales, too."

If these two recent photographs do not look like "hell" to you, please be assured that they are actual, modern-day pictures of Jesus' "hell." Here's the biblical reality and reason why.

This valley's name in Hebrew and in Old Testament and New Testament times was *Gei Ben-Hinnom*, which means the Valley of the Son of Hinnom, or simply *Gei-Hinnom*. A transliteration of this compound word as well as a slight corruption and contraction gave rise to the word *Gehenna*. *Gehenna* in Aramaic is the word Jesus employed eleven times during his earthly ministry (of its twelve uses in the New Testament). Most all Bible versions translate Jesus' *Gehenna* as "hell." As we saw in our last chapter, *Young's Literal Translation* does not. It translates this word directly as Gehenna.

Ironically, *The World Book Encyclopedia* in its article on "Hell" observes what has transpired over the past nineteen intervening centuries. "Hell is no longer prominent in the teachings of Judaism, but Gehenna became the hell of Christianity and Islam."[4] Notably, Islam's "hell" is also derived from a similar corruption and contraction of the same Hebrew compound word *Gei-Hinnom* or *gehinnom*. In the Qur'an, the related and transliterated Arabic word is *Jahannam* or *Jehennam*. It is translated into English as "Hell," "Hell-fire," or "blazing fire." This translation contrasts with their word *jannah*, which is an afterlife, garden-like Paradise enjoyed by righteous and perfected Muslims, but not by non-Muslims.

To this day, this same valley surrounds old Jerusalem on the southwest side and bears the name *Gehenna*. You can go to this "hell" without dying. Israel's Ministry of Tourism hopes that you will. It conducts daily tours and would be delighted to assist you in making your travel plans. Listen to how they attractively recast and pitch *Gehenna*.

> It's not easy to find something good to say about the Hinnom Valley in Jerusalem, whose bad press from biblical days has followed it down through the ages. After all, it was here, right around the corner from the First Temple, that the people of Judah offered their children to the fire god Molech and to Ba'al (Jer. 31; 32:35), for which, Jeremiah warned them, they would pay with the destruction of the Temple and exile . . . . In light of the sacrifices to the fire god, the latter name gave rise to the word "Gehenna," which over time became a synonym for hell . . . . Bad press or not . . . it also makes for one of the most picturesque walks you can take in the Holy City . . . . stroll through Gehenna . . . . have a wonderful view of the Mount of Olives and the Judean Desert.[5]

Four Original, Biblical-Language Words

Ironically, the two authors of the tradition-upholding and hell-defending book, *Sense and Nonsense About Heaven & Hell*, emphasize a basic principle with which I wholeheartedly agree. "The first step in understanding what the Bible teaches about Hell is to read what it says."[6] And truly, there is no other credible source. So, and in keeping with our ground rule #1 – *Sola Scriptura*, let's go to the Bible.

W.E. Vine's Expository Dictionary of Biblical Words identifies four original-language words found in the Old and New Testaments that have been variously translated in different versions of the Bible as "hell."[7] They are: **Gehenna, Sheol, Hades, and Tartarus**.

In this and the next two chapters we will address each one of these words and places, and in this order. We start with *Gehenna* because it is the word Jesus most used, the word most often rendered as "hell" by most Bible translations, and the word most employed to build a doctrine of hell as a fiery afterlife place of eternal conscious punishment. But is this what *Gehenna* really pointed and points to?

[handwritten annotation: "How often did Jesus use "real, literal, familiar" "this world" concepts, places, people, things to teach spiritual realities?"]

Gehenna—a Big and Sad Part of Jewish History

One of the biggest problems with *Gehenna* being an other-worldly, afterlife place is, it was and still is a proper noun and the name of a real, literal, familiar, this-world place. Just like the Mount of Olives, the Judean Desert, Calvary, Bethlehem, or Gethsemane, all these places were and are still located in the immediate vicinity of Jerusalem. As the two above photographs show, *Gehenna* today is a beautiful and partially but densely populated suburb of this modern-day city.

Thus, and inescapably, we must now ask an embarrassing question. By what hermeneutic (rule or principle of interpretation) or from what textual basis do translators change *Gehenna* into an other-worldly, afterlife place and translate it into a totally different, non-associated word? Like our Rio Grande Valley of Texas, the Grand Canyon of Arizona, or the Mississippi River in the middle of America, or the Mount of Olives, the Judean Desert, Calvary, Bethlehem, or Gethsemane in Israel, which are all proper nouns, names, and this-world places, why aren't translators true to the word? They don't translate these other proper nouns and local place names as something entirely different. Is there some legitimate textual imperative that we are missing for translating *Gehenna*, differently, as "hell?" Perhaps a little more history will help.

Long ago, a man named Hinnom lived in this valley (*Gei*). And, like many valleys throughout the world, it was originally named after him— the "Valley of Hinnom." Later, it was named after his son (*Ben-Hinnom*), the "Valley of the son of Hinnom." Again, *Gehenna* is a transliteration of a compound word and a slight corruption and contraction derived from the Hebrew *Ge Hinnom,* meaning "Valley of Hinnom," or *Gehenna.*

Gehenna also suffered through a long, sad, and sordid history. In Bible times, it was a horrific place and reeked of a horrible stench. Why? Because, allegedly and arguably, it was the local city garbage dump of Jerusalem.[8] Hence, fires were kept burning to dispose of the garbage and worms ate this waste as well as the carcasses of sacrificed animals deposited there from the Temple (see Heb. 13:11), and the bodies of criminals who had been executed (see Jer. 31:40a). All these things and more were tossed into this fiery garbage dump.

One of the biggest problems with *Gehenna* being an other-worldly, afterlife place is, it was and still is a proper noun and the name of a real, literal, familiar, this-world place.

Additionally, *Gehenna* had been the place of pagan sacrifices and burnings of Israeli children as they were offered to the gods of Baal(s) and Molech (see Jer. 7:30-31; 19:2, 4-5; 32:35). Let's also take special note from these just-referenced, Old Testament passages that these sacrifices and burnings were not "commanded" nor "mentioned" by God. They never "enter [his] mind." And God termed these acts "evil" and "detestable." Nowadays, and perhaps ironically, the church has, or soon will have, God Himself doing these same "evil" and detestable" acts to multiple billions sentenced and cast into an eternity of fiery punishment and suffering in a *Gehenna* "hell."[9] *No comparison whatsoever.*

Next, is a biggie! *The Israelites were committing murder while worshipping pagan gods.*

Jeremiah's Three *Gehenna* Prophecies *The NT sheds light on the OT*

No, the opposite is true *We begin to understand OT thru' the NT*
Most Bible students are well aware of the axiom that so much of the New Testament comes to light when we begin to understand it through a deeper appreciation of the Old Testament and its Jewish background.

The following three prophecies were inspired by God and delivered through the Old Testament prophet, Jeremiah. They laid down the prophetic groundwork and set the stage for the time and nature of the fulfillment of Jesus' uses of this familiar valley and its proper name *Gehenna*. All three prophecies speak of the same future event and are contained in the pre-exilic book of Jeremiah (written 604 B.C.). As we shall see, they firmly establish this valley and its name *Gehenna* as a symbol for a future, divine, but *this-world* judgment. They also describe the stark and extreme horror of an earthly military defeat. Let's see if these three prophecies render our modern-day concept of this valley being a metaphorical symbol of an afterlife "hell" as highly suspect. (The **bold** emphasis below is mine.)

Gehenna Prophecy #1 – Jeremiah 7:32-34

> *So beware, the days are coming, declares the Lord, when people will no longer call it **Topheth** or the **Valley of Ben Hinnom**, but the **Valley of Slaughter**, for they will **bury the dead** in Topheth until there is no more room. Then the **carcasses** of this people will become **food** for the birds of the air and the beasts of the earth, and there will be no one to frighten them away. I will bring **an end** to the sounds of joy and gladness and to the voices of bride and bridegroom in the towns of **Judah** and the streets of **Jerusalem**, for the **land** will become **desolate**.*

Topheth was a particular site and a "high place" located within the Valley of Hinnom outside of Jerusalem. Topheth means a "place of fire," "cremation" or "burning." It may also have been derived from the Hebrew root word "toph," meaning a drum. Scholars believe the beating of percussion instruments was used to drown out the cries and screams of infants and children being burned alive by the priests of the Ammonite god, Molech. It is also believed that a brazen image of Molech was erected at Topheth. It had the head of a bull with two horns and the body of a man. The idol's stomach was enlarged, hollowed out, and used as a furnace for the fire. During the sacrifices, not only doves, pigeons, and lambs, but also their own children were placed into the arms or stomach of the idol. It is not known when the Israelites started their idolatry and infanticide sacrifices to Molech. Later on in Jewish history, Josiah eventually put an end to these nefarious practices and restored pure worship to God—"He desecrated Topheth, which was in the Valley of Ben Hinnom, so no one could use it to sacrifice his son or daughter in the fire to Molech" (2 Ki. 23:10—of course, we moderns are far too sophisticated to be involved in these kinds of cruel and horrific practices today, aren't we?[10])

Fittingly in this passage of Scripture, the Lord through the prophet Jeremiah renames this valley "the valley of slaughter." And as it's graphically described here, this place was worse than a graveyard. Decent burial was not provided. The dead bodies cast into this dump laid unburied and became carrion for birds of prey, scavenging animals, and maggots. Lastly, Jeremiah prophesies a future-coming divine judgment and destruction that will leave the towns of Judah and the streets of Jerusalem and the land desolate.

The questions we must raise here are: Was this prophecy fulfilled several years later in the 587 B.C. fall of Jerusalem to Babylonians (see Jer. 39:1f; 52:1f)? Or, was it fulfilled in the A.D. 66-73 destruction and desolation left by the Romans? Or, is it yet-unfulfilled? Jeremiah's next two prophecies repeat many of these same words and phrases and elaborate on this future-coming and *this-world* judgment event.

Gehenna **Prophecy #2 – Jeremiah 19:1-15**

*This is what the Lord says: "Go and buy a **clay jar** from a potter. Take along some of the elders of the people and of the priests and go out to the **Valley of Ben Hinnom**, near the entrance of the Potsherd Gate. There proclaim the words I tell you, and say, 'Hear the word of the Lord, O kings of Judah and people of Jerusalem. This is what the Lord Almighty, the God of Israel, says: Listen! I am going to bring **a disaster** on this place that will make the ears of everyone who hears of it tingle. For they have **forsaken me** and made this a place of foreign gods; they have **burned sacrifices** in it to gods that neither they nor their fathers nor the kings of Judah ever knew, and they have filled this place with **the blood of the innocent**. They have built the **high places** of Baal to burn their sons in the fire as offerings to Baal—something I did not command or mention, nor did it enter my mind. So beware, the days are coming, declares the Lord, when people will no longer call this place Topheth or the Valley of Ben Hinnom, but the **Valley of Slaughter**.*

*"'In this place I will **ruin** the plans of Judah and Jerusalem. I will make them **fall by the sword before their enemies**, at the hands of those who seek their lives, and I will give their **carcasses** as food to the birds of the air and the beasts of the earth. I will **devastate this city** and make it an **object of scorn**; all who pass by will be appalled and will scoff because of all its wounds. I will make them **eat the flesh** of their sons and daughters, and they will eat one another's flesh during the stress of the **siege** imposed on them by the **enemies** who seek their lives.'*

*"Then **break the jar** while those who go with you are watching, and say to them, 'This is what the Lord Almighty says: I will **smash this nation and this city** just as this potter's jar is smashed and **cannot be repaired**. They will **bury the dead** in **Topheth** until there is no more room. This is what I will do to this place and to those who live here, declares the Lord. I will **make this city like Topheth**. The houses in **Jerusalem** and those of the kings of **Judah** will be defiled **like this place, Topheth**— all the houses where they burned incense on the roofs to all the starry hosts and poured out drink offerings to other gods.'"*

*Jeremiah then returned from Topheth, where the Lord had sent him to prophesy, and stood in the court of the Lord's temple and said to all the people, 'This is what the Lord Almighty, the God of Israel, says: 'Listen! I am going to bring on this **city** and the **villages** around **it every disaster** I pronounced against them, because they were stiff-necked and would not listen to my words.'"*

For the second time, this physical valley is renamed "the valley of slaughter." Targeted is the same prophetic and terrible future-coming judgment because of the detestable practices being performed here. The image of smashing the jar is a symbolical representation of the city and the state being irrevocably broken and destroyed. Bernhard W. Anderson in his textbook, *Understanding the Old Testament*, confirms this understanding and adds, "in this way he [Jeremiah] dramatically demonstrates that Jerusalem would be broken into fragments, and that the destruction would be so great that the accursed valley would have to be used for a burial place."[11]

Likewise, the two phrases "like Topheth" and "like this place, Topheth" apply and expand the wickedness and guilt of this "high place" and the symbolism of future-coming, fiery judgment beyond this valley and onto the greater area of Jerusalem and Judah. This national judgment will involve a massive siege, disaster, slaughter, ruin, falling by the sword before enemies, devastation, eating of flesh, carcasses thrown into this valley and being eaten by birds and animals, and ultimately "desolation."

So, again we question, was this national judgment literally fulfilled in this world in 587 B.C. or in A.D. 66-73? Or, is it yet-unfulfilled and its language employed as a symbol of some greater judgment? Answers offered by commentators are mixed:

Barnes' Notes

Vs. 1 – "In solemn procession he must bear the vessel out to the place of doom, the valley of Gehenna. There he was to break the vessel; and just as all the art of the potter would be of no avail to restore the broken fragments, so did God proclaim the final destruction of Jerusalem such as it then was, and of that generation which inhabited it."
Vs. 9 – "Fulfilled to the letter **both** in the siege of Jerusalem under Nebuchadnezzar [in 587 B.C.] and that long after under the Roman Titus [A.D. 70]."

Adam Clarke Commentary

Vs. 11 [cannot be repaired] "that cannot be made whole again [*KJV*] – This seems to refer rather to the final destruction of Jerusalem **by the Romans**, than to what was done by the Chaldeans/Babylonians. Jerusalem was healed after 70 years; but nearly 1800 years have elapsed since Jerusalem was taken and destroyed by the Romans; and it was then so broken, that it could not be made whole again."

<u>*Jamieson, Faussert, and Brown Commentary*</u>

Vs. 15 – "The valley of Hinnom, the scene of the Jew's greatest guilt, was made the scene of the denunciation of their doom, and was to be the scene of its execution (Jer. 19:4) . . . as the scene of unmingled woe. Once it resounded with the cries of 'innocent' (Jer. 19:4) children cruelly put to death; hereafter it was to resound with the death-groans of adult men who richly merited their retributive punishment . . . . and to be burnt with fire by the enemy. As the Jews 'estranged' the place (Jer. 19: 4) which was God's from Him who was its rightful owner, so was the land to be estranged from them and given to strangers, while they themselves must sojourn as captives and strangers in a strange land. . . . **Whatsoever people or state** is broken by God, is 'like a potter's vessel' broken to pieces, so that it 'cannot be made whole again' (Jer. 19:11) by man. But what is impossible to man is possible to God, and He will surely keep His promise of restoring Israel, broken and scattered as the Jews have long been."

Jeremiah's third *Gehenna* prophecy provides the defining key for determining the actual time and nature for the fulfillment of this future-coming and divine-judgment event.

<u>*Gehenna* Prophecy #3 – Jeremiah 31:38-40</u>

> *"The days are coming," declares the Lord, "when this city will be **rebuilt** for me from the Tower of Hananel to the Corner Gate. The measuring line will stretch from there straight to the hill of Gareb and then turn to Goah. **The whole valley** where **dead bodies** and ashes **are thrown**, and all the terraces out to the Kidron Valley on the east as far as the corner of the Horse Gate, **will be holy to the Lord. The city will never again be uprooted or demolished."*

For the third time, Jeremiah prophesies of this coming-judgment event. But this time he adds a change in that this "Valley of Slaughter" would become "holy to the Lord." What does that mean? In other words, the grim associations linked to this valley of Hinnom (*Gehenna*) and city would become a thing of the past as it is transformed. Once again, does this sound like an eternal, afterlife "hell" to you?

Also pinpointed in this third prophecy was the future reality that the city of Jerusalem would be rebuilt to "never again be uprooted or demolished." What does that mean? It cannot mean the city that was rebuilt after the return from Babylon captivity. That city was "uprooted" and totally "demolished" again by the Romans in A.D 70-73. *Adam Clarke Commentary* suggests that this valley and city being made "holy" would happen, "when the people shall have the law written in their hearts. . . ."

Twice, later and using similar "the-time/days-is/are-coming" language, Jeremiah prophesies more about this coming future time. He associates it with the coming of the New Covenant.

> *"**The time is coming**," declares the Lord, "when I will make a **new covenant** with the house of **Israel** and with the house of **Judah**. It will not be like the covenant I made with their forefathers when I took them by the hand to lead them out of Egypt, because they broke my covenant, though I was a husband to them," declares the Lord.*

> *"This is the covenant I will make with the house of Israel after that time," declares the Lord. "I will put **my law in their minds** and write it **on their hearts**. I will be their God, and they will be my people. No longer will a man teach his neighbor, or a man his brother, saying, 'Know the Lord,' because they will all know me, from the least of them to the greatest," declares the Lord."*
>
> (Jer.31:31-34).

> *"'**The days are coming**,' declares the Lord, 'when I will fulfill the gracious promise I made to the house of **Israel** and to the house of **Judah**. "'In those days and at that time I will make **a righteous Branch sprout from David's line**; he will do what is just and right in the land. In those days Judah will **be saved** and Jerusalem will live in safety. This is the **name** by which it will be called: **The Lord Our Righteousness.**'*

*For this is what the Lord says: 'David will never fail to have **a man** to sit on the **throne** of the house of Israel, nor will the priests, who are Levites, ever fail to have **a man** to stand before me **continually** to offer burnt offerings, to burn grain offerings and to present sacrifices.'"* (Jer. 33:14-18)

Barnes' Notes commentary stresses that "Jeremiah's words [here] are to be spiritually understood. The city is one that renders holy unto Yahweh what was before unclean." This time is then compared with "the time of the 'New Jerusalem' (Rev. 21:27)." In concurrence and around A.D. 48, the Apostle Paul spoke of this same new and holy city. In his book to the Galatians, he portrayed this city as a then-present and/or coming reality and part of the change of covenants (Old to New) that was also taking place back, then and there. He termed this city "the Jerusalem that is above is free, and she is our mother" (Gal. 4:26). He next compares this city to "the present city of Jerusalem" which he writes is "in bondage" (Gal. 4:25 *KJV*) or "in slavery" (*NIV*). Later, around A.D. 57, in his letter to the Corinthians he writes this about the soon-coming national judgment event, which both Jeremiah and Jesus prophesied would come upon the Jewish people, "Time is short . . . . The world in its present form is passing away" (1 Cor. 7:29, 31). What world was passing away? It was the world of Old Covenant biblical Judaism that had been made "obsolete" by Jesus' death, burial, resurrection, and ascension to heaven.

The valley of Hinnom, the scene of the Jew's greatest guilt, was made the scene of the denunciation of their doom, and was to be the scene of its execution.

The writer of the book of Hebrews, around A.D. 65 adds, "By calling this covenant 'new,' he [Jesus] has made the first one obsolete; and what is obsolete and aging will soon disappear" (Heb. 8:13). And it all happened *exactly* as Jeremiah and Jesus, along with Daniel, had prophesied and every New Testament writer and the early Church expected. (For more on this prophetic fulfillment, see my book, *The Perfect Ending for the World* – pp. 109-202).[12]

Gleanings from *Gehenna*

What can we glean so far from and about *Gehenna*? Especially, what do we make of Jeremiah's three *Gehenna* prophecies? Below are seven gleanings, or takeaways, from this chapter that I believe we should etch in our minds. In my opinion, they are irrefutable insights. Once again, and most importantly, they provide the historical and prophetic precedent in setting the stage for Jesus' prophetic use of this valley's name and place in the New Testament. But you be the judge:

Gleaning #1 – For 1st-century Jews, *Gehenna* was a real, literal, familiar, *this-world* place, (and not an other-worldly, afterlife place). Arguably, it also was the all-purpose and burning garbage dump of Jerusalem whose sight and smell was ever-present before them.

Gleaning #2 – It had a long, sad, sordid, and well-known past history.

Gleaning #3 – It became a *this-world* symbol for a terrible, fiery, future-coming, and divine national judgment of Judah and Jerusalem.

Gleaning #4 – This prophesied, future-coming judgment would be brought by means of a disastrous military defeat by *this-world*, earthly enemies.

Gleaning #5 – This judgment would have a starting point and an ending point, would not last "forever and ever," but would be permanent and leave the land "desolate" and in "ruin."

Gleaning #6 – This valley and city would subsequently be restored and become "holy to the Lord" and "righteousness."

Gleaning #7 – Do not *Gehenna's* biblical history and Jeremiah's three prophecies render as highly suspect our modern-day concept of Jesus' *Gehenna* being a metaphorical, other-worldly, afterlife place of eternal conscious punishment and torment that we have come to know as "hell?" Would you agree or disagree? Hell yes? Hell no?

With these seven *Gehenna* gleanings in mind, it's time for us to revisit Jesus' hell, which, again, is *Gehenna*. In our next chapter, we will re-address Jesus' eleven usages and teachings that are focused on this earthly valley. We will be asking two demanding questions: 1) Is there any textual basis or historical validation for a shift in meaning and translating *Gehenna* as "hell?" 2) Is a 1st-century, this-world fulfillment—that's consistent with Jeremiah's three prophecies and the New Covenant reality—supportable and documentable?

Jeremiah's three *Gehenna* prophecies . . . . provide the historical and prophetic precedent in setting the stage for Jesus' prophetic use of this valley's name and place in the New Testament.

Let's also keep in mind the basic hermeneutical principle of "letting Scripture interpret Scripture." Perhaps, and just perchance, the Jewish background we've uncovered in this chapter will put Jesus' use of this proper noun and familiar earthly place of *Gehenna* into a textual and historical context and time perspective different than what we've known or been told and taught before. Hell yes? Hell no?

Chapter 3

Revisiting Jesus' Hell

Jesus is credited by many Christian writers and scholars as being "the chief proponent of the doctrine of hell."[1] But is He? Dr. Billy Graham believes that "no one taught about hell or warned us against it more than Jesus."[2] But did He? Senior Managing Editor for *Christianity Today* magazine, Mark Galli, claims that "though Christ's words about hell are clear, emphatic, and repeated, our temptation is to think he didn't mean what he said."[3] But what did He really say? Rightly, Galli warns believers about "radically reinterpreting Christ's words about hell, stripping them of their straightforward meaning."[4]

Again, the word Jesus most often used and is most often translated as "hell" was *Gehenna*. And *Gehenna* was and still is today a real, literal, familiar, and this-world place with a long, sad, sordid, and well-known past history. In Jesus' day, it was located in the immediate vicinity of Jerusalem and was the focal point of Jeremiah's three and as-yet-unfulfilled prophecies. But Galli traditionally insists that "over time Gehenna also became the name of the place where sinners were punished after death."[5] But is it? And "God revealed most of the details we know about hell later, in the New Testament."[6] But did He?

In this regard, Chan offers some good advice for us to adhere to: "if truth is what we are after, we need to stick to what Jesus actually said." And "to understand Jesus' statements in the context of the world He lived in. We need to enter Jesus' world . . . if we're to figure out what He meant when He spoke of hell."[7] Therefore, to help us keep the proper, textual, contextual, and historical details in the forefront of our minds we will replace the questionable translation of "hell" with the original, proper noun, and name *Gehenna* everywhere Jesus used it (although He used it in Aramaic). As we revisit Jesus' eleven *Gehenna* usages and teachings, and James' single use, keep asking yourself these three questions:

1. How would Jesus' original hearers have understood this word—i.e., what did *Gehenna* mean to them?
2. Did Jesus ever indicate that He was using this word differently?
3. By what hermeneutic or upon what textual basis do we nowadays understand Jesus' *Gehenna* as "hell" and a metaphor pointing to an afterlife, other-worldly place, dimension, or state of eternal conscious punishment?

Also remember as we proceed, and as Robert W. Yarbrough accurately emphasizes that "because Jesus is the central authority for Christians, his teachings are of utmost significance." So do his words about *Gehenna* present "an insurmountable hurdle for revisionists to overcome?"[8] as Yarbrough further proclaims, or not?

Jesus' Two *Gehenna* Usages with 'This Generation'

Let's start with Jesus' last two uses of the word *Gehenna* (chronologically #10 and #11). Contextually, they are the clearest and most definitive usages. Again, the **bold** emphasis below is mine.

#10 – Matthew 23:15

> *"Woe to you, teachers of the law and Pharisees, you hypocrites! You travel over land and sea to win a single convert, and when he becomes one, you make him twice as much a son of **Gehenna** as you are."*

Was this a vague metaphorical reference to an afterlife place called hell? Jesus knew what *Gehenna* was back then. So did these Jewish teachers and the Pharisees. They could see it and perhaps smell it everyday. They were also familiar with this valley's sordid history and

Jeremiah's three as-yet-unfulfilled *Gehenna* prophecies. If Jesus was using this word and this valley in a different way than it is found and translated in the Jewish Old Testament Scriptures (*Gei Ben-Hinnom*), wouldn't that make Him appear like a false teacher? As we have seen, his Jewish contemporaries most likely did not understand this valley as a symbol of everlasting torture in the afterlife. Then was Jesus merely using *Gehenna* as a symbol of moral corruption and foulness? Eighteen verses later, Jesus gets more poignant and specific.

#11 – Matthew 23:33

> *"You snakes! You brood of vipers! How will you escape being condemned to* **Gehenna***?"*

This verse marks Jesus' 11th and final use of the word *Gehenna*. Three verses later, He time restricts this terrible condemnation to occur with his "this generation." Jesus tells them, "So upon you will come all the righteous blood that has been shed on earth . . . . I tell you the truth, all this will come upon this generation" (Matt. 23:35-36). Two verses later, Jesus emphatically declares the result of this *this-world* judgment, "Look, your house is left to you desolate" (Matt. 23:38; also see Luke 21:20-32). Please note that Jesus' "desolate" here directly ties back to Jeremiah's "desolate" in his first *Gehenna* prophecy (see again Jer. 7:32-34). Jesus speaks further of this same, soon-coming, and national judgment and desolation in Matthew 24, Mark 13, and Luke 21 and pinpoints his "this generation" for its fulfillment (Matt. 24:34; Mark 13:30; Luke 21:32).[9]

In Luke's account Jesus instructs his original hearers what to do, "When you see Jerusalem surrounded by armies, you will know that its desolation is near. Then let those who are in Judea flee to the mountains, let those in the city get out, and let those in the country not enter the city. For this is the time of punishment in fulfillment of all that has been written" (Luke 21:20-22). "All that has been written" (i.e., the whole Old Testament) would certainly have included Jeremiah's three *Gehenna* prophecies.

Likewise, the writer of Hebrews, writing around A.D. 65, knows this dreadful and destructive judgment is coming soon when he writes, "By calling this covenant 'new,' he has made the first one obsolete; and what is obsolete and aging will soon disappear" (Heb. 8:13). Peter, writing around A.D. 65-67, claims the time is very close as he exhorts his contemporaries that "the end of all things is at hand" . . . . For it is time for judgment to begin with the family/house of God . . ." (1 Peter 4:7a, 17a). John, writing around A.D. 67-68, leaves no doubt, this judgment is right there, "This is the last hour . . . we know it is the last hour" (1 John 2:18).

Jesus' "desolate" here directly ties back to Jeremiah's "desolate" in his first *Gehenna* prophecy (see again Jer. 7:32-34).

After burning the Temple and the entire city in A.D. 70, the Romans removed every stone, one-by-one from the Temple complex. over the next three years. This massive deconstruction was in fulfillment of another prophecy by Jesus that "not one stone here will be left on another" (Matt. 24:2). Then they plowed up the hill of the sanctuary. Thus was typologically fulfilled the prophecy of Micah: "Zion will be plowed like a field, Jerusalem will become a heap of rubble, the temple hill a mound overgrown with thickets" (Mic. 3:12; also Jer. 26:18).[10]

Josephus, the Jewish historian for the Romans and our only eyewitness account of this period, described the utter destruction and desolation of Jerusalem as follows:

> Caesar gave orders that they should now demolish the entire city and temple. . . . it was so thoroughly laid even with the ground by those that dug it up to the foundation, that there was left nothing to make those that came thither believe it had ever been inhabited. This was the end which Jerusalem came to by the madness of those that were for innovations; a city otherwise of great magnificence, and of mighty fame among all mankind.[11]

Over the next fifty years the entire country was left desolate and devoid of most of its inhabitants. The people had been killed, died, or were sold into slavery. Everything was utterly destroyed—"to the uttermost" (1Thess. 2:16 *KJV*).

No country or people ever suffered the magnitude of God's wrath and judgment that befell Old Covenant Israel. Not only did Israel cease being the nation of the living God, it ceased being a nation for nineteen centuries until its rebirth as a secular nation in 1948. The world of biblical Judaism, however, perished forever. It all happened forty years from the time Jesus told his disciples, "Look, your house is left to you desolate" (Matt. 23:38) and "not one stone here will be left on another" (Matt. 24:2).

This fulfillment is more than coincidence. Not only did Jesus cite his "this generation" as the one headed for this national judgment (Matt. 24:34), He also used the *this-world*, physical valley of *Gehenna* as both a literal reality and figurative symbol for it. Josephus also recorded that as a result of the Jewish-Roman War of A.D. 66-70, the local Valley of Hinnom and garbage dump of Jerusalem—known as *Gehenna*—was literally heaped with dead, unburied bodies of Jews that were tossed into its fires during and after that time.[12] Only in this time-restricted and this-world context do Jesus' warnings about a real, coming, and shocking judgment make sense, literal sense.

Jesus' Nine Other *Gehenna* Usages in Chronological Order

#1 – Matthew 5:21-22

> *"You have heard that it was said to the people long ago, 'Do not murder, and anyone who murders will be subject to judgment. But I tell you that anyone who is angry with his brother will be subject to judgment. Again, anyone who says to his brother, 'Raca,' is answerable to the Sanhedrin. But anyone who says, 'You fool!' will be in danger of the fire of **Gehenna**."*

This marks the first time Jesus uses the word *Gehenna* during his earthly ministry. Please note, there is not the slightest hint that He is using the name of this place any differently or in a new and unfamiliar way from how the prophets and his contemporaries had been using and understood it. Rather, Jesus speaks calmly and in a straightforward manner. And given Jewish history and the Old Testament background covered in our last chapter, do you really think our ideas of *Gehenna* being an other-worldly, afterlife, and spirit/soul realm "hell" would have come into the minds of Jesus' original audience upon hearing these words? Let's not forget that the Jews already had a name for an afterlife holding place of the dead. It was Sheol in Hebrew and Hades in Greek. How confusing would it have been to a 1st-century Jewish mind if by *Gehenna* Jesus meant another, other-worldly place?

Most significantly, the Jewish Septuagint (a 2nd-century B.C. Greek translation of the Old Testament from Hebrew to Greek), never translated Sheol as *Gehenna*. The word Hades was used, instead. (We'll cover both Sheol and Hades in our next chapter.) Why is this important? Because the Septuagint demonstrates that the Jews back then did not associate *Gehenna* with or as being an other-worldly place.

Seriously, what in Jesus' passage above would have prevented an original 1st-century hearer from immediately thinking of this valley southeast of Jerusalem and its association with a coming, *this-world*, national judgment and fiery destruction as prophesied by their prophet Jeremiah? However, this specific place and prophetic meaning is a reality and concept foreign to or forgotten by most Gentiles today. And yet other Jewish prophets prophesied of this same, future-coming time and judgment event—see Moses in Deuteronomy 31:29 through 32:1-43, or Daniel 12:7-13, Micah 1:2-7, and Malachi (3:1-5; 4:1-3).

John the Baptist also prophesied of it: "The ax is already at the root of the trees, and every tree that does not produce good fruit will be cut down and thrown into the fire . . . . His winnowing fork is in his hand, and he will clear his threshing floor, gathering the wheat into his barn and burning up the chaff with unquenchable fire" (Matt. 3:10, 12).

Notably, and once again, it was standard operating procedure for the Jews to literally judge, execute, and dump the bodies of criminals (murders, troublemakers, etc.) into this valley (see Jer. 31:40a). In the eyes of an ancient Jew, not having one's body properly buried but left exposed, eaten by worms, and burned was a sign of great shame and a punishment from God. So when Jesus speaks literally here of "murder, anger, judgment, Raca (an Aramaic term of contempt), you fool, and the Sanhedrin," what justifies switching the judgment consequence of "the fire of *Gehenna*" from being this-worldly to being non-literal, metaphorical, and other-worldly?

After all, the type of person who thinks and behaves in this offensive manner and commits these kinds of crimes tells us a lot about that his heart and how he thinks and feels about God (see Mark 7:20-23). Most likely, that person would not listen to Jesus. Nor would he follow Jesus or obey his later instructions to leave Jerusalem and escape the forthcoming judgment of *Gehenna*. And that literal fire of *Gehenna* was literally burning in that literal valley right there in front of their literal eyes. At best, a switch of meaning must be considered assumptive, if not an outright and unwarranted imposition upon the text. Would you agree or disagree? Hell yes? Hell no?

#2 & #3 – Matthew 5:29-30 (2X)

*"If your right eye causes you to sin, gouge it out and throw it away. It is better for you to lose one part of your body than for your whole body to be thrown into **Gehenna**. And if your right hand causes you to sin, cut it off and throw it away. It is better for you to lose one part of your body than for your whole body to go into **Gehenna**."*

Twice in this passage Jesus uses *Gehenna*. And it's obvious He is speaking figuratively and "overstates here for rhetorical effect" about one's right eye and right hand. But as Yarbrough further notes, "even as a figure of speech his words are graphic."[13] Then are *Gehenna* and one's body also employed figuratively? Or, is this a mixed reference of figurative and literal?

Let's note that Jesus' main point here was "sin," literal sin. And even though He prescribes a figurative remedy, the force of meaning was not for this person to physically maim himself in order to enter into the Christian life, but for a person to literally stop doing that sin. If one didn't stop, the consequence of this rebelliousness could be that "your whole body" might literally and someday be thrown "into *Gehenna*."

Another relevant part of Jewish history comes from the prophet Isaiah, who preceded Jeremiah by more than one hundred years (740-687 B.C.). Isaiah both prophesied of and later recorded a mass dumping into *Gehenna* of 185,000 literal dead bodies of Assyrian soldiers who had been sent to attack and capture Jerusalem. They were killed by a plague sent by the Lord. This occurred at the end of the 8th century B.C. (circa 701-691 B.C.). Here's how Isaiah foretold and then recorded it:

"The voice of the Lord will shatter Assyria; with his scepter he will strike them down. Every stroke the Lord lays on them with his punishing rod will be to the music of tambourines and harps, as he fights them in battle with the blows of his arm. Topheth has long been prepared; it has been made ready for the king. Its fire pit has been made deep and wide, with an abundance of fire and wood; the breath of the Lord like a stream of burning sulfur, set it ablaze (Isa. 30:31-33).

"You conceive chaff, you give birth to straw; your breath is a fire that consumes you. The peoples will be burned as if to lime; like cut thornbushes they will be set ablaze. . . . The sinners in Zion are terrified; trembling grips the godless: "Who of us can dwell with the consuming fire? Who of us can dwell with everlasting burning?" (Isa. 33:12).

"Then the angel of the Lord went out and put to death a hundred and eighty-five thousand men in the Assyrian camp. When the people got up the next morning – there were all the dead bodies!" (Isa. 37:36).

The *Adam Clarke Commentary* explains that "Here the place where the Assyrian army was destroyed is called Topheth by a metonymy; for the Assyrian army was destroyed probably at a greater distance from Jerusalem, and quite on the opposite side of it."

Isaiah also used similar catastrophic language to describe the destruction of Edom:

"Edom's streams will be turned into pitch, her dust into burning sulfur; her land will become blazing pitch! It will not be quenched night and day; its smoke will rise forever. From generation to generation it will lie desolate; no one will ever pass through it again" (Isa. 34:9-10).

Once again, given and honoring the Jewish understanding of *Gehenna* from their history and prophets, and in anticipation of the fulfillment of Jeremiah's three *Gehenna* prophecies, how can we explain what Jesus was talking about in this above passage? Was Jesus really calling some people to physically dismember themselves during this life so that they would end up in heaven yet without some of their physical limbs or both eyes? Or was He really teaching them that keeping one's body intact while continuing to sin would eventually put you in an other-worldly hell? Or, is there a third and more practical option?

As we shall continue to see, the sins of the majority of Jews and, particularly, their sin of rejecting Jesus as their Messiah, caused them to disregard his prophetic warnings and not to follow his instructions to flee Jerusalem when they saw the two primary signs of the soon-coming national judgment starting to take place:

1) **Sign #1**—Jerusalem surrounded by armies (Luke 21:20-21). History records that four times and within a forty-year period after Jesus spoke these words Jerusalem was surrounded by foreign armies.

2) **Sign #2**—the abomination that causes desolation standing in the holy place, the Temple (Matt. 24:15-16). The Jewish historian, Josephus, records numerous abominations in the Temple perpetrated by both the apostate Jewish priesthood as well as the Roman armies—all of which led up to Jerusalem's desolation. He also reports that as a consequence of their unbelief and disobedience, 1.1 million Jews were killed in the fall and destruction of Jerusalem during the Jewish-Roman War of A.D. 66-70. This tally does not include those killed in countless skirmishes against the Jews in foreign cities, or in the Galilean campaign, or those who died in the Diaspora of disease, famine and persecution. Ninety-seven thousand more Jews went into foreign captivity.[14]

Thus, those who held onto false hopes, rejected Jesus as the Messiah, disregarded his prophetic words, and stayed in the city personally suffered this severity of national judgment in apt fulfillment of Jesus' words. And *Gehenna* was the dumping ground where many thousands of these dead bodies from Jerusalem literally and infamously ended up rotting and burning during and after this city's fiery destruction—exactly *as* and *when* Jesus had said, and exactly as the bodies of many infamous criminals and defeated foreign armies previously had been cast into

Gehenna, along with the carcasses of sacrificed animals and the offal of the city.[15]

#4 – Matthew 10:28

*"Do not be afraid of those who kill the body but cannot kill the soul. Rather, be afraid of the one who can destroy both soul and body in **Gehenna**."*

This verse and the next one are quite similar and repetitious. Here, the body and the soul are treated as separate and distinct entities. The first emphasis is upon those "who can kill the body but cannot kill the soul." A Roman soldier or a Zealot Jew could and did kill many bodies. They also killed Christ's body. Jesus' point here was to tell them to fear God. Only God is the "one who can destroy both soul and body in *Gehenna*"—or anywhere else for that matter: on the sea, on mountains, in other cities and towns, or in the countryside, etc. But let's especially note what Jesus did not say here. He did not say "punish" or "torment" the soul "forever" or for "eternity" in some afterlife, other-worldly place. Then does this destruction of the soul indicate an extinction of being, or annihilation of a person in the afterlife? Or, is it to be understood that *only* God is able to do this if He desires? We'll address this issue of annihilation in Chapter 12. But here let's note that in the very next three verses, Jesus relates to them "don't be afraid" because in "the will of your Father . . . . you are worth more than many sparrows" and He will protect them (Matt. 10:29-31).

5 – Luke 12:4-5

*"I tell you, my friends, do not be afraid of those who kill the body and after that can do no more. But I will show you whom you should fear: Fear him who, after the killing of the body, has power to throw you into **Gehenna**."*

These two verses are similar to the singular verse above, but with a change at the end—"throw you into *Gehenna*." So, what does this statement mean? Jesus elaborates a few verses later. "I have come to bring fire on the earth, and how I wish it were already kindled!" (Luke

12:49). "Hypocrites! You know how to interpret the appearance of the earth and the sky. How is it that you don't know how to interpret this present time?" (Luke 12:56).

Once again, this "fire" literally happened, and on a massive scale, as the Temple and the city were engulfed in flames started by Roman soldiers. This all took place "on the earth" and back then and there during that "this present time"—forty years later to be exact—as Jesus would time-specify the week before his crucifixion (see again usages #10 and #11 above and Matt. 23 & 24).

In the Luke 12:49 verse the Greek word for "earth" is *ge*. It's the standard word for land, or ground, or a region but not necessarily the whole planet, and often used to speak of the Promised Land (see Matt. 2:6; 2:20; Acts 7:3). Hence, this fiery judgment of which Jesus spoke was not far off in time or place. It was imminent, earthly, and local. Let's note, once again, that nothing in this verse or in the immediate context surrounding it speaks of an afterlife or other-worldly realization.

6 – Matthew 18:8-9

"If your hand or your foot causes you to sin, cut it off and throw it away. It is better for you to enter life maimed or crippled than to have two hands or two feet and be thrown into eternal fire. And if your eye causes you to sin, gorge it out and throw it away. It is better for you to enter life with one eye than to have two eyes and be thrown into the fire of **Gehenna**.*"*

7, 8 & 9 – Mark 9:42-49 (3X)

"And if anyone causes one of these little ones who believe in me to sin, it would be better for him to be thrown into the **sea** *with a large millstone tied around his neck. If your hand causes you to sin, cut it off. It is better for you to enter life maimed than with two hands to go into* **Gehenna**, *where the fire never goes out. And if your foot causes you to sin, cut it off. It is better for you to enter life crippled than to have two feet and be thrown into* **Gehenna***. And if your eye causes you to sin, pluck it out. It is better for you to* **enter the kingdom of God** *with one eye than to have two eyes and be thrown into*

Gehenna, where 'their worm does not die, and the fire is not quenched.' Everyone will be salted with fire. "

Since these two passages and three uses (#7, 8 & 9) are similar to and repetitions of Matthew 5:29-30 (#2 & 3 addressed above), here we'll focus on the four major additions (highlighted above in **bold**) that further describe and shed light on *Gehenna*.

First, is this "sea," hell? Of course not. And no Bible version translates it that way. Like *Gehenna*, the sea is another real, this-world place into which alive or dead human bodies could be and were thrown. And with a millstone tied around one's neck you'd sink quickly from sight and become fish food.

Second, and contrary to some traditional beliefs, the phrase "enter the kingdom of God," does not mean to enter heaven. Throughout his earthly ministry, Jesus presented, taught, modeled, and conferred upon his followers the kingdom of God as a then-and-there present, earthly reality. Thus, and in perfect harmony and consistency, the Apostle Paul taught that "we must go through many hardships to enter the kingdom of God" (Acts 14:22). Those hardships were and are this-world hardships. Likewise, this kingdom is a this-world domain. Many of these hardships are documented throughout the pages of the New Testament.

Third, "where 'their worm does not die, and the fire is not quenched.'" Some manuscripts also contain these two phrases at the end of verses 44 and 45. These expressions are regarded as some of the most horrible descriptions found in the Scriptures. Most Bible readers have been led to believe they describe conditions of endless conscious punishment of the wicked in an afterlife place they call "hell." But these words are a verbatim quote from part of the prophet Isaiah's very last verse of his Old Testament book. Traditionally, they, too, have been attributed to an other worldly place called "hell" and to teach eternal torment. But Isaiah's last verse reads in full as follows: "And they will go out and look upon the dead bodies of those who rebelled against me; their worm will not die, nor will their fire be quenched, and they will be loathsome to all mankind" (Isa. 66:24).

Factually, this verse could not be speaking of departed people suffering the eternal torment of being roasted with fire and crawled over by worms in an afterlife place called "hell," since alive people could not "go out and look upon" them there. It must refer to the dead bodies being consumed by fire and worms (maggots) in a this-world, burning garbage dump and the decaying, worm-infested pile of waste of *Gehenna* located just outside of Jerusalem. Nothing in Jesus' usage of this language indicates a different sense than that of the prophet Isaiah. And recall, once again, that Jesus also proclaimed, "When you see Jerusalem surrounded by armies, you will know that its desolation is near . . . . for this is the time of punishment in fulfillment of all that has been written" (Luke 21:20, 22). "All that has been written" is code for all the Old Testament scrolls. This would have included the scroll of Isaiah as well.

Fourth, the expression "the fire is not quenched" also has a historical background (see Matt. 3:12; Luke 3:17). And the Jews had never heard this language used in any other way than for a this-world, national judgment. Below are three examples of past uses and fulfillments:

Ezekiel 20:47-48 – Regarding God's promised judgment on Judah.

> *"Say to the southern forest: 'Hear the word of the Lord. This is what the Sovereign Lord says: I am about to set **fire** to you, and it will **consume** all your trees, both green and dry. The **blazing flame will not be quenched**, and every face from south to north will be scorched by it. Everyone will see that I the Lord have **kindled** it; it will **not be quenched.**"*

Babylon fulfilled these very words in the destruction of Jerusalem in 586-7 B.C. And the Jews were carried off into captivity.

Jeremiah 21:10-12 – Prophesied of this same future-coming national judgment event with similar unquenchable, fiery language.

> *"I have determined to do this city **harm and not good**, declares the Lord. It will be given into the hands of the king of Babylon, and he will **destroy it with fire**. Moreover, say to the royal house of Judah, 'Hear the word of the Lord: O house of David, this is what the Lord says:*
>> *"Administer justice every morning;*
>> *rescue from the hand of his oppressor*
>> *the one who has been robbed.*
>> *or my wrath will break out and burn like **fire***

because of the evil you have done—
burn with no one to quench it.
I am against you, Jerusalem,
you who live above this valley
on the rocky plateau, declares the Lord—
you who say, "Who can come against us?
Who can enter our refuge?"
I will punish you as your deeds deserve, declares the
Lord.
*I will kindle a **fire** in your forests*
*that will **consume everything** around you."*
(Also see Isa. 34:5-10; Jer. 4:4; 7:20; 17:27; Lam. 4:11;
2 Ki. 22:17; 2 Chron. 34:25)

This same "not be quenched" fire and burning certainly belonged to this world and went out long ago after it consumed and devoured everything these temporal judgment verses say above.

Amos 5:4-6 – Amos prophesied of another similar judgment promised by God. It was to come on the northern kingdom of Israel at the hands of the Assyrians.

*"This is what the Lord says to the house of Israel: "Seek me and live; do not seek Bethel, do not go to Gilgal, do not journey to Beersheba. For Gilgal will surely go into exile, and Bethel will be reduced to nothing." Seek the Lord and live, or he will sweep through the house of Joseph like **a fire**; it will devour, and Bethel will have **no one to quench** it."*

This prophecy was fulfilled in 722 B.C. when the ten northern tribes were carried into captivity. Thus, both of these unquenchable fires which consumed the two sections of Israel were unstoppable. But these burnings did end, literally. This fire is not burning today. It went out after accomplishing its purpose.

Fifth, the expression "eternal fire" is also used in the New Testament book of Jude to reflect upon the divine judgment inflicted upon Sodom and Gomorrah which "serve as an example of those who suffer the punishment of eternal fire" (Jude 7). And that fire also expired long ago.

Just like the "unquenchable fire," this fire is not endless. It only burned until it had consumed its object.

Perhaps, with this Jewish background in mind, we can better appreciate John the Baptist's words about how Jesus would baptize with "fire" and burn up chaff "with unquenchable fire" (see again Matt. 3:11-12). His inspired proclamation sets the stage for and re-introduces this familiar language into that 1st-century, contemporary scene.

Therefore, when Jesus spoke of unquenchable fire and worm not dying here in Mark 9:43, his Jewish listeners, knowing this history and being familiar with this figure-of-speech language, would have immediately associated it with a future-coming, *this-world*, national judgment upon Jerusalem and Judah. Remember, that's the only way they had ever heard this language used. So, if Jesus meant something different by it, why didn't He say so? At the least, He should have clarified the matter and avoided possible confusion. Fact is, He issued no changes, clarifications, or disclaimers. And whenever He spoke of the afterlife, He used these two words—heaven or Hades.

Nevertheless, we cannot take this figure-of-speech "fire" literally to a fault even though these literal divine judgments often involved literal fire. In all the various times that God had previously brought this type of judgment on Israel and other nations, this fire consumed and devoured the object of God's wrath. But that literal burning and God's judgment also eventually ended. Thus, and historically, this fire was *not* employed by God for the purpose of punishing and torturing the departed and conscious souls of people forever and ever in an other-worldly, afterlife place. It had nothing to do with the afterlife. But it had everything to do with this life on this earth for the people involved.

Therefore, when Jesus spoke of unquenchable fire and worm not dying . . . his Jewish listeners . . . would have immediately associated it with a future-coming, *this-world*, national judgment.

Paradoxically, a fire that would not be quenched does not necessitate a fire that would burn unendingly or eternally in either this world or the afterlife. Hence, unquenchable does not mean it never stops. It means it would burn and cannot be stopped or put out until it accomplished its divine purpose. Then, when it has done its work and all is burned up and there is nothing more to burn, it goes out. Occasionally, this unquenchable fire comes in world history—against nations, cities, peoples, and even individual people. Like God's acts of grace, mercy, and love, his judgments and "raging fire" are ongoing aspects of his character and sovereignty and are unstoppable (Heb. 10:26-27).

Look, for instance, at what Daniel saw in his vision of heaven:

"As I looked, thrones were set in place, and the Ancient of Days took his seat. His clothing was as white as snow; the hair of his head was white like wool. His throne was flaming with fire, and its wheels were all ablaze. A river of fire was flowing, coming out from before him . . . . I kept looking until the beast was slain and its body destroyed and thrown into the blazing fire" (Dan. 7:9-11).

Not only did the earthly cities of Sodom and Gomorrah experience this fire of God, but the Bible says "they serve as an example of those who suffer the punishment of eternal fire" (Jude 7). Why do these two former *earthly* towns serve as "an example" and constant warning for all time? It is because "It is a dreadful (fearful) thing to fall into the hands of the living God" (Heb. 10:31), here and now in this world—not to mention, there and later in the afterlife.

In sum, only God has the power to cast someone, or ones, into this earthly "fire" that can "not be quenched." The Bible never uses this "fire-cannot-be quenched" language in association with conscious everlasting suffering for all eternity in an other-worldly, afterlife place. Once again, a this-earthly understanding is in perfect harmony with Jeremiah's three *Gehenna* prophecies. And this fulfillment was to occur within the generation in which Jesus was crucified (Matt. 23:36; 24:34).

Fifth, "everyone will be salted with fire." Being salted is not the same as being thrown into the salt shaker or having the salt poured on you, so to speak. Most likely back then, this metaphor meant everyone will be affected by this massive judgment and disaster. And they were. Even those who obeyed Jesus' instructions to flee Jerusalem and this fiery national judgment were affected by being totally uprooted and possibly the loss of family and friends who refused to leave. But, as we shall also see in later chapters of this book, everyone, most certainly, will go through and be tested by fire (1 Cor. 3:12-15).

James' Single Usage

#12 – James 3:6

> *"The tongue also is a fire, a world of evil among the parts of the body. It corrupts the whole person, sets the whole course of his life on fire, and is itself set on fire by* **Gehenna**.*"*

James pens this letter in A.D. 60. It's the only place *Gehenna* is used outside of Jesus' usages in the Gospels. Obviously, the degenerating conditions and the soon-to-arrive four sieges of Jerusalem from A.D. 66 to A.D. 70 were to adversely affect the minds and tongues of many trapped inside the city walls. They would not be obeying Jesus' warnings to flee and, most likely, would speak negatively of him. Therefore, they would suffer the ultimate penalty in the subsequent destruction and desolation of this renowned Temple and city of the living God.

Others, however, have suggested that James was only employing *Gehenna* here as a figure, symbol, or synonym of all that was horrible, filthy, and morally corrupt in the mind of a Jew at that time. Thus, James was only emphasizing how a corrupt, wicked, and foul tongue inflames and defiles the whole body, which, of course, is true. But James goes on and prophesies further about the tongue (Jas. 3:9-12) and about this coming judgment calling it "the day of slaughter" (Jas. 5:5). Moreover, he puts his contemporaries on imminent notice that "the Lord's coming is at hand . . . . The judge is standing at the door!" (Jas 5:7-9).

Once again, this judgment happened, exactly *as* and *when* Jesus had said and exactly *as* and *when* the early Church and every New Testament writer, including James, expected—as they were guided into "all truth" and told "what is yet to come" by the Holy Spirit (John 16:13).[16]

What Questions Should We Now Be Asking?

So nowadays does *Gehenna* apply to us? Fact is, the word *Gehenna* was never spoken of to the Gentiles by Jesus. And Paul, who wrote fourteen epistles, never mentioned it once, nor does John, Peter, Jude, or Luke in Acts. Nor was any Gentile ever threatened with the prospect of *Gehenna*. That's a strange silence if *Gehenna* is "hell," strange, indeed. But that's not a strange silence if *Gehenna* was particular and only applied to the bodies and souls of 1st-century Jews living in Jerusalem during the A.D. 66-70 Roman-Jewish War?

Furthermore, since *Gehenna* was and still is a proper noun and name for a real, this-worldly, physical location just outside Jerusalem, why did it need translated at all? We don't translate other proper nouns and place names in the New Testament—such as Gethsemane, Calvary, and Bethlehem, which are also located in the immediate vicinity of Jerusalem—as something entirely different. Why only this one?

This judgment happened, exactly *as* and *when* Jesus had said; and . . . the early Church and every New Testament writer, including James, expected.

What justification forces us to interpret and understand the real earthly place of *Gehenna* otherwise? Is there any textual evidence or indication that requires us to think that *Gehenna* has any application or relevance beyond how 1st-century Jews understood it? After all, they were more familiar with this valley and its use and history in the Old Testament (especially Jeremiah's three prophecies) than we are. And today its fire is gone, the worms are gone, and it's no longer used as a garbage dump. That *Gehenna* was not eternal. In the absence of any such evidence, isn't it plain that Jesus was warning them that their city would soon be destroyed? By what hermeneutic (rule or principle of interpretation) do we suddenly turn this valley in Jerusalem into an afterlife, other-worldly place of eternal conscious punishment?

Another fact is, Jesus never said the English word "hell." He said *Gehenna*. Therefore, how could He believe in "hell?" Is not, then, "hell" an improper translation for *Gehenna*? Why not simply take this word and place in its most literal, face-value sense and leave it un-translated—then it would not be so confusing or misunderstood?

Seriously, does translating *Gehenna*, literally and exactly, as *Gehenna* and understanding it both literally and symbolically as a *this-world*, fiery national judgment involve any scriptural impossibilities or conflicts with other passages? I know of none. Besides, a *this-world* judgment event is exactly what happened there. It seems our modern-day, passed-down, and popular translation and concept of *Gehenna* as "hell" is far different than Jesus' uses and teachings.

In defense of the traditional view, Yarborough frankly states that "Jesus' words on hell seem fairly straightforward."[17] The authors of the book *Hell Under Fire* merely maintain and want us all to believe that hell just "developed" via a "transferred use of this place name for the final state of the lost."[18] Well, who did this "developing?" And by what and whose authority? Was it possibly the Roman Catholic Church in subsequent centuries?

In my opinion it makes better sense and is most reasonable to understand Jesus' *Gehenna* as it meant the same to the Jews in Jesus' day as it meant to the Jews in Jeremiah's day—i.e., a place, a term, and a symbol for a coming national judgment upon them and all the literal horror of being rejected and abandoned by God to an enemy who would cause their dead bodies to be thrown into the burning, worm-infested piles of waste and decay of the city garbage dump named *Gehenna*.

Sharon Baker confirms and summarizes this 1st-century Jewish perception of *Gehenna* in writing these words:

> When Jesus spoke of Gehenna, his hearers would think of the valley of rotting, worm-infested garbage, where the fire always burned, smoke always lingered, and if the wind blew just right, a smell that sickened the senses wafted in the air. The word "Gehenna" called to mind total horror and disgust. . . . a place to which no one wanted to go.[19]

Before closing this chapter, let's also note that none of the above passages associated *Gehenna* with Satan or demons or spoke of people being tormented there. For me, the bottom line is this. All the Old and New Testament usages of this valley named *Gehenna* render our modern-day concept of it being an other-worldly, afterlife place called "hell" as highly suspect, at best. So, where am I wrong on this? Would you agree or disagree? Hell yes? Hell no?

Yarbrough, along with most traditionalists, most likely would disagree insisting that my historical reasoning and biblical support are simply "a sign of misguided sentimentality rather than the discovery of a truer meaning in Jesus' words."[20] No doubt, he would further contend that I am allowing "the sensibilities of our age to redefine what his words mean."[21] But how can that be if I am simply going back to the original and undiluted meaning of a word in its historical context?

Packer, of course, is supportive of Yarbrough's position. Unfortunately, he erroneously argues that "every New Testament author mentions hell as well" (which they don't). He rhetorically asks, "How could our Lord and his prophets have been any clearer? What more could they have said to put everyone out of doubt about their meaning?"[22] Well, I ask the same two questions but for different reasons—the reasons we've covered in these last two chapters.

A Metaphorical Irony?

Ironically, I find it quite, if not totally inconsistent, that traditionalists, like Albert Mohler, Jr., rail against 18th-century Enlightenment skeptics and modern-day liberal theologians for "arguing that hell should be viewed metaphorically, not literally."[23] Of course, these liberals take this stance to dismiss hell as an afterlife reality as well as its consequences. Instead, they prefer to cite various "hell-on-earth" atrocities.

But then traditionalists turn around and do the very same thing, do they not? They argue that *Gehenna* is to be understood metaphorically, and not literally, as the afterlife place of eternal conscious punishment for all the lost. This interpretative switch rings quite hollow. Why is this same methodology invalid in the former instance and not invalid in the latter? Doesn't this methodology cut both ways?

And yet, if *Gehenna* is not "hell" but *Gehenna*—a real, *this-world* place and city garbage dump and a symbol of fiery national judgment— you may now, and rightly so, be wondering from where in the hell did we come up with the word "hell?" And what about Sheol, Hades, and Tartarus? How do they fit in with this hell-talk and doctrine? Do they point to hell, or not? It is to this task of further re-discovery we next turn as we re-explore the shocking etymology of hell, the afterlife compartments of Sheol, Hades, and Tartarus, as well as some other hellish problems.

Chapter 4

Shocking Etymology and Other Hellish Problems

W hat's the opposite of these words: "to torment and punish forever?" How about "to cover, conceal, and protect for a temporary period of time?" Shockingly, perhaps for some, this latter phrase is the etymology and original meaning for our modern English word "hell." Moreover, it comes from a pagan source and not from the Bible. It also has little, if any, resemblance to our modern-day images of hell.

Etymology is the study of the origin, history, and derivation of words. *The New Encyclopedia Britannica* confirms this little-known etymology this way: "Hell, the abode or state of being of evil spirits or souls that are damned to postmortem punishment. Derived from an Anglo-Saxon word meaning "to conceal," or "to cover . . . ."[1] *Webster's Dictionary* explains that "hell" comes from middle English, old English, and old high German, (*hel, helle, helan*) and arose during the Anglo-Saxon pagan period (A.D. 400 – 1100).[2]

Our word helmet is derived from this same etymology, root, and meaning.[3] A helmet covers, conceals, and protects the head. It certainly does not torment or punish one's head.

Similarly, the word "hel" or "helle" was used in Europe during the middle ages when potato farmers would "hel" their potatoes. That is, during the winter they would cover, conceal, and protect their potatoes by digging holes, putting their potatoes in the ground, and covering them with dirt. These farmers referred to this process as "putting their potatoes in hel"—again, for the purpose of care and protection, and not torment and punishment.

Today, my wife conceals and protects the potatoes she buys at the grocery by storing them in a dark place so they won't sprout buds and go soft and bad as quickly as they would in a lighted and open area. In some parts of England it is also said that to cover a building with a roof of tiles or thatch was "to hel the building." That job was done by people called "helliers." Therefore, to hel a house meant to cover and protect it with a roof. I'm told that the term heling a house is still used in the New England portions of the United States.

Ironically, but in keeping with the etymology and original meaning of hell, we are still "helling" most dead people today. How so? We "hell" a person every time we conceal, cover, and protect the body of someone who has died (Christian or non-Christian, alike) by laying them in a casket, closing the lid, placing the casket in a vault, lowering the vault into the ground, and covering the vault with dirt. Of course, this meaning could not be applied to cremation, which does not cover and protect the body. It destroys it.

Thus, the origin and basic meaning of the word "hell" had nothing to do with an other-worldly, afterlife place or with a place of eternal torment and punishment with no hope of escape. That connotation or derivation had to come later. But the modern-day meaning evolved, or devolved, depending on your perspective, from referring to the common earthly grave of all deceased human beings into its meaning today of being a nether-world place of eternal conscious torment and punishment for only the damned.

Consequently, most of our thinking about hell and hellfire today does not come from either the Bible or from its etymology and historical usage. Of course, words can and sometimes do change their meaning over time. Therefore, etymology may or may not be a certain guide. Fact is, our modern-day word "hell" is derived more from Dante's *Divine Comedy* and Milton's *Paradise Lost* as well as from the nether-world beliefs of other ancient religions. For instance, the Babylonians and Assyrians believed the nether world was a place where gods and demons of great strength and fierceness presided over the damned. The Egyptians believed the Other World was a place of pits of fire for the damned.

Consistent with the background on hell that we have been discussing so far, Anglican theologian N.T. Wright admits and surmises:

- "The point is that when Jesus was warning his hearers about Gehenna, he was not, as a general rule, telling them that unless they repented in this life they would burn in the next one . . . .
- "Rome would turn Jerusalem into a hideous, stinking extension of it own smoldering rubbish heap . . . .
- "It is . . . with difficulty that we can extrapolate . . . of a warning about what may happen after death itself . . . .
- "Jesus simply didn't say much about the future life . . . .
- "We cannot therefore look to Jesus's teaching for any fresh detail on whether there really are some who finally reject God. . . ."[4]

So if our traditional and "scripturally based" case for "hell" using *Gehenna*, "unquenchable fire," and a changed meaning for "hell" is, at best, highly suspect, then is there nothing to fear after this life is over? Are all the other afterlife warnings in the Bible to be dismissed as meaningless, misleading, and incorrect? Is there no postmortem justice? What about the other three biblical words sometimes translated as "hell"—Sheol, Hades, Tartarus? And what about other "hell" associated terminology like: "weeping and gnashing of teeth," "fire and brimstone," "outer darkness," "the abyss" or "bottomless pit," the "lake of fire," and, "eternal punishment?" Will these places and phrases support our traditional understandings about "hell," or not? Let's see.

Sheol—the Temporary Unseen Place of the Dead

For Old Testament Jews, Sheol was the temporary, afterlife, and holding place of the souls of all dead people. It's portrayed as a dark and shadowy dungeon in which there is no activity worthy of mention, nor were there any moral distinctions. The old *King James Version* of the Old Testament translates Sheol's 65 appearances as: "hell" 31 times, "the grave" 31 times in a generic sense, and "the pit" 3 times. Most modern translations no longer translate any of Sheol's uses as "hell," preferring instead, "the grave," "the pit," or simply "death." All of which prompts

Moody Church senior pastor, Erwin Lutzer, to concede that "this inconsistency in translation has caused some to be confused regarding what sheol really means."[5]

In the original Hebrew, the term Sheol means "unseen." Notably, this unseen afterlife place in the Old Testament was not a place of punishment. Jacob was there (Gen. 37:35: 42:38; 44:29, 31). Righteous Job longed for it (Job 14:13). David spoke of going there (Psa. 49:14-15). And even Jesus went there (Psa. 16:10; Acts 2:24-31).

In these cases and more, dead souls were "unseen" because they were in the other-worldly abode of the departed in Sheol. And they were all awaiting the general resurrection of the dead on the "last day" (John 6:39, 40, 44, 54; 11:24). According to Jesus, the reason they were still waiting was because heaven was not open yet (John 3:13; 13:33, 36). Then, writing around A.D. 57, the Apostle Paul in 1 Corinthians 15:54-55 cites portions of these two Old Testament Sheol passages in expectation of the imminent fulfillment of the resurrection of the dead:

1) Paul – "Where, O death, is your victory? Where, O death, is your sting?" Quoted from Hosea 13:14 – "I will ransom them from the power of the grave (Sheol); I will redeem them from death. Where, O death, are your plagues? Where, O grave (Sheol), is your destruction?"

2) Paul – "Death has been swallowed up in victory." Quoted from Isaiah 25:8 – "he will swallow up death forever. The Sovereign Lord will wipe away the tears from all faces; he will remove the disgrace of his people from all the earth. The Lord has spoken."

"This inconsistency in translation has caused some to be confused regarding what sheol really means."

Sheol is also used in a figurative sense to speak of national or city judgments—i.e., in terms of the vanishing of a nation or city. Isaiah 14:15 prophesied of Babylon being "brought down to the grave, to the depths of the pit." Ezekiel 26:19-21 prophesied of Tyre being made a "desolate city" and brought down to the "ocean depths" and "to the pit" in the "earth below." Historically and spatially, this nation and this city did not go to a particular location—this-worldly or other-worldly. They simply were destroyed and disappeared.

Likewise, in Deuteronomy 32:22 and following verses, Sheol language is coupled with a fiery national judgment that God would bring on Israel in her latter/last days because of her idolatry (Deut. 31:29; 32:29). This, too, has no application to an afterlife "hell." In a broader figurative application, Sheol also was used to refer to any gloomy or miserable state, degraded condition, or extreme suffering without reference to its cause.

Therefore, *Collier's Encyclopedia* correctly writes about the Hebrew "Sheohl" [sic]. Again, the **bolds** are mine:

> First it (Hell) stands for the Hebrew Sheohl of the Old Testament and the Greek Hades of the Septuagint and New Testament. Since Sheohl in Old Testament times referred simply to the abode of the dead and suggested no moral distinctions, **the word 'hell,' as understood today, is not a happy translation.**[6]

Correspondingly, *The Encyclopedia Americana* has this to say about our modern-day confusion and misunderstandings:

> Much confusion and misunderstanding has been caused through the early translators of the Bible persistently rendering the Hebrew Sheohl and the Greek Hades and Gehenna by **the word hell**. The simple transliteration of these words by the translators of the revised editions of the Bible has not sufficed to appreciably clear up **this confusion and misconception.**[7]

Some scholars cite the Greek teaching of the immortality of the human soul and the nether world, which probably began to infiltrate Jewish teachings around the time of Alexander the Great, for the reason that the Hebrew Sheol corresponds with the Greek Hades. Both were viewed synonymously as being the unseen place of the dead, and not a place filled with fire, torture, and screams of torment. Rather, they were understood to be a place of gloom and darkness (Job 10:21), of resting and silence (Psa. 115:17), with neither pain nor pleasure, and neither reward nor punishment. And all the dead were there in this invisible world or state of the dead without distinction—the good and the bad, rich and poor, Jews and Gentiles, kings and paupers. All "slept" together in this shadowy spirit-realm abode awaiting resurrection. Yet it was not

seen as a place of separation from God. Scripture states God was there
(see Psa. 139:7-8; Amos 9:1-2).

Hades—the Equivalent of Sheol

Hades is the New Testament Greek equivalent of the Old Testament
Hebrew Sheol. This is confirmed in the Septuagint, the Greek translation
of the Old Testament Hebrew Bible, where Sheol is translated as Hades.[8]
And Hades, like Sheol, refers to things unseen in that common resting
place of all the dead—i.e., departed spirits/souls.

In the New Testament the word Hades occurs ten times—Matt.
11:23; 16:18; Luke 10:15; 16:23; Acts 2:27, 31; Rev. 1:18; 6:8; 20:13,
14. The *King James Version* (old and new) translates Hades as "hell."
Most modern translations like *NIV, NASB, ASV*, and *YLT* leave it un-
translated as "hades" or render it as "the grave" so that it might be
distinguished from "hell."

Vine's Expository Dictionary of Biblical Words adds these important
and clarifying remarks: "Hades . . . it corresponds to 'Sheol' in the O.T.
and N.T., it has been unhappily rendered 'Hell'. . . . It never denotes the
grave, nor is it the permanent region of the lost; in point of time it is, for
such, intermediate between decease and the doom of Gehenna . . . . the
signification of the temporary destiny of the doomed."[9]

Incorrectly, the Apostle's Creed states that "He [Christ] descended
into hell"—a translation and expression that conveys a wrong idea.
Biblically, Christ descended into Hades, as we shall shortly see.

But in contrast with Sheol, Hades is not morally neutral. In his
parable of the rich man and Lazarus in Luke 16:19-31 (not the Lazarus
Jesus raised from the dead in John 11), Jesus depicts Hades as a two-
compartment holding place of dead and departed souls awaiting their
resurrection. And they are separated by a great gulf. Lazarus resided in
the righteous side, a place of "comfort" called "paradise" (also see Luke
23:43; 2 Cor. 12:4) or "Abraham's bosom/side" (Luke 16:22-23 –
KJV/NIV). The rich man, however, was confined in the unrighteous side,
a place of doom and punishment. And, indeed, in Jesus' parable, the rich
man was suffering and conscious of his punishment. This depiction is
different from what we found in Sheol.

Some scholars attack this parable's credibility and applicability. They contend that while Jesus often taught people in parables or illustrations as a way for them to grasp a point or principle, these stories, and particularly this story, were not meant to be taken as literal accounts, a detailed geography, or that it represented an accurate depiction of afterlife reality at that time. They further claim that Jesus' reference to two compartments represents the influence of Greek thought. Consequently, they argue that Jesus' focus here was not upon teaching about literal attributes of an other-world, afterlife holding place of the dead. Rather, it was a fabricated illustration about wealth and poverty that was used to ridicule the indifference of Pharisees, to convey the principle of how they and we should show mercy to those who suffer, and to demonstrate how to compassionately treat people in this life.

Three factors, however, mitigate against this reductionistic understanding and criticism. 1) Why would Jesus use this illustration if He knew it wasn't true? 2) Why would He use it if the Pharisees to whom He was talking did not hold to this belief? 3) Why didn't those Pharisees challenge Jesus on this view of Hades and the afterlife? The reason is, they all held this same view. It coincided with their belief.

The 1st-century Jewish historian, Josephus, confirms this solidarity of belief in his treatise on Hades that he wrote toward the end of that century. In this treatise he laid out the most common Jewish position on Hades, Tartarus, and heaven, which was current in Jesus' day as well. And even though there is an authorship controversy,[10] here's a portion from what Josephus wrote. It's titled: "An Extract out of Josephus' Discourse to the Greeks Concerning Hades:"

> Now as to Hades, wherein the souls of the righteous and unrighteous are detained . . . a *subterraneous* region . . . . a place of custody for souls, in which angels are appointed as guardians to them, who distribute to them *temporary punishments*, agreeable to everyone's behavior and manners . . . . it is prepared for a day aforedetermined by God, in which one righteous sentence shall deservedly be passed on all men. . . . while the just shall obtain *an incorruptible* and never-fading *kingdom*. These are now indeed confined in Hades, but not in the same place wherein the unjust are confined . . . [Re: the just] while they wait for the rest and *eternal* new *life in heaven*, which is to succeed this region. This place we call *The Bosom of Abraham*. But as to the unjust, they are dragged by force to the *left hand* by the angels allotted for

punishment. This is the discourse concerning Hades, wherein the souls
of all men are confined until a proper season, which God hath
determined, when he will make a resurrection of all men from the dead
. . . .[11]

The Jewish Talmud also contains a sizeable amount of material and
sheds more light on this popular view of Hades in Judaism at that time.
Additionally, modern-day scholars and authors (Edersheim, Schaff,
Schurer, and others) have further documented this view. In a nutshell,
therefore, Jesus' parable illustration in Luke 16 is an accurate
representation of the 1st-century Jewish view of this temporary place of
separation for all the dead (righteous and unrighteous). There, the
righteous awaited a redeemer to remove them from Sheol/Hades and take
them to heaven.

And yet, confusion about the afterlife permeates the Church today.
Once again, Senior Pastor Erwin Lutzer, in this book *One Minute After
You Die,* exemplifies this confusion when he writes:

No one is yet in hell. Someday, hades will be thrown into hell, but that
has yet not happened . . . . But after the Ascension of Christ believers
are said to go directly into heaven. In other words, the two regions of
hades no longer exist side by side; there is reason to believe that
Abraham's Bosom is in heaven today . . . . Hades, as far as we know,
now has only one region, and that is where unbelievers enter. I believe
it is still an abode for departed spirits, a temporary intermediate state
where those who have not received God's forgiveness must wait until
further notice.[12]

For Pastor Lutzer, the rich man in Hades whom Jesus mentioned in
his Luke 16 parable "is still there awaiting the final judgment of the lake
of fire."[13] And when that supposed future time comes, "the news that
awaits them [him] will not be encouraging."[14]

But what if that time of judgment already came, nineteen centuries
ago—exactly *as* and *when* Jesus specified and every New Testament
writer and the early Church expected as they were guided into all truth
and told about the things to come by the Holy Spirit (John 16:13)—and
Pastor Lutzer, as well as most Bible-reading and believing Christians,
have just missed it?

The Emptying Out of Hades

Here's a quick look at an alternative view. It's a chronological and highlighted recap of how the righteous side of Hades may already have been emptied out over nineteen centuries ago.[15]

First, and immediately after his crucifixion, Jesus descended into Hades—the righteous side of the holding place of spirits/souls of the dead. It was not a place of torment, nor was it "hell"—a mistranslation. We know this from Acts 2:27, 31 where Peter directly quotes from Psalm 16:10 regarding Sheol. We also know that Jesus spent the better part of three days and three nights there (Matt. 12:40). During that time between his death and resurrection, He preached to the spirits of the righteous dead held captive in that afterlife prison (1 Pet. 3:19-20; 4:6; Eph. 4:9).[16] But this understanding of these passages is contested.[17]

Second, Jesus came out of Hades via his resurrection from the dead and in fulfillment of David's Psalm 16:10 prophecy that the Messiah would not be left in Hades and his body would not see decay.

Third and next, the "firstfruit" group was raised from the dead as Matthew's gospel recorded. "The tombs broke open and the bodies of many holy people who had died were raised to life. They came out of the tombs, and after Jesus' resurrection they went into the holy city and appeared to many people" (Matt. 27:51-53; 1 Cor. 15:20, 23; from the typology of Lev. 23).

Fourth, "when he [Jesus] ascended on high, he led captives in his train" or "led captivity captive" (Eph. 4:8, *NIV KJV*) up into heaven with Him. This could very well have been, or at least included, that same "firstfruit" group.

Fifth, on the "last day" singular (John 6:39, 40, 44, 54; 11:24) of the "last days" plural in which they were living back then and there (Heb.1:1-2), the rest of the harvest of righteous dead souls were taken out of the righteous compartment of Hades, by-passed earth, were transported directly to heaven, received their judgment of rewards/loss (Heb. 9:27; 1 Cor. 3:10-15) and their new "spiritual body" (1 Cor. 15:44) which "God gives" (1 Cor. 15:38). Regardless of whether you think this has already happened (as I do) or is yet to happen (as most Christians do), the biblical fact is this. The righteous side of Hades either was or will someday be emptied out by Jesus Who is "the Living One," "was dead" and is now "alive for ever and ever," and holds "the keys to death and Hades (Rev. 1:18).[18]

This past or yet-future fulfillment leaves us with only the unrighteous compartment of Hades still occupied. What was, or still is, to become of that other side and the deceased spirits/souls imprisoned therein? Scripture tells us that they, too, were to be resurrected (Dan. 12:2). Thirty-some years after Jesus' and the firstfruits' resurrection, the Apostle Paul makes this nearness declaration during his defense before the governor, Felix: "There will be a resurrection of both the righteous and the wicked" (Acts 24:15). Unfortunately, this customary and familiar translation is also a traitor. The original Greek literally reads, "there is *to be about to be* a resurrection of both the righteous and the wicked." "To be about to be" is a double intensification of imminence (nearness) language missed by all reductionistic "will be" translations.

Then where did or where will someday the souls of the unrighteous go when resurrected out of that other compartment of the hadean realm? John, in the Bible's last book of Revelation tells us that "death and Hades" itself as well as those whose "name was not found written in the book of life" would be "thrown into the lake of fire" (Rev. 20:13-15). Once again, and regardless of one's eschatological view (past or future fulfillment), Revelation's lake of fire is the final destination and surviving reality for Hades and those spirits/souls still contained within it.

Contrary to much popular belief, this emptying out of Hades and its being cast into the lake of fire was precisely what Jesus was talking about when He proclaimed and prophesied during his earthly ministry that "the gates of Hades will not overcome it (his church)" (Matt. 16:18). He was not, as is usually assumed, talking about evil forces operating in our physical world.

Then where did or where will someday the souls of the unrighteous go when resurrected out of that other compartment of the hadean realm?

It's further possible that this casting of death, Hades, and non-believers into the lake of fire was also what the Apostle Paul was talking about when he prophesied that "the last enemy to be destroyed is death"

(1 Cor. 15:26). In Scripture, the word "death" means "separation." *Vine's Expository Dictionary of Biblical Words* defines death as "the separation of the soul . . . from the body . . . . the separation of man from God" and especially notes that death "never denotes non-existence."[19]

Therefore, Hades—the temporary abode of all the dead, the realm of the departed, the unseen world of disembodied spirits—was viewed by the Jews of Jesus' day as a place of separation of the soul from the presence of God. But someday this was to change as part of God's plan of redemption. And even though Christians largely and correctly agree that Christ defeated sin on the cross and with his resurrection, the hadean realm remained operative throughout the New Testament. This is why, in my opinion, the afterlife place of Hades was Paul's "last enemy"—and not physical death itself. The Bible plainly teaches that "man is destined to die once, and after that the judgment" (Heb. 9:27). This reality does not change. What changed, or changes, was the emptying out of Hades and its being cast into the lake of fire. Hadean death (that separation) was the only remaining obstacle standing between the saints and their postmortem entrance into the presence of God in heaven. Again, it either was or still is to be defeated on the "last day."

Doesn't this exposition better explain, scripturally and historically, why "death and Hades" are so closely associated in the Revelation (Rev. 1:18, 6:8; 20:13-15)? Fact is, Hades was to the spirits/souls sequestered there (separation from God and the Temple where He dwelled on earth), what the grave was to the body (separation from the soul). But then on the "last day" singular of the "last days" plural, everything changed or will change someday, depending on your eschatological view.

In my opinion, Hades was completely emptied out by Jesus Who holds "the keys to death and Hades" (Rev. 1:18), and Who had been there before for the better part of three days and three nights. Next, Hades itself was thrown into the lake of fire, along with those still in it (Rev. 20:13-15). Of course, most Christians believe all these things are yet to happen. But past or future, this "last enemy" of "death"—i.e., separation in the hadean realm—was or will be someday absorbed into the lake of fire.

If, however, my past-fulfillment view is correct, no saint is still sequestered in the righteous side of Hades today waiting for a future resurrection day and the opening of heaven (see again John 3:13). Then does Hades still exist if it's in the lake of fire today? Or will it still exist when it goes into this lake of fire someday? Is it still operative as it was in Bible times? We'll discuss the lake of fire in a moment and the question of who does or does not go into it in Parts III and IV.

A final note: Hades, like Gehenna and Sheol before, is also used twice by Jesus in a figurative manner to prophesy of a future, this-world judgment—i.e., the calamity, suffering, and vanishing of the city of Capernaum (see Matt. 11:23 and Luke 10:15). No Bible commentator or translation suggests that this city went into an afterlife place of endless punishment termed "hell."

Tartarus—Who Knows What This Means, Was or Is?

Our fourth and final biblical word usually translated as "hell" is the Greek word, *Tartarus*. It's found only once in the Bible and never used in the Septuagint. *Young's Literal Translation* renders it directly as "Tartarus." Furthermore, this single usage only refers to it as a place of incarceration of fallen angels/demons awaiting further judgment by God. Human souls are not mentioned. "For if God did not spare angels when they sinned, but sent them to hell (Tartarus), putting them into gloomy dungeons (into chains of darkness) to be held for judgment;" (2 Pet. 2:4; also see Jude 13).

Paradoxically, Tartarus in the original Greek language is not a noun. It's a participle—i.e., making a verb from a noun. Scholar, John McRay, recognizes this linguistic fact and contributes this bit of wisdom:

> I have transliterated the Greek participle *tartarize* here because its exact meaning is debatable . . . . The Greek text literally says that God "delivered them to pits of nether gloom [gloomy dungeons – *NIV*] having *tartarized* them . . . ." Whether a final state of punishment or an interim state of punishment is indicated here is not specified. However, it is clear that the punishment is currently in progress and will continue until the parousia and the final day of judgment. [20]

With no other biblical use, the *Adam Clarke Commentary* recommends "we must have recourse to the Greek writers for its meaning." Of course, relying on Greek writers means opening a can of mystical worms. Clarke lists several Greek writers but focuses on the *Iliad* (viii., lin. 13 and circa 720 B.C.) in which Homer writes without any explanation, "threatening any of the gods who should presume to assist either the Greeks or the Trojans, that he should either come back wounded to heaven, or be sent to *Tartarus*."

Clarke's commentary next compares Peter's use of *Tartarus* with Homer's mythological prison, thusly:

> On the whole, then, . . . in St. Peter, is the same as . . . *to throw into Tartarus*, in *Homer*, only rectifying the poet's mistake of *Tartarus* being in the bowels of the earth, and recurring to the original sense of that word above explained, which when applied to *spirits* must be interpreted *spiritually*; and thus I . . . will import that *God* cast the apostate angels out of his presence *into that . . . blackness of darkness* . . . .

McLaren thinks *Tartarus* was "the place in Greek thought below Hades, also a place of divine punishment."[21] But in reality, all we know is that Tartarus is where God sent the evil, sinning angels. Perhaps, it was a name for the unrighteous compartment in Hades. But the one thing we can say for sure is, in the Bible *Tartarus* is not a noun. It's a participle that is traditionally mistranslated as the noun "hell."

Other 'Hell' Associated Phraseology and Terminology

In our last chapter, we utilized the basic hermeneutical principle of "letting Scripture interpret Scripture" to show that the phrase "unquenchable fire"—which is frequently associated with hell—was never used for anything other than a this-world, national judgment. And that fire always ended. In this section, we will address other biblical expressions and images that have likewise been misconstrued. Over the centuries, most of us have been told and taught that these literally refer to people suffering unending conscious punishment and torment in an other-worldly, afterlife place called "hell." Let's test this assertion and see if it's well-founded or unfounded.

"Weeping and Gnashing of Teeth"
Jesus employed this phrase several times (Matt. 8:12; 13:42, 50, 22:13; 24:51; 25:30; Luke 13:28). But in the Old Testament this language is used exclusively to speak of this-world events. For instance, in Isaiah

22:12 weeping speaks of the time Jerusalem would be destroyed by Babylon in a national judgment. In Job 16:9 *KJV* "the gnashing of teeth" speaks of an adversary about to kill his victim. In the *NIV* it is God Who gnashes his teeth. (Also see Psa. 35:16; 37:12; Lam. 2:16; Acts 7:54). The Psalmist used it from the victim's standpoint in Psalm 112:10.

James 5:1 uses it to depict the weeping of the rich in fear of God's coming national judgment on Jerusalem A.D. 66-73 (also see Jas. 5:5-9). John in Revelation 18:9 adopts similar weeping language, to again speak of a coming national judgment and impending destruction. Then why should Jesus' usages be any different? Unless He clarified that He was using it differently, which He did not do.

"Fire and Brimstone" (*KJV*)
See uses in Rev. 9:17, 18; 14:10; 19:20; 20:10; 21:8. Luke 17:29 employs this terminology to refer to the destruction of Sodom. Similarly, Isaiah 30:33 used this language for the coming national judgment on Assyria. Isaiah 34:9 used it for the future national judgment on Edom. Psalm 11:6 for a general judgment on the wicked. Ezekiel 38:22 for the national judgment on Gog, a pagan earthly nation opposed to God's people. And some believe Revelation 14:9-11 speaks of the coming national judgment on Jerusalem.

Surprisingly, the Greek word translated as "brimstone" or "sulfur" is *theion* and comes from the root word *theos* for "God" and *theios* for "godlike."(More on this tidbit when we cover the lake of fire, shortly.)

"Outer Darkness" (*KJV*)
Jesus spoke of "outer darkness" in three places in Matthew 8:12; 22:13; 25:30. The *NIV* translates this as "outside, into the darkness." But why wouldn't the original 1st-century audience have understood these words as outer space or something? After all, that literal outer darkness was literally above their heads and before their eyes every night. Also, wouldn't fire in hell produce light, and not darkness? McLaren in pondering this conundrum suggests that "all these images can't be taken literally at the same time—I mean, you can't have literal fire and darkness, right?[22]

In support of the traditional "hell" view, the authors of *Hell Under Fire* offer this explanation. "Various descriptions contain elements in tension with each other, those descriptions are in all likelihood metaphorical." Next, however, they dismiss this literal tension of mixed metaphors by washing their hands of the problem and conceding, "we are not under constraint to resolve how utter darkness can also have perpetually burning flames."[23] In their opinion, "metaphors are used precisely in order to describe realities greater than themselves." Of course, these authors are also quick to assure us that "hell itself is not metaphorical but real." It's just that "these vivid metaphors point to a reality more awful than themselves, indeed, terrible beyond mere words."[24]

Timothy Keller agrees. But we have to hunt to find his explanation buried in a footnote in the back of his book, *The Reason for God*. There he volunteers that "each metaphor suggests one aspect of the experience of hell. (For example, 'fire' tells us of the disintegration, while 'darkness' tells us of the isolation.) Having said that does not at all imply that heaven or hell *themselves* are 'metaphors.'"[25]

Interestingly, and to the contrary, the three expressions of "outer darkness" are also used in conjunction with the expression "weeping and gnashing of teeth." And as we have seen above, this latter language is associated with a this-world event, particularly national judgments and impending destruction. Destruction, of course, could certainly be characterized as a "darkening." Today, for example, we say things like "the lights were turned out" or "the stage/screen went dark"—meaning there was nothing left to be seen. But the bottom line about "the exact nature of hell" is, "the Bible doesn't give us much beyond these few, bare truths. . . . fire? darkness? conscious torment? annihilation?—is not as clear."[26]

"The Abyss or Bottomless Pit"

This mysterious expression is used nine times in the New Testament: Luke 8:31; Rom. 10:7; Rev. 9:1, 2; 9:11; 11:7; 17:8; 20:1, 3. The Septuagint (2nd century B.C. Greek translation of the Old Testament) uses this term in Genesis 1:2 to speak of the original deep-and-darkness of the earth and its waters at the beginning of creation. It is never translated as "hell." Instead, it's a metaphor for judgment and punishment/torment and even the grave. The Old Testament equivalent Hebrew word *tehome* is used 36 times and translated as "great deep, depths" (Gen. 1:2; Job 28:14; 38:16; Psa. 33:7; 36:6). These are references to the deepest parts of the sea and figuratively understood to

mean "the farthest extreme from heaven (Gen. 49:25; Deut. 33:13)."[27]
David Chilton further elaborates:

> Jonah spoke of the Abyss in terms of excommunication from God's
> presence, a banishment from the Temple (Jon. 2:2-6). The domain of
> the Dragon (Job 41:31; Ps. 148:7; Rev. 11:7; 17:8), the prison of the
> demons (Luke 8:31; Rev. 20:1-3; . . . Jude 6), and the realm of the dead
> (Rom. 10:7) are all called by the name *Abyss*.[28]

The New Testament application of this term is best understood, in
my opinion, as being a spirit-realm confinement area, prison, or dark
abode of demonic spirits. It must not be confused with Sheol, Hades, or
Gehenna to which it is never conjoined or equated. And, we must re-
emphasize, it is never translated as "hell."

"The Lake of Fire"
Finally, is this our place of "hell?" The expression "lake of fire" is only
found in the Bible's last book of Revelation. Most Christians assume that
this lake is "hell." No doubt, this is because "the most well-known
imagery used to describe hell is fire."[29] Yet many theologians and
scholars admit they don't know what the lake of fire is. Writing in one of
the world's most prestigious theological journals, Glenn Peoples
confesses that "whatever the lake of fire signifies, it must be a fate that
can be applied to both personal entities (such as the devil or lost human
beings) *as well as* impersonal entities (such as the beast)."[30]

WARNING: What you are about to read may be more shocking than
the little-known etymology of hell with which we began this chapter.
Most likely, Revelation's lake of fire is totally opposite in meaning from
what we think of as hell. Does this seem impossible? Let's see.

First, read Revelation 20:14-15 and 21:8 and let's agree that Hades
is either now or will someday be located, ultimately and finally, in this
"lake of fire."

Second, let's especially note that *Gehenna* and *Tartarus* are not
thrown into this lake of fire—although many today equate *Gehenna* with
both hell and the lake of fire. For instance, William Hendriksen in his
well-respected book, *More Than Conquerors*, asserts that "after the
judgment, hell is called 'the lake of fire.'"[31] But how does he know this
to be true? He doesn't say. He just makes the assertion.

Third, "death and Hades" (and equivalent Sheol) being thrown into this lake of fire does not necessitate their termination or annihilation. But it does change their location.

Fourth, the lake of fire is contained in a book filled with signs and symbols. So it should not be surprising that it, too, is a sign and a symbol pointing to some literal reality other than itself. But the book of Revelation does not decipher this imagery for us as it does some of its other signs and symbols (for example see: Rev. 1:20; 17:15; 19:8). And many prominent Christian theologians connect fire to hell. However, by again using the analogy of Scripture—letting "Scripture interpret Scripture" we can gain a better insight.

Fifth, the book of Revelation contains both this lake and a "river of the water of life" (Rev. 22:1, 17). Generally, most of us think of a lake as being a large body of water and larger than a river since many rivers flow into lakes. Hence, a lake of fire would be a lot of fire. And from other scriptures we know that Jesus is spoken of as being "living water" (John 4:10-12) and the Holy Spirit as "streams (or rivers – *KJV*) of living water" (John 7:38-39).

Most likely, Revelation's lake of fire is totally opposite in meaning from what we think of as hell.

In a like manner, the prophet Daniel's vision of God's throne in heaven contains this scene. "His throne was flaming with fire and its wheels were all ablaze. A river of fire was flowing coming out from before him" (Dan. 7:9b-10a). The writer of Hebrews further tells us that "our God is a consuming fire" (Heb. 12:29; also see Deut. 4:24; Isa. 33:14). In many places in the Old Testament fire is associated with God (see for instance: Exod. 24:17; Deut. 32:22; Isa. 30:27; 33:14; Lev. 10:1-2; Ezek. 1:27; 8:2; Hos. 6:5; Luke 12:49). Likewise, God speaks "out of the midst of the fire" (Deut. 4:12, 15, 33, 36; 5:4; 22, 24, 26; 9:10; 10:4). In the New Testament, fire is commonly used as a reference to God or his messengers (see Rev. 1:14; 2:18; 10:1; 15:2; 19:12; Matt. 3:11; Luke 12:49; Acts 2:3; 7:30; 1 Cor. 3:13, 15; Heb. 1:7). Make no mistake, these and many other verses confirm that "fire comes from God, surrounds God, and *is* God."[32] Our God is a consuming fire!

This lake is also filled with brimstone—the "lake of fire and brimstone" (see Rev. 20:10; 21:8; also see 14:10). Let's recall, again, that the Greek word for brimstone or sulfur is *theion*. And this word may very well define the nature or character of this fire. It is derived from the root word *theos* for "God" and *theios* for "godlike; divine." Therefore, by the analogy of Scripture, the "lake of fire" is most probably a symbol for God Himself and his judgment. And "death and Hades" as well as Satan, the beast, the false prophet, and "anyone's name . . . not found written in the book of life" (Rev. 19:20; 20:10, 13-15; 21:8) were or are to be thrown into this lake of fire. In Chapters 16 and 17 we'll expand upon the many possible applications (positive and negative) and durations of this understanding of Revelation's "lake of fire."

Sixth, if this understanding is correct, then "death and Hades" are now, or will be someday, not in a place of separation from or absence of God, but in God Himself. Perhaps this is why the third angel in Revelation 14, when discussing "the wine of the wrath of God, which is poured out without mixture into the cup of his indignation," further reveals that "he shall be tormented with fire and brimstone in the presence of the holy angels, and in the presence of the Lamb" Who is Jesus (Rev. 14:10-11, *KJV*).[33] If this place of torment is not hell—i.e., a place of eternal separation from God as it is traditionally posited—what does this verse mean? For one, this judgment may not be a pleasant experience, in this world or in the afterlife, if for no other reason than "it is a dreadful thing to fall into the hands of the living God" (Heb. 10:31). But it could also mean an afterlife refinement, cleansing, or purification by fire. Furthermore, it is most likely that everybody is going to get some fire in the afterlife (see again Mark 9:49; 1 Cor. 3:13-14; 1 Pet. 1:7). We'll have much more to say about this possibility later in the book.

Seventh, and regardless of your eschatological view, the lake of fire is the final, superseding, surviving, ultimate, and ongoing reality where "death and Hades" reside in some form. And as you have seen, we can make a stronger case that the lake of fire is God Himself in some way, form, or dimension than we can for it being a place of separation from Him and called "hell." Then what about punishment in the afterlife? Is this not something to be feared?

The lake of fire is God Himself . . .

"Eternal Punishment/Eternal Life"

Only one verse in the Bible couples these two phrases together. Jesus warned his hearers, "Then they will go away to eternal punishment, but the righteous to eternal life" (Matt. 25:46).

Traditionalists argue like this: "if no eternal punishment, then no eternal life; whatever eternal means for life, it must equally mean for punishment." And granted, the same Greek adjective (*aionios*) is used for both words translated as "eternal." But where does this punishment take place? This verse does not say, nor does Daniel 12:2 or 2 Thess. 1:7-9, which present similar scenarios. What then prevents this punishment from taking place in the lake of fire, which as we have seen above may be in God Himself and not in a place of separation from Him called "hell?" And for what purpose or purposes? Again, we'll have much more to say on these afterlife possibilities and prospects in chapters 11, 16, and 17.

'Come Now Let Us Reason Together' (Isa. 1:18a)

Based upon what we've covered so far, how solid or substantial do you now think the biblical and historical support is for the church's traditional beliefs about hell?

Is *Gehenna* hell? (yes or no?) Is Sheol hell? (yes or no?) Is Hades hell? (yes or no?) Is Tartarus hell? (yes or no?) Is the lake of fire hell? (yes or no?) Are human souls/bodies being tormented in hell presently? (yes or no?) If not now, will they someday be? (yes or no?) Then where are they now?

It's amazing to me how void of biblical support is the huge traditional belief and foundational doctrine of Christianity called "hell." So where am I wrong on this? I keep asking myself, why would Jesus confuse his original audience (and us today) by introducing another other-worldly place of the dead when God had already revealed Sheol/Hades as the other-worldly holding place of the dead back then? Even more confusing, why would He do so by using a familiar name and a proper noun of a this-world place that was located in the immediate proximity of Jerusalem—i.e., *Gehenna*?

A Critical Objection

According to Francis Chan, "first-century Jews believed in hell. . . . as a place of punishment that awaits the wicked." He insists that this belief "was nearly unanimously held. This is undeniable. This is the first-century *Jewish* view of hell. And this Jewish world is the one Jesus grew up in." Therefore, "if we want to understand Jesus in light of His own first-century context, then we need to understand what this context believed about hell. This will keep us from reading back into the New Testament our own ideas about what Jesus was saying about hell." [34]

He also clarifies that "the typical afterlife scenario among Jews in Jesus' day was that after the wicked die, they go to a place called hades, sometimes called sheol. This is not the same thing as 'hell.' Hades . . . . is a place where the wicked wait until judgment day. After they are judged, the wicked are then thrown into hell as punishment for their sins." [35]

In other words, Chan's view conflicts with what I have been presenting in this and the previous two chapters. He is claiming that Jesus' *Gehenna* was, indeed, our traditional and modern-day concept and reality that we call "hell." He summarizes that "no Jew would have scratched his head wondering what Jesus was getting at. The everlasting fire of gehenna is a place of punishment for all who don't follow Jesus in this life." [36] It's "their final state." [37] And, "Jesus agreed with His Jewish contemporaries about the realities of hell." [38]

My Response: At best, Chan's alleged association of *Gehenna* with hell is a weak connection and a major stretch for these ten reasons:

1. The *Hastings' Dictionary of the Bible* notes about **"GEHENNA: . . .** No systematic eschatological statement has, however, been preserved for us from Jewish times, much less on which may be said to represent a general consensus of opinion." [39]

2. Chan cites only one reference from the Apocrypha (15 inter-testament books written between 200 B.C. to A.D. 100) that directly associated *Gehenna* with a final afterlife place of torment (4 Ezra or 2 Esdras 7:32-36). [40] I found no other direct associations in the Apocrypha, although there are several references to fire, flames, torments, and judgment, etc. *The Old Testament Psuedigrapha* (the Apocrypha and other sacred

writings written 200 B.C. to A.D. 200) contains ten vague and unsubstantiated references to an abyss or unnamed valley. The only possible exception in which the word Gehenna is used in the English translation is *Ascension of Isaiah* 4:14. This scarcity of usage and association hardly substantiates Chan's claim.

3. No doubt, some influence and confusion could have crept into Jewish thinking from Greek, Egyptian, and other pagan sources. In this regard, *The Anchor Bible Dictionary* comments about Hades, Hell: "While Greek ideas about the afterlife probably did not influence the origins of Jewish expectations of retribution after death, later Jewish writers sometimes incorporated particular terms and concepts from the Greek and Roman Hades into their own pictures of the afterlife. . . . Thus Hades . . . is not confused with the place of eternal torment for the wicked after the day of judgment, which was usually known as Gehenna."[41]

4. *The Anchor Bible Dictionary* also further suggests that "Gehenna may have naturally lent its name to the underworld realm of the god Molech who was worshipped there. . . . Other reasons given for the association are the fact that the Valley of Hinnom was noted for the fires of the Molech cult and later contained the continually burning fires of a refuse dump. Although Gehenna does not have these associations in the OT, the OT is the primary source of the association, particularly the prophecies of Jeremiah regarding the dead bodies of the wicked cast into Gehenna (7:29-34; 19:6-9; 32:35). . . . By at least the 1st century C.E. there emerged a metaphorical understanding of Gehenna as the place of judgment by fire for all wicked everywhere. . . . This understanding divorced Gehenna from its geographical location, but retained its fiery nature. Gehenna had become hell itself"[42] Or had it? As we have seen, Jeremiah's prophecies pointed toward a this-world, national judgment event within the generation of Jesus' contemporaries. Most likely, this occurred in circa A.D. 70.

5. In Scripture, *Gehenna* is not cast into the lake of fire; nor is Hades cast into *Gehenna*. Why not, if *Gehenna* is our "hell" and the final afterlife destination of the wicked?

6. In Josephus' treatise on the most common Jewish position on Hades, Tartarus, and heaven, which we discussed and presented

an excerpt (pp-81-82 above), *Gehenna* is never mentioned and no such connection made. In fact, Josephus never mentioned *Gehenna* in any of his extensive writings—"The LXX, Philo, and Josephus do not have the term;"[43]

7. The Septuagint does not translate Sheol as *Gehenna*, but as Hades.

8. Jesus' time-restricted the fulfillment of his *Gehenna* warnings to his "this generation" (see again Matt. 23:15, 33, 36 in Chapter 3).

9. Jesus wasn't using *Gehenna* any differently than Jeremiah used it in his three *Gehenna* prophecies—a national, this-world judgment (see again Chapter 2).

10. Lastly, Jesus prophesied, "when you see Jerusalem surrounded by armies, you will know that its desolation is near. . . . For this is the time of punishment in fulfillment of all that has been written" (Luke 21:20, 21). "All that has been written" would have included Jeremiah's three *Gehenna* prophecies.

Concluding Thoughts

McLaren offers a valid speculation for why many Christians are or will be fearful about even questioning, let alone testing, this belief. He writes "if so many Christians have been so wrong about hell, how can they be right about anything?" Perhaps, as he sarcastically suggests, we should take a dismissive attitude and decree that "it's not really that central."[44] Or maybe we could console ourselves with this bit of patronizing, "a person can't just go rethinking things all the time." Or, perchance, we should face up to the possibility that we might be using our understanding of hell "to minimize the importance of justice on earth"[45] and by extension, to excuse ourselves from our biblically mandated role to contribute to making this happen. Of course, it is easier to sooth our complacency by believing that the injustices of this world will be paid for in the next world and leave it at that.

For me, however, the following two popular authors are more biblically in tune in this regard than are many generations of Bible readers:

Anglican scholar, N.T. Wright, as he concludes:

> Most of the passages in the New Testament which have been thought
> by the Church to refer to people going into eternal punishment after
> they die don't in fact refer to any such thing. The great majority of
> them have to do with the way God acts *within* the world and history.
> Most of them look back to language and ideas in the Old Testament,
> which work in quite a different way from that which is normally
> imagined.[46]

The unheard-of Wm. Paul Young—until his three-million-copies
bestseller, *The Shack*, hit the market:

> "So you suppose, then, that God does this easily, but you cannot?
> Come now, Mackenzie. Which three of your five children will you
> sentence to hell?" [God commanded.]
> "I can't. I can't. I won't!" Mackenzie screamed. "Could I go instead?
> If you need someone to torture for eternity, I'll go in their place.
> Would that work? Could I do that?"
> "Now you sound like Jesus. You have judged well, Mackenzie. I am so
> proud of you! And now you know Papa's heart . . . who loves all his
> children perfectly" [replied God.][47]

By now your head and perhaps your heart may be swimming in a sea
of further questions. Are the hell passages really hell passages? Or, is all
this "hell" stuff biblically bankrupt? Are we clinging to an unscriptural
belief? Have false theories of hell done unfathomable damage to untold
millions and billions? Have we been obeying God purely out of fear of a
false concept? Are those who have turned their backs on God because
they cannot believe a loving God would send people to eternal
punishment ultimately going to end up there, anyway?

Is all this "hell" stuff biblically bankrupt? Are we clinging to an unscriptural belief?

These are good questions and we will be addressing them. But,
maybe, perchance, perhaps, conceivably, there is one thing we can now
all agree upon . . .

Are the Italians Truly Right?

Are the translators traitors? At least in regards to the four original, biblical-language words variously translated as hell—"traduttore, traditore"—"translator, traitor"—"all translators are traitors."

Do you also remember our revealing statistic and graphic illustration in Chapter 1, page 23? It showed translation matches for the word "hell" going from a high of 54 down to 0? In closing this last chapter of Part I "Does Hell Really Exist?" can we now agree that "hell" is not just a poor or blatant mistranslation of the English transliterated words for: Gehenna, Sheol, Hades, and Tartarus, nor is it merely misleading; but it is an outright substitution of a totally unrelated word and a perversion and corruption of the text by translators, all of which has created centuries of confusion? Would you now agree or disagree? Hell yes? Hell no?

In my opinion, none of these four words should be translated as hell any more than it would be proper for these other proper nouns—Calvary, Gethsemane, Bethlehem, or Jerusalem, New York, or the Grand Canyon—to be so translated. But this is exactly what translators have done. Proper nouns for real earthly places should all be left un-translated. *Gehenna* is not hell. *Gehenna* is *Gehenna*. It was true back then. It's still true today. Would you now agree or disagree? Hell yes? Hell no?

Likewise, the etymology and original meaning of the word hell ("to cover, conceal, and protect" for a temporary time period) has little or nothing in common with our modern-day and popular concept of eternal conscious punishment and torment.

So what are your thoughts now? At the least, would you now agree that our traditional notions of hell are far from decisive, are not clearly taught in the Bible, and our efforts to maintain this view are now made more difficult by the insights we've unveiled so far? Hell yes? Hell no? If "hell no" is your answer, then where am I wrong on this? Please be assured, I am open to correction, provided it's civil and biblical.

CAUTION: Traditionalists fear that if there is no hell, then there was no need for the cross. And if there was no need for the cross, there is no need for Jesus. Wittmer phrases his fear this way:

I appreciate that the looming threat of hell can make us uncomfortable, but if we eliminate this from the Scriptures we deflate the true and even more astonishing biblical story. A world without the real possibility of hell, of eternal death would increasingly resemble the contrived world of the film *The Truman Show*, comically and tragically unrealistic.[48]

But, as we will further see, this fear is premature and mistaken. It would be erroneous for you or anyone to jump to this conclusion at this point. There is plenty from which to be saved. And this change of view does *not dispose* of the need for Jesus and his work on the cross. Nor does it *demean* the importance of Christian morality in this life *or suggest* that moral values are to be cast aside. Moreover, many scriptures speak of loss, suffering, and punishment in the afterlife—and not just for un- or non-believers, but also for believers.

Now, it's on to Part II and the greater issue—one contested even more than hell. That is, the final and eternal destiny of those who have not or do not believe—i.e., have never heard about or have heard but rejected Jesus Christ. Biblically, what now becomes of them?

PART II: THE GREATER ISSUE CONTESTED

Chapter 5

The 'All' Controversy

E very now and then in Christian circles a strange-sounding idea pops up.[1] It's deemed "heretical" and "not an option for evangelicals because it lacks biblical warrant."[2] In the contemporary church, it's only held by a small and fringe minority. It's the doctrine and belief that eventually everyone who has ever lived on planet Earth will be saved and spend eternity with God.

Upon first hearing, most evangelical Christians reject this possibility without a moment's thought. To them, it seems so obviously false. Often they are shocked that anyone would believe such an absurdity, especially people in the church. After thinking about it for a few moments, however, some agree that God could save everyone if He wanted to, but they insist that He doesn't want to and that the Bible clearly teaches He will not save everyone. At least this is what they have been told, taught, and led to believe the Bible says.

But here's a bigger, broader, and more "hell-of-a-problem" than hell. I call it "the 'all' controversy." In several places in the Bible, God actually says that He wants to save everyone and that He will accomplish everything He desires. Even more troubling—and in my opinion the irony of ironies and the paradox of paradoxes—is that this belief, which sounds so strange to us today, just may have been "the prevailing doctrine of the Christian church during its first five hundred years."[3]

"*Hell no!*" you say. "*Hell yes*, it was!" Christian Univeralists retort. One thing we can know for sure, however, is, this issue is not something we can simply ignore or take too lightly.

It's called "Universalism," and also "Universal Salvation," "Universal Reconciliation," "Final Universal Restoration," or "Final Holiness." But it's not a uniform belief system, as some assume—except for the end product of all people being saved, eventually. Several varieties of Universalism have been and are currently espoused. The differences between varieties basically involve the questions of "how" this saving process happens, "where" it happens, and "why."

Five Main Positions

Below are the five main positions or basic views in the Christian church today regarding the salvation of human beings. Please keep in mind that throughout church history as well as today, educated and dedicated Christians have subscribed to each of the last four views.

1) Pluralist Universalism – All will be saved in the end regardless of what they believe, don't believe, in whom they believe, what religion they do or don't belong to, or how they live their lives—it doesn't matter. This position also rejects Christ's role and work in bringing about salvation.

2) Christian Universalism (also called Evangelical Universalism[4] or Exclusive Universalism) – Because of God's expressed desire, will, power, grace, mercy, and love and Jesus Christ's saving work, all people who have ever lived or will live on planet Earth, eventually and ultimately, will be reconciled to God, saved, and reside with Him forever in the afterlife. However, most adherents hereto do believe in some real and afterlife place of temporary (not eternal) punishment and/or purification.

3) Inclusivism – Holds that salvation extends beyond those who have heard of Christ in this life but not necessarily to all—i.e. "positing the possibility of salvation for sincere devotees of faiths in which Jesus Christ is either unknown or rejected as the divine Savior."[5] In other words, there are many ways to God and "people who have not knowingly accepted Christ may nevertheless be saved by his sacrifice on the cross, for God can read their hearts"[6] Other variations of this position provide

no preeminent role for Jesus Christ, whatsoever. [We're not going to deal with this position since it's basically a hybrid between Universalism and Exclusivism.]

4) Annihilationism (also called Pseudo-Universalism or Conditional Immortality) – Holds that the human soul/spirit is not naturally immortal but mortal and not capable of the eternal life that transcends death. Therefore, only those saved by Jesus during their earthly lives receive eternal life (immortality) after death. All others will cease to exist in any form (body, soul, or spirit) either immediately after death and judgment, or after death, judgment, and a time of suffering divine punishment.

5) Exclusivism or Restrictivism – This position is the opposite of the four above and the prevailing position in the church today. Some Exclusivists, however, also subscribe to a form of Annihilationism. It holds that only those who have heard of Jesus and have consciously put their trust and faith in Him in this life before they die (by election or freewill) will be saved. The rest will be condemned to eternal conscious punishment and torment in a literal afterlife place called "hell."

First Six Hundred Years—a Universalist Perspective

Since most people and most Christians don't realize that Christian Universalism has held a significant place in the Christian tradition from the post-apostolic period to the present time; and since so much controversy seems to be aroused when this view is presented today, I feel it's prudent to briefly review the early history of salvation beliefs through the church's first six hundred years. We'll do so in a highlighted and bulleted manner and from a Christian universalist perspective, utilizing some of their own words and speech. Of course, some historians contest some of these facts and events, as we will see. One reason for these differences is because much of this material may have been suppressed throughout church history and not allowed to be heard, discussed, and assessed.

So whether you agree or disagree with this presentation, I think you'll find that this perspective does provide some interesting food for thought, if not a cause for pause. Also, we should note that at the time of the Protestant Reformation in the sixteenth century the sect known as Anabaptists adopted Christian Universalism and John Calvin wrote a tract condemning it. Later on, in the eighteenth and nineteenth centuries, it enjoyed a significant renaissance in Western Europe and America.

Overview

- The eventual and universal salvation for all people through Jesus Christ was "the prevailing doctrine," mainstream teaching, and majority belief "of the Christian church during its first five hundred years."[7]
- Many Christian martyrs laid down their lives for this belief that even those who were persecuting, torturing, and killing them would eventually be saved.
- The plain, face-value understanding of over one hundred and twenty verses in the Bible are cited by Christian Universalists to support their doctrinal belief.

Early Church Fathers

- Most leading historians acknowledge that the early church was dominated by Universalists. For example, see Philip Schaff's *History of the Christian Church*, volumes 1 & 2.[8]
- The majority (most, best, and ablest) of the early church fathers believed, taught, and wrote about this doctrine. These include:
- **Clement of Alexandria** (A.D. c. 150 - c. 220), was the head of the school in Alexandria, Egypt, and tagged by some historians as "the first Christian scholar" in the post-biblical period, who led the church into "the true knowledge of Christianity."[9] He gave the world the first, post-biblical, and comparatively complete statement of Christian doctrine in A.D. 180. It contained the doctrine of Universal Salvation. He also taught and wrote that departed souls could be purified beyond the grave and that punishment in Hades is remedial and restorative. There, these punished souls are cleansed by spiritual fire and God's punishments are saving, disciplinary, and lead to conversion.

- **Origen** (A.D. c. 185 - c. 254) was Clement's student at the school in Alexandria, his successor, and a distinctive Universalist. Christian Universalists and many historians feel that "Origen was the greatest scholar of his age and the most learned and genial of all the ante-Nicene fathers . . . . one of the greatest theologians and saints the church ever possessed . . . [who] loved the truth so as to suffer for it."[10] His written presentations of Christianity contained the doctrine of Universal Salvation as "a fundamental and essential element."[11] Origen's "greatest contribution was to develop a comprehensive understanding of the Biblical Gospel that was based on belief in God's plan for the ultimate redemption and restoration of all as the foundation of the Christian message." He "died as a martyr, enduring torture at the hands of the Roman government for his faith in Christ, during a time of great persecution of the Christian community. Most of Origen's copious writings have been lost or destroyed . . . ."[12] St. Athanasius (c. 293-373), the Archbishop of Alexandria and a student of Origen, defended him as orthodox. Schaff confirms that "the true, independent followers of Origen drew from his writings much instruction and quickening . . . . Such men were Pamphilus, Eusebius of Caesarea, Didymus of Alexandria, and in a wider sense Athanasius, Basil the Great, Gregory of Nazianzum, and Gregory of Nyssa; and among the Latin fathers, Hilary, and at first Jerome, who afterwards joined the opponents . . . . adhered to Origen's doctrine of the final salvation of all created intelligences."[13] He has also been characterized by non-universalist writers, thusly and variously:

  ➤ "Without a doubt the most controversial figure in the development of early Christian eschatology."[14]
  ➤ "a magnetic teacher. He accepted invitations to travel from many quarters. Students from hundreds of miles came to capture something of his wisdom . . ."[15]
  ➤ "one of the early Church's finest biblical scholars."[16]
  ➤ "a Christian scholar of extensive travel and great learning, devoted his life to the study of the Scriptures. He wrote so extensively that at times he employed as many as twenty copyists. In his extant writings, Two-Thirds of the entire

New Testament can be found in quotations . . . . the most
learned man of the ancient church.[17]
➢ "the real founder of universalism."[18]

- **Gregory Nazianzum** (A.D. c. 328 - c.391), who presided over
  the church council in Constantinople, in which the Nicene Creed
  was finally formed (A.D. 381), was a Universalist. Schaff states
  that this Gregory "was one of the champions of orthodoxy" and
  "labored as powerfully for the victory of orthodoxy as for true
  practical Christianity."[19]
- **Gregory of Nyssa** (A.D. c. 332 - c. 395), who "was devoted to
  the memory of Origen"[20] and "only second to Origen as an
  advocate of universal restoration,"[21] and added the words, "I
  believe in the life of the world to come" to the Nicene Creed,
  was also a Universalist. Schaff terms this Gregory "a profound
  thinker of the school of Origen"[22] and relates this description
  about this Gregory's written beliefs, "Gregory adopts, for
  example, the doctrine of the final restoration of all things. The
  plan of redemption is in his view absolutely universal, and
  embraces all spiritual beings . . . . Unbelievers must indeed pass
  through a second death, in order to be purged from the filthiness
  of the flesh. But God does not give them up, for they are his
  property, spiritual natures allied to him. His love, which draws
  pure souls easily and without pain to itself, becomes a purifying
  fire to all who cleave to the earthly, till the impure element is
  driven off. As all comes forth from God, so must all return into
  him at last."[23]
- Hence, both Gregories were avowed Universalists. The first
  presided over the Council of Constantinople and the latter added
  clauses later. The quite-appropriate question modern-day
  Universalists now ask is: Why would such an important church
  council, in ancient or modern times appoint an avowed
  Universalist to preside over its deliberations or select another to
  guide its final form if their view of salvation was considered a
  heretical view?
- Clement, Origen, the Gregories and many others were "not only
  the greatest among the saints in their maturity, but were reared
  from birth by Christian parents, and grew up 'in the nurture and

admonition of the Lord.'" As a result, "these ancient believers in final restoration lived and toiled and suffered, in an atmosphere of joy and hope, and were not loaded with a painful and crushing burden of sorrow in view of the endless misery of innumerable multitudes."[24] As we shall see, not only their salvation beliefs but also their lives were in stark contrast to those who opposed them.

Four of the Six Theological/Catechetical Schools

- During the second and third centuries, Alexandria in Egypt was the second largest city in the world, and its so-called "catechetical school"[25] and church was the seat of world learning, culture, and thought. It was also the center of Christian theology. And Universal Salvation was its teaching. It was here that Clement, Origen, and their followers exerted their influence.

- Five other major theological schools also existed in the church at large at this time. Three more schools taught Universal Salvation. One of those, in Caesarea, leaned toward Origen's view. The two others, in Antioch and Edessa/Nisibis, both in modern-day Turkey, leaned toward the universalistic view of Theodore of Mopsuestia (A.D. 350-429). And one, in Carthage in Northern Africa that was the Roman Empire's third most important city, favored eternal punishment. The sixth, in Ephesus in modern-day Turkey, favored annihilation of the wicked.

- Thus, four of the six Christian theological schools taught the doctrine of Universal Salvation. However, historian Shelley pinpointed the Alexandrian school and church claiming that "during the third and fourth centuries few . . . exerted more influence."[26]

No Condemnation—Why Not?

- None of the four great General Councils of the church, which were held during these five hundred years, ever addressed, named, or condemned this belief for being heretical—although they did so for many prevailing heresies of their times.

- None of the early-church Fathers (previously mentioned) or others were ever denounced by the church for espousing a heresy in regard to their belief in Universal Salvation or postmortem purification and conversion.
- No creed or declaration of Christian opinions during that same time period contained anything contradictory toward, incompatible with, or condemnatory of the doctrine of Universal Salvation.
- No word or hint of endless punishment and/or torment for anyone in the afterlife is contained in any of these creeds.
- Irenaeus (A.D. 120 - 202) in his principal work, "Against Heresies," did not regard Universalism as a heresy and nowhere named or condemned it as a heretical belief.
- Others (such as Ignatius, Hippolytus) also wrote against the prevalent heresies of their times and never named Universalism as one of them.
- Thus, "for more than five hundred years, during which Universalism had prevailed, not a single treatise against it is known to have been written. And with the exception of Augustine, no opposition appears to have been aroused against it on the part of any eminent Christian writer."[27]
- Many of Origen's other theological teachings were condemned as errors, but his doctrine of Universal Salvation never was mentioned or condemned.
- Many teachings of the three Gnostic sects that flourished in the Second Century, all which accepted Universal Salvation and were in full agreement with Clement, Origen and the Alexandrine school, were bitterly opposed by the "orthodox" fathers. But their Universalism was never condemned.
- Of course, some during this time did teach endless punishment for a portion of humankind and others taught the eventual annihilation of the wicked in the afterlife. But they were in the minority. And notably, the church did not rebuke them nor dogmatize on man's final destiny as we do today.
- During the 1st century, "the concept of eternal damnation to a tormenting hell was largely unheard of among Christians . . . especially those of a Jewish background, who knew this was not

taught in the Hebrew scriptures—and it only gradually came to be believed by some Christians in the second and third centuries as more Gentiles from a Greco-Roman background converted to the faith of Christ bringing some of their pagan ideas along with them."[28]

- Although the doctrine of endless punishment for the wicked was not fully developed until Protestantism, prayers for the dead and wicked dead were widely practiced in the early church. Modern-day Universalists argue that this practice would have been "absurd if their condition is unalterably fixed at the grave."[29]

- Thus, early Christianity was "molded, guided and sustained by the influence and power of Universalism." It "represents the prevailing religious faith of the three first and three best centuries of the church,"[30] which was "most remarkable for simplicity, goodness and missionary zeal."[31]

- So modern-day Universalists appropriately ask: Why didn't a single church council for the first five hundred years condemn Universal Salvation when they condemned many other teachings as heresies?

- Why didn't a single Christian writer of the first three centuries of Christianity declare Universalism a heresy?

- Why didn't a single early creed express an idea to the contrary nor mention everlasting, endless punishment?

- To the contrary, early Christianity was "a religion of sweetness and light"[32] and "a religion of joy and not of gloom, of life and not of death."[33] But this type of Christianity would soon begin to change, drastically—from Augustine (A.D. 354-430) onward and ripening into the Popery and Roman Catholicism.

The Rise of Opposition

- During the second and third centuries, **Tertullian** (A.D. 160 - 220) and the African school in Carthage had been the main exception to the almost total void of any opposition to or condemnation of the doctrine of Universalism.

- Tertullian, it is believed, "was probably the first of the fathers to assert that the torments of the lost will be of equal duration with the happiness of the saved." And yet somewhat inconsistently in his "fifty arguments for the Christian religion . . . not once does he state that endless punishment was one of those doctrines. And, he speaks of the sinner as being able after death, to pay 'the uttermost farthing.'"[34]

- It is also documented that "Tertullian and other prominent defenders of the doctrine of endless punishment were reared as heathen, and even confess to have lived corrupt and vicious lives in their youth." Additionally, he "had a pagan education in Roman law and rhetoric, but lived a heathen into mature manhood, and confesses that his life had been one of vice and licentiousness." After converting to Christianity in later years. "He lived a moral and religious life . . . but the heathen doctrines he retained rendered his spirit harsh and bitter."[35]

- Universalists further claim that "the great transition of Christianity to Churchianity may be said to have begun with **Constantine** (A.D. 272-337), who legalized Christianity in the Roman Empire in A.D 313, at the beginning of the Fourth Century." But, according to Universalists, this dramatic change also brought in "pagan principals held by the masses [that] modified and corrupted the religion of Christ . . . ."[36]

- Schaff negatively notes that "from the time of Constantine church discipline declines; the whole Roman world having become nominally Christian, and the host of hypocritical professors multiplying beyond all control."[37]

- Then comes **Augustine** (A.D. 354 - 430). Universalists charge that "he was a great fountain of error destined to adulterate Christianity and change its character for long ages . . . . many centuries."[38]

- From a personal character standpoint, "he himself informs us that he spent his youth in the brothels of Carthage, after a mean, thieving boyhood. He cast off the mother of his illegitimate son . . . whom he ought to have married, as his sainted mother . . . urged him to do . . . . His mother allowed him to live at home during his shameless life, but that when he adopted the Manichaean heresy she forbade him her house. And afterward, when he became 'orthodox', though still living immorally, she received him in her home."[39]

- Augustine changed the language of Christianity from Greek to Latin—all of which Universalists say brought about distortions and corruptions of prior Christian truth claims, introduced a long train of errors and evils, and subverted the current belief in Universal Salvation cherished by Clement, Origen, and the Alexandrine Christians.

- Amazingly, "Augustine did not know Greek. This he confesses. He says he 'hates Greek' . . . . admits that he had 'learned almost nothing of Greek,' and was 'not competent to read and understand' the language . . . . that such a man should contradict and subvert the teachings of such men as Clement, Origen, the Gregories and others whose mother-tongue was Greek, is passing strange. But his powerful influence, aided by the civil arm, established his doctrine till it came to rule the centuries."[40]

- Universalists further charge that Augustine's hatred and "misunderstanding of a foreign language" brought in "mistranslations of the original Greek Scriptures."[41]

- They summarize that "the triumph of Latin theology was the death of rational exegesis"[42]

- Nevertheless, Augustine "is the first writer to undertake a long and elaborate defense of the doctrine of endless punishment, and to wage a polemic against its impugners." In doing so, "Augustine assumed and insisted that the words defining the duration of punishment, in the New Testament, teach its endlessness . . . . that *aeternus* in the Latin, and *aionios* in the original Greek, mean interminable duration." When challenged that "*aionios* does not denote eternal, but limited duration, Augustine replied that though *aion* [age] signifies limited as well as endless duration, the Greeks only used *aionios for endless.*"[43] But this is not what the early-church fathers, who were steeped in the Greek language, taught that it meant.

- "And it was the immense power Augustine came to wield that so dominated the church that it afterwards stamped out the doctrine of universal salvation."[44]

- Hence, Augustine became "the most important church theologian after Origen." Yet he "was a man who converted to Christianity from a pagan background . . . who *could not even read Greek* and thus had no command of the language in which the New Testament was written and in which the early Christians had read the Bible."[45]

- Now, for the rest of the story, according to Universalists. "In no other respect did Augustine differ more widely from Origen and the Alexandrians than in his intolerant spirit . . . [and in] the persecution of religious opponents. . . . He was the first in a long line of Christian persecutors . . . to advocate the right to persecute Christians who differ from those in power . . . . the principle which led to Albigensian crusades, Spanish armadas, Netherlands' butcheries, St. Bartholomew massacres, the accursed infamies of the Inquisition, the vile espionage, the hideous bale fires of Seville and Smithfield, the racks, the gibbets, the thumbscrews, the subterranean torture-chambers used by churchy torturers."[46]

- And yet . . . "Even in the Fifth Century Universalism as regards mankind was regarded as a perfectly tenable option . . . . though there were sporadic assaults on the doctrine of universal restitution in the fourth and fifth centuries; they were not successful in placing the ban of a single council upon it; even to the middle of the Sixth Century."[47]

- In sum, the early church fathers had derived their Universalism directly and solely from the Greek-language-written Scriptures. But the change to the Latin language changed things.

- Therefore, "universal salvation was the prevailing doctrine in Christendom as long as Greek, the language of the New Testament, was the language of Christendom."[48].

- "Univeralism was least known . . . when Latin was the language of the Church in its darkest, most ignorant, and corrupt ages."[49]

- "The Greek tongue soon becomes unknown in the West and the Greek fathers forgotten."[50]

- Even so, "as late as A.D.400, Jerome says, 'most people' . . . and Augustine 'very many' . . . believed in Universalism, notwithstanding that the tremendous influence of Augustine, and the mighty power of the semi-pagan secular arm were arrayed against it."[51]

Doctrine or Duty of 'Reserve'

- Increasingly, during this time, many who believed in Universalism "felt that the opposite doctrine was necessary to alarm the multitudes."[52] In other words, "the wise could accept truths not to be taught to the multitudes"[53] and "false threats were necessary to keep the common people in check."[54]
- It is termed the doctrine or duty of "reserve." In Latin it was known as *fraus pia* and meaning "fraud + pious, honesty, holy, godly." Hence, the truth was intentionally held *in reserve* from the ignorant masses and false doctrine was taught to them for their own good—i.e., to control and deter them from sin and to secure obedience and restraint lest they take advantage of God's goodness. Meanwhile, the chosen few, the elite, secretly held on to what they believed and did not entrust this truth to the masses. The fear of eternal punishment, it was felt, must be kept always before people's eyes "as the prop of human and divine authority."[55]
- Bottom line is, the doctrine or duty of "reserve" was a wretched and deceptive practice of teaching known falsehoods—that the elite did not believe would be executed—for the attainment of a greater good.

Sixth Century Onward

- The year A.D. 544 has often been cited as "the first time" the doctrine of Universal Salvation was formally "condemned and anathematized as heretical."[56]
- Supposedly, this occurred during a local council in Constantinople where fifteen anathemas were charged against Origen (who died in A.D. 254). One of those fifteen was his view of Universal Salvation. It must be pointed out that this council was boycotted by the Pope and called instead by the East Roman (Byzantine) Emperor, Justinian.
- Universalists, however, disagree with this account. Here is their take. "Historians and writers on the state of opinion in the early church have quite often erred in declaring that an ecclesiastical

council pronounced the doctrine of universal salvation heretical, as early as the Sixth Century."[57]

- They contend that "in 544-6, a condemnation of Origen's views of human salvation was attempted to be extorted from a small, local council in Constantinople by the emperor Justinian, but his edict was not obeyed by the council. . . . The council voted fifteen canons, not one of which condemns universal restoration . . . . not one of the nine anathemas ordered by Justinian was sanctioned by the council . . . . Justinian was unable to compel the bishops under his control to condemn the doctrine he hated, but which they must have favored."[58]

- Furthermore, they maintain that "the age of Justinian . . . that condemned Origen, is conceded to have been the vilest of the Christian centuries. The doctrine of a hell of literal fire and endless duration had begun to be an engine of tyranny in the hands of an unscrupulous priesthood, and a tyrannical emperor, and moral degradation had kept pace with the theological declination . . . . Contrasted with the age of Origen it was as night to day."[59]

- The historical fact is, "Origen was officially declared a heretic in 553 [at a Second Council of Constantinople, a fifth overall council]. The legacy of the greatest early church theologian and his illuminating writings were thus cast out of the church, and with this travesty the destruction of original Christian theology and its replacement by Roman Church tradition was virtually complete."[60]

- From this time on, "Origen could no longer be tolerated, and was at length condemned"[61] and "the doctrine of eternal punishment reigned."[62]

- "Latin became the language of Christianity, and Augustine's system and followers used it as the instrument of molding Christianity . . . . and Augustinian inventions of original and inherited depravity, predestination, and endless hell torments, became the theology of Christendom."[63]

- Consequently, "the broad faith of the primitive Christians paled and faded before the lurid terrors of Augustinianism. It vanished in the Sixth Century . . . . It remained in the East a while . . . and only ceased when Augustinianism and Catholicism and the power of Rome ushered in and fostered the darkness of the Dark Ages."[64]

- "The modern orthodox views as to the doctrine of eternal punishment, as opposed to final restoration, were not fully developed and established till the middle of the Sixth Century, and that they were not established by thorough argument, but by imperial authority."[65]
- Origen, "this chief Universalist of the centuries immediately succeeding the apostles was, by general consent, the most erudite and saintly of all the Christian fathers. Historians, scholars, critics, men of all shades of thought and opinion emulate one another in exalting his name, and praising his character."[66]
- No one "did more and suffered more for the truth of Christ than any man after the first century of our era"[67]
- "Origen did more than any other man to win the Old World to the Christian religion."[68]
- "With the possible exception of Augustine, Origen is the most distinguished and the most influential." But "in the Sixth Century it [the church] disowned its author."[69]
- Universalists feel that "Origen's death is the real end of free Christianity."[70]

Comparisons and Conclusions

- "The most powerful minds (300 to 400 A.D.) adopted the doctrine of universal restoration, and those who did not adopt it entered into no controversy about it with those who did."[71]
- "The principal ancient Universalists were Christian born and reared, and were among the most scholarly and saintly of all the ancient saints."[72]
- "The most celebrated of the earlier advocates of endless punishment were heathen born, and led corrupt lives in their youth. Tertullian one of the first, and Augustine, the greatest of them, confess to having been among the vilest."[73]
- In retrospect re: Universalism: "this teaching was the strongest where the language of the New Testament was a living tongue, in the great Greek fathers; . . . and declines as knowledge and

purity decline. On the other hand, *endless penalty is most strongly taught precisely in those quarters where the New Testament was less read in the original, and also in the most corrupt ages of the church.*[74]

- "The contrast between Origen's system and Augustine's is as that of light and darkness; with the first Fatherhood, Love, Hope, Joy, Salvation; with the other, Vengeance, Punishment, Sin, Eternal Despair. With Origen God triumphs in final unity; with Augustine man continues in endless rebellion, and God is defeated, and an eternal dualism prevails . . . . The doctrine of endless punishment assumed in the writings of Augustine a prominence and rigidity which had no parallel in the earlier history of theology."[75]

- "The submergence of Christian Universalism in the dark waters of Augustinian Christo-paganism, after having been the prevailing theology of Christendom for centuries, is one of the strange phenomena in the history of religious thought."[76]

- Hence, the doctrine and belief of Universal Salvation "is not, as many think . . . something new, but is towards the position of the early Christians . . . . It is a re-birth, a restoration of Christianity to its primitive purity . . . . back to those earliest ante-Nicene authorities, the true fathers of the church."[77]

- Today, Christian Universalists ask a poignant question: If the doctrine of Universal Salvationism was the creed of the majority (perhaps a large majority) of Christians in the East and the West and did not hinder the early church for its first five hundred years . . . "Why should it now?"[78]

- In conclusion, modern-day Christian Universalist, Gary Amirault, comparatively writes: "When one looks at the lives of those church leaders who brought the doctrine of 'Eternal Torment' into the church, we find a long string of envyings, power plays, persecutions, character assassinations, book burnings, murders, and tortures. They became like the God they created—tormentors! . . . . They exchanged the truth for a lie and brought darkness to the world—the Dark Ages. . . . Idolatry, corruption, rewritten history, inquisitions, crusades, relics (cutting up dead bodies of Saints and making money off of them as good luck charms), indulgences (selling certificates to sin), pogroms, witch hunts, Mary worship, corrupt popes, and torment—much torment—all in the name of Jesus Christ."[79]

- Schaff concludes of those times that they "amounted therefore in great measure to a paganizing and secularizing of the church . . . . the temporal gain of Christianity was in many respects cancelled by spiritual loss . . . . it smuggled heathen manners and practices into the sanctuary under a new name."[80]

History Contested and Other Condemnations

In stark contrast to the historical perspective presented above, some modern-day, exclusivist evangelicals hold a quite different view of this same period in church history and the prevalence of universalism as a belief therein. They contend that:

- "Only a tiny minority of Christians have ever espoused universalism."[81]
- "The standard view [Exclusivism] . . . . has been the nearly unquestioned doctrine of the church from the beginning."[82]
- "Over the centuries, alternatives to the standard view have cropped up here and there, and no more so in the last couple of centuries."[83]
- "universalism has been a decidedly minority view in church history and contemporary evangelicalism."[84]
- "As for Clement and Gregory, it is a matter of historical debate whether they were universalists."[85]
- "Universalism . . . . has been a belief ascribed to by only a minuscule number of Christians and has been rejected time and again by the church."[86]
- "advocates were always a minority."[87]
- "Until the nineteenth century, almost all Christian theologians taught the reality of eternal torment in hell. Here and there, outside the theological mainstream, were some who believed that the wicked would be finally annihilated . . . . Even fewer were the advocates of universal salvation, though these few included some major theologians of the early church."[88]

- "Although this view has had a fairly long history, only recently has it had any sort of popularity. For much of its earlier history, it existed virtually on the fringes of Christianity. Only in the past two or three decades has there been any real interest in it within what would ordinarily be called orthodox or evangelical Christianity."[89]

Not surprisingly, most modern-day evangelicals also adamantly contend that "no biblical Christian can be a universalist (believing that all mankind will ultimately be saved)."[90] They passionately warn that "this widespread notion, popularized as it is, may be the single most significant problem contributing to the resistance to active missions . . . ."[91]

In an article tantalizingly titled, "Don't Get Brainwashed," J. Lee Grady not only terms Universalism a "heresy" and an abandonment of "biblical orthodoxy" but also characterizes it as "a powerless message that can't change anyone."[92]

Other evangelicals today have variously characterize it as . . .

- "Poison for the church"
- "Going against the very nature of God"
- "Nullifying the sacrifice of Christ"
- "Negating the need for God/Christ"
- "A slippery slope downward 'toward theological liberalism in which all confidence in Scripture is lost and the uniqueness of the Christian gospel evaporates.'"[93]

On the other hand, some notable names are not so sure about all this. For instance, the much-admired C.S. Lewis showed an inclusivist-universalist leaning when he wrote, "we do know that no man can be saved except through Christ; we do not know that only those who know Him can be saved through Him."[94]

Even the revered evangelical author, Dallas Willard, who is said to have universalist-postmortem leanings, has been quoted in *Christianity Today* magazine, thusly, "He says he doesn't believe anyone will be saved except by Jesus, but he adds, 'How that works out, probably no one knows.'"[95]

Recent church historians have perceptively made these "unbiased" observations about this contested time period in early church history:

- "This period [A.D. 100-300], however, the age of extraordinary expansion before Christianity moved from the catacombs to the imperial courts, serves to remind us that the church is truly catholic only when it is impelled by the gospel to bring all men to living faith in Jesus Christ."[96]
- "It was in the work of Clement and Origen . . . that this intellectual strategy developed. It enabled Christianity to engage and to persuade those with scholastic interests. At the same time, it opened the door for the importation into Christian thinking of ideas that the main body of the Church later came to denounce as heresy."[97]
- "Another disputed point, at the end of the Patristic age and beyond, was the actual *extent of eschatological salvation* . . . . but bitterly contested by others from Origen's time onwards. . . . Both positions have found their passionate defenders throughout Christian history, and continue to be proposed in our own time. Both remain enshrouded in the double, mutually limiting mystery of God's providential love and the genuineness of human freedom."[98]

So Who's Right?

Obviously, a huge difference of opinion exists between the prevailing belief and doctrine of the early church and that of the modern-day church on this issue of the extent of God's grace . . . and wrath in the afterlife destiny of all people.

So who's right?

Fact is, many verses in the Bible plainly state (at face value) that all humankind will be saved. But evangelical Christians, like the revered Billy Graham, disagree. "The Bible does not teach that every person will go to Heaven when he or she dies. Instead, it teaches the reality of Hell (which is eternal separation from God), and warns us of the seriousness of turning our backs on God."[99]

Without a doubt, the universalist message is a profound challenge to the exclusivist position. But after being held at bay in the conservative church for such a long time, the debate is heating up again. Millard J Erickson recently acknowledged that these "long-accepted positions are no longer going unchallenged" and "even groups as conservative as the Evangelical Theological Society are stirred by debate regarding these matters. . . . Because this is not only a matter of theology but also deeply affects such fields as missions. . . ."[100]

A huge difference of opinion exists between the prevailing belief and doctrine of the early church and that of the modern-day church.

But our time is not the first time Exclusivism has been potently challenged. Jesus challenged the exclusiveness of the Pharisees in his day. The Roman Catholic Church has backed off its exclusivism doctrine of *extra ecclesiam nulla salus*: outside the [Apostolic Roman Catholic] Church there is no salvation—i.e. only practicing Catholics may be saved. Today it has kept but modified this dogma into a more inclusive position. No longer does it dispute that people can be saved outside of the Roman Catholic Church. In both of these above cases, something was clearly wrong and needed to be corrected. Perhaps, a similar view-widening effort is now underway in the church with the renewed debate over the extent of salvation and condemnation.

Please be advised, however, that this issue and debate is most divisive and an emotionally driven controversy. Therefore as we move along, let's keep 1 Thessalonians 5:21 well in mind as our guide to "Test everything. Hold on to the good." Unfortunately, this has not been well-practiced in the past. Erickson in the Preface of his excellent book on this topic correctly reflected:

> Firm positions are taken, sometimes without real appreciation for the type of considerations that motivate those of opposite persuasions. In many cases, more is read into the Scripture than is exegetically supported there. . . . Probably the emotional factor has overwhelmed the rational.[101]

Fair and Balanced Methodology

What is, or should be, the true Christian doctrine on this matter of salvation and the extent of God's grace . . . and wrath in the afterlife? The answer goes to the heart of Christian theology and Christianity itself. Essentially, this whole debate and controversy boils down to the meaning of one of the smallest words in the Bible—the word "all." Does all always mean "all?" Or does all sometimes mean "not all" and only "some?"

Christians throughout church history have come to radically differing conclusions on this matter. Another fact is that during most of the centuries of church history "exclusivism has been the historic position of much of the church, and for that reason alone it merits our deepest respect."[102] And yet the salvation of all humankind through Jesus Christ might possibly have been the prevailing doctrine and the belief of the vast majority of Christians, including the leadership, for Christianity's first five hundred years. Moreover, many Christians since this time have found Christian Universalism's appeal attractive. Today, however, this view is definitely in the minority and considered heretical—and rightly so. Heresy is defined as "a belief different from the accepted belief of a church, school, profession, or other group."[103] But as we've seen, this may not have always been true. One thing, however, is for sure. Christian Universalism is almost as old as Christianity itself.

Therefore, in our next Chapter 6 let's proceed in our journey of re-discovery by looking at the scriptures used in support of Christian Universalism. Then in Chapter 7 we'll do the same for Exclusivism. As we shall see, both views employ many specific biblical texts and theological arguments in defense of their position. And each believes that their view is the plain and obvious teaching of Scripture, and that the other side's view is not. Not surprisingly, both sides also have their own way of interpreting and understanding these verses, which contrasts with how the other side handles them. Additionally, each side has problem texts as the other side is more than willing to point out.

Nevertheless, over the ages, Christians have been convinced by all of these arguments siding with either one side or the other. The great preacher Rev. Charles Spurgeon, in writing against the renaissance of Universalism taking place in 1800s admitted, "God the Universal Father, and all men universal sons. Now I must confess there is something very pretty about this theory, something so fascinating that I do not wonder that some of the ablest minds have been wooed and won by it."[104]

Then, in PART III, we'll breakdown these disagreements and the debate into seven argument areas. We'll analyze and weigh the relative strengths and weaknesses of argument within each area. In PART IV, we'll propose a solution of synthesis and offer some concluding comments and suggestions. I, however, make no pretense that this effort is exhaustive. But it is extensive.

My overall purpose for using this methodology is to represent each side and view, fairly and adequately, to pose some hard questions, to practice critical thinking, and to take an objective and critical assessment of the evidence—i.e. *Sola Scriptura*. To my knowledge, this type of approach and extent of scope has not been done in any book of which I'm aware—*until now*. Nor is this type of approach allowed in most churches. But in this book we are not so constrained, thank God.

Additionally, I propose that we don't take these conflicting positions lightly or without compassion for those who may be hurt by hearing another biblically based position in opposition to their own. Some, however, if not many, on both sides are not willing to do this. For instance, Philip Gulley, a Quaker pastor, best-selling Christian author, and a Universalist, rejects scriptural authority in this regard. In a recent article in *The Indianapolis Star*, Gulley claims:

> the theory of "ultimate reconciliation" is not derived from the Bible but from experience. . . . If you were to lay down on paper all the verses about damnation and net total all the verses about eternal forgiveness and reconciliation, there is more about damnation. . . . And there are people who believe that if there is more in Scripture about one point of view, then it must be true. I am not willing to let Scripture be that final authority.

At best, Gulley is naïve when he "sincerely thinks the universalistic love message will revolutionize our society if not our world" without the support of Scripture and by resorting to only philosophical arguments from "experience."[105]

Throughout the centuries of debate and divisiveness over the issue of the extent of God's salvation and condemnation, essentially two kinds of arguments have been employed by both sides—scriptural and philosophical. And both kinds of arguments are heavily influenced and empowered by emotion—on both sides. The classic philosophical argument, again utilized by both sides, is, "I just can't believe a God of love, grace, mercy, love, justice, etc. would do this (fill in the blank).

In contrast, our analysis and synthesis methodology will be based solidly and solely on the final authority of Scripture and exegetical arguments. It's to this task of re-examining the two competing and conflicting views—Universalism vs. Exclusivism—that we next turn.

To my knowledge, this type of approach and extent of scope has not been done in any book of which I'm aware—*until now.*

Admittedly today, only a small minority of evangelical Christians accept the doctrine of Christian Universalism. The vast majority believe in Exclusivism. Certainly, those who subscribe to Calvin's doctrines of election and limited atonement reject all forms of Universalism. But as you are about to see, Christian Universalism is not as "anti-biblical," "faith-destroying," and "false-teaching" as some say. Likewise, the case for Exclusivism and eternal conscious punishment—the prevailing doctrine and view—is not as "open-and-shut" as many others would like us to think.

Chapter 6

Scriptural Landscape for Universal Salvation

C hristian Universalists recommend that readers or listeners respond to each scripture they present in support of their view by answering "true or false" after each is read or heard. They feel this involvement technique better drives their point home. Exclusivists immediately retort that it's not that simple. As we've noted, Exclusivists have "tried to dismiss all of the universalistic texts in the Bible with a single, almost off-handed remark."[1] They simply contend that "I don't think you can persuasively argue for universalism from Scripture."[2] You have to look at "the broader context of Scripture." By that they mean the scriptures they use to counter and correct this contrary view. We will cover those scriptures in our next chapter.

Christian Universalist Gregory MacDonald explains this scriptural swordfight and point-counterpoint conundrum this way:

> Most of the debates for and against universalism in the past have been proof-text debates. The universalist will quote his or her favourite [sic] texts to prove that universal reconciliation is taught in the Bible. The traditionalists will counter with their own proof texts . . . . Obviously, such texts are important and will have to be considered.[3]

This is why J.I. Packer finds Universalism "wanting, suffering from poor biblical interpretation and internal inconsistencies."[4] Well, we shall see for ourselves. But one thing most Christian theologians do agree on is: "Universalism is a challenge to Christian orthodoxy . . . . [And] in recent years . . . universalism had made something of a comeback."[5]

Since this chapter presents the Christian Universalist's position, we will honor and adhere to their advice and insert a **T or F?** (True or False) following each scripture verse or verses. For ease of comprehension, we will utilize a scripture-by-scripture format interjecting supportive commentary and critical objections, where and when appropriate, to give this presentation a more lively, interactive, and point-counterpoint flow and feeling.

To help us sort through approximately a hundred and twenty scriptures used by Christian Universalists, I've arranged them into these seven categories:

1. 'Alls' in Parallel
2. Single 'All' and 'Every'
3. Reconcile 'All Things'
4. Double 'Alls'
5. Possible Foreshadowings in the Old Testament
6. God's Stated Character, Nature, Will, Desire, and Purpose
7. The 'Especially' Most-Difficult 'All' of All

All **bolds** below are mine.

Verses Cited for Universal Salvation

<u>'Alls' in Parallel:</u>

*"Therefore, just as sin entered the world through one man, and death through sin, and in this way death came to **all men**, because **all** sinned . . . . Consequently, just as the result of one trespass was condemnation for **all men**, so also the result of one act of righteousness was justification that brings life for **all men**. For just as through the disobedience of the one man **the many** were made sinners, so also through the obedience of the one man **the many** will be made righteous"* (Rom. 5:12, 18-19) – **T or F?**

Christian Universalists like Thomas Talbott stress that "I do not know how Paul could have expressed himself any more clearly than that .... the whole point of such a parallel structure, so typical of Paul, is to identify a single group of individuals and to make two parallel statements about that single group of individuals, and the effect is therefore to eliminate any possibility of ambiguity."[6]

Thus, Christian Universalists feel that "a universal salvation is affirmed there." And that this is "the natural reading of the text and the context supports it."[7] Likewise, Paul's parallel use of the expression "the many" has the same unity of force and scope of group as the "all men" in verses 12 and 18. This second parallel structure contrasts "the one" and "the many"—singularity and plurality. The difference between "all men" and "the many," as Talbott explains, is "'the many' . . . includes all human beings except for the first and second Adam."[8] But this second parallelism is presented in an even more convincing way. Here Paul draws a strong correspondence between the universal condemnation resulting from Adam and the equivalent and universal enlivening resulting from Christ.

These two strong parallelisms prompt Christian Universalist Gary Amirault to ask, "Why do many Christians not see what is plainly written .... all are justified by Christ's righteous act. No one 'decided' to die in Adam, it was 'reckoned' to us. Equally, no one 'decided' to 'receive eternal life,' it is also 'reckoned' to us."[9] Hence, Christian Univerialists insist that "all men" and "the many" that were made sinners are the "all" of the human race. They are the same. Therefore, dittos for "all men" and "the many" made righteous and given life. The structure of these two parallelisms demands that the same group is compared between Adam and Christ. And no disclaimers are made or remarks added to differentiate the subjects cited into two different groups.

Thus, Paul's teaching here is two simple parallel statements of fact. The same "all" and "the many" group that is affected by Adam's transgression is locked together in parallelism with Christ's justification. And because not one single person escapes Adam's sin, likewise, not one single person is denied Christ's righteousness. Bottom line is, the same "all" and "the many" who died in Adam will "all" be saved through Jesus Christ. This is the undeniable point of the paralleled comparison, Christian Universalists believe. The two "alls" and two "the manys" are all equivalent.

Critical Objection: False, say Exclusivists. The "alls" and "the manys" are not equivalent nor the same group. They appeal to "the broader context of Scripture" and their claim there is "no second chance" after death. Thus, the first "all" and the first "the many" is all, but the second "all" and second "the many" could not possibly be everyone. Other Exclusivists contend that the second "all" and "the many" mean "*some* people of all *types* will be saved (i.e., Jews and Gentiles)"[10]—i.e., for all people-groups.

Christian Universalists readily challenge Exclusivists to produce one scripture to prove their "no second chance" claim. They further maintain that the gospel of the "Good News" is a lot better and greater than many have been led to believe. Therefore, just as the one sin of Adam resulted in condemnation for all people, Christ's righteous act was just as far-reaching. If this is not true, they argue, then Adam was more powerful than Christ. His sin was universal in its effects, but Christ's redemption is not. So they ask, did Adam's sin far surpass Christ's righteous act? Apparently so, if the Exclusivists are right. But apparently not, if the parallel construction is right, as they further castigate Exclusivists for playing word games here—i.e., "all" does not mean "all" always. Again, this is the essence of "the 'all' controversy."

Armirault is astonished by exclusivist reasoning here as he asks, "Isn't it amazing how low people will stoop to degrade our Savior just so they can hang onto those traditions (Hell or Annihilation) which make the word of God of no effect?" Christian Universalists continue their argumentation by citing Romans 5:20 – "Where sin abounded, grace abounded much more" to further support their position.

*"For if **the many** died by the trespass of the one man, how much more did God's grace and the gift that came by the grace of the one man, Jesus Christ, overflow to **the many!**"* (Rom. 5:15) – **T or F?**

Here, once again, "the many" is set in a parallelism. Whatever group died because of Adam's trespass is the same group that benefits from Christ's work. This is in perfect harmony with Paul's pairing of "the first man Adam . . . of the dust of the earth" and "the last/second man from heaven" (1 Cor. 15:45, 47).

Amirault also highlights the "how much more" phrase. It's not how much less. Jesus' power to save is not less than Adam's power to condemn. He charges that Exclusivists "make the transgression of the first Adam greater than the redeeming act of Jesus?"[11] Also, the *King James Version* leaves out the definite article *oi*—the "the" before "many." This omission "has caused some great misunderstandings."[12]

Again, the reason why Paul chose to use "the many" here instead of all, as he did in Romans 5:18, was because both Adam and Jesus are excluded from those who were imputed death through Adam. Neither Adam nor Jesus had an earthly father. Thus, the sin imputed to all in Adam was *not* imputed to either Adam or Jesus. They both came into this world without sin. Furthermore, Jesus wasn't "made righteous" by his own act. Therefore "the many" is everyone else who was condemned in Adam who are also made alive in Christ, which, again, is everyone except Adam and Jesus Christ.

*"For as in Adam **all** die, so in Christ **all** will be made alive. But each in his own turn . . . . "* (1 Cor. 15:22-23a) – **T or F?**

This is the fourth foundational verse used in a parallelism structure supporting, if not confirming, the Christian Universalist position that God elects everyone to salvation, and not just a few. Also cited to further bolster their position are these Old and New Testament verses referring to how "a matter must be established by the testimony of two or three witnesses" (see Deut. 19:15; 17:6; Matt. 18:16; 2 Cor. 13:1; 1 Tim. 5:19; Heb. 10:28).

So in this verse we find another parallelism with the same comparative truth. It, however, is clearer and more straightforward than what was presented in Romans 5:12, 15, 18-19 above. Here, also, the effect of Christ's work is compared to being as great as Adam's sin. No shift in relevance or meaning is evident in the text itself. Like the other parallelisms, the two "alls" stand together in a parallel with their meanings of equal extent and scope.

So Christian Universalists consistently maintain their position that the first "all" is the same as the second "all." And that one "all" could not mean less than the other "all." In other words, "the remedy must necessarily be equal to the disease, the salvation must be as universal as the fall."[13]

Critical Objection: Most commentators disagree and attempt to show that Paul's second "all" is more restrictive than the first "all" and only applies to those who belong to Christ. All agree, of course, that the "all die" is universal.

But Exclusivists cling to their "broader-context-of-Scripture" stance and persist in their belief that "there is, therefore, no contextual evidence to justify the view that all people will be in Christ and will be made alive."[14] Johnson agrees and adds this bit of perplexing rationality, "what the Bible says and what it teaches are not the same thing. Only the overall teaching of the Bible (on a particular issue) can be considered authoritative for Christian faith, not the apparent teaching of any specific passage. Individual passages must be placed in the context of the broader teaching of the Scripture as a whole."[15]

So Johnson proposes "three solutions" for Paul's parallelisms: 1) Paul is only expressing "a genuine universalist hope here." 2) "Paul is speaking in broad, general terms." 3) "perhaps Paul envisions Christ as the beginning of a whole new creation. Adam heads the old creation, and in it all who have come from him, who belong to him, die. Christ, by contrast, heads a new creation (2 Cor. 5:17). One enters it by being reconciled to God in Christ (2 Cor. 5:18-19) . . . . There is no one else in the new creation. . . . In this sense, the two 'alls' in 1 Cor. 15:22 are compatible if not exactly coordinate."[16]

Christian Universalists counter that it's continually amazing "the very lengths to which some have gone in an effort to explain away Paul's straightforward statements about all human beings . . . ."[17] They warn that "none of us should underestimate, perhaps, the power of the faulty philosophical ideas that we bring to the text and thus impose upon it."[18]

For Christian Universalists, this ultimate reality and understanding is, of course, incompatible with a "hell" of eternal conscious punishment and somewhat incompatible (arguably) with a permanent annihilation of any soul. Amirault additionally ponders, "If Hell is a real place of merciless endless torture, since God knows the beginning from the end, why didn't God just kill Adam and Eve and end the long terrible chain of misery that passed to their offspring before it began? After all, the Scriptures say that all died BECAUSE of Adam."[19]

*"For God has bound **all men** over to disobedience so that he may have mercy on **them all**"* (Rom. 11:32) – **T or F?**

This fifth parallelism is, again, a clear and concise statement of God's ultimate intention, it is argued. And acceptance of this paired and shared reality is required by the emphatic parallelism. Elsewhere, Paul clearly points out that God saved and saves us "according to his mercy" (Tit. 3:5; 1 Cor. 7:25; 1 Tim. 1:13, 16).

*"for **all** have sinned and fall short of the glory of God, and are justified freely by his grace through the redemption that came by Christ Jesus"* (Rom. 3:23-24) – **T or F?**

In this sixth and final parallel construction referencing universal salvation, we find a major and highly significant difference. Here we have only one "all." It is the singular subject of the entire sentence. Therefore, Christian Universalists contend, this singular-subject treatment demands that whoever the "all" group is who "have sinned" *must be* the same group that is "justified freely."

They further contend and conclude that these above six sets of parallelism scriptures make it abundantly clear that Christ's purpose, goal, will, and work was to reconcile all who died due to Adam's transgression which is every single one of us.

Critical Objection: The majority of the church today does not agree. Jesus will not save all mankind (Calvinism) or cannot due to Satan's power to deceive and man's power of free will (Arminianism). "Some evangelicals have objected that some universalist interpretations of texts seem rather strained. In many cases I agree, and I shall attempt to avoid such forced interpretations . . . ."[20]

Single 'All' and 'Every':

Obviously, the below, single-usage passages do not have the same force as the double usages in the parallelisms above. But they don't conflict with them, either, Christian Universalists maintain.

*"who gave himself as a ransom for **all men** . . . ."* (1 Tim. 2:6) – **T or F?**

He died for all without exception.

*"For the grace of God that brings salvation has appeared to **all men**."* (Titus 2:11) – **T or F?**

*"But Jesus turned and rebuked them, and he said, 'You do not know what kind of spirit you are of, for the Son of Man did not come to destroy **men's lives but to save them**."* (Luke 9:56 – only in some manuscripts) – **T or F?**

Jesus didn't condemn them. Rather, He condemned his own disciples for behaving the way the typical exclusivist Christian behaves today. "Much of the Church world is in the same foul spirit John and James were in . . . . [they want] unbelievers burned instead of saved."[21]

*". . . he might taste death for **everyone**"* (Heb. 2:9) – **T or F?**

None are excluded because "God is no respecter of persons" (Acts 10:34 *KJV*). He saves everybody.

*". . . because we are convinced that one died for **all**, and therefore **all** died. And he died for **all** . . . ."* (2 Cor. 5:14-15) – **T or F?**

Things said in plain words need to be believed, argue Christian Universalists. Likewise, Christ is the judge of "all" (2 Cor. 5:10; Acts 17:31; Rom. 2:16), for "all have turned away" (Rom. 3:12), and "all have sinned" (Rom. 3:23). The "alls" are of equal extent. If *all* were dead, then Christ died for *all*.

*"The true light that gives light to **every man** was coming into this world"* (John 1:9) – **T or F?**

Somehow, somewhere, at some time, and in someway Christ enlightens every one who comes into the world.

*"Now I want you to realize that the head of **every man** is Christ, and the head of the woman is man, and the head of Christ is God"* (1 Cor. 11:3) – **T or F?**

*"We proclaim him, admonishing and teaching **everyone** with all wisdom, so that we may present **everyone** perfect in Christ"* (Col. 1:27, 28) – **T or F?**

"I do not want you to be ignorant of this mystery . . . . Israel has experienced a hardening in part until the full number (fullness – *KJV*) *of the Gentiles has come in. And so **all Israel** will be saved . . . . for God's gifts and his call are irrevocable"* (Rom. 11:25-26) – **T or F?**

If "all Israel" means a mass conversion of a last generation of Israelites or the salvation of every Israelite who ever lived, as many Exclusivists believe (and in contrast to a remnant of Jews and/or Gentiles), then doesn't this just add weight to the Christian universalist application of this reality to all humankind? And thus it is written . . .

*"that at the name of Jesus **every knee** should bow, **in heaven** and **on earth** and **under the earth**, and **every tongue** confess that Jesus Christ is Lord, to the glory of God the Father"* (Phil. 2:10-11) – **T or F?**

In this passage, all in heaven, on the earth, and under the earth are enumerated as subjects of the exalted Christ. Who—dead or alive—is excluded from this? No one! say Christian Universalists. Thus, this acknowledgement of Christ is universal. There are no exceptions. Paul's text here is taken from Isaiah which reads:

> *"Before me **every knee** will bow; by me **every tongue** will swear. They will say of me, 'In the Lord alone are righteousness and strength.' **All** who have raged against him will come to him and be put to shame. But in the Lord **all** the descendents of Israel will be found righteous and will exult"* (Isa. 45:23b-25; also partially quoted in Rom. 14:11).

But Paul's text, which he applies to Jesus, goes considerably farther than Isaiah's—from only the living to including the dead—i.e., "under the earth" (see also Rev. 5:3, 13)

Critical Objection: "the statement is one of purpose, and it does not necessarily follow that the purpose will be fulfilled. The point is simply

that God intends Christ shall have the same honour [sic] from all people
as that to which he himself is entitled"[22]

Critical Objection: "Here . . . there is still a division between
opponents and the righteous. There is a question perhaps whether those
who are 'put to shame' will then be saved, but the passage does not say
so; . . . Universalists argue that the confession in Philippians 2:11 is not
'forced' but voluntary and salvific, but who could possibly come to this
conclusion in the light of [Phil.] 1:28 and 3:19?"[23] And yet a little later in
a seeming contradiction, Marshall acknowledges and even italicizes his
comment about the word *confess* in Philippians 2:10-11 that "*Every use
of this word in the New Testament connotes a voluntary confession. . . .* is
willing and, sometimes, joyful acknowledgement. It will not do to
suppose that the humble confession of Phil. 2:11 is a reluctant and forced
confession from Jesus' conquered enemies."[24]

Critical Objection: Exclusivists further disagree over what this
bowing and confessing means. They contend it does not mean what it
seems to mean—i.e., that all are saved. Rather, many will be forced to do
this against their will and, therefore, this is not an act of faith and
acceptance of Christ resulting in salvation. After all, the devils believe
and tremble (Jas. 2:19 *KJV*). Are they saved? Exclusivists chide.

Christian Universalists characterize this force-submission
explanation as "somewhat question-begging," since all creatures that
confess Jesus Christ is Lord elsewhere in Paul's letters "is always in a
context of salvation" (see 1 Cor. 12:3; Rom. 10:9). "There are no
examples in Paul of an involuntary confession of Christ's Lordship,"
they point out. Furthermore, "the word translated as 'confess'
(*exomologeomai*) is a word almost always meaning 'praise.'"
Consequently, "there is no good linguistic reason to think Paul was using
it in any other way here." Hence, "the universal salvation that Isaiah
extended only to the living is now extended to the dead."[25]

Moreover, and as Talbott also notes, "throughout the Septuagint" this
verb "implies not only confessions, but the offer of praise and
thanksgiving as well."[26] But he adds, "if they do not do this sincerely and
by their own choice, if they are forced . . . against their will, then their
actions . . . bring no glory to God; a Hitler may take pleasure in *forcing*
his defeated enemies to make obeisance against their will, but a God who
honours [sic] the *truth* could not possibly participate in such a fraud."[27]

*"For God did not send his Son into **the world** to condemn **the world**, but to save **the world** though him"* (John 3:17) – **T or F?**

Note that the *King James Version* reads "might be saved." But Christian Universalists explain that while Exclusivists say "might" expresses uncertainty and means "maybe, " its use in Matthew 26:56; Mark 3:14-15; John 9:3; 17:2; 1 John 4:8-9 leave no meaning of doubt or uncertainty here. Instead, they maintain, once again, that God loves *all* and gave Christ to die for *all*. Condemning was not the intent, purpose, or result of Christ's coming into the world. Thus, Christ is truly and fully "the Savior of the world" (John 4:42; 1 John 4:14; 1 Tim. 4:10—again, a triple witness of Scripture; see also John 1:29; 6:51). They further contend that "the world" here is the whole world and contains "all" and "every man" in the world, not just a part of the world.

Critical Objection: Exclusivists challenge back that "Savior of the world" means the "potential" savior of the world. He won't actually save all the world. Rather, this verse only points to the universal scope of the salvation Jesus brings.

Christian Universalists counter that Satan has deceived and recruited others to cause the world to doubt this glorious truth and salvation reality.

*"As for the person who hears my words but does not keep them, I do not judge him. For I did not come to judge **the world** but to save it"* (John 12:47) – **T or F?**

And not just part of it – but "Savior of the world"—the whole world.

*"Look, the Lamb of God, who takes away the sin of **the world**"* (John 1:29)

Why is sin singular? Christian Universalists ponder. Their answer: because all of us became condemned by one sin and not by our sins, plural. Sin was imputed to us. It was not our fault. Therefore, "in Adam all die." Also see John 6:33 – "life to the world." Again, not just part of it – but "Savior of the world"—the whole world.

*"That God was reconciling **the world** to himself in Christ, not counting men's sins against them . . . ."* (2 Cor. 5:19) – **T or F?**

Baker sarcastically writes, "Notice it says *the world*! Not just a select few. . . . Do you see the contradiction? God's good purpose and will is to redeem the world. God has the power to do so. Yet God goes against the divine will to save all and creates, preserves, and populates a place of punishment where the wicked and the unrepentant dwell, unredeemed, unreconciled, and unrestored for all eternity. . . . In fact, traditional views of hell do not bring God glory; they usurp God's glory by diminishing God's power!"[28]

Remember, Christian Universalists insist that the extent of this reconciliation is the same as the extent of these sins —"for all have sinned" (Rom. 3:23; 5:12). God the Father and God the Christ are big enough to reverse and restore everything Adam's fall lost.

*"He is the atoning sacrifice for our sins, and not only for ours but also for the sins of **the whole world**"* (1 John 2:2; also John 6:51) – **T or F?**

Did Jesus pay the full price for our sin/sins and for the whole world, or not? Once again, the scope is the same—"For the Son of Man came to seek and to save what was lost" (Mark 19:10; Luke 19:10). All are lost. All are saved. "Here is a trustworthy saying that deserves full acceptance: Christ Jesus came into the world to save sinners . . . ." (1 Tim. 1:15), the "ungodly" (Rom. 5:6), "for all, the righteous for the unrighteous" (1 Pet. 3:18). He did not come just to open the door for the possibility of some to choose (Arminianism), or to close the door for those not elected (Calvinism). He came to save all, for "all have sinned" (Rom. 3:23). Will Christ fail to accomplish the full reversal of Adam's transgression? No, say Christian Universalists. Yes, say Exclusivists.

*"But I, when I am lifted up from the earth, will draw **all men** to myself"* (John 12:32) – **T or F?**

This prophecy not only foreshadowed the manner of Jesus' death, it also foretold the effect. All men would be drawn to Him! And, as Stetson insists, "God is in the process of saving all souls and making them new in the image of Christ . . . . He won't stop until He finishes the job."[29] But how this is happening, going to happen, or might happen—to draw *all* people to Himself, not *some*, but *all*—is a matter of further exploration.

*"In the last days, God says, I will pour out my Spirit on **all people***" (Acts 2:17; quote of Joel 2:28) – **T or F?**

There is no restraint of scope. Following Pentecost, his Spirit has been poured out on "all people."

*"And the angel said unto them, Fear not: for, behold, I bring you good tidings of great joy, which shall be to **all people**"* (Luke 2:10 – KJV) – **T or F?**

"Is endless misery 'good tidings of great joy, which shall be to ALL people? queries Amirault.[30]

*"In thee shall **all nations** be blessed"* (Gal. 3:8 – KJV) – **T or F?**

*"but now revealed and made known through the prophetic writings by the command of the eternal God, so that **all nations** might believe and obey him –"* (Rom. 16:26) – **T or F?**

*"Who will not fear you, O Lord, and bring glory to your name? For you alone are holy. **All nations** will come and worship before you, for your righteous acts have been revealed"* (Rev. 15:4) – **T or F?**

"Notice that John [Paul as well] does not say that people *from* all nations (a description which would fit the church, [Rev.] 5:9; 7:9) will come and worship, but that all nations will come and worship. . . . there is no suggestion of *forcible* worship in this text," remarks Christian Universalist, MacDonald.[31]

Critical Objection: "Scholars generally deal with the texts . . . that 'all' here signifies 'all kinds of people' (such as both Jews and Gentiles) rather than 'all individual people . . . .'"[32]

But Christian Universalists counter that many Christians have been seduced by Satan's lies and have tried to interpret the "all men," "all mankind," "all nations," etc. type language to mean "all of some sort" or "all sorts of men" instead of realizing that is not what the passage plainly says. Notably, none of the leading Bibles translate these phrases this other way. They mean what they say—"the totality of things."

*". . . so that **the world** may believe that you have sent me"* (John 17:21) –
T or F?

This universal statement in Jesus' prayer for all believers is another
indication that the whole world of all men and women is the focus of
Christ's redemptive purpose.

Jesus prayed, *"Father forgive **them**; for they know not what **they** do"*
(Luke 23:34) – **T or F?**

Of those who crucified Christ, back then and there, did the Father
forgive them? Or did Jesus not get his prayer answered? And by
extension, if it is true that we all have crucified Christ, has God not
forgiven all of us as well?

*"It was not through the law that Abraham and his offspring received the
promise that he would be heir of the world. . . . Therefore, the promise
comes by faith, so that it may be by grace and may be guaranteed to **all**
Abraham's offspring – not only to those who are of the law but also to
those who are of the faith of Abraham. He is the father of us **all**"* (Rom.
4:13, 16) – **T or F?**

Agreeably, this "all" is limited to only those who are "of the law"
and "of the faith of Abraham." "The others," Paul later tells us, "were
hardened" by God Who "gave them a spirit of stupor, eyes so that they
could not see and ears so that they could not hear, to this very day"(Rom.
11:7-8; also 2 Cor. 3:14). Hence, they were like "branches" that were
"broken off" (Rom. 11:17). This includes people who died several
thousands of years ago. But the greater good news, according to
Scripture and the Christian Universalists, is that "God is able to graft
them in again"—somehow, someway, someday by reversing their
"unbelief" that He caused them to have (Rom. 11:23; also see 9:16-21)
and instilling faith via his drawing and enabling powers (John 6:44; 65).
Seriously, how much human free will is involved in these verses?

*"I will call them 'my people' who are **not my people**; and I will call her
'my loved one' who is **not my loved one**," and, "It will happen that in
the very place where it was said to them, 'You are not my people,' they*

will be called 'sons of the living God'" (Rom. 9:25-26; from Hosea 2:23 and 1:10) – **T or F?**

Of course, this first applied to a Jew-Gentile remnant and oneness. But is that all it can apply to? If God has done this before, why can't He do it again, and again, and again, and in an even greater fashion, especially when it's in keeping with his expressed will, desire, and purpose that all should be saved and none perish—as we shall shortly see?

*"For since the creation of the world God's invisible qualities – his eternal power and divine nature – have been clearly seen, being understood from what has been made, so that **men** are without excuse"* (Rom. 1:20) – **T or F?**

Termed general revelation, and along with the law "written on their hearts" (Rom. 2:15; also Heb. 11:6), some Universalists and Inclusivists believe this knowledge is sufficient not only for producing guilt but also for instilling saving knowledge. But Christian Universalists do not so believe (see again Chapter #5, p 104).

Reconcile 'All Things':

*"and through him [Christ] to reconcile to himself **all things**, whether things on earth or things in heaven, by making peace through his blood, shed on the cross"* (Col. 1:20) – **T or F?**

Nothing is excluded from "all things," right? So Christian Universalists ask: Where, pray tell, are all the billions of people you think are left out of this Scripture and are going to burn in Hell for all eternity? Christ "created all" and will reconcile the same "all" (Col. 1:16-20).
    Critical Objection: As Talbott notes, "we could hardly ask for a clearer or more specific statement. . . . But consider how some have tried to limit and minimize the victory. A standard argument . . . is that in Colossians 1:20 and Philippians 2:10-11 Paul had in mind, not reconciliation in the full redemptive sense, but a pacification of evil

powers, a mere subjugation of them against their will. . . . The very suggestion seems incoherent."[33]

Plainly, Christian Universalists persist; universal reconciliation is the goal of Christ's redemptive work. Moreover, some throughout church history have believe that "all things" might include more than humans— i.e., all rational creatures—evil spirits, fallen angels, perhaps even animals?

But Wittmer protests that "these [all things] texts can't bear the weight that advocates of post-mortem salvation place on them." And it certainly "does not necessarily mean . . . every last plant, animal, or person that ever lived."[34]

*"Then I heard **every creature** in heaven and on earth and **under the earth** and on the sea, and all that is in them, singing: 'To him who sits on the throne and to the Lamb be praise and honor and glory and power for ever and ever"* (Rev. 5:13) – **T or F?**

What's this all about? (See also Rev. 5:3 and comments again on Phil. 2:10, p-135f.)

*"Whom the heaven must receive until the times of restitution of **all things**, which God hath spoken by the mouth of all his holy prophets since the world began"* (Acts 3:21 *KJV* / "everything" *NIV*) – **T or F?**

*"The Father loveth the Son, and hath given **all things** into his hand"* (John 3:35 *KJV*) – **T or F?**

*"but in these last days he has spoken to us by his Son, whom he appointed heir of **all things**, and through whom he made the universe"* (Heb. 1:2) – **T or F?**

*"The Son is the radiance of God's glory and the exact representation of his being, sustaining **all things** by his powerful word . . . ."* (Heb. 1:3; also 2:7-8) – **T or F?**

*"Jesus knowing that the Father had given **all things** into his hands, and that he was come from God, and went to God;"* (John 13:3 *KJV*) – **T or F?**

"... *according to the working whereby he is able even to subdue **all things** unto himself"* (Phil. 3:21 *KJV*) – **T or F?**

"***All things** are delivered unto me of my Father; ...*" (Matt. 11:27 *KJV*) – **T or F?**

"*And hath put **all things** under his feet, and gave him to be the head over **all things** to the church"* (Eph. 1:22 *KJV*) – **T or F?**

"*Who is the image of the invisible God, the firstborn of every creature: For by him were **all things** created, that are in heaven, and that are in earth, visible and invisible, whether they be thrones, or dominions, or principalities, or powers: **all things** were created by him, and for him: And he is before **all things**, and by him **all things** consist"* Col. 1: 15-17 *KJV*) – **T or F?**

"*Moreover, the Father judges no one, but has entrusted **all judgment** to the Son"* (John 5:22) – **T or F?**

In sum, and according to Scripture, Jesus Christ created all things, is heir of all things (Heb. 1:2), has authority over all things, subdues all things, judges all things, and reconciles all things – **True of False?** challenge Christian Universalists.

Hence, MacDonald explains that "the 'all' of 'all things' is then expanded upon to show that it encompasses all things 'in heaven and on earth, visible and invisible.' That is to underscore the breadth of Christ's creating work. . . . The next thing to notice about the salvation is that it extends as wide as creation. . . . The 'all things' that are reconciled in v. 20 are, without any doubt, the same 'all things' that are created in v. 16. In other words, every single created thing. It is not 'all without distinction' (i.e., some of every kind of thing) but 'all without exception' (i.e., every single thing in creation)."[35]

Over the centuries, Christian Universalists have debated whether these principalities and powers include angelic beings or human power structures. We will not address this aspect of salvation in this book. Instead, I will adopt the thinking of MacDonald here who further writes: "little hangs on that debate . . . so I will pursue the question no further."[36]

Critical Objection: Schaff explains Paul this way: "He is a conditional universalist; he teaches the universal need of salvation, and the divine intention and provision for a universal salvation, but the actual salvation of each man depends upon his faith or personal acceptance and appropriation of Christ."[37] Notably, most Christian Universalists would not disagree with Schaff's explanation here.

Critical Objection: Senior Pastor, Kevin DeYoung, flatly disagrees with Christian Universalists. In a critical paper titled "God Is Still Holy and What You Learned in Sunday School Is Still True: A Review of *Love Wins* by Rob Bell," he writes: "In Ephesians 5:6 he [Paul] warns that the wrath of God comes upon the sons of disobedience. The uniting of all things does not entail the salvation of all people. It means that everything in the universe, heaven and earth, the spiritual world and the physical world, will finally submit to the lordship of Christ, some in joyful worship of their beloved Savior and others in just punishment for their wretched treason. In the end, God wins."[38]

Double 'Alls':

*"Here there is no Greek or Jew, circumcised or uncircumcised, barbarian, Scythian, slave or free, but Christ is **all, and is in all**"* (Col. 3:11) – **T or F?**

*"When he has done this, then the Son himself will be made subject to him who put everything under him, so that God may be **all in all**"* (1 Cor. 15:28) – **T or F?**

*"one God and Father of all who is over **all and through all and in all**"* (Eph. 4:6) – **T or F?**

Here again, Christian Universalists maintain that "all in all" is God's ultimate intention and plan. "If Hell is real and a place of eternal separation from God, why would Paul . . . say the goal of God's creative plan was to ultimately be "all IN all?"[39]

God's goal, therefore, is universalism—for the Father's will someday to be all in all and all in each individual, cleansed from every sin and evil, restored to God from a state of enmity, and serving Him by consent. And not just a few, or many, or most—but the perfect harmony of "all in all." Eventually, all of God's enemies will be conquered and subdued—for Christ "must reign until he has put all his enemies under his feet" (1 Cor. 15:25).

One Christian Universalist in a Facebook response and email to me understands this "all in all" phrase this way: "Theologically, it can only mean one thing. 100% are in Christ, and subsequently God is in 100% of all things."[40]

Possible Forshadowings in the Old Testament:

Christian Universalists believe that the plain words in the following verse when taken at face value harmonize perfectly with universalistic scriptures in the New Testament.

*"O give thanks unto the Lord; for he is good; for his **mercy** endureth for ever"* (1 Chron. 16:34 *KJV*).

*"and the dust returns to the ground it came from, and **the spirit returns to God** who gave it."* (Eccl. 12:7).

*"For the Lord will **not cast off for ever**; But though he cause grief, yet will he have **compassion** according to the multitude of his **mercies**. For he doth not afflict willingly nor grieve the children of men"* (Lam. 3:31-33 *KJV*).

*"I will **not accuse forever**, nor will I always be angry, for then the spirit of man would grow faint before me—the breath of **man that I have created"*** (Isa. 57:16).

*"The Lord will lay bare his holy arm in the sight of **all the nations**, and **all the ends of the earth** will see the salvation of our God"* (Isa. 52:10).

*"And the glory of the Lord will be revealed, and **all mankind** together will see it. For the mouth of the Lord has spoken"* (Isa. 40:5 – in *KJV* "all flesh;" also see Gen. 6:12-13; Psa. 145:21; Luke 3:6).

*"**All the nations** you have made will come and worship before you, O Lord; they will bring glory to your name"* (Psa. 86:9).

"On this mountain the Lord Almighty will prepare a feast of rich food for ***all peoples***, *a banquet of aged wine—the best of meats and the finest of wines. On this mountain he will destroy the shroud that enfolds* ***all peoples***, *the sheet that covers* ***all nations***; *he will swallow up death forever. The Sovereign Lord will wipe away the tears from* ***all faces***; *he will remove the disgrace of his people from all the earth. The Lord has spoken"* (Isa. 25:6-8).

"Abraham will surely become a great and powerful nation, and ***all nations*** *on earth will be blessed through him"* (Gen. 18:18).

". . . and ***all the peoples*** *of the earth will be blessed through you"* (Gen. 12:3b; also 28:14).

"You open your hand and satisfy the desires of ***every living thing***. *The Lord is righteous in all his ways and loving toward* ***all he has made"*** (Psa. 145:16, 17).

"The earth is the Lord's, and ***everything in it***, *the world, and* ***all*** *who live in it;"* (Psa. 24:1).

*"****All kings*** *will bow down to him and* ***all nations*** *will serve him."* (Psa. 72:11).

"I revealed myself to ***those who did not ask for me***; *I was found by* ***those who did not seek me***. *To a nation that did not call on my name, I said, 'Here am I, here am I.'"* (Isa. 65:1).

Critical Objection: "'All (the) nations' is a figure of speech by which the *whole* world is substituted for a *part* of it . . . . The sense . . . is not 'all' without exception but 'all' without distinction."[41]

"The Lord is gracious and compassionate, slow to anger and rich in love. The Lord is ***good to all***; *he has* ***compassion on all*** *he has made.* ***All*** *you have made will praise you, O Lord;* ***your saints*** *will extol you"* (Psa. 145:8-10).

*"**All the ends of the earth** will remember and turn to the Lord, and **all the families** of the nations will bow down before him, for dominion belongs to the Lord and he rules over the nations. **All the rich** of the earth will feast and worship; **all** who go down to the dust will kneel before him – those who cannot keep themselves alive"* (Psa. 22:27-29).

*"O you who hear prayer, to you **all men** will come. When we were overwhelmed by sins, you atoned for our transgressions. Blessed is the man you choose and bring near to live in your courts . . ."* (Psa. 65:2-4a).

*"Say to God, 'How awesome are your deeds! So great is your power that **your enemies** cringe before you. **All the earth** bows down to you; they sing praise to you, they sing praise to your name"* (Psa. 66:3, 4).

*"No longer will a man teach his neighbor, or a man his brother, saying, 'Know the Lord,' because they will **all** know me, **from the least of them to the greatest**,' declares the Lord"* (Jer. 31:34; quoted in Heb. 8:11).

Critical Objection: Regarding "what kind of universalism is found in the Old Testament?" Surprisingly, one Christian Universalist admits that it's not "the salvation of each and every individual who has ever lived." He explains that "the Old Testament is interested primarily in groups (Israel and national groups) rather than individuals." But he hedges in adding, "this does not mean that we cannot infer the fate of individuals," which he believes the New Testament definitely teaches.[42] Johnson adds, "the kind of universalism we find in the Old Testament is the broader definition . . . . [where] God loves all people, and the nations as a whole are called to praise and honour [sic] God."[43]

God's Stated Character, Nature, Will, Desire, and Purpose:

The scriptures presented in this section and the next are termed "difficult texts" by Exclusivists because they express God's character, nature, will, desire, and purpose.

*"'He is patient with you, **not wanting anyone** to perish, but **everyone** to come to repentance."* (2 Pet. 3:9) – **T or F?**

This is God the Father's stated desire (see vss. 5-8)

*"Who wants **all men** to be saved and to come to a knowledge of the truth"* (1 Tim. 2:4) – **T or F?**

This is "God our Savior's" stated desire (see vs. 3). Thus, Christian Universalists contend that we must recognize, honor, and submit to God's sovereignty in this matter, regardless of how we feel about it. After all, who are we to say that our omnipotent God is not able or is unwilling to accomplish what He desires? Or, that He fails in the end? How vain, how arrogant is it for us to claim and expect that his will and desire will not be met or achieved?

Critical Objection: Exclusivists insist that these two verses only mean God *hopes* this will come to pass in the future. As Parry and Partridge argue, "texts . . . expressing God's *desire* to save all . . . [are] not a prediction of what will actually happen."[44] Galli further equivocates that "when it comes to things eternal, we don't know all that God wants or what God wants most. . . . It's not easy to figure out what God ultimately wants . . . ."[45]

*"If you had known what these words mean, 'I **desire mercy, not sacrifice**,' you would **not** have **condemned the innocent**"* (Matt. 12:7).

And yet, according to Christian Universalists, this is exactly what Exclusivists are doing. That will not do. Universal reconciliation "is something *already* accomplished in Christ. In Christ the whole creation is *already* reconciled! Now obviously, this salvation has not worked its way through the whole creation yet," they concede, but eventually it will.[46]

So will God really have his own stated desire thwarted for all eternity, as apparently most of mankind has already or will reject his offer for salvation? Christian Universalists further cite the following passages from throughout the Bible where God Himself or his prophet— ("Surely the sovereign LORD does nothing without revealing his plan to his servants the prophets" – Amos 3:7) emphatically declare God's character, nature, will and purpose on this matter.

*"I say: My **purpose will stand**, and I **will do all that I please** . . . . What I have said, that will **I bring about**; what I have **planned**, that will **I do**"* (Isa. 46:10-11) – **T or F?**

What possibly could be clearer than this declarative statement directly from God?

*"so is my word that goes out from my mouth: It will not return to me empty, but will **accomplish what I desire** and **achieve the purpose** for which I sent it"* (Isa. 55:11) – **T or F?** –

Another direct statement from God. And Jesus is the Word, isn't He (see John 1:1-4)?

*"The Lord Almighty has sworn, 'Surely, as I have **planned**, so it **will be**, and as I have **purposed**, so it **will stand**. . . . For the Lord Almighty has **purposed**, and who can **thwart** him? His hand is stretched out, and who can **turn it back?**"* (Isa. 14:24, 27) – **T or F?**

*"But the **plans** of the Lord **stand firm** forever, the **purposes** of his heart through all generations"* (Psa. 33:11) – **T or F?**

*"Our God is in heaven; and he **does whatever pleases** him"* (Psa. 115:3) – **T or F?**

*"the LORD **does whatever pleases** him, in the heavens and on the earth, in the seas and all their depths"* (Psa. 135:6) – **T or F?**

*"He **does as he pleases** with the powers of heaven and the peoples of the earth. No one can hold back his hand or say to him: 'What have you done?'"* (Dan. 4:35) – **T or F?**

Oh really? exclaim Christian Universalists. Isn't this exactly what the Exclusivists are trying to do?

*"But he stands alone, and who can oppose him? He **does whatever he pleases**"* Job 23:13) – **T of F?**

*"Then Job replied to the LORD: 'I know that you can do **all things; no plan** of yours can be **thwarted**"* (Job 42:1-2) – **T or F?**

*"It is of the Lord's **mercies** that we are not consumed, because his **compassions fail not**"* (Lam. 3:22 *KJV*) – **T or F?**

*"who hath saved us, and called us with an holy calling, not according to our works, but according to his own **purpose** and **grace**, which was given us in Christ Jesus before the world began"* (2 Tim. 1:9 *KJV*) – **T or F?**

*"he predestined us to be adopted as his sons through Jesus Christ, in accordance with his **pleasure** and **will**"* (Eph. 1:5) – **T or F?**

*"And he made known to us the mystery of his **will** according to his good **pleasure**, which he **purposed** in Christ to be put into effect when the times will have reached their fulfillment—to bring **all things** in heaven and on earth together **under one head**, even Christ. In him we were also chosen, having been predestined according to the **plan** of him who **works out everything in conformity** with the **purpose of his will**"* (Eph. 1:9-11) – **T or F?**

*"In him we were also chosen, having been predestined according to the **plan** of him who works out **everything** in **conformity** with the **purpose** of his **will**"* (Eph. 1:11) – **T or F?**

*"Because God wanted to make the **unchanging nature** of his **purpose** very clear to the heirs of what was promised, he **confirmed** it with an oath"* (Heb. 6:17) – **T or F?**

So if God saved them back then and there, "according to his own purpose and grace" (2 Tim. 1:9), why not everyone else as well, eventually, as he has so confirmed many times what He desires and will accomplish?

*"who gave himself for our sins to rescue us from the present evil age, according to the **will** of our God and Father"* (Gal. 1:4) – **T or F?**

Jesus came "to do the will of him who sent me" (John 6:38b). He is still doing it—"on earth as it is in heaven" (Matt. 6:10)—isn't He?

*"for it is God who works in you to **will** and to act according to his good purpose"* (Phil. 2:13) – **T or F?**

Critical Objection: Parry and Partridge counter: "the claim that God will ultimately achieve *all* his purposes for creation is one that orthodox Christians disagree over . . . . God has given humans freedom to choose to reject his purposes for them. If humans keep on rejecting God's offer of salvation, God could only save them by disregarding their freedom, and thereby treating them not as persons but as objects."[47]

In contrast, Calvinists maintain that God always achieves his purposes. They just delimit his purpose to being only saving some—those He has predestined, the elect. As MacDonald notes, "those who subscribe to a strong Calvinism with its doctrine of election and limited atonement would certainly deny it."[48]

Notwithstanding, the Arminian theology of "free will" seems to offer the best possible *philosophical* explanation as the reason why God does not achieve his purpose of universal salvation. But really and truly how "free" is free will if "no one can come to me unless the Father who sent me draws him" and "has enabled him" (John 6:44, 65)?

Thus, Christian Universalists counter this exclusivist objection by characterizing it as "a poor contender when placed along side the universalist interpretation."[49] Amirault further challenges that "if the demands of divine justice are opposed to the requirements of mercy, is God divided against Himself?"[50] But exactly how all this happens, many Christian Universalists are willing to place in the category of "the secret things [that] belong to the LORD our God . . . ." (Deut. 29:29; also see Rom. 9:19-21; 4:17; Eph. 1:5, 9, 11; 2:7; Matt. 6:10) and leave it in the realm of mystery:

> *"Oh, the depth of the riches of the wisdom and knowledge of God! How unsearchable his judgments, and his paths beyond tracing out! Who has known the mind of the Lord? Or who has been his counselor? . . . .For from him and through him and to him are all things. To him be the glory forever! Amen"* (Rom. 11:33, 34, 36).

Oh, the wonder of it! Oh, the mystery of it! Whether we understand it, agree with it, or not, Jesus Christ is, indeed, the Savior of the whole world! For who has known the Lord's mind?

The 'Especially' Most-Difficult 'All' of All:

*". . . we have put our hope in the living God, who is the Savior of **all men**, and **especially** of those who believe"* (1 Tim. 4:10) – **T or F?**

Two categories of people are presented here—one within the other. But according to this scripture, all people in both categories will be saved – again, **T or F?** As Amirault queries, "Can God be 'especially the Savior of them who believe,' unless He is actually the Savior of all (1 Tim. 4:10)?"[51]

The very next verse emphatically directs us to "command and teach these things" (1 Tim. 4:11). Christian Universalists believe they are doing just that and Exclusivists are not. But one thing is for sure. This verse is "especially" the most difficult verse for Exclusivists. As Sanders frankly admits, "universalists do . . . have some arguments that are not easily overcome."[52]

Critical Objection: Exclusivists must say that "especially" (*NIV*) or "specially" (*KJV*) means "just" or "only" those who believe. Problem is, the Greek word used here is *malista* (*Strong's* #3122). It means "most of all" or "chiefly" or "in the greatest degree." It does not mean "just," "only" or "exclusively." Big difference!

And everywhere else this word is used in the New Testament it means the same thing and is used in this same manner:

- I Timothy 5:8 – "But if any provide not for his own, and *specially* for those of his own faith . . . ."
- Titus 1:10 – singles out some from among many unruly and vain talkers and deceivers as *"specially* they of the circumcision."
- Philemon 16 – "a brother beloved, *specially* to me."
- Gal. 6:10 – "let us do good to all men, *especially* unto them who are of the household of faith."
- Acts 25:26 – "Wherefore I have brought him forth before you, and *specially* before thee, O king Agrippa . . . ."
- Also see Acts 26:3; 1 Tim. 5:17; 2 Tim. 4:13.

Onto the Other Side of the Story

If you answered "True" to some, many, most, or even all of the above scriptures, perhaps you can better understand those who have or currently believe in Universal Salvation—that ultimately everyone will be saved. This eventual reality, they contend, is God's plan of redemption and his ultimate victory. But regardless of your degree of agreement or disagreement, the Exclusivist claim that Christian Universalism is "not an option for evangelicals because it lacks biblical warrant"[53] is, at best, "especially" difficult to maintain in light of the scriptural landscape we have just reviewed, if not patently untrue.

Fact is, the above scriptures stand as a perpetual challenge to every form of Exclusivism. And Christian Universalists wonder why Exclusivists resist these plain statements, pervert the Word of God, and continually undervalue God's grace and the redemptive work of Christ. Also, and hopefully by now, you can better understand, as Parry and Partridge have acknowledged, why "the pull of universalism arises from claims internal to Christian theology itself and is not obviously an alien import."[54]

A customer review on Amazon.com of Thomas Talbott's Christian universalism book, *The Inescapable Love of God* commented appropriately:

> The book of Romans . . . turns out to support the belief that God has predestined ALL to be conformed to the image of His Son! It is startling to see how we have overlooked so many verses and mis-read others, based on our preconceptions.[55]

Johnson affirms that "the case for universalism is stronger than is usually realized. God's saving love for the world is a prominent biblical theme from Genesis through Revelation." And while he acknowledges that "eventually, everyone will confess Jesus Christ as Lord," he humbly concedes that "we do not know how God's judgment works out with respects to individuals."[56]

Soren Kierkegaard, (1813 – 1855), a Danish Christian philosopher, theologian, and religious author who was vitally interested in human psychology summarized his feelings on this matter this way: "If the others are going to hell, then I am going along with them. But I do not believe that; on the contrary, I believe that we will all be saved, I, too, and this awakens my deepest wonder."[57]

Ludlow contributes that Kierkegaard's hope for universal salvation "was based neither on a philosophical system, nor on philosophical objections to the notion of eternal punishment, but on a profound faith in the saving power of Christ."[58] Hilborn and Horrocks chime in that "with the growth of systematic universalist theologies across various traditions in recent years, evangelical biblical scholars have been led to re-investigate the key verses cited in defense of the view that all will be saved."[59]

Christian Universalists wonder why Exclusivists resist these plain statements, pervert the Word of God, and continually undervalue God's grace and the redemptive work of Christ.

In a nutshell, one universalist website called "The True Gospel" headlines that "Redemption" is "A Declaration for All Not a Choice for a Few"[60] But most Christians today do not believe this. Nor do they understand the above scriptures in the manner which Christian Universalists understand them. Instead, they side with Lutzer as he espouses, once again, the traditional, evangelical, and exclusivist line that "Universalism has never been widely accepted by those who take the Scriptures seriously."[61] Therefore for Exclusivists, and as Christian Universalists repeatedly charge, Jesus ends up losing most of those for whom He died.

But as the writer of Proverbs aptly puts it, "The first to present his case seems right, till another comes forward and questions him" (Prov. 18:17). Or, as I like to paraphrase it, "One story sounds right, until you hear the other side." It is to that other side of the story we now turn. Once again, its major argument against all we have presented in this chapter is an appeal to "the broader context of Scripture." Yes, there are many other scriptures used by Exclusivists that support their view. Let's next take a close and critical look at this compelling, competing, and most-prominent position.

Chapter 7

Scriptural Landscape for Exclusive Salvation

I t's referred to as "the broader context of Scripture," or more specifically, the "broader context of the New Testament teaching about sin and its consequences."[1] Boa and Bowman Jr. in their *Sense & Nonsense About Heaven & Hell* tome frame their exclusivist position, in contrast to the Christian Universalism position covered in our previous chapter, thusly:

> The case against Christian universalism is based on a mass of biblical texts . . . that approach the subject from a variety of angles. . . . In fact, these texts appear to limit the number of people who will be saved to a minority of the human race. . . . Close attention to the wording and background of these statements often shows that they are actually contradictory to the notion of universal salvation.[2]

Again, for ease of comprehension, we will utilize a scripture-by-scripture format interjecting supportive commentary and critical objections, where and when appropriate, to give this presentation a more lively, interactive, and point-counterpoint flow and feeling.

To help us sort through approximately a hundred or so scriptures used by Exclusivists, I've arranged them into these three categories:

1. Many to Condemnation and Destruction
2. Only the Few Who Believe
3. Have Life

Again, all **bolds** below are mine.

Verses Cited for Exclusivism

Many to Condemnation and Destruction

*"Enter through the narrow gate. For **wide** is the gate and **broad** is the road that leads to **destruction**, and **many** enter through it. But **small** is the gate and **narrow** the road that leads to **life**, and only a **few** find it"* (Matt. 7:13-14).

What could be clearer? Exclusivists proclaim. Therefore, only a few will be saved.

Critical Objection: Stetson argues back that "Jesus does not say the people who don't find the narrow gate to heaven will *forever* be left out. That is an assumption . . . . So even if most people do take the broad road to destruction, that doesn't mean they cannot someday find their way back to the straight and narrow path that leads to the gate of heaven."[3]

Also, let's note that Jesus doesn't mention hell or heaven here at all. That's assumptive as well. He only contrasts destruction and life. Christian Universalists caution, that we should not make more of this than it actually says. And the words "destruction" and "life" have many different meanings.

*"By the same word the present heavens and earth are reserved for **fire**, being kept for the day of **judgment** and **destruction** of **ungodly men**"* (2 Pet. 3:7).

Critical Objection: Neither hell nor the afterlife are mentioned here, either. A strong case can be made that this verse actually refers to the impending divine judgment of the earthly nation of Israel in circa A.D. 70 rather than to individual people in the afterlife.[4]

Stetson adds that "if God didn't want people to destroy their children with fire (Jer. 32:35), surely He would not do this to His own children—human beings—in a fiery eternal torture chamber beyond the grave. It would be absurd to think that God holds mere humans to a higher moral standard than His own divine perfection!"[5]

*"For the message of the cross is foolishness to those who are **perishing**, but to us who are being **saved** it is the power of God"* (1 Cor. 1:18).

Again, two distinct groups with two different afterlife destinies are affirmed.

Critical Objection: Amirault counters that "if the wages of sin is eternal punishment in Hell, then Jesus would have to be eternally punished if in fact He died for my sins. But the Bible says the wages of sin is death which is exactly what Jesus did – died . . . . Is Jesus presently being eternally tortured in place of those who accepted Him as Lord?"[6]

In other words, "if Jesus died in our place to save us from this fate, wouldn't Jesus have to be eternally punished if in fact He took our punishment upon Himself? But He's NOT being eternally punished. He DIED which is what the penalty of the wages of sin is, DEATH, NOT everlasting life of unending torture or eternal death (annihilation)."[7]

Critical Objection: "The Lord Jesus suffered on the cross for about 6 hours then died physically. He did not suffer forever. . . . Why would God require a lost person to suffer for their personal sins forever, while Christ's suffering for the World . . . was temporary?"[8]

Critical Objection: Stetson concurs that "if condemnation to a never-ending hell is the penalty for sin, then why doesn't Jesus have to burn in hell forever if he died to pay the penalty for our sins?"[9]

Jones, in quoting theologian Jack Cottrell, simply believes and points out that "at the cross Jesus 'suffered the equivalent of eternity in hell for every sinner.'"[10]

*"Then they will go away to **eternal punishment**, but the righteous to **eternal life**."* (Matt. 25:46; also John 5:28-29; Rom. 2:7-8; Matt. 13:30, 40-43, 49-50).

All men will not ultimately be saved as this verse clearly compares and contrasts two different afterlife destinies. The vast majority will die and face everlasting punishment in hell—because whatever the word "eternal" means when applied to life in this statement by Jesus, it means the same when applied to punishment.

Critical Objection: "Infinite punishment for finite crimes just doesn't seem just. I could never torture people endlessly, especially my own children. How can you say the God will do that to His children? This seems hideous. You make God look like a monster worse than Hitler, not a loving Father Who would even die for His enemies!"[11]

Also, "as we are commanded 'to overcome evil with good,' may we not safely infer that God will do the same? Would the infliction of endless punishment be overcoming evil with good?"[12]

Critical Objection: Stetson thinks Christianity has been perverted into being the "bad-news gospel that passes for the Good News of Christ in the minds of many souls . . . . that God really is a monster."[13] He also believes that, "we become like the God we worship. If we worship a cruel God, we will be cruel. If we worship a vengeful God, we will take revenge on those we see as His enemies. If we worship a sadistic God, we will delight in tormenting those who do not worship Him or who disagree with our religious views . . . . Instead of the Good News of God's loving Fatherhood and the destiny of all people to be saved . . . . people who called themselves Christians only knew a gospel of terror and hatred. [which] They had been taught by the churches to believe in . . . ."[14]

*"Then he will say to those on his left, '**Depart from me**, you who are **cursed**, into the **eternal fire** prepared for the devil and his angles"* (Matt. 25:41; 7:23; Luke 13:27).

Part of the reality of hell and its curse is exclusion from fellowship with Christ and being in continuous persecution someday in the presence of Satan and his demons.

Critical Objection: Again, Christian Universalists protest this interpretation and understanding saying, "How can you say burning someone alive forever is 'just' or 'fair; for everyone who hasn't accepted Jesus Christ? Even we humans fit the punishment to the crime . . . . Is just being born into this world grounds for being endlessly tortured. . . . This is not justice—this is insanity!"[15]

What then is the meaning of this passage? It doesn't sound like exclusion from Christ, who is the Lamb of Revelation.

*"If anyone worships the beast and his image and receives his mark on the fore-head or on the hand, he, too, will drink of the wine of God's fury, which has been poured full strength into the cup of his wrath. He will be tormented with burning sulfur **in the presence of the holy angels and the Lamb*** (Rev. 14:10-11).

*". . . Fear him who, after the killing of the body, has power to throw you into **hell** [Gehenna] . . . ."* (Luke 12:5).

If we aren't saved from something, then Jesus died in vain.

*"If your hand causes you to sin, cut it off. It is better for you to enter life maimed than with two hands to go into **hell** [Gehenna], where the fire never goes out"* (Mark 9:44; also 45-48).

This grotesque verse stresses the seriousness and unendingness of hell.

*"But anyone who says, 'You fool!' will be in danger of the fire of **hell** [Gehenna]"* (Matt. 5:22).

Hell is a real place, dimension, and state of being.

Critical Objection: These three verses are *Gehenna* verses, not "hell" verses. See again, all twelve *Gehenna* verses we covered in Chapter 3.

*"He will **punish** those who do not know God and do not obey the gospel of our Lord Jesus. They will be punished with **everlasting destruction** and **shut out** from the presence of the Lord and from the majesty of his power"* (2 Thess. 1:8-9).

It's inescapable. Once again, two groups of people are mentioned here and are mutually and permanently separated from one another. The group spoken of in this passage suffers the divinely revealed alternative to salvation and eternal life in heaven.

Critical Objection: Amirault fires back, "If anyone deserved to go to Hell, it was us Christians for our hypocrisy and lack of concern for the lost[16] . . . don't you deserve to go to Hell yourself for being so callused and non-caring?"[17]

Critical Objection: Talbott chimes in with this piece of logic. "(Contrary to repeated declarations in the New Testament)," doesn't this make God "every bit the 'respecter of persons'?"[18]

*"and so that all will be **condemned** who have **not believed** the truth but have delighted in **wickedness**"* (2 Thess. 2:12).

Critical Objection: Baker asks some poignant questions: "why do we find it so easy to buy into the violence of hell when Jesus told us to love our enemies? Sometimes we even seem to take a certain satisfaction in the thought that God will be violent toward sinners and send them to eternal punishment. I just don't get it. Why do we want to hold on to hell, and why do we feel justified in doing so? We don't seem to think about how horrible it makes God look."[19]

*"Their destiny is **destruction**, their god is their stomach, and their glory is in their shame. Their mind is on earthly things"* (Phil. 3:19).

A wrong focus in this life produces a destiny in the afterlife of permanent destruction.

Critical Objection: "If Hell is real, does not judgment triumph over mercy and thus contradict this Scripture (James 2:13b)?"[20]

*"For certain men whose **condemnation** was written about long ago . . . are **godless** men, who change the grace of our God into a license for **immorality** and **deny** Jesus Christ our only Sovereign and Lord"* (Jude 4).

All the wicked will suffer forever in hell.

Critical Objection: Baker protests: "Even the government considers torture a criminal action! How can we condone it just because God is doing it?"[21]

*"How much **more severely** do you think a man **deserves** to be **punished** who has trampled the Son of God under foot, who has treated as an unholy thing the blood of the covenant that sanctified him, and who has insulted the Spirit of grace?"* (Heb. 10:29; also 6:4-6).

There may be degrees of punishment in hell, but the duration is forever.

Critical Objection: Baker mockingly contributes that "we cling to traditional views of hell, in which our loving God exacts eternal punishment for temporal sin—an extreme case of the punishment *not* fitting the crime—and we consider this to be 'justice.'"[22]

*"But there were also **false prophets** among the people, just as there will be **false teachers** among you. They will secretly introduce **destructive heresies**, even denying the sovereign Lord who bought them – bringing swift **destruction** on themselves"* (2 Pet. 2:1).

Universalism is one of those "destructive heresies," if not the #1 heresy. Woe to those who hold it or even entertain it.

*"**Woe** to them! They have taken the way of Cain . . . . They are . . . **twice dead**"* (Jude 11-12).

How could this be said if God was going to save them all, eventually someday?

*"And I will put **enmity between** you and the woman, and between your offspring and hers . . . . "* (Gen. 3:15).

Early in the Genesis account God told us that there would be a separation between those who belonged to Satan (the serpent) and those who belong to Jesus (the offspring or seed of the woman, the body of Christ).

*"You **belong** to your father, the **devil** . . . . "* (John 8:44).

Jesus told the religious Jews who were seeking to kill Him exactly to whom they belonged.

*"Not everyone who says to me, 'Lord, Lord,' will **enter the kingdom of heaven**, but **only** he who does the will of my Father who is in **heaven**. **Many** will say to me on that day, 'Lord, Lord, did we not prophesy in your name, and in your name drive out demons and perform many miracles?' Then I will tell them plainly, 'I never knew you. **Away from me, you evildoers!**"* (Matt. 7:21-23).

This hard saying of Jesus indicates that many who appear to follow Jesus during their earthly lives, back then and there and here and now, will not be saved.

Critical Objection: Note in the above passage that the "kingdom of heaven" and "heaven" are not the same thing, as many have confused. The kingdom of heaven was and still is a then-and-there, here-and-now reality of the rule, reign, and will of God being done on earth. Hence, Jesus was not saying here that only a few will find salvation and enter heaven.

*". . . but whosoever speaketh a word against the Holy Ghost, it shall **not be forgiven** him, neither in **this world**, neither in the **world to come**."* (Matt. 12:32, *KJV*).

Exclusivists term this verse "the death blow to universalism." It's known as "the unpardonable sin." Mark 3:29 puts this statement of Jesus into a somewhat milder form saying, "but is in danger of eternal damnation."

Critical Objection: The *King James Version* is a bad translation here. The word "world" is *aion* and means an "age." The *New International Version* translates this properly as *"either in this age or in the age to come."* And these two ages deal with earthly time and realities—that is, neither in the Old Covenant Mosaic age or in the "age to come" of the New Covenant Christian age that was being ushered in by Jesus, the Messiah. This has nothing to do with the postmortem afterlife as Exclusivist Marshall so proposes and confuses: "after death followed by entry into the Age to Come (or 'the Kingdom of God'; or 'eternal life') or exclusion."[23]

Only the Few Who Believe

"For God so loved the world that he gave his one and only Son, that **whoever believes** *in him shall* **not perish** *but have* **eternal life"** (John 3:16).

It's the most quoted and best-known verse in the Bible. Clearly, it says that belief in God's Son is the only means of attaining eternal life. It's the differentiating criteria between being saved and being lost, eternally. Only "whoever believes" receives eternal life. This is the extent of Christ's atonement. Salvation is not extended to the entire human race of all ages. Those who do not believe "perish."

Critical Objection: "If Hell is real and the greatest part of humanity went there, how could you HONESTLY say that 'Love NEVER fails?' Seems like love fails most of the time according to your understanding of things (1 Cor. 13:8)."[24] Also note, that Exclusivists like to avoid the *very* next verse, which reads, "For God did not send his Son into the world to condemn the world, but to save the world through him (John 3:17).

"This righteousness from God comes through faith in Jesus Christ **to all who believe.** . . . *"* (Rom. 3:22; also Rom. 1:16).

Again, belief in Jesus Christ is clearly the criterion that limits who is saved and receives this righteousness from God. This and many other scriptures assert that the promise of salvation is only for "all who believe."

"Whoever **believes** *and is* **baptized** *will be* **saved,** *but whoever does* **not believe** *will be* **condemned"** (Mark 16:16; also John 5:28-29).

Consistently, the substance of the gospel is an absolute connection between belief and salvation.

Critical Objection: Note: the word "condemned" or "damned" (*KJV*) is the Greek word *katakrino*. It means "to judge against, i.e., sentence: – condemn, damn.) (*Strong's* #2632*).* The degree and duration of this are not specified. And the idea of eternal torment (which is enthusiastically preached from many pulpits) has probably done more to cause the name of God to be blasphemed than any other teaching on earth, including evolution, according to some Christian Universalists.

Critical Objection: "It's a plain fact that the colder less loving one is the easier it is to teach Hell while the more loving one becomes the harder it is to talk about Hell. Is heaven full of cold unloving people?"[25]

Critical Objection: *"the image of God we hold in our heads and hearts matters* because that image dictates our behavior. It enables us to condone, justify, or even engage in violent acts against our 'neighbors.' Seeing God as a violent judge, who throws multitudes of people into the eternal fires of hell for punishment without end, contributes to our own behavior. . . . affects the way we think and live."[26]

"for, 'Everyone who calls on the name of the Lord will be saved'" (Rom. 10:13).

This often-cited verse under girds the mighty mission mandate and message for Christians to evangelize the lost. But, again, it's only those who call on the name of the Lord. And how can they call on Him unless they know about Him (Rom. 10:14-15).

"Yet to all who received him, to those who believed in his name, he gave the right to become children of God" (John 1:12).

How could it be any clearer? argue Exclusivists. Only those who receive Christ and his atoning work and believe on Him in this life fulfill the condition that God has consistently and persistently prescribed for salvation—*"today* is the day of salvation" (2 Cor. 6:2), and not some postmortem day.

Critical Objection: But what about "those who die as infants or children and don't have an opportunity to respond in faith to Christ? What about those who have never heard the gospel, either before the advent of Jesus or since—people raised in cultures that have never seen a church or a Christian preacher? How are they to believe?"

While Galli recognizes that "we so desperately want to answer these questions," he simply believes "God has not revealed what he will or will not do in these cases."[27] Furthermore, "the so-called age of accountability is not expressly taught in Scripture."[28]

*"I told you that you would die in your sins; if you **do not believe** that I am the one I claim to be, you will indeed **die in your sins**"* (John 8:24).

Again, these words of Jesus couldn't be clearer.

*"I tell you the truth, he who **believes** has everlasting **life**"* (John 6:47).

Sure God wants everyone to be saved, but not all will believe. They resist his will and go to hell. It's not God Who sends them there. It's their choice.

Critical Objection: Amirault caustically counters, "if my daughter is in Hell because she did not get 'born again' then I'd rather go to Hell and be with her than to be with your God because there would be more love in Hell than near your vindictive God."[29]

*"Whoever **believes** in the Son has **eternal life**, but whoever rejects the Son will not see life, for God's **wrath** remains on him"* (John 3:36; also 3:18).

More clear and emphatic words from Jesus Himself documenting that eternal life is effectual only for those who believe.

Critical Objection: Amirault again caustically comments that since "most people don't get 'born again,' doesn't that make abortionists the greatest evangelists of all since they kill babies before they can enter the world to begin their life of sin? (Gory thought, but think about it.)"[30]

*"that everyone who **believes** in him may have **eternal life**"* (John 3:15; also 5:24).

*" 'Yet there are some of you who do **not believe**.' For Jesus had known from the beginning which of them did **not believe** and who would **betray** him. He went on to say, 'This is why I told you that no one can come to me unless the Father has **enabled** him.' From this time many of his disciples turned back and no longer followed him. 'You do not want to leave too, do you?' Jesus asked the Twelve. Simon Peter answered him, 'Lord, to whom shall we go? You have the words of **eternal life**'"* (John 6:64-68).

It is God Who "enables" some to believe and others not to believe (also see John 6:44).

*"For God did not appoint us to **suffer wrath** but to **receive salvation** through our Lord Jesus Christ"* (1 Thess. 5:9).

The "us" here are believers. Outside the Christian faith there is no salvation.

Critical Objection: "If all things were made for GOD's pleasure, is it conceivable that God would derive pleasure from seeing those He created endlessly tortured?"[31]

Critical Objection: "If the greatest part of mankind eventually goes [to Hell], wouldn't Jesus be considered a great failure considering the fact He was sent to save the whole world?"[32]

Critical Objection: "Would not the salvation of half of mankind glorify God more than the salvation of one-fourth? Would not the salvation of nine-tenths of mankind glorify God more than the salvation of one-half?"[33] But if "God fell short of His goal to save all . . . [isn't] God . . . a failure?"[34]

Critical Objection: "If God is the Father of all men, will He do less for His children than earthly parents would do for theirs?"[35]

*"Christ is the end of the law so that there may be righteousness for everyone who **believes**"* (Rom. 10:4; 1 Tim. 1:16).

Again, here's the condition and the extent of atonement and redemption.

Critical Objection: "Does the belief of endless misery cause the believer to 'rejoice with joy unspeakable and full of glory?' – (1 Pet. 1:8)."[36]

*"I know my sheep and my sheep **know me** . . . . and I lay down my life for the **sheep** . . . . but you do **not believe** because you are **not my sheep**"* (John 10:14-15, 26-28).

Jesus only died for his sheep. That's not everyone. All men are not his sheep.

Critical Objection: Baker pitches a different perspective. She writes, "we get our ideas of justified violence from the image of God we carry around with us, which we develop out of our traditional interpretations . . . . We cast Hitler as *the* villain in history, the archetype of a horribly evil person. But our traditional views of hell cast God as worse, as one who tortures and puts billions and billions of people through a second death, not for a few days, months, or years, but for *all* eternity, forever and ever and ever! Their only offense? Not confessing Jesus as Savior. They are no worse than we are: all sin and fall short of God's glory. But for a temporal error, shall they endure endless torture and torment? We call this God's justice?"[37]

Critical Objection: Christ also said, "I have other sheep that are not of this sheep pen" (John 10:16). Wittmer counters that this does not mean "Jesus has come to save people who remain in other religions. . . . Jesus is merely telling his Jewish audience that he has come to bring both Jews and Gentiles (the 'other sheep') to faith in him."[38]

"This is my blood of the covenant, which is poured out for **many** *for the forgiveness of sins"* (Matt. 26:28).

His blood is not poured out for all—only for those many who believe.

". . . to give his life as a ransom for **many***"* (Mark 10:45; Matt. 20:28).

This "many" is for his Church (Eph. 5:25), for the many who believe, and for the children God gave him (Tit. 2:14). Like many other verses, this verse expresses the very same intention and purpose of Christ. Christ did not die "for all men" as some verses seem to say and the Christian Universalists claim. He died for no more than God gave Him.

". . . I am not praying for the world, but for **those** *you have* **given me***, for they are yours. . . . Father, I want* **those** *you have* **given me** *to be with me where I am . . . ."* (John 17:2, 9, 24; also 6:37, 39).

God has not given everybody to Jesus, only some.

*"The Lord knows **those** who are **his** . . . ."* (2 Tim. 2:19).
    Not all are his!

*"And this is the will of him who sent me, that I shall **lose none** of all that he has **given me**, but raise them up at the last day"* (John 6:39).

    Not all are his!

*"Jacob I loved, but Esau I **hated** . . . . I will have **mercy** on whom I have mercy, and I will have **compassion** on whom I have compassion. . . . Therefore God has mercy on whom **he wants** to have mercy, and **he hardens** whom **he wants** to harden"* (Rom. 9:13, 15, 18; Exod. 33:19).

Christian Universalism's main presupposition is that God loves everybody, while ignoring his wrath. But this verse teaches otherwise (also see Mal. 1:2-3).

Calvinists claim that God's desire and purpose in salvation is limited to a small group of foreordained, or elected people, "the elect" to eternal life (Acts 13:48; Rom. 8:30; 9:11; Eph. 1:4;). And that "he will certainly accomplish this purpose" verses "the other side . . . who insist . . . that what God desires he will certainly achieve . . . [as] all people will be saved."[39] God not only destined or chose certain individuals for mercy, but chose other individuals for wrath and destruction (Rom. 9:21-23). Therefore, Calvinists have to interpret words such as "all," "world," and "everyone" in a limited way. The others are the reprobates and go to damnation (2 Pet. 2:12; 1 Pet. 2:8; Jude 4; Matt. 25:32). So, Christ died only for the elect who *will* believe.

Arminians have a greater problem. While they agree with Christian Universalists that Christ died for all sinners, and that God's grace is universally extended and available to everyone, they maintain that it is also conditional and based on if they *should* hear and believe. Hence, God's will, desire, and purposes are thwarted by human free will, desire, and purposes.

Critical Objection: "If . . . God only loves those who love Him, what better is He than the sinner?"[40] "If God hates the sinner, does the sinner do wrong in hating Him?"[41]

Critical Objection: "that Christ died only for the elect" is an "erroneous idea."[42]

Critical Objection: "The idea that God is as much glorified by the damnation of the lost as by the salvation of the saints as held by some Calvinists is hard to reconcile with Ezekiel 18:23: 'Do I take any pleasure in the death of the wicked? declares the Sovereign Lord. Rather, am I not pleased when they turn from their ways and live?'"[43]

*"But he who **stands firm** to the end will **be saved**"* (Matt. 24:13).

What is left unsaid but strongly implied here is that he who does not, will not be saved.

*"No one can come to me unless the Father who sent me **draws** him . . . . unless the Father has **enabled** him"* (John 6:44, 65).

No question, God is in control of all this, or at least knows in advance who will or will not receive salvation.

Critical Objection: "the concept of Hell . . . . violates the nature of God . . . .the wisdom of God, the pleasure of God, the promises of God . . . the power of God . . . . the full power of the cross of Christ . . . . goes against our conscience and our hearts. Finally, it has the ring of something the subtlest of all creatures would concoct . . . the greatest lie ever told."[44]

Have Life

*"He who has the Son **has life**; he who does not have the Son of God does **not have life**"* (1 John 5:12).

These plain words and this plain truth differentiate two groups of people—saved and unsaved—and two different afterlife destinies.

*"**My sheep** hear my voice; I know them, and they follow me. I give them **eternal life**, and they shall **never perish**; **no one can snatch** them out of my hand"* (John 10:27-28).

Only believers are Christ's sheep, hear his voice, follow Him, and have eternal life. All others perish.

"Whoever does not love does not know God, because God is love. This is how God showed his love among us: He sent his one and only Son into **the world** *that we* **might live through him***"* (1 John 4:8-9).

Most of the world "might" but will not.

Critical Objection: "How does the threat of endlessly torturing us convince us that God loves us and that we should love Him with all our heart, soul, mind and strength?"[45]

"For just as the Father raises the dead and gives them **life***, even so the Son gives* **life** *to whom* **he is pleased** *to give it"* (John 5:21).

Critical Objection: "If Hell is real and the devil and all his works and people are to be thrown into it to stay alive forever, doesn't that violate . . . [the] statement that He came to 'destroy' the works of the devil? (1 John 3:8)"[46]

Critical Objection: "If . . . universalism is a heresy, why is it that those who believe God loves all and will save all find it easier to love all people than those who believe most people are going to Hell? (Think this through very carefully.)"[47]

The Lines Are Drawn

The lines seem clearly and strongly drawn between the two sides in this centuries-old debate and theological stand-off. On one side, Christian Universalists lament the idea "that only a handful of the billions who have lived and died on this planet will finally make it into heaven is certainly N-O-T 'good tidings of great joy that will be for all the people.'"[48]

As Thayer sarcastically puts it, "Who can believe this?"[49] He adds:

> . . . remember that this is under the government of a God who has all the resources of wisdom, power, and spiritual influences to prevent it . . . . From all this there is but one refuge; and that is, the utter rejection of a doctrine so plainly opposed to the spirit of the Gospel, and to the commandment of faith and love and the full and hearty reception of the

divine truth that God is the Father of all, Christ the Saviour of all, and Heaven the final home of all . . . ."[50]

Exclusivists in turn argue that Christian Universalists have "lifted a whole bunch of scriptures out of their contexts and built a 'spoof-text' argument" and "are twisting Scripture to their own destruction."[51] They further admonish that "of course, evangelicals want all people to be saved, but we dare not promise universal salvation without a word from God," which, of course, they believe has not be given.[52]

"that only a handful of the billions who have lived and died on this planet will finally make it into heaven is certainly N-O-T 'good tidings of great joy that will be for all the people.'"

Christian Universalists counter back that "universalism is not as bankrupt of biblical support as some suggest . . . . Any case for Exclusivism must do justice to these and similar passages."[53]

Another with universalist sympathies philosophically writes:

Fundamentalist traditions are strong. But I have a problem with the idea that God had no better plan than to create mankind, give them the power to reproduce, only so in the end about 1 out of a thousand will be saved—and all the others, most who never even heard of him—they will need to be punish forever. In the end, with this view, Satan would be a greater soul winner than Jesus.[54]

Another philosophically concludes:

Make no mistake about it; the only way to put out the raging fire of hatred in our world is to put out the fire of hell in people's hearts . . . . The fact is, the exclusive salvation and eternal damnation of fundamentalism is nothing more than a lie—a powerful lie with a long history, but a lie that must finally be defeated by the truth . . . . The Bible teaches that God has an unfailing plan to save *all* people . . . . That, my friends, is the Good News of Christian Universalism. That is the original Gospel of Jesus Christ. . . . . discover it and embrace it. And when we do, our hearts will overflow with joy and our Christianity will make perfect sense for the first time, in a way we will want to shout from the rooftops.[55]

Philip Schaff aptly summarized the conflict between the Christian universalist and exclusivist positions this way:

This doctrine of a divine will and divine provision of a universal salvation, on the sole condition of faith, is taught in many passages which admit of no other interpretation, and which must, therefore, decide this whole question. For it is a settled rule in hermeneutics that dark passages must be explained by clear passages, and not vice versa . . . . To these passages should be added the divine exhortations to repentance, and the lament of Christ over the inhabitants of Jerusalem who 'would not' come to him (Matt. 23:37). These exhortations are insincere or unmeaning, if God does not want all men to be saved, and if men have not the ability to obey or disobey this voice. . . . It is impossible to restrict these passages to a particular class without doing violence to the grammar and the context.

For a solution, Schaff suggested . . .

The only way of escape is by the distinction between a revealed will of God, which declares his willingness to save all men, and a secret will of God which means to save only some men. Augustine and Luther made this distinction. . . . But this distinction overthrows the system which it is intended to support. . . . A man who says the reverse of what he means is called, in plain English, a hypocrite and a liar. . . Nor does it remove the difficulty when he [Calvin] warns us to rely on the revealed will of God rather than brood over his secret will.[56]

Yes, the lines are drawn quite firmly. But is a better solution than Schaff's solution a possibility? The first step in that direction must be to analyze, re-evaluate, and weigh the strengths and weaknesses of the seven major arguments in this stalemated debate and centuries-long stand-off. It is to that task we next turn in Part III – "Analysis of Conflicting Arguments."

PART III: ANALYSIS OF CONFLICTING ARGUMENTS

Chapter 8

Dispute over Universal Language?

NOTE TO READER: Throughout this and the next six chapters of PART III, we will analyze and weigh the strength argument presented by both sides. After each chapter, we will vote on which view has the strongest argument with the advantage going to either Christian Universalism, Exclusivism, or, inconclusively, to a Draw. We will also keep a running tally at the end of each chapter. I think you will be astonished at the results. I was astonished the first time I went through this material with my Bible study group. And each of us cast a vote as we finished up each chapter's discussion and analysis. Please feel free to cast your vote as well and keep your own running tally.

Another thing you will notice is an intensification of argumentation, conflict, and emotion as we progress through each of these seven argument areas. But since we have been able to sensibly deal with the so-called "hell" texts in Part I, we should be able to deal just as sensibly with the arguments presented by both sides in these seven chapters, don't you think?

As we proceed, please keep in mind that we are delving into a mystery (see again Rom. 11:33-36). And everything regarding this mystery has not been revealed by God to us in his Word. Therefore, let's proceed with a high degree of humility. In this re-discovery endeavor, arrogance and dogmatism are out of place.

WARNING: Some may feel that parts of these chapters are too involved, too deep, or, perhaps, over their heads of what they are comfortable handling, academically and/or intellectually. Truly, some of this material is not simple surface stuff. That's okay. Skim it, take a rest, come up for air, and hit it again some time later. Don't expect this pursuit of truth to be easy. Some unlearning, no doubt, will be necessary. It was for me. And, once again, unlearning is the hardest form of learning.

But I believe enough has been revealed by God in his Word that we can viably attempt to offer a resolution to this mystery and possibly reconcile this divisive and stalemated debate. Let us see.

One of the Smallest Words

First, we must grant that Christian Universalists do have "a battery of proof texts from the Bible to support their deductive arguments," as the Exclusivist authors *Sense & Nonsense About Heaven & Hell* pejoratively put it.[1] And "in some sense Christ died for the whole world . . . . *for all . . . . for every one*."[2] But what is that sense? That's the key issue of argumentation in this chapter.

Secondly, and as Christian Universalist MacDonald admits, "there has been tremendous confusion amongst biblical scholars over the term 'all'" and other simple and similar expressions such as: "all men," "the many," "everyone," "every man," "every knee," "every tongue," "the world," "the whole world," "all people," "all nations," "all things," "every creature," "all in all," "all the nations," "all mankind," "all peoples," "every living thing," "all kings," "all the ends of the earth," "all the families of the nations," and "all the earth" (see again Chapter 6). "So it is worth spending a little time clarifying it. It is commonplace to find scholars suggesting that 'all' can sometimes mean 'all without distinction; rather than 'all without exception,' and thus 'all people' can mean 'all *types* of people (i.e., Jew and Gentile) and does not necessarily mean ' all individual people.'"[3]

But as we have seen, some Christian Universalists argue that "all" means all (everyone) always. Exclusivists argue back that "the gospel is addressed in general terms to all humanity."[4] This is how and why "God is a universalist. From Genesis to Revelation, God's saving purposes always have in view all human beings. . . . This broad universalism sets the overall tone for the Bible's teaching on salvation. . . . [But] only those who have made a conscious decision in this life to accept Christ as their personal Saviour will be saved and that everyone else, i.e., the vast majority of human beings who have ever lived (with exceptions usually made for the mentally handicapped and small children) will endure a hell of eternal conscious punishment."[5]

As a result of this disagreement, what we find is that one of the smallest words in the Bible is one of the most difficult to interpret and understand. The dispute revolves around this basic question: when does "all" mean "all" and when does "all" not mean "all?" When does it mean only "some" or "all of some sort?" John Owen tried to capture the essence of this "all" controversy this way:

> . . . those terms of the *world, all men, all nations, every creature,* and the like, used in the business of redemption and preaching of the gospel . . . . Upon these expressions hangs the whole weight of the opposite cause, the chief if not the only argument for the universality of redemption . . . ."[6]

Later on Owen revealed more of his exclusivist bent in claiming that "the whole strength of this [universalist] argument lies in turning indefinite propositions into universals, concluding that because Christ died for sinners, therefore he died for all sinners."[7]

The dispute revolves around this basic question: when does "all" mean "all" and when does "all" not mean "all?" When does it mean only "some" or "all of some sort?"

Make no mistake; this small word "all" is the most significant word in this debate. The Greek word for "all" is *pas.* It's consistently defined with a singular meaning. *Strong's Concordance* defines it as meaning "all, any, every, the whole."[8] *Vine's* says regarding the Old Testament Hebrew equivalent that "All . . . *kōl* . . . [means] 'all; the whole' . . . . The word can be used alone, meaning 'the entirety,' 'whole,' or 'all' (Exod. 29:24)." But it also "can signify everything in a given unit whose members have been selected from others of their kind (Gen. 6:2)."

Regarding the New Testament use, "PAS radically means 'all' . . . 'every,' every kind or variety . . . . the whole of one object . . . . Used without a noun it virtually becomes a pronoun meaning 'everyone' or 'anyone.'"[9]

Bauer, Arndt, Gingrich, and Danker defines it when used with a noun as "emphasizing the individual members of the class denoted by the noun *every, each, any,* scarcely differing in meaning from the plural 'all;'" with a noun in the plural as "*all men, everyone;*" with a noun in the singular, "*the whole, all.*" with a noun in the plural, "*all.*" used without an article, "*everyone without exception. . . .*"[10]

Exclusivists like Owen, nonetheless, insist that a distinction is sometimes mandated when universal language "is not universally collective of all of all sorts, but either distributive, for some of all sorts, or collective, with a restriction to all of some sort."[11] In other words, they insist that there are times when everyone on earth, everyone who ever lived, or the entire human race is *not* the object of "all" or of the similar expressions. They further contend that this language must mean that salvation is open or available to all and every kind or class of man in a representative and global sense and merely designates that humanity at large will be drawn to Christ. But not all will actually be saved. Hence, Douglas Moo maintains in *Hell Under Fire* that what Scripture presents "is a universalism of people groups, not of individuals."[12]

Thirdly, and perhaps most importantly, evidence of a restrained, restricted, or limited-sense meaning is found in other verses and contexts in the Bible. Here are a few of those instances (all **bolds** are mine):

Everyone . . .

"*and when they found him, they exclaimed: '**Everyone** is looking for you!'*"(Mark 1:37).

But everyone in the whole town of Capernaum was not out looking for Jesus that morning.

"*They came to John and said to him, 'Rabbi, that man who was with you on the other side of the Jordan—the one you testified about—well, he is baptizing, and **everyone** is going to him'*" (John 3:26 – "*and **all men** come to him – KJV*).

But not everyone in the Judean countryside were going to Jesus to be baptized.

*". . . Since that time, the good news of the kingdom of God is being preached, and **everyone** is forcing his way into it"* (Luke 16:16).

But everyone, like the Pharisees for instance, was not doing this at that time, either.

*"for **everyone** held that John really was a prophet"* (Mark 11:32).

The Pharisees didn't.

*"Though I am free and belong to no man, I make myself a slave to **everyone**, to win as many as possible. . . . I have become all things to **all men** so that by all possible means I might save some"* (1 Cor. 9:19, 22).

Paul was not in servitude to every single person nor all things to all men in all the cities and countries he visited.

   All . . .

*"**all** the ends of the earth will remember and turn to the LORD, and **all** the families of the nations will bow down before him,"* (Psa. 22:27).

Over the many centuries, many have come to and died on earth without bowing down before him.

*"**All** kings will bow down to him and all nations will serve him"* (Psa. 72:11).

All kings have not done this.

*"**all** the ends of the earth have seen the salvation of our God."* (Psa. 98:3b).

The natives in what would become North America, for example, had not seen at that time, nor at the time of Jesus.

"For with fire and with his sword the LORD will execute judgment upon all men, and many will be those slain by the LORD" (Isa. 66:16).

All men throughout history have not received this type of judgment.

"And afterward, I will pour out my Spirit on all people . . . ." (Joel 2:28a; quoted in Acts 2:17).

But only "about three thousand" were saved at this fulfillment at Pentecost out of approximately one million or more in Jerusalem at the time (Acts 2:41).

"For the grace of God that brings salvation has appeared to all men (Tit. 2:11).

Multiple millions throughout the Roman Empire never saw Jesus while He was alive nor after his resurrection during his post-resurrection comings/appearings.

People went out to him from Jerusalem and all Judah and the whole region of the Jordan" (Matt. 3:5).

Obviously, not everyone did—just some people from every region.

"News about him spread all over Syria, and people brought to him all who were ill . . . ." (Matt. 4:24).

Obviously, once again, not everyone in every area in Syria heard about Jesus, nor was every single ill person in Syria brought to Jesus for healing.

"Then you will be handed over to be persecuted and put to death, and you will be hated by all nations because of me. . . . And this gospel of the kingdom will be preached in the whole world as a testimony to all nations, and then the end will come" (Matt. 24:9, 14).

At most, this included the nations of the then-known world (*oikoumene* in the Greek, meaning "land (i.e., the [terrene part of the] globe, specifically the Roman Empire).[13] Other scriptures confirmed that this preaching of the gospel was fulfilled in the 1st century (see Col. 1:6, 23; Acts 1:8; 2:5; 24:5; Rom. 1:8; 10:18; 16:26; Jude 3).[14] But it wasn't preached in what would become North America, or Australia, or China, etc.

*"At dawn, he appeared again in the temple courts, where **all the people** gathered around him, and he sat down to teach them* (John 8:2).

It was only all the people who were present, then and there. This certainly was not all the people in Jerusalem that morning.

*". . . I always taught in synagogues or at the temple, where **all** the Jews come together. . . ."* (John 18:20).

Not every Jew practiced the Jewish faith and attended synagogue or temple events, even back then.

*"There are different kinds of working, but the same God works **all** of them in **all men*** (1 Cor. 12:6).

Not all men have all the gifts of the Spirit. This is hyperbole.

World or **whole world** . . .

*"So the Pharisees said to one another, 'See this is getting us nowhere. Look how **the whole world** has gone after him!'"* (John 12:19).

Not everyone was pursuing Jesus.
For more hyperbolic usages, see again Matt. 24:14; also Luke. 2:1; Rom. 1:8; 11:12; 1 John 5:19; Rev. 12:9)[15]

Gleanings from Restricted Uses

What should we glean from the above mixture of possible meanings of the small words "all," "everyone," "world?" At the very least, this implies caution should be used before assuming that universal terms literally mean "every single individual" or "all" all the time. The meaning of each use must be determined by its context.

In our modern-day world, we often use universal expressions in an exaggeration or hyperbolic manner. For example: All of Indiana and Indianapolis (where I live) was excited about the Colts beating the Chicago Bears and winning Super Bowl XLI in 2007. But my wife wasn't. She couldn't have cared less. And how about these familiar statements?

- All Americans love hamburgers. (No they don't.)
- I do this ___(fill in the blank)___ all the time. (No, you don't.)
- On a church sign, "All Welcome." (Are they setting up 6 billion chairs?)
- Perhaps you can think of more.

Fourthly, other biblical uses of universal terms like "all" do have universal meanings and apply in both a collective and universal sense. Here are some examples generally agreed upon by both sides:

"'*All* authority in heaven and on earth has been given to me*" (Matt. 28:18).

"*Not at all! Let God be true and **every** man a liar*" (Rom. 3:4).

*There is **no one** righteous, not even one; there is **no one** who understands, **no one** who seeks God*" (Rom. 3:10b-11).

This universal application is arguable.

"*for **all** have sinned and fall short of the glory of God*" (Rom. 3:23).

"*For **all** must appear before the judgment seat of Christ, that **each one** may receive what is due him for the things done while in the body, whether good or bad*" (2 Cor. 5:10).

"***All** Scripture is God-breathed and is useful for teaching, rebuking, correcting and training in righteousness*" (2 Tim. 3:16).

Hence, the word "all" or "every," or "world" cannot be made into "some" or "few" or "everyone" in every case. The quandary remains—when is "all" all, and when is it not all?

Fifthly, what do we do with all the multiple "alls" in these verses? They appear to offer up a mixed bag of "alls?" So how do we parse out these "alls?"

"one God and Father of all, who is over all and through all and in all" (Eph. 4:6).

"Love the Lord your God with all your heart and with all your soul and with all your strength. . . . To love him with all your heart, with all your understanding and with all your strength, and to love your neighbor as yourself is more important than all burnt offerings and sacrifices" (Mark 12:33; from Deut 6:5).

A general rule of language is that if a word has a certain meaning in a sentence, if it is used again in the same sentence, it means the same thing. So how do you explain all the "alls" in these above two passages?

Fact is, the word "all," and other universal expressions like it, in and of itself and themselves, cannot determine its scope or meaning, or that intended by the speaker or writer. Thus, context and common sense are cited as the qualifiers and quantifiers of the scope and meaning of these words in any particular Bible passage.

Sixthly, this subjective variability means that the scope and meaning of equivalent expressions of universal language is highly contingent upon reading one's preferred theology and/or emotions into the text instead of taking the text at literal face value, or allowing it to stand on its own. So Exclusivists spiritualize these words to mean something other than their literal sense—i.e., only a portion of humankind. While Christian Universalists take them literally, almost everywhere. Who is correct?

The *Worldwide Perspectives* missions' manual exemplifies this first eisegetic (reading ones own ideas into a passage) tendency with its exclusivist comments on the "all men" in John 12:32:

On the surface, this statement could be interpreted to mean that everyone in the world will become a Christian. Since we know that this is quite unlikely, the statement probably means instead that some of all kinds of men will be drawn to Jesus when they learn that His death atoned for their sins.[16]

Seventhly, and as we have seen, is the general appeal of the traditional exclusivist position to the overall and broader biblical context—i.e., their interpretation of that context. As textbook writer, John Murray, termed it, "the context determines the scope."[17] This appeal, however, is not only biased, it's a two-way street. Exclusivists insist that these universal words do not mean what they literally say because of the broader context of Scripture and the nature of God forbid it. Thus, "for all men of course means 'for all those in Christ,'"[18] Christian Universalists counter that an even broader context is the nature, will, and desire of God, which demands it, and these words literally do mean what they literally say (see 2 Pet. 3:9; 1 Tim. 2:4; John 3:17). We'll address this area in chapter 14. For now, and once again, note how both sides appeal to a "broader context."

Let's Vote

In my opinion, this first area of argumentation in the Christian Universalist-Exclusivist debate is a stand-off, a toss-up, and an inconclusive gray area. So for me, it's a Draw, at least for now.

Strength-of-argument advantage: Draw.

Grudem acknowledges this stalemate. He writes that "the 'all' is not explicitly restrictive by a specific phrase such as 'all of God's people,' but this is clearly the sense in the overall context. Of course, in other contexts, the same word 'all' can mean 'all people without exception,' but this must be determined from the individual context in each case."[19] In other words, context rules. But who determines what and whose context rules? Grudem concedes that "the question of the extent of the atonement, for the specific scriptural texts . . . can hardly be said to be conclusive on either side."[20]

Further compounding this dilemma, as Grudem voices, are "the statements 'Christ died for his people only' and 'Christ died for all people' are both true in some sense." But in what sense are they both true? He adds, "too often the argument over this issue has been confused because of various senses that can be given to the word 'for' in these two statements."[21] So from Grudem's perspective, we now add the meaning of another, small, and simple three-letter word into this confusing mix.

No doubt, the true meaning of these universal-language-type words and passages will perpetually resist a formulistic resolution. Given their ambiguity and elasticity, neither side can conclusively prove or defend its position here. Again, the fact that these words can mean a certain thing in any one place and something different in another is the crux of "the all controversy." This realization also forced John Owen to conclude "that no strength of argument can be taken from the word [*all*] itself."[22]

And yet Gary North writes regarding 1 Timothy 4:10 – "who is the Savior of all men, and especially of those who believe"—"This is probably the most difficult verse in the Bible for those who deny universal salvation from hell and who also deny common grace."[23]

"The question of the extent of the atonement, for the specific scriptural texts . . . can hardly be said to be conclusive on either side."

Douglas Moo in *Hell Under Fire* sums up this stand-off like this:

> We conclude that none of the verses usually cited as evidence that Paul taught universalism must be interpreted in that way. Could they be so interpreted? Of course—but only by isolating them from the entire fabric of Paul's teaching[24]

Once again, Moo presents a "broader-context" argument that Christian Universalists answer by asking this challenging question: "Can God be 'especially the Savior of them who believe,' unless He is actually the Savior of all? (1 Tim. 4:10)."[25]

Exclusivist, evangelical, and conservative theologian Erickson rightly admits about the Christian Universalist position: "Could it be? Yes, most certainly that is a possibility. Is it true, however? That is the real question. . . . the burden of proof for a view such as this, which at least on its surface conflicts with some other teachings of Scripture, rests on those who advance it."[26]

In concluding this first argument area, Grudem offers this bit of wise counsel:

> Our knowledge of the issue comes only from incidental references to it in passages whose concern is with other doctrinal or practical matters. In fact, this is really a question that probes into the inner counsels of the Trinity and does so in an area in which there is very little direct scriptural testimony—a fact that should cause us to be cautious.[27]

All of which brings us to our second area of argumentation and one that may have the potential to break this stalemate and clear up this massive gray area. Let us see.

STRENGTH-OF-ARGUMENT ADVANTAGE SCORECARD

	Christian Univ.	Excl.	Draw
Dispute over Universal Language?			✓
RUNNING TALLY	0	0	1

(How do you vote?)

Chapter 9

Power and Point of Parallelism?

C hristian Universalists place paramount importance on twelve clauses arranged in six syntactical parallel structures encompassing eight verses of Scripture. These structures are termed *parallelisms* and were commonly used in Hebrew writings.

In this chapter, we will analyze the six salvation-extent parallelisms presented in Chapter 6. They are found in, again: Rom. 3:23-24; 5:12, 15, 18-19; 11:32; and 1 Cor. 15:22. These parallelisms form the origin and mainstay of the Pauline theme for Universal Salvationism. The crux of the issue we must address within them, once again, concerns the definition and meaning of the words "all," "all men," and "the many," which are contained twice in each parallelism, except for one. The question is: are these words, when used in the first clause of each parallelism, equally balanced with and mean the same as their use in the second clause, or not?

> In this regard, MacDonald issues this proclamation and challenge: We must be open to the possibility that we have misread the Bible. . . .
> Reason, I suggest, would lead us to *seek* a universalist interpretation of specific biblical texts. Typically such an interpretation is ruled out *a priori* and thus not even considered. . . . We need to look again at these so-called universalist texts . . . and ask whether they may *actually* mean what they seem to mean when taken at face value.[1]

It is to this re-assessment task we now turn.

About Parallelisms

Henry A. Virkler in his textbook, *Hermeneutics*, states about the Hebrew parallelism that it is "a feature which may shed light on the meaning of words that are in question."[2] The emphasis here, however, must remain on Virkler's use of the word "may," given the amount of disagreement inherent in the understanding of Paul's six parallelisms that we are considering. Vickler next identifies three basic types of parallelisms:[3]

Synonymous parallelism = the second line of a stanza repeats the content of the first but in different words.
     Example: "He does not treat us as our sins deserve or repay us according to our iniquities." (Psa. 103:10)
     [Especially note the two uses of "us."]

Antithetic parallelism = the idea of the second line sharply contrasts with that of the first line.
     Example: "The wicked borrow and do not repay but the righteous give generously." (Psa. 37:21)

Synthetic parallelism = the second line carries further or completes the idea of the first line.
     Example: "The Lord looks down from heaven on the sons of men to see if there are any who understand, any who seek God." (Psa. 14:2)

Regarding the literary use of a parallelism, *The Anchor Bible Dictionary* contributes:

Parallelism is the most prominent rhetorical figure in ancient Near Eastern poetry, and it is also present, although less prominent, in biblical prose. It can be defined as the repetition of the same or related semantic content and/or grammatical structure in consecutive lines or verses. . . . parallelism is a matter of relationships between lines and/or parts of lines.[4]

In his book, *The Dynamics of Biblical Parallelism*, Berlin further elaborates:

> . . . the essence of parallelism . . . is a *correspondence of one thing with another*. Parallelism promotes the perception of a relationship between the elements of which parallelism is composed, and this relationship is one of correspondence. . . . in general it involves repetition or the substitution of things which are equivalent on one or more linguistic levels.[5]

So if we reread Paul's six parallelisms with the above information in mind, do we still have a stand-off, a toss-up, and an inconclusive draw? Or does the double employment of these words in a strong textual parallelism make a differentiation between them more difficult to support?

Christian Universalists bemoan what they think should be obvious. These verses are not difficult to understand. The problem is, men don't want to believe them. Twice in each parallelism, except for one, the "all," "all men," and "the many" subjects are correspondingly paired and strongly drawn together in a comparison of the effects of Adam's transgression with Christ's redemption. Let's also note that these six parallel comparisons contain plain words, simple sentence constructions, and straightforward, resultant consequences. These comparisons are not easy to sidestep, take away from, or alter the relationship drawn. They do provide Christian Universalists with a compelling argument—although it is not unanswerable, as we shall further see.

The hermeneutic (interpretive principle or approach) one invokes in understanding these parallel texts is crucial. Unquestionably, the dual "all," "all men," and "the many" stand in a balanced, structural, and grammatical parallelism. And as the *Anchor Bible Dictionary* lays out, all six parallelisms utilize "sets of parallel terms . . . fixed or shared word pairs . . . [that] answer one to another in corresponding lines."[6] For example in 1 Corinthians 15:22 "in Adam all" who died corresponds with and is compared to "in Christ all" who are made alive. Hence, "In [this] grammatical parallelism the syntax of the lines is equivalent."[7]

So, how can interpreters make one side of this parallel less inclusive or more exclusive than the other? Wouldn't they be hard-pressed to do so? And since the first "all" is universal in its impact (there is no disagreement here – see Rom. 3:1-12, 23), how then are we to handle the second "all?"

Regarding the parallelism of Romans 5:18, John Murray, a conservative, a Calvinist, and a textbook writer, in his book on Romans, answers these questions, thusly:

> There is no possibility of escaping the conclusion that, if the apostle meant the apodosis to be as embracive in its scope as the protasis, then the whole human race must eventually attain to eternal life. There is no escape from this conclusion in distinguishing between the objective provision and subjective appropriation. Nor is it possible to evade this inference by placing upon the justification of life an attenuated interpretation such as would be compatible with everlasting perdition.[8]

<u>NOTE TO READER</u>: The definition of an "apodosis" is "the clause stating the result in a conditional sentence – 'If I were rich, I would help the poor.' The latter half is the apodosis. A "protasis" is "the clause stating the condition in a conditional sentence." (the first half)."[9]

Yet, on the next page, and in typical exclusivist style, Murray changes his tune and this verse's meaning by resorting to the "broader-context-of-Scripture" argument when he writes:

> When we ask the question: Is it Pauline to posit universal salvation? The answer must be decisively negative (*cf.* II Thess. 1:8, 9). Hence we cannot interpret the apodosis in verse 18 in the sense of inclusive universalism, and it is consistent with sound canons of interpretation to assume a restrictive implication.

Likewise, and to be consistent, Murray restricts the second clause in 1 Corinthians 15:22 by merely asserting that "the parallel does not demand this."[10] In other words, it *cannot* mean this!

Grammatically, it is correct that Paul's God-inspired, parallel statements (depending on the type of parallelism they are) can mean two different things. And, therefore, there are two different ways of interpreting and understanding them.

Christian Universalists claim that in these parallelisms the "all(s)," "all men(s)," and "the many(s)" are the constant; the "in Adam-die" and "in Christ-made alive" are the variables. This understanding is further strengthened by the word "so" that connects the same subject (see 1 Cor. 15:22). Also, this understanding is consistent with a rule of language that if a word has a certain meaning in a sentence, if it is used again in the same sentence, it means the same thing. Of course, this understanding comes from a normal, face-value, and literal reading—the "all" of the first clause is the same "all" of the second clause. But in the Exclusivist view, this interpretation and understanding is not the case.

Exclusivists, while siding with Donald Guthrie in his textbook, *New Testament Theology*, and regarding 1 Corinthians 15:22, admit that "on the face of it this seems to imply not only a universal resurrection, but also a universal salvation" and that "the 'all' in this verse is paralleled in the statement 'as in Adam all die."[11] But to the contrary, they also claim that "close attention to the wording and background of these statements" shows "they are actually contradictory to the notion of universal salvation." They further assert that "universalists misread this."

Instead, they propose, along with Boa and Bowman in *Sense and Nonsense about Heaven & Hell*, that "Paul is here contrasting what happens to all who are 'in Adam' (they 'die') with what happens to all who are 'in Christ' (they 'will be made alive'). He does not say, nor does he mean, that absolutely everyone is now or ever will be 'in Christ.' The people who are 'in Christ' are those 'who have hoped in Christ in this life' (v.19) . . . they are 'those who are Christ's' (v. 23)."[12]

In other words, the "alls" are qualified by what it means to be "in Adam" and "in Christ," respectively. In their view, Paul limits the application of grace to only those who have obeyed the gospel and believed in Christ.

Adding more weight to this exclusivist position is the ambiguity of universal language (see again Chapter 8) that "in some contexts 'all' does not mean all human beings . . . . the words 'all' and 'world' can be used in a variety of contexts to which the universalistic interpretation is not sufficiently sensitive."[13]

The "all" of the first clause is the same "all" of the second clause. But in the Exclusivist view, this interpretation and understanding is not the case.

Guthrie adds regarding 1 Corinthians 15:22, "the two statements may, however, be understood to mean that all who are 'in Adam' will die and all who are 'in Christ' shall be made alive. Paul is affirming 'not the universality of the law, but the universality of its *modus operandi* within the compass in which it works.' The emphasis falls not on the 'all' taken by itself, but the 'all' joined with 'in Adam' and 'in Christ.'" He concludes, that this "cannot be held to teach universal salvation."[14]

Theologian Sam Frost presents his take and exclusivist case in this manner:

> Rather, 'in Christ' is an adverbial phrase that modifies the verb . . . or whole clause 'shall be made alive.' . . . Paul is comparing two bodies, those who have solidarity with the body of Adam ('all those who are dying/falling asleep') and those 'in Christ' (all those who are being made alive).[15]

In a similar manner, Leon Morris in his textbook, *The Epistle to the Romans*, equivocates "the many" in Romans 5:19 by first acknowledging a Christian universalist understanding that it "corresponds to the same expression at the beginning of the verse [vs. 18]." But Morris traditionally takes this to only mean "a great number."[16]

Christian Universalist Talbott retorts: "I still see no way to explain away the clear universal thrust . . . . the suggestion that . . . the second 'all' does not mean 'all,' while the first 'all' does, is patently unsatisfactory. The syntax of Paul's sentence, its parallel structure, and the construction 'For as . . . even so' seems to me to put the matter beyond dispute."[17]

Four additional problems further complicate this debate. They are briefly:

1) There is clearly a difference between a person being "in Christ" and having Christ "in you"—see John 15:1-10; 1 John 2:5-6; John 14:12.
2) The switching of groups within these parallelisms may be akin to the circular type of reasoning dispensationalists use to qualify and defer Jesus' "this generation" in Matthew 24:34 as being some future generation that will see "all these things" happening about which Jesus spoke.[18]
3) Even Exclusivist Douglas J. Moo admits that "Romans 5:18 seems to affirm universalism . . . even more clearly" than 1 Cor. 15:22. He cites "one key difference between these texts is that 'life' in Romans 5:18 does not refer to resurrection but to

spiritual or eternal life (cf. 5:17, 21) . . . . The extent of eternal life will match the extent of death and condemnation." But he bails himself out of this seeming conundrum via a familiar device – "In response, we must reiterate . . . that such a view requires that Paul contradict himself on a rather fundamental point within the same letter.[19] . . . . But Paul is clear elsewhere . . . that escape from that judgment comes only via a vital connection, by faith with Christ."[20]

4) The New Testament emphatically affirms that all people will be raised—some "to live" and some "to be condemned" (John 5:29; also see Acts 24:15). But what does "condemned" actually and totally mean? Is it possible someone can be condemned and still be saved, eventually?

Christian Universalists Fire Back with Guns Blazing

Christian Universalists are not intimidated or thrown off message by these exclusivist attacks. They adamantly support and defend their belief that these two compared "all" groups are the same—if one is universal, the other is universal. And they insist that "made alive" speaks of salvation (1 Cor. 15:22, 42-57).[21]

Generally, both sides in this great debate agree that all humankind come into this world in the same lost condition and under the same curse because all are in Adam's sin without having personally sinned. And since this sin has been imputed to them by God, likewise, Christ's death and righteousness is correspondingly imputed.

So is it then not only possible but logical, ask Christian Universalists, that "God hath concluded all in unbelief that He might have mercy on all (Rom. 11:32)?"[22] In other words, since "no one 'decided' to die in Adam, it was 'reckoned' to us," isn't it possible that "equally no one 'decided' to 'receive eternal life,' it is also 'reckoned' to us"?[23]

Consistently, they maintain that honoring and following Paul's strong parallel constructions and by God's grace, mercy, and love, this same group is the object of Christ's redemption. Eventually, all humankind who were born dead in Adam will be saved by Christ— somehow, in some way, by some means known only to God as He draws and enables every single person (John 6:44, 65).

The historical reality is that many throughout church history, and perhaps the majority for its first five hundred years, have believed that the strength of argument here favors Christian Universalism. The paralleled constructions are that straightforward. Neither their meanings nor rules of interpretation suddenly and dramatically change in mid-stream, i.e., in mid-parallel. No qualifications are made and no exclusions are warranted by the text. No amount of scripture twisting can get around the parallel placement of these two contrasting yet corollary truths. And what Christ accomplished is just as universal in its reach and effectiveness as the consequences of Adam's sin. If this is not so, Christian Universalists chide, then was Adam's sin and disobedience more far-reaching than Christ's sacrifice and obedience? And if so, wouldn't that mean that Adam had more power than Christ?

Consistently, they maintain that honoring and following Paul's strong parallel constructions and by God's grace, mercy, and love, this same group is the object of Christ's redemption.

The whole point and power of the balanced and synonymous parallelisms, employed six times, demands that Christ's redemptive work be commensurate with the effect of Adam's sin on the totality of humankind. Thus, this universal application confirms that Christ's "one act of righteousness" was big enough to reverse all Adam caused. How else, they argue, can grace abound much more than sin (Rom. 5:20-21), unless grace delivers all from sin's effects?

The Adam-Christ Parallel

Another load of scriptural ammunition seemingly leaning towards Christian Universalists, is to appreciate and honor the scriptural parallel between Adam and Christ—"So it is written: 'The first man Adam became a living being'; the last Adam, a life-giving spirit" (1 Cor. 15:45 from Gen. 2:7). Therefore, Christian Universalists ask these four questions:

1. Why did Paul refer to Jesus as "the last Adam?"
2. What do they have in common?
3. How does Adam foreshadow Christ?
4. And why and how can, or should, Jesus be compared to Adam?

First and foremost, Adam and Jesus are the only two men to enter the world sinless. (Eve also entered sinless.)

Here is what, why, and how they address it. The "first man Adam," by his sin and disobedience, brought death to all humankind. By contrast, the second Adam (Jesus), a type and by his sacrifice and obedience, brought life to all humankind. If this is not true, is Jesus then a lesser type than Adam? No, of course not, "because Christ on the Cross represented all mankind in the same way that Adam, the first man, did when he was expelled from the Garden. Paul called Jesus 'the last Adam' (1 Cor. 15:45) and 'the second man' (vs. 47), the culmination of the human condition and its collective restoration . . . . Note that the power of the cross is to reconcile *all things* . . . ."[24]

Talbott agrees, "What the second Adam does for every human being is thus equal to and, according to Romans 5:17, even greater than what the first Adam has done."[25] MacDonald frames this comparative in this manner. "Christ's act of righteous obedience on the cross totally reverses the results of Adam's act of disobedience in Eden. . . . [they] are the *very same* 'all people.'"[26]

Hence, Christ's obedience and Adam's disobedience are related because both of them involve *all* of humanity, without exception. Not one of us chose to be involved in Adam's condemnation. Therefore, God sent Christ to save the *same* people. Consequently, *all* will be saved, eventually, Christian Universalists insist.

Furthermore, they argue, traditional Christianity limits Christ's work to only a few who "accept" their salvation now—i.e., during this life—which destroys the scriptural parallel between the first Adam and the last Adam—i.e., the imputation of sin and righteousness. Hence, Exclusivists must confess—*all* condemned, *few* saved.

The Position of 'All'

Another Christian Universalist shot across the exclusivist bow is the position in the sentence of the word "all" in 1 Corinthians 15:22. Its position is critical, they maintain. But Exclusivists essentially move the second "all" to a position before Christ—"all in Christ"—instead of its inspired position (in the original Greek as well) after Christ—"in Christ all"—in an obvious attempt to invent "proof" of eternal torment applying only to those who do not believe in this life. In other words, it's not as they say "all in Christ will be made alive," but rather as the scripture literally reads, "so in Christ all will be made alive." Again, it's an exact parallelism—"in Adam all die, so in Christ all will be made alive." "In Christ" does not modify "all." Rather, it's an adverbial phrase modifying "will be made alive." And none of Paul's parallelism texts place such a contextual limitation on the scope of Christ's salvation as only being for "all in Christ." Big difference!

Such twisting of words, Christian Universalists further maintain, destroys the beautiful parallel and makes these parallel structures, their balanced relationship, and Adam's foreshadowing of Christ into nonsense. Such "shenanigans," it is alleged, produce an out-of-balance parallelism and an erroneous conclusion. One conclusion is exegetical (a scholarly explanation from the text of a passage) and covers *all*. The other conclusion is eisegetical (reading one's own ideas into a passage) and covers only a *few*. What kind of parallel is that, they complain?

Talbott summarizes his view on this verse this way:

> Another explicit statement of Paul's that many try to explain away is 1 Corinthians 15:22 . . . . Paul in no way restricts himself . . . . Nor did he say merely that all those *in Christ* would be made alive. To the contrary, he said that in Christ shall all be made alive. And the whole point of the parallel construction here, as in Romans 5:18, is to pick out a single group . . . all human beings (see v. 21).[27]

Likewise, Christian Universalists charge, "if people are burning in hell, Adam did not *foreshadow* Christ, he *eclipsed* Him. . . . Religion makes Adam more powerful than Christ. . . . What an insult to our Savior! . . . If these plain verses aren't reliable, then God is not reliable."[28]

Concluding Salvos

Exclusivists fire back that God doesn't owe humanity anything. We all deserve death and God didn't have to save any of us. The fact that God chose to save some is mercy upon mercy and grace upon grace.

Ironically, Exclusivist Grudem in his *Systematic Theology* textbook properly recognized that the word "all" is sometimes explicitly restricted by a specific phrase in which it is used and/or by appealing to the ambiguity of its other uses (see Chapter 8, p-12-13). But then in his chapter on "The Atonement," he never addresses any of Paul's six parallel construction passages employing the words "all," "all men," and "the many." He ignores them, completely—not only in that chapter but throughout his entire textbook. Such avoidance is not scholarly. But it is revealing.

On the other hand, Paul Rowntree Clifford sides with the Christian Universalists:

> The universalist emphasis in the New Testament on both our corporate guilt and our corporate redemption transcends all those passages that have been interpreted as according a privileged status either to those who claim to be better than others or to those who claim to merit the favor of God because of their profession of faith. Thus the Christian hope is that in the world beyond this earthly one, at the name of Jesus every knee shall bow, and every tongue confess him to be the king of glory.[29]

What about this argument? Christian Universalists might further support their literal position with an argument by analogy. If "all" doesn't mean "all"—especially in Paul's six parallel construction passages—then perhaps the definite article "the" doesn't mean "the" but only an indefinite "a" in Jesus' statement, "I am *the* way and *the* truth and *the* life" (John 14:6). If we are willing to accept the one, by what hermeneutic do we preclude the other?

What about this argument? Exclusivists demand a balanced and synonymous parallelism understanding in Jesus' two uses of the word "eternal" in his "eternal punishment" and "eternal life" declaration in Matthew 25:46. Then why not be consistent with the "alls" in Paul's six parallelisms as well?

Perhaps, it's our "traditions of men" that have blinded us, once again (Mark 7:13; Matt. 15:6 *KJV*), and made an equivalent "all" understanding, which is seemingly preserved in at least five of Paul's six parallelisms, difficult for us to see and believe? But let's not depreciate this textual construct and its power, point, and purpose too quickly. Indeed, parallelism is a most-compelling argument. And it is intentionally employed six times, utilizing plain and commonly used language. These six constructions cannot be written off on a theological or emotional whim, even if one wants to avoid an unpleasant or unfavorable conclusion.

The Clincher?

What possibly might be the proverbial "800-pound gorilla" in this area of argumentation and one that just might tip the scales in the Christian Universalist's favor is Paul's parallelism in Romans 3:23-24. Notably, it comes first in his epistle and sets *the precedent*. Most significantly, Paul's "all" here is only mentioned *once*. It is the singular subject of his entire statement. However, the same two consequences, results, and conclusions apply to this singular "all" group. And since Scripture cannot contradict Scripture and assuming Paul is consistent, the force of this singular "all" in this verse must override any divergent or dichotomous interpretation or understanding arising from his dual use of "all(s) later on—as being two different groups—i.e., one inclusive and one exclusive.

In my opinion, this precedent-setting verse cannot be stressed too strongly. What a critical function this singular "all" verse performs. But if Paul's dualistic use of "all(s)" in five later verses are two different subject groups—one inclusive and one exclusive, then Romans 3:23-24 is not only contradictory, it's a false statement.

Let's Vote

In sum, the analogous comparison and syntactical, synonymous, and parallel construction presents a strong claim, if not a demand, that the singular "all," and the two "all(s)," the two "all men(s)," and the two "the many(s)" are all on equal footing.

If the singular "all" in Romans 3:23-24 is honored, there can be no difference between their respective identities. The two groups of humankind are equivalent and should not be positioned or understood antithetically. The acceptance of this conclusion is also supported by the force of the parallel comparison drawn between Adam and Christ.

The force of this singular "all" in this verse must override any divergent or dichotomous interpretation or understanding arising from his dual use of "all(s) later on—as being two different groups—i.e., one inclusive and one exclusive.

Therefore, a balanced equality is the most natural reading and meaning of the repetition. Since the former group represents all humankind, the latter does as well. They are of equal extent and scope. And given Paul's precedent of Roman 3:23-24, no textual possibility exists for escaping this conclusion without throwing Paul into contradiction. Given his precedence, how can we evade, soften, devalue, pervert, or explain away the strong and plain inference of these six synonymous parallelisms? And so for me, although we can't be dogmatic about this, the strength-of-argument advantage here must go to . . .

Strength-of-argument advantage: Christian Universalism.

Interestingly, Philip Schaff, who was not a Christian Universalist, certainly and conspicuously, starts off sounding like one until his caveat as he concludes about this matter:

The Divine Intention and Provision of Universal Salvation.—God sincerely wills . . . that all men, even the greatest of sinners, should be saved, and come to the knowledge of truth through Christ, who gave himself a ransom for all. The extent of Christ's righteousness and life is as universal as the extent of Adam's sin and death, and its intensive power is even greater. The first and the second Adam are perfectly parallel by contrast in the representative character, but Christ is much stronger and remains victor of the field, having slain sin and death, and living for ever as the prince of life. Where sin abounds there grace super-abounds. . . . and thus righteousness passed unto all men on condition of faith by which we partake of his righteousness. God shut up all men in disobedience, that he might have mercy upon all that believe.[30]

Christian Universalists believe that this is exactly what will occur— eventually all will believe. Somehow, in some way, at some time, and by some means known only to God all these conditions (and more) will be met. Everyone will "willingly" believe and be saved. And yet it is a fact that not all people become believers and enter into salvation in this life. So Christian Universalists explain that the Apostle Paul here is not concerned with how God will bring about this salvation or how it will be received, but rather with the universality of it through Christ. The point being made here is that the scope of God's mercy is the same as the scope of his condemnation (see Rom. 11:32).

But exclusivists still complain and challenge back, "is there any evidence that suggests that God will bring all people to faith, whether in this world or after death. But . . . we have found none."[31]

This brings us to our next area of argumentation.

STRENGTH-OF-ARGUMENT ADVANTAGE
SCORECARD

	Christian Univ.	Excl.	Draw
Dispute over Universal Language?			✓
Power and Point of Parallelism?	✓		
RUNNING TALLY	1	0	1

(How do you vote?)

Chapter 10

One Way or Many Ways?

This will be our shortest chapter. Why so? It is because little if any disagreement exists between Exclusivists and Christian Universalists in this area of argumentation. MacDonald, a Christian Universalist, assures us of this fact:

> The [evangelical] universalist will happily concur that reconciliation is only for those who are in Christ through faith. There is no salvation outside of Christ, and one is included in Christ through faith. However the universalist will also maintain that, in the end, everyone will be in Christ through faith.[1]

One notable exception, which we noted in Chapter 5, is Philip Gulley—novelist, theologian, Quaker pastor, and former bestselling author with an evangelical Christian publisher, Multnomah. His "books charmed readers across the country" until Gulley challenged "the belief that there is only one way to salvation." He now believes that "God will save all people – every Christian, Jew, Buddhist, Hindu, Muslim, atheist. Everybody, even if they never accept Jesus as Lord. And he has written a book about it."[2] Not surprisingly, Multnomah "dropped Gulley citing theological differences." Gulley also volunteered, as we have seen, that he is "not willing to let Scripture be that final authority."[3]

In Chapter 5 we covered the four varieties or variations of universalism. They vary on questions of how, by whom or what, when, and so on. In 2008, the Pew Forum on Religion and Public Life reported that "65 percent of Americans believe many religions can lead to eternal life."[4]

But the New Testament Scriptures speak loudly, clearly, and consistently on this one point. The way of salvation is *only* through the Person and work of Jesus Christ. And none of the supportive scriptures are ambiguous, contrary, or contested in this regard (see for example: Heb. 7:25; John 1:12; 3:16; 6:35; 11:25; 12:46; 14:6; 20:31; Acts 16:31; Rom. 3:22-26; 6:3-4, 23; 10:9-12, 17; 1 Tim. 2:5-6; and many more).

Therefore, in this debate over the extent of salvation, we will dogmatically maintain and insist that it is only and exclusively "at the name of Jesus every knee should bow, in heaven and on earth and under the earth, and every tongue confess that Jesus Christ is Lord, to the glory of God the Father" (Phil. 2:10-11; also Rev. 5:3, 13).

But how this salvation and/or submission reality someday, somehow, somewhere is occurring and/or will occur, and to what extent, remains for us to keep to re-exploring. So will Jesus Christ ultimately be so acknowledged by everyone who ever lived? And if He will, eventually, be the choice of every person who ever lived, doesn't this at least imply that every single person will be saved—even (gasp) Judas, Pontius Pilate, Hitler, Stalin, Mao, Idi Amin, and Pol Pot? This possibility has been pejoratively termed the "monsters-in-heaven-with-us" problem or argument.

Two Critical Factors

For now, let's especially note two critical factors:

1) Whatever redemptive scheme is the correct one, God's provision of it is the same for all. That is, all must come to the cross of Christ and receive Him as Savior. Salvation is individually and explicitly received by grace through faith (Eph. 2:8-9) and by personal belief (John 3:16) in only the Person, name, and work of Jesus Christ. He, and He alone, is the object and the mediator of God's plan of redemption.

Galli is spot-on when he asserts that "if God were to save anyone without faith, he would be acting contrary to his own words."[5] In the broad realm of Universalism this is known as: "Christocentric" or "Christian Universalism" or "Evangelical Universalism"—that eventually everyone will be saved by God but only through Christ and his death on the cross, resurrection, and judgment whether they recognize and believe in Him in this life or not.

All must come to the cross of Christ and receive Him as Savior.

Make no mistake; this is an exclusivist position. It must be distinguished from "all-roads-lead-to-Rome" or "Pluralistic Universalism"—i.e., via many ways, all religions, or it doesn't make any difference what you think, believe, or do, and even includes atheists. Consequently, in this pluralistic variety of Universalism, no confession in Jesus as Savior is needed to go to heaven. And Jesus provides no preeminent role. As it stands, this is truly biblical heresy because it blatantly contradicts the way of salvation for humankind presented throughout the Scriptures.

So by definition and undeniably, Scripture presents an "exclusive" position in that salvation is attained from and received exclusively through Christ, even if inclusively all are eventually so reconciled to God. Of course, this exclusivism is what stirs the ire of many in our modern-day, religious, secular, and pluralistic societies.

2) The realm for the realization of the reality of "every knee" bowing and "every tongue" confessing is not limited to this earth. It includes those "in heaven" and "on earth" as well as "under the earth" (Phil. 2:10; also Rev. 5:3, 13). Nor can this salvation be scripturally limited to only being made effectual during our physical lives on earth.

Again, how this has been, is, and/or will be effectuated is open for legitimate and further discussion. And Galli is also spot-on when he asserts that "the Bible teaches nothing about conversion after death."[6] But Jones is not on target when he claims that "The Bible teaches that when people die, their eternal destiny is determined by the choice either to accept Christ as the payment for their sins, or to reject him."[7]

Nowhere does Scripture ever state that one must believe and make a decision for Jesus during this life and before death, or that there is no other opportunity (second chance) to go to heaven. The Bible is silent here. And this silence speaks volumes for those who have ears to hear. Moreover, it gives God all the latitude He desires to save anyone He wants, postmortem in the afterlife, and without violating his Word, the

Scriptures. For one, it opens wide the door of possibility for millions of infants being saved after death,[8] and for billions of un-evangelized, those who never had a chance to hear of Jesus or never heard an effective gospel presentation, to finally hear, believe, and receive Him as Savior.

Five Categories of Human Beings—the Un-evangelized

The authors of *Sense & Nonsense About Heaven & Hell* identify "five categories of human beings who are (usually) understood to have never heard about Jesus Christ during their mortal lifetime:

(1) *Old Testament people.*
(2) *Young children who have died.* [I would add aborted babies here.]
(3) *Mentally incapable people.* [I would change this to mentally disabled people.]
(4) *Pre-Christ heathen.*
(5) *Post-Christ heathen.* "

Again, these are characterized as the "unevangelized"[9]—because none of these have heard nor understood that belief in Jesus of Nazareth's future or past death and resurrection was necessary for salvation (more on this in Chapter 13 re: the "Missions Problem"). And so, Christian Universalists and many Exclusivists reason that God cannot be truly just in condemning these people if they never had a chance to hear and decide (Rom. 10:14-17).

Nowhere does Scripture ever state that one must believe and make a decision for Jesus during this life and before death, or that there is no other opportunity (second chance) to go to heaven.

Yet the exclusiveness of Jesus Christ and distinctiveness of Christianity eliminate a common assumption of many other Universalists and all Pluralists that people can be saved through other religions, other names, other ways, or by general revelation (Rom. 1:18-20f; Psa. 19:1-6), or by common grace (Matt. 5:44-45; Acts 14:17; 17:26-28; Rom. 2:4; Ps. 145:9, 15-16), etc.

Regarding "all things" being reconciled to Christ (Col. 1:16-20), who and/or what is included, how this might be effectuated, and whether this goes beyond human beings has been debated for centuries. For instance, does this redemption include Satan and demons? In my opinion, probably not—see Hebrews 2:16, Christ did not die for angels and they did not die "in Adam" as all do humans. Do all things on earth include animals, dirt, rocks, trees, flowers, and other inanimate objects like stars and planets? Some Christians think it might. They believe in "cosmic" salvation. But I think not.[10] Or does reconciliation occur through subjugation—being brought under his direct authority? But everything already is under his authority, isn't it? Correctly and dogmatically, both Exclusivists and Christian Universalists hold that "salvation requires an explicit acceptance of Christ's redemptive work through faith."[11] So, wouldn't that preclude animals, dirt, rocks, trees, flowers, and other inanimate objects?

As Douglas J. Moo appropriately concedes, "Paul affirms that God's nature and purposes demand that all creatures be finally subject to his authority, but the nature of that submission is not spelled out."[12]

Critical Objection: *"Then why did Jesus have to die on the cross if not to save us from eternal hell?"*

Stetson terms this objection "the single most important question that Christian Universalists must answer if we are to successfully explain our view of the Gospel to sincere believers in Christ."[13] He assures his reader that "there is a good reason for the cross of Christ other than what fundamentalists teach. . . . it proves God's love is unfailing and conquers all evil." He insists that "the cross is not a dividing line, permanently excluding some people from the love of their Creator. No, the cross is a ladder to heaven through which all people may eventually return to the Father who sent His Son, the Lord Jesus, into our world."

Over several pages, Stetson pontificates on this matter "in some detail" and offers interesting answers and insights. Below is a condensed and bulleted recap of his major points. See how many you can agree with, or not:

- "Before Jesus died on the cross and rose again from the grave, it was very difficult for people to believe in the goodness of God. People usually feared God and knew He was great and mighty, but did not necessarily love Him."
- "God seemed to arbitrarily favor some people and not others. . . ."
- When bad things happened, people thought God was punishing them or had abandoned them—they had no concept of a loving Father in heaven who cares about the welfare of each and every one of us and wants to save us through divine grace."[14]
- "God chose to allow Jesus to suffer and die a death of torture on the cross."[15]
- "Even in Old Testament times God did not really like the bloody sacrifices people offered Him according to religious law" (see Hos. 6:6; Isa. 1:11).
- "God wanted people to move beyond this primitive form of religion once and for all . . . to progress to higher levels of spirituality, once they had the opportunity to hear about Christ."[16]
- "universal reconciliation. . . . is made possible because of the incarnation of God in Christ, and the cruel death God experienced on the cross while in human form."
- "By dying on the cross, God could reach both the living and the dead by showing all people how much He loves us."
- Thereby, "God can truly empathize with the anguish of human existence. Empathy is the beginning of mercy, and without mercy there can be no forgiveness."
- "Because of the cross, God truly knows the human condition. He has lived it, in the person of Jesus Christ. God knows suffering and injustice. He knows the cruelty of evil. God can relate to man and his struggles in a much more intimate way, because He has been a man. Yes, God loves us *that much*—so much that He was willing to go through the cross to reach our hearts."[17]
- "This is why the cross was necessary for our salvation. . . . Indeed, it is because of Jesus' sacrificial death that we can truly

love God. Without it, we could only fear God and tremble in anticipation of punishment for our inherent sinfulness. . . ."

- Thus, "Paul taught, 'that God was reconciling the world to Himself in Christ, not counting men's sins against them.' (2 Cor. 5:19)."[18]

- "The resurrection was the culmination of God's plan to prove His love for all people. If Jesus had not conquered death and shown this publicly, he would have gone down in history as just another radical Jewish false prophet who was executed by the Romans for treason. We never would have known he was the divine being he claimed to be, and we never would have understood God's absolute power to change evil into good."[19]

- "The cross of Christ is a symbol of hope for all people, that God loves every one of us and will not abandon us even when we lose faith and abandon Him. Even the most hopeless souls— even the unbelieving and sinful dead—have hope in the saving power of Jesus Christ."

- "God's love is infinite and can overcome all obstacles. . . . for *all* of us."

- "So if you think universal salvation is impossible for God, think again. God never gives up on anyone; He has a plan to make all things right. That's the whole point of the cross. It has nothing to do with saving people from an endless torture in hell."[20]

Let's Vote

Even Stetson's Christian universalist position is an exclusive position because for him, as well as for the Exclusivists, salvation is *only* through the Person, work, and name of Jesus Christ and no one else (John 20:31). So for me it's . . .

Strength-of-argument advantage: Exclusivism.

STRENGTH-OF-ARGUMENT ADVANTAGE
SCORECARD

	Christian Univ.	Excl.	Draw
Dispute over Universal Language?			✓
Power and Point of Parallelism?	✓		
One Way or Many Ways?		✓	
RUNNING TALLY	1	1	1

(How do you vote?)

Chapter 11

How Long Is 'Eternal' in Eternal Punishment?

If it's true that 1 Timothy 4:10b is the "most difficult verse in the Bible for those who deny universal salvation" to handle[1]—"who is the Savior of all men, and especially of those who believe." Then this verse is the most difficult and challenging for those who hold to Universal Salvationism—"Then they will go away to eternal punishment, but the righteous to eternal life" (Matt. 25:46).

Exclusivists steadfastly contend that "the symmetry is stark and simple. . . . Jesus clearly teaches 'punishment in an individual, eternal sense.'"[2] In other words, whatever "eternal" means as an adjective for "life," it must also mean as an adjective for "punishment." How ever long eternal is for life, it is likewise as long for punishment. Some term this verse "the Achilles' heel" for Universalists[3] and lay down the gantlet that "the task for the universalist is to circumvent the seemingly clear New Testament teaching on eternal punishment."[4] But then they preempt their challenge by charging that "universalist speculation about eternal punishment is more than a little incoherent."[5] Or is it? The inescapable irony here, however, is those Exclusivists who advocate this same dual meaning for "eternal" do not follow this same consistency of logic with their treatment of the dual "alls" in Paul's five parallelisms we covered in Chapter 9.

Fact is, "eternal" is coupled with punishment seven times in the New Testament. And for many Christians, this coupling is a large part of the "good news" that after death the vast majority of people go to a place, a state, or a dimension called "hell" where they will suffer horrible punishment and torment, forever and ever, and with no chance of escape.

As sad and tragic as this destiny may be, in their minds it justifies the Christian faith. After all, if there was not an awful place like hell to be saved from, many heaven-bound Christians feel their faith would be meaningless and Christ would have died in vain. Equally sad and ironic, most of these Christians do not seem to care much about what happens to these unbelievers. Consequently, they do little to forewarn or communicate this destiny of condemnation to them—i.e. by personal witnessing. So why shouldn't this all-to-common, ambivalent attitude and lack of evangelistic enthusiasm be called for what it probably is—hypocrisy?

Other Christians find repugnant the idea of eternal conscious punishment for a temporal, God-imputed state of sin and/or sins committed during a short lifetime. They argue that a perfectly just God administering appropriate justice would demand no more than an equally long period of punishment to counterbalance a life in the sin state.

Hence, the authors of *Sense & Nonsense About Heaven & Hell* acknowledge that "the range of beliefs [here] about Hell is much more varied and complex. There are plenty of opinions, even among those professing faith in Christ, as to what will happen to the wicked or unrighteous." They cited the following as examples of this variance:

- "They will suffer everlasting punishment.
- They will suffer temporal punishment, and then be annihilated.
- They will simply be annihilated.
- They will suffer temporal punishment, and then some will be saved.
- They will suffer temporal punishment and then all will be saved.
- They will not suffer any punishment, but all will be saved."[6]

Another fact is, most, if not all, Christian Universalists accept and believe that there will be divine punishment after death, although it will not last forever and ever.

The Key Word under Dispute

Essentially, the subject of this dispute is the meaning of one Greek word—the adjective *aionios*, which is translated as "eternal" in such verses as Matthew 25:46 (eternal punishment) and as "everlasting" in 2 Thessalonians 1:9 (everlasting destruction). But literally it does not mean "eternal." It means "age enduring" or "that which pertains to an age. . . . the same term is also used repeatedly in the Septuagint and occasionally in the New Testament in contexts where it could not possibly mean 'eternal' or 'everlasting'"[7]

Therefore, Christian Universalists consider eternal to be a "pervasive mistranslation of a key word in the Bible" that has "change[d] an entire religion, turning a positive message into something very negative."[8] They are quick to point out that *aionios* does not always mean eternity or forever. It may also mean "enduring for an indefinite, short, or long period, an age," since, grammatically, an adjective gets its meaning from its base noun, and no adjective can have a greater force or a difference in meaning than the noun from which it is derived. For example, "hourly" cannot be expanded to mean "yearly," or vice versa.

NOTE TO READER: The rest of this chapter, and perhaps the next chapter as well, may be more technical than some are used to. But the issue at stake is crucial and demands nothing less than this intense word study.

Aionios' base noun is *aion. Strong's Concordance* variously defines *aion* as "an *age*; by extension. *perpetuity*—age, course, eternal, (for) ever (-more), world."[9]

Vine's defines it as "an age, era, signifies a period of indefinite duration, or time viewed in relation to what takes place in the period. The force attaching to the word is not so much that of the actual length of a period, but that of a period marked by spiritual or moral characteristics. . . . It is sometimes wrongly rendered 'world.'"[10]

Bauer, Arndt, Gingrich, and Danker also defines it variously as "1. very long time, eternity" or "2. a segment of time, age. 3. the world."[11]

Another fact is that an age has a beginning and an end. No age lasts forever, is eternal or everlasting. Ages come and go. Comparatively, for instance, the word "college" is used as both a noun and an adjective. If you went to college (noun) you had college (adjective) years. They had a beginning and an end, did not last forever, and were not eternal or everlasting. The same is true for *aion* (age) and *aionios* (age-enduring). Even with this grammatical grounding, the understandings and opinions of scholars vary.

Not surprisingly, therefore, while Morris recognizes that "the word we translate as 'eternal' (*aionios*) means literally 'pertaining to an age (*aion*)," he equally believes "the word could mean 'everlasting.'"[12]

Ladd merely assigns *aionios'* meaning to the afterlife in writing quite ambiguously that this "very word involves an eschatological expectation. It is primarily the 'life of the age to come.'"[13]

Dispensationalist, John MacArthur, insists on the traditional understanding that it "denotes something perpetual, something never-ending."[14]

Another Exclusivist, Edward E. Stevens, presents this scope argument against a limited duration understanding. He cites that the word *aionios* is used "sixty-six times" in the New Testament. "Of these . . .

- 51 instances . . . of the happiness of the righteous.
- 2 of God's existence.
- 6 of the church, the Messiah's kingdom.
- Remaining 7 of the future punishment of the wicked.

He concludes, therefore, "if in these seven instances, we attach to the word the idea of limited duration, consistency requires that the same idea of limited duration should be given it in the fifty-one cases . . . ."[15] But is such a broad-brushed conclusion justifiable?

In keeping with the above varied definitions, Ephesians 2:7 states that there are many "coming ages" (plural), more than just one. Ephesians 1:21 talks about "this present age" and "the one to come." But in Ephesians 3:21, the literal Greek employs an idiomatic phrase combining both a singular and plural—"into all generations of the age of the ages." And Romans 16:25 mentions "long ages past."

Hence, Murray J. Harris remarks on the adjective *aionois*: "The use of *aionios* in Philemon 15 ("that you might get him back *permanently*") [forever – *KJV*] shows that the word need not mean "eternal."[16]

Even more insightful is the Old Testament Hebrew equivalent word for the Greek word *aion*. It's the Hebrew word *olam*. *Olam* is translated as *aion* in all cases in the Septuagint. Thus, *aion* and *olam* are synonymous, corresponding equally with each other. Christian

Universalist, Amirault, presents the following exegetical and compelling argument in noting how *olam* was employed many times in a time-limited fashion in the Old Testament:

> Some of the Old Testament Scriptures which were used to support the "everlasting"ness of the Old Covenant were: Exodus 40:15 which describes the Aaronic Priesthood as "everlasting" yet Hebrews 7:14-18 declares an end to it being replaced by the Melchizedek Priesthood; the children of Israel were to "observe the Sabbath throughout their generations, for a perpetual covenant" (Exodus 31:16), yet Paul states there remains "another day" of Sabbath rest for the people of God (Heb. 4:8, 9); the Law of Moses was to be an "everlasting covenant" (Leviticus 24:8) yet we read in the New Covenant the first was "done away" with and 'abolished" (2 Corinthians 3:11, 13), and God "made the first old" (Hebrews 8:13).
>
> The Hebrew word which is translated "everlasting" and "perpetual" in the above Old Testament passages is the word "*olam*." This same word was used by the King James Bible translators to make Jonah stay in the "belly of hell for*ever*" where the "bars of the earth closed behind me forever" yet in the same verse God brought his life "up from the pit!" (Jonah 2:2, 6). In verse 1:17 the King James translation clearly says Jonah was in the fish for 3 days and nights. How could this be *forever*?
>
> The King James Bible, as well as many others, tells us that a bondslave was to serve his master "forever." (Exodus 21:6) It also tells us that God would dwell in Soloman's Temple "forever" (1 Kings 8:13). I began to see there was not only a problem with Old Testament Scriptures contradicting New Testament ones, but even within the Old Testament itself. Passages such as God dwelling in Solomon's Temple "forever" clearly contradict history which shows that Solomon's Temple was destroyed long ago.
>
> . . . The classical *Wilson's Old Testament Word Studies* by William Wilson gives as the meaning of "olam," "*duration of time which is concealed or hidden*," in other words, an unknown length of time. This unknown length of time could be 3 days and nights as in the case of Jonah, or the length of a man's life, or as long as the period of time the Aaronic Priesthood [sic] was in effect, which was around 1600 years.[17]

Many more things and people in Old Covenant times were spoken of as *ad olam* or *olam*: The Sabbath (Exod. 12:24); the nation of Israel (Isa. 45:17), David's throne (2 Sam. 7:13), the house of Eli and his father's house (1 Sam. 2:30), the scapegoat ceremony (Lev. 16:29), the Passover (Lev. 16:29, 31, 34), an ear-pierced slave (Exod. 21:6), the house of Levi as priests (Num. 18:19), and Jerusalem as the capital city (Psa. 132:13, 14). But the Old Covenant ended, as did the nation of Israel (Jer. 18:9, 10), and so did these other specific examples.

Hanson's perspective is further illuminating:

> So of *aionion*; applied to Jonah's residence in the fish, it means seventy hours; to the priesthood of Aaron, it signifies several centuries; to the mountains, thousands of years; to the punishments of a merciful God, as long as necessary to vindicate his law and reform his children; to God himself, eternity. Human beings live from a few hours to a century; nations from a century to thousands of years; and world, for aught we know, from a few to many millions of years, and God is eternal. . . . In other words it practically denotes indefinite duration.[18] [For many more examples see Hanson's *Aion-Aionios*, pp. 28-36.]

This variety of scriptural precedence forced Hanson to decide that "the word has a great range of meaning."[19] And "if these hundreds of instances must denote limited duration why should the few times in which punishments are spoken of have any other meaning? . . . the very few times in which it is connected with punishment it must have a similar meaning. . . . it only has the sense of endless when the subject compels it, as when referring to God. . . ."[20] Hence, claiming that *aionios* punishment is "eternal" punishment in the seven times these two words are coupled would be, at best, interpretation by exception.

**"The word has a great range of meaning" . . . .
claiming that *aionios* punishment is
"eternal" punishment in the seven times
these two words are coupled would be, at best,
interpretation by exception.**

One Legitimate Exception

One major and legitimate exception exists in both the Hebrew and Greek language. It's whenever *olam* and *aion* are used "in the plurals,"[21] The following excerpt from my book, *The Perfect Ending for the World* explains:

> In Ephesians 3:21, however, the verse contains both the singular "age" and the plural "ages." The reason for this double employment is because neither the Hebrew nor Greek language had a separate word for the concept of eternity, foreverness, or endlessness. That's why throughout the Old and New Testaments both of these ancient languages used a range of phrases employing the word "age" in a hyperbolic and idiomatic fashion.[22] The more this word was employed in a phrase, the more intensified was the meaning of what might best be translated as *forever*. Examples of these phrases in an increasing and intensifying order are:
>
> > "unto the age" (singular)
> > "unto the ages" (plural)
> > "unto the age of the age" (double singular)
> > "unto the age of ages" (singular and plural)
> > "unto the ages of the ages" (double plural)
>
> Hence, this double use of age (singular) and ages (plural) in Ephesians 3:21 is a way of saying forever. One thing, however, is for sure. This idiom cannot mean its opposite. Therefore, "world without end" or "for forever and ever" are preferred translations that emphasize the concept of permanence, eternalness, endlessness, everlastingness, perpetuity. These translations clash with any idea of an end of the world, end of human history, or end of time.[23] The world, time, and the present new-covenant age simply do not have an end.[24]

For our purposes in this book, the message we want to take away from the above exposition is this, and as Hanson rightly demonstrates, "that neither of the words, of itself, denotes eternity."[25] "Eternity can only be meant here as ages piled on ages imply [sic] long, and possibly endless duration."[26]

Back in the 1800s, Hanson conducted an extensive word study for his 1878 book appropriately titled, *Aion-Aionios*. In it, he elaborates on the reason for this multiple employment:

... the pure idea of eternity is too abstract to have been conceived in the early ages of the world, and accordingly *is not found expressed by any word in the ancient languages.* But as cultivation [sic] advanced and this idea became more distinctly developed, it became necessary in order to express it to invent new words in a new sense . . . . *The Hebrews and other ancient people have no one word for expressing the precise idea of eternity.*[27]

Even in the Greek classics, written more than six centuries before the Septuagint, Hanson documents that they "never used *aion* to denote eternity . . . . never once in the sense of endless duration."[28] Then he adds that "nothing can be plainer than that Greek Literature, at the time the Hebrew Old Testament was rendered into the Greek Septuagint, did not give to *Aion* the meaning of endless duration.[29]

As a result of his work, he terms it "absurdity" that "God has hung the great topic of the immortal welfare of millions of souls on the meaning of a single equivocal word. Had he [God] intended to teach endless punishment by one word, that word would have been so explicit and uniform and frequent that no mortal could mistake its meaning. . . . Instead of denoting every degree of duration, as it does, it never would have meant less than eternity."[30]

Hanson next detailed that:

Out of more than five hundred occurrences of our disputed word in the Old Testament, more than four hundred denote limited duration, so that the great preponderance of Old Testament usage fully agrees with the Greek classics. The remaining instances follow the rule given by the best lexicongraphers, that it only means endless when it derives its meaning of endlessness from the nature of the subject with which it is connected. . . . The fact that the word is so seldom, and by so few applied to punishment, and never in the Old Testament to punishment beyond death, demonstrates that it cannot mean endless."[31]

So Hanson rhetorically asked, "Had God intended endless punishment . . . . would he for thousands of years conceal so awful a destiny from millions whom he created and exposed to it?[32] He continues developing his case by noting that "the Jews who were contemporary with Christ, but who wrote in Greek, will teach us how they understood the word. Of course, when Jesus used it, he employed it as they understood it." He particularly cites Josephus' and Philo's usages, and surmises, "We thus have an unbroken chain of Lexicongraphy, and Classic, Old Testament, and Contemporaneous Usage, all allowing to the word the meaning we claim for it. Indefinite duration . . . ."[33]

He dutifully concludes, "Speaking to those who understood the Old Testament, Jesus and his Apostles employed such words as are used in that book, in the same sense in which they are there used. Not to do so would be to mislead their hearers unless they explained a change of meaning."[34] And, of course, neither Jesus nor any New Testament writer ever made any such disclaimer or qualification.

W.E. Vine's An Expository Dictionary of Biblical Words agrees about the "440 times in biblical Hebrew and in all periods" that the word *olam* was used that it denotes a variety of meanings like these:

- "First, in a few passages the word means 'eternity'"
- "Second, the word signifies 'remotest time' or 'remote time.'"
- "for a long time."
- "With the preposition *ad*, the word can mean 'into the indefinite future' . . . . 'as long as one lives.'"
- "In the largest number of its occurrences . . . . This construction is weaker and less dynamic in emphasis . . . as it envisions a 'simple duration.'"[35]

Ralph L. Smith concurs that "the word *olam* is ambiguous and should not be understood as 'eternity' . . . . 'Everlasting in the Old Testament means 'as far as one can see or comprehend and beyond'"[36]

In sum, the concept of eternal (as unending) in the adjective form of *aionios* is definitely weakened by its various meanings and the uses of the comparable Hebrew noun *olam*. Therefore, when the base noun's (*aion*) definitions are recognized, this lends credence to its adjective form meaning an indeterminate length of time with a beginning and an end. In other words, *aionios* could be any length of time or of no specific duration since the duration of an "age" would be a period of time of unknown length determined by, in any case, the fact, condition, person, or scope of the subject to which the term applies. However, as Baker points out, "it never means an eternity . . . . [it] means an age, a specific period of time, a short period of time in comparison to all 'eternity.'"

Then she charges, however, that "we are inconsistent with our translation of this Greek word."[37]

Hanson further conjectures that "ignorance of the real meaning of the word on the part of those who were not familiar with Greek, subverted the current belief in universal restoration, cherished . . . by Clement and the Alexandrian Christians."[38] Hence, *aionios* is "mistranslated in the New Testament, [as] 'everlasting,' eternal.'[39]

Applying *Aionios* to Punishment

Only seven times in six scriptures in the New Testament does the adjective word *aionios* describe punishment, fire, destruction, or judgment (Matt. 18:8; 25:41, 46; 2 Thess. 1:9,; Heb. 6:2; Jude 7).

So Hanson rightfully asks, "Now if God's punishments are . . . endless how can we explain the employment of . . . . a word whose uniform meaning everywhere else is limited duration? The idea is preposterous. . . . No. The New Testament usage agrees with the meaning in the Greek classics, and in the Old Testament."[40]

With this wide variety of base-noun meanings in mind—from "eternal" to "an age" to a "course" to "world"— it is no wonder that translating *aionios* exclusively as "eternal" has caused problems in understanding. Granted, in some uses *aionios* may mean forever. But in other uses it may only mean a short or long time period. Unshackling ourselves from the traditional, but inadequate, translation allows an interpretation that would harmonize with Universal Salvationism's contention that hell, or punishment and/or refinement somewhere in the afterlife, is not a permanent destiny for its inhabitants.

The counter argument, however, is another parallelism argument. But this time, the parallelism construction and logic are defended by Exclusivists when they bring up Matthew 25:46 (also note Heb. 6:2; Rev. 20:10). Hanson terms it "the great proof-text of the doctrine of endless punishment"[41]—*"Then they will go away to **eternal** punishment, but the righteous to **eternal** life."*

Paradoxically, the same Exclusivists who argue that the first "all" is *not* the same as the second "all" in Paul's five parallelisms (Chapter 9), argue here that the first "eternal" and the second "eternal" *must be* the same. Thayer credits Augustine (A.D. 354-430) as "the first to argue that *aionios* signified strictly *endless*. . . . he brings Matt. xxv. 46 as proof, arguing that if the 'everlasting punishment' was not endless, the 'eternal life' was not. And this criticism has been handed down from his time to the present, and is still employed with great confidence."[42]

With this wide variety of base-noun meanings in mind—from "eternal" to "an age" to a "course" to "world"— it is no wonder that translating *aionios* exclusively as "eternal" has caused problems in understanding.

Thayer observantly relates that "the history of the doctrine of Endless Punishment, in its effects on the character and action of those believing it, is one of the most painful and shocking in the annals of mankind."[43] He next illustrates how "a savage creed, if left unchecked to do its legitimate work, will beget a savage temper and a corresponding conduct; or, in a word, that 'a corrupt tree cannot bring forth good fruit.'"[44] In his follow-up chapter, appropriately titled "The Doctrine Creates a Cruel and Revengeful Spirit – Illustrated from History,"[45] he documents many examples in subsequent church history.

Nonetheless, Exclusivists, like Murray J. Harris, are convinced to the contrary that the dual phrases and same word used therein make the meaning unmistakable. Whatever "eternal" means in its connection with "life" in the phrase "eternal life," it must likewise mean and be "identical in duration" in its linkage with "punishment."[46] In other words, however long "eternal" life is for the righteous, that's how long the punishment is for the wicked, the parallelism argument goes. Hence, the unending joy of the redeemed stands in contrast to the unending torment of the wicked.

Do you grasp the irony here?

Again, it's another parallelism argument like Universalists use for their "all" argument. But here, Exclusivists argue for an equally balanced parallelism, while they deny this understanding for all five of Paul's dual "all" parallelisms.

Matthew 25:46 Revisited

Surprisingly for some, Matthew 25:46's parallelism does not carry the same force as Paul's six "all" parallelisms for at least twelve reasons:

1.) This verse, as well as its whole chapter, has been susceptible to numerous interpretations and proven difficult, ambiguous, and obscure enough to prohibit dogmatizing about it.

2.) The adjective *aionios* is the only common factor here. But, as we have seen, it is quite equivocal in its meaning—i.e., has a variety of meanings, where as, "all" is less unequivocal in its meaning. And, arguably, the focus of Paul's six parallelisms is on a single homogeneous "all" group with a common condition. But in Matthew 25:46 a consistency of one meaning ("eternal") is not demanded, *per se*, by the meaning of the word *aionios* itself.

3.) Admittedly, the destinies of two different groups are being addressed. But this may only be temporary for one group—"age-lasting" or "age-long," "lasting for an age, an indefinite period of time." While, at the same time and for the other group, it can be "forever," "everlasting," or "eternal." Once again, and according to Christian Universalists, "the problem started when the Bible was translated into Latin. Aionios was rendered as the Latin word *aeternus*, meaning eternal." This was done "based on the proclamation of the Roman Emperor Justinian in 544 C.E. that hell lasts forever. He described it in Greek as *ateleutetos* (another word meaning 'endless'), rather than aionios." Lamentably, "the legacy of this error has lasted for centuries and done untold damage to the Christian faith."[47]

4.) Only one such parallel is found. Moreover, it is legitimately debatable whether this is a parallelism. If it is, it is certainly not as strong as Paul's six parallelisms. And as Jesus confirmed, "every matter may be established by the testimony of two or three witnesses." Even this statement of Jesus is confirmed three times in Scripture (Matt. 18:16 from Duet. 19:15; also 2 Cor. 13:1). And, "a cord of three stands is not easily broken" (Eccl. 4:12). But, again, this parallelism—if it is one—is found *only once*.

5.) Jesus' afterlife parable in Luke 16 of the rich man and Lazarus in Hades shows that some do face conscious negative consequences after they leave this physical realm. But like the "unquenchable fire," the *aionios* punishment may be a perpetual reality but not necessarily ceaseless or unending for each individual going through it.

6). Why does Psalm 30:5 say that God's "anger lasts only for a moment, but his favor lasts a lifetime?" Dittos for "For men are not cast off by the Lord forever. Though he brings grief, he will show compassion, so great is his unfailing love" (Lam. 3:31-32)? And "God is love" (1 John 4:8, 16). And "love never fails" (1 Cor. 13:8a). "Will not the judge of all the earth do right?" (Gen. 18:25).

These and more biblical insights are cited by Christian Universalists as reasons why they believe they "have discovered the God of a more joyful Christianity than the bad-news gospel that passes for the Good News of Christ in the minds of many souls. . . . The fire of hell has burned into the core of their being, leaving them scarred and scared."[48]

7). Why doesn't the Apostle's Creed, the oldest creedal statement of the Church of Rome, utter a word about punishment or the duration of punishment? It only mentions "to judge the quick and the dead" and "the life everlasting" (*aionion* life and no mention of *aionion* death or punishment). Hanson describes this omission as "incredible that this declaration of faith . . . should not convey a hint of so vital a doctrine as that of endless punishment, if at that time that dogma was a tenet of the church . . . . And this is all that the most ancient creeds contain on the subject."[49]

The Nicene Creed, likewise, "does not contain a syllable referring to endless punishment, though the doctrine was then professed by a portion of the church . . . it was not generally enough held to be stated as the average belief."[50]

Hanson explains that since the Alexandrian fathers held to "God as Father, punishment was held to be remedial, and therefore restorative, and final recovery from sin universal. It was only . . . under the baneful reign of Augustinianism, that Deity was hated, and that Catholics transferred to Mary, and later, Protestants gave to Jesus that supreme love that is due alone to the Universal Father."[51]

8). Amirault confidently asks that since "we are commanded 'to overcome evil with good' (Rom. 12:20, 21), may we not safely infer that God will do the same?" Or, he adds, "would the infliction of endless punishment be overcoming evil with good?"[52] Or, would "the infliction of endless misery be returning evil for evil, would it be right for God to inflict it?"[53]

9) Hanson reports that "Josephus, writing in Greek to Jews, frequently employs the word that our Lord used to define the duration of punishment (*aionios*), but he applies it to things that had ended or that will end. . . . . He applies it to the imprisonment of John the Tyrant; to Herod's reputation; to the glory acquired by soldiers; to the fame of an army as a 'happy life and *aionian* glory.' He used the words as do the Scriptures to denote limited duration, but when he would describe endless duration he uses different terms."[54] Therefore, "Christ carefully avoided the words in which his auditors expressed endless punishment (*aidios, timoria* and *adialeiptos*), and used terms they did not use with that meaning (*aionios kolasis*).[55]

10) Hanson further spells out that "the word by which our Lord describes punishment is the word, *kolasin*, which is thus defined: 'Chastisement, punishment.' 'The trimming of the luxuriant branches of a tree or vine to improve it and make it fruitful.' 'The act of clipping or pruning—restriction, restraint, reproof, check, chastisement.' 'The kind of punishment which tends to the improvement of the criminal is what the Greek philosophers called *kolasis* or chastisement.' 'Pruning, checking, punishment, chastisement, correction. . . . but we pity those afflicted with such misfortune.'"[56]

Stetson agrees and expounds that "the word *kolasis* has the connotation of beneficial disciplinary correction, such as a parent might punish a child for wrongdoing with the purpose of reform. This is in sharp contrast to *timoria*, meaning punitive or vindictive punishment. Kolasis comes from a root word meaning 'to prune,' as a tree or plant. . . . so God is going to prune the souls of sinners, cutting away the parts that are corrupted by sin, in order to transform the person into a more holy and fruitful son or daughter of God. Kolasis is loving, parental discipline with the goal of helping the one being subjected to it. That's a far cry from the fundamentalist doctrine of damnation!"

"The word *kolasis* has the connotation of beneficial disciplinary correction, such as a parent might punish a child for wrongdoing with the purpose of reform. This is in sharp contrast to *timoria*, meaning punitive or vindictive punishment."

Hence for Stetson, "aionios kolasis should not be translated as 'eternal punishment,' but should be understood to mean a limited period of time in which a person will receive divine judgment for reformation and improvement of character. If Matthew had meant to suggest that Jesus taught eternal torment, he probably would have written *aidios timoria*."[57]

He determines, therefore, that "'Eternal torment' is simply not Biblical. It is an invention of church tradition that became established in the mass consciousness of Christianity because of centuries of faulty Bible translations."[58]

Talbott's Christian-universalist take is somewhat different. He says eternal life means "a special quality of life, associated with the age to come . . . eternal punishment is a special form of punishment, associated with the age to come. . . . In that respect, the two are exactly parallel. But neither *concept* carries any implication of unending temporal duration; and even if it did carry such an implication, we would still have to clarify what it is that lasts forever. . . . So it all boils down, perhaps, to how we understand divine punishment and its essential purpose. Is it an end in itself? Or is it a means to an end, indeed a means of grace . . . ?"[59]

Critical Objection: Chan disagrees, although he confesses that "part of me wants to believe that this is true." He offers "three reasons" why "the word means 'punishment.'"[60] But Bible dictionaries, concordances, commentaries, and lexicons are mixed in their support or lack of support for the above redemptive claims about the Greek word *kolasis*. For instance, *Liddell and Scott* offers this variety of possible meanings for this word group: "to be chastised, punished, prune, check, correction."[61]

Interestingly, however, this same God Who applies *kolasis* also inflicts "discipline" (*paideia*) and "punishes (*mastigoo*) everyone he accepts as a son" (Heb.12:5-7; also see Prov. 3:11-12). *Paideia* is quite similar in meaning to *kolasis* as Christian Universalists described in #10 above, and for good reason. They believe this is how God operates in both this life and in the afterlife:

- *Paideia, Strong's* #3809 from #3811 means "tutorage, i.e, education or training disciplinary correction:—chastening, chastisement, instruction, nurture."
- *Paideuo, Strong's* # 3811 (Heb. 12:6, 7) means to "train up a child, educate, discipline (by punishment):—chasten, instruct,

learn, teach," (Also used in 1 Cor. 11:32; 2 Cor. 6:9; Heb. 12:6, 10; Luke 23:16, 22).

- *Mastigoo, Strong's* #3146 (Heb. 12:6) means "flogs/scourges" 11)

If the punishment of Matthew 25:46 is of a limited duration, then how do Christian Universalists explain *aionios'* use with "life" (*zoe*) in the same scripture?

Hanson merely states that life eternal "is not endless, but is a condition resulting from a good character. The intent of the phrases is not to teach immortal happiness, nor . . . endless punishment. Both phrases, regardless of duration, refer to the limited results wronging or blessing others, extending possibly through Messiah's reign until, 'the end' (1 Cor. 15). . . . *that is all that we can etymologically or exegetically make of the word in this passage.*"[62]

And yet he further elaborates that "the word may denote both limited and unlimited duration in the same passage, the different meanings to be determined by the subject treated. . . . it . . . does not usually denote endless existence, but the life of the gospel, spiritual life, the Christian life, regardless of its duration. . . . Its duration depends on the possessor's fidelity. It is no less than the *aionion* life, if one abandons it in a month after acquiring it. It consists in knowing, loving and serving God." However, he cautions, "how often the good fall from grace. Believing, they have the *aionion* life, but they lose it by apostasy. Notoriously it is not, in thousands of cases, endless. The life is of an indefinite length. . . ."[63] (Especially note: Matthew 24:13 and Hebrews 6:4 in this regard.) He surmises, "The word may mean endless when applied to life, and not when applied to punishment, even in the same sentence, though we think duration is not considered so much as the intensity of joy or the sorrow in either case."[64]

Next, Hanson cites other words used in the Bible to denote the soul's immorality and happy existence, and which are never applied to punishment. He adds: "They would have been affixed to punishment had the Bible intended to teach endless punishment."[65]

Stetson explains these realities this way: "Does 'eternal life' . . . in Mat. 25:46 and similar verses mean that our life with God in heaven only lasts for an age? No," he answers. "We can be sure that the life in heaven is eternal because of the following verse in the Bible: 'When the perishable has been clothed with the imperishable, and the mortal with immortality, then the saying that is written will come true: 'Death has been swallowed up in victory.' (1 Cor. 15:54). This is referring to the life of the resurrection. The Greek words translated as 'imperishable' (*aphtharsia*) and 'immortality' (*athanasia*) really do mean what they say in English." He concludes, "so the point Jesus was making in verses like Mat. 25:46 is that sinners will spend a period of time being judged and corrected by God—the aionian chastisement, surely not a pleasant process—while the righteous people will be enjoying the blessings of God, the aionian life in Christ. Eventually, everyone will be reconciled and redeemed and will live eternally in heaven, but before that happens, some will receive judgments for an age while others are receiving rewards."[66]

12) Regarding the origin and development of the doctrine of endless punishment, Hanson discloses that "though the Old Testament does not contain the doctrine, Josephus . . . assures us that the Pharisees of his time accepted and taught it. Of course they must have obtained the doctrine from uninspired sources. . . . Nothing is better established in history than that the doctrine of endless punishment, as held by the Christian church in mediaeval times, was of Egyptian origin . . . and . . . adopted by the Greeks and Romans."[67] Notably, Moses, for instance, "was educated in all the wisdom of the Egyptians" (Acts 7:22), and yet he had nothing to do with this common Egyptian doctrine in his biblical writings.

Hanson further reports that "classic scholars know that the heathen hell was early copied by the Catholic church . . . . the heathen writers declare that the doctrine was invented to awe and control the multitude. Polybius writes: 'Since the multitude is ever fickle . . . there is no other way to keep them in order but by fear of the invisible world. . . .'"[68] Hanson terms this intentional falsification, "the corruption of Christianity."[69]

Regarding the source of this doctrine and the two facts that the Old Testament does not contain it and it was already a pagan doctrine, Hanson appropriately asks, "How can it be supposed that the Latins were correct in claiming that the Greek Scriptures teach a doctrine that the Greeks themselves did not find therein? And how can the Greek fathers in the primitive church mistake [sic] when they understand our Lord and his disciples to teach universal restoration?" He follows these two questions immediately by reminding his readers that "it may be well to note here, that after the third century the descent of the church into errors of doctrine and practice grew more rapid. The worship of Jesus, of Mary, of saints, of relics, etc. followed each other. . . . Thus theology became more hard and merciless—hell was intensified, and enlarged, and eternized—heaven shrunk, and receded, and lost its compassion—woman (despite the deification of Mary) was regarded as weak and despicable—the Agapae were abolished and the Eucharist deified, and its cup withheld from the people—and woman deemed too impure to touch it!"[70]

"How can it be supposed that the Latins were correct in claiming that the Greek Scriptures teach a doctrine that the Greeks themselves did not find therein?"

Thus, Hanson claims, "there was no controversy among Christians over the duration of punishment of the wicked for at least three hundred years after the death of Christ. Scriptural terms were used with their Scriptural meanings . . . the endless duration of punishment was not taught until heathen corruptions had adulterated Christian truth . . . the antidotal truth of universal salvation assumed . . . through Clement, Origen, and other Alexandrine fathers. . . . The doctrines of Prayer for the Dead, and of Christ Preaching to those in Hades, and of Mitigation, were humane teachings of the primitive Christians that were subsequently discarded."[71]

Next, of course according to Hanson, was development of the duty or doctrine of "reserve . . . . a certain accommodation as necessary . . . to make use even of falsehood for that attainment of a good end"[72] Or, in other words, "to teach false doctrines to the masses with the mistaken idea that they were needful."[73] And all because the Roman Catholic Church "dare not entrust the truth to the masses, and so held it in reserve—to deter men from sin"[74] (see again Chapter 5, p-115).

Critical Objection: Despite this knowable background, Exclusivists, like Marshall, stay their course maintaining and insisting that "there is scholarly agreement that in the New Testament *aionios* does mean 'never-ending' (like *aidios*), although the force of this term may be conditioned by the context; there is no good reason to take it otherwise here. If punishment is not everlasting, neither is the life given to the righteous (Matt. 26:45b)."[75]

But Johnson, a co-contributor in the same book with Marshall, feels otherwise. He acknowledges "the problem of whether *aionios*, 'eternal,' refers to a qualitative state (the life or punishment appropriate to the age to come) or quantitative (everlasting in duration)." But he sides with "either or both meanings are possible. There is no reason to assume or read into the passage that some are lost forever. Their punishment in eternity, punishment that all deserve . . . may burn away all that keeps them from the full realization of the image of God in which they were created." He poignantly asks, "Will anyone finally persist in refusing God's love?"[76]

Gleanings about *Aionios*

As a result of a flexible meaning for the Greek adjective *aionios*, Christian Universalists can affirm the biblical doctrine of hell (or punishment/chastisement somewhere)—and its conscious purification and/or scourging for the unsaved and wicked beyond death—without subscribing to endless torture, condemnation, and confinement. This possibility softens the difficulties of explaining hell's (or somewhere else's) fairness and God's love and justice. No longer must God be portrayed as a perpetual and disproportional torturer of temporal-finite sins with eternal-infinite punishment.

Variable durations may also better answer the infamous question of why God would send anyone to hell (or somewhere else). As Hanson once again reminds us, "a punishment cannot be endless, when defined by an adjective [*aionios*] derived from a noun [*aion*] describing an event, the end of which is distinctly stated . . . ."[77]

Daley reports that Origen (185–254—an early Christian scholar and theologian, and one of the most distinguished of the early fathers of the Christian Church, and a Christian Universalist—see again Chapter 5, pp-107f), "at least raises serious questions about the eternity of punishment of sinners. In his *Commentary on John* . . . he declares himself unsure whether those who are 'bound and cast into outer darkness' will remain there forever or will someday be released; 'it does not seem safe to me to pass judgment,' he remarks. . . . And 'eternal' *(aionios)* as he used it, seems to refer to long but limited periods of time or 'ages' . . . rather than to eternity in the Augustinian sense of timeless existence, or even to endless duration."[78]

Hanson also quotes Clement's insistence that afterlife/postmortem punishment "is remedial and restorative, and that punished souls are cleansed by fire. The fire is spiritual, purifying the soul. God's punishments are saving and disciplinary . . . leading to conversion. . . . and especially since souls, although darkened by passions, when released from their bodies, are able to perceive more clearly because of their being no longer obstructed by the paltry flesh."[79]

Hanson next highlights Clement's "three causes" for why "the good God punishes: First, that he who is punished . . . may become better than his former self; then that those who are capable of being saved by examples may be drawn back, being admonished; and thirdly, that he who is injured may not readily be despised, and be apt to receive injury. And there are two methods of correction, the instructive and the punitive, which we have called the disciplinary."[80]

Another reason there may be varying durations and degrees of punishment/purification in the afterlife is because not all sins may be demeaned as equal. Numerous scriptures imply this possibility. Hence, varying durations and/or degrees of retribution/restoration appropriately may be in the offing and in proportion to one's knowledge, opportunity, and wickedness. For example:

"How much more severely do you think a man deserves to be punished who has trampled the Son of God under foot, who has treated as an unholy thing the blood of the covenant that sanctified him, and who has insulted the Spirit of grace?" (Heb. 10:29).

"But because of your stubbornness and your unrepentant heart, you are storing up wrath against yourself for the day of God's wrath. God 'will give to each person according to what he has done'" (Rom. 2:5-6; from Psa. 62:12; Prov. 24:12).

"But woe to that man who betrays the Son of Man! It would be better for him if he had never been born" (Mark 14:21).

"They devour widows' houses and for a show make lengthy prayers. Such men will be punished more severely" (Mark 12:40; Luke 20:47).

"That servant who knows the master's will and does not get ready or does not do what his master wants will be beaten with many blows. But the one who does not know and does things deserving punishment will be beaten with few blows . . . ." (Luke 12:47-48).

"But I tell you, it will be more bearable for Tyre and Sidon on the day of judgment than for you" (Matt. 11:22, 24; 10:15).

Exclusivist, Kenneth L. Gentry, Jr. while maintaining that "this torment is of endless duration" at least agrees that "the degree of this torment is proportioned according to the extent of one's rebellion."[81]

Another reason there may be varying durations and degrees of punishment/purification in the afterlife is because not all sins may be demeaned as equal.

Critical Objection: What about "the unforgivable sin"—*"Anyone who speaks a word against the Son of Man will be forgiven, but anyone who speaks against the Holy Spirit will not be forgiven, either in this age or in the age to come"* (Matt. 12:32; Mark 3:29; Luke 12:10)?

A possible and compatible answer in harmony with the material we have been addressing could be: "Not be forgiven" does not necessitate endless punishment, only a punishment. Once that punishment is over, one has still not been forgiven; he or she is still guilty of the offense. But he or she has paid the penalty. Hanson critically adds this tidbit about this sin, "endless damnation is not thought of, and cannot be extorted from the language."[82]

Erickson harmoniously broadens our perspective here in noting, "There will be no mere forgetting of sins. They have to be faced . . . . The consequences of sin will have to be paid. . . . [But] the will of God extends beyond this life."[83]

What about Punishment for Believers?

Many Exclusivists teach that for believers "God only forgives our sins when we repent and trust Christ for our salvation, but he also forgets them." They cite Jeremiah 31:34, for instance, "I will forgive their wickedness and will remember their sins no more."

But below are a few other verses to the contrary. They may involve afterlife punishment, or at least a loss of rewards, for believers (more on this in Chapter 17 and Appendix A):

> *"That servant who knows the master's will and does not get ready or does not do what his master wants will be beaten with many blows"* (Luke 12:47).

> *"Not many of you should presume to be teachers, my brothers, because you know that we who teach will be judged more strictly"* (Jas. 3:1).

> *"It would have been better for them not to have known the way of righteousness, than to have known it and then to turn their backs on the sacred commandment that was passed on to them"* (2 Pet. 2:21).

> *"But I tell you anyone who is angry with his brother will be subject to judgment . . . anyone who says, 'You fool!' will be in danger of the fire of hell [Gehenna]"* (Matt. 5:22).

> *"But the subjects of the kingdom will be thrown outside, into the darkness, where there will be weeping and gnashing of teeth"* (Matt. 8:12; also 22:13).

> *"If any man builds on this foundation using gold, silver, costly stones, wood, hay or straw, his work will be shown for what it is, because the Day will bring it to light. It will be revealed with fire, and the fire will test the quality of each man's work. If what he has built survives, he will receive his reward. If it is burned up, he will suffer loss; he himself will be saved, but only as one escaping through the flames"* (1 Cor. 3:12-15).

In the parable of the talents, it was not a stranger but a servant—and not an immoral but an unprofitable one—who was to be cast into outer darkness, where there is weeping and gnashing of teeth (Matt. 25:14-30).

Consequently, Origen also taught that,

> God's consuming fire works with the good as with the evil, annihilating that which harms His children. This fire is one that each one kindles; the fuel and food is each one's sins . . . . When the soul has gathered together a multitude of evil works, and an abundance of sins against itself, at a suitable time all that assembly of evils boils up to punishment, and is set on fire to chastisement. . . . It is to be understood that God our Physician, desiring to remove the defects of our souls, should apply the punishment of fire. . . . Our God is a 'consuming fire . . . thus He enters in as a 'refiner's fire' to refine the rational nature, which has been filled with the lead of wickedness, and to free it from the other impure materials which adulterate the natural gold or silver, so to speak, of the soul. Our belief is that the Word [Christ] shall prevail over the entire rational creation, and change every soul into his own perfection. . . . For stronger than all the evils in the soul is the Word, and the healing power that dwells in him and this healing he applies, according to the will of God, to every man.[84]

One more insight to note with Ladd is, "Paul never discusses what he believes about the fate of the wicked." But he had "much to say about the destiny of those in Christ . . . ."[85]

What about Purgatory?

Conceivably and perhaps appropriately, Hanson characterizes Purgatory appropriately as another corruption given to us by the Roman Catholic Church:

> There can be no doubt that the Catholic doctrine of purgatory is a corruption of the Scriptural doctrine of the disciplinary character of all God's punishments. Purgatory was never heard of in the earlier centuries. It is first fully stated by Pope Gregory the First, "its inventor," at the close of the Sixth Century. "For some light faults we

must believe that there is before judgment a purgatorial fire." This theory is a perversion of the idea held anciently, that all God's punishments are puragative; . . . That the condition of the dead was not regarded as unalterably fixed is evident from the fact that prayers for the dead were customary anciently, and that, too, before the doctrine of purgatory was formulated. . . . Even Augustine accepted the doctrine. He prayed after his mother's death, that her sins might be forgiven, and that his father might also receive pardon. ("Confessions," ix, 13)."[86]

Let's Vote

Despite the variety of meanings and length of durations for the Greek word *aionios*, some Exclusivists contend that this Christian universalist argument "is just another of Satan's lies to deceive the elect into thinking there is nothing to fear." They continue to charge that "Universalists have tampered with the meaning of the word in order to twist certain scriptures into harmony with their preconceived opinions."

On the other hand, other Exclusivists concede . . . "I will grant that it [the word "aion"] does not always mean forever. The context has to be taken into very careful consideration. It can mean 'forever' or it can simply mean a generation, era, or age of time with indefinite time limits assigned to it."[87]

"There will be no mere forgetting of sins. They have to be faced . . . . The consequences of sin will have to be paid. . . . [But] the will of God extends beyond this life."

Most likely, many Exclusivists will oppose my presentation of verses implying afterlife punishment for believers, which we briefly alluded to above, as undercutting the sufficiency of Christ's saving work and flying in the face of Romans 8:1, which assures us that "there is now no condemnation for those in Christ Jesus." However, I must point out a manuscript discrepancy with this verse. Some later manuscripts attach a contingency clause that reads, "who do not live according to the sinful nature but according to the Spirit." So I ask you, how many believers live their lives in accordance with this clause? Consequently, we should not be so sure that this verse (in its entirety) alleviates the possibility of afterlife punishment and/or refinement for believers.

In concluding this chapter, and in my opinion, four things appear biblically and reasonably sure:

- *Varying durations and degrees of afterlife punishment and/or purification are possible for everyone.*
- *Everyone will be judged and punished/refined* "by what they had done" (Rom. 5:6; Rev. 20:12-13). This judgment will involve an evaluation of everything that each person has done during their life and will include "every careless word" (Matt. 12:36; also see Eccl. 12:14; Rom. 14:10, 12; 2 Cor. 5:10).
- Jesus, in paying the penalty for our sin and sins, was and is not being eternally punished for them.
- In unison, most Christians agree that God is sovereign, merciful, and just. Therefore, some contend his punishment(s) in the afterlife will be likewise. But eternal punishment for temporal sin(s) is none of these things.

Chan, however, takes a powder, so to speak, when he asks. "What about the word *aionios*? "Bible scholars have debated the meaning of this term for what seems like an eternity, so we're not going to settle the issue here. It's important to note that however we translated *aionios*, the passage still refers to punishment for the wicked, which is something that Universalists deny."[88] But as we have shown, Christian Universalists going back to early church fathers certainly don't deny this punishment. In all fairness, and one page later, Chan does relent in writing, "the debate about hell's duration is much more complex than I first assumed. While I lean heavily on the side that says it is everlasting, I am not ready to claim that with complete certainty. I encourage you to continue researching."[89] And so we shall.

Hanson provides a suitable summary for this chapter by concluding, "How could universal salvation have been the prevailing doctrine in that age of the church unless the word applied to punishment in Matt. xxv:46 was understood by Christians to mean limited duration? . . . . Augustine . . . was the first known to argue that *aionios* signified endless." And it was said of him, he "was very imperfectly acquainted with the Greek language[90] . . . . Hence the word did not mean endless duration among the early Christians for about six centuries after Christ."[91]

"But oh how the simple meanings of words have been corrupted by theologians!"[92] Is this really what happened? Here's my vote . . .

Strength-of-argument advantage: Christian Universalism.

STRENGTH-OF-ARGUMENT ADVANTAGE SCORECARD

	Christian Univ.	Excl.	Draw
Dispute over Universal Language?			✓
Power and Point of Parallelism?	✓		
One Way or Many Ways?		✓	
How Long Is 'Eternal' in Eternal Punishment?	✓		
RUNNING TALLY	2	1	1

(How do you vote?)

Chapter 12

The Annihilation Option?

Most Exclusivists today do *not* consider Universalism of any type to be the dominant challenge to their popular and traditional position of unending conscious punishment in hell. They consider Annihilationism to be "the dominant challenge in our day."[1]

WARNING: this area of argumentation is quite vague, ambiguous, and a massive gray area, as you will see. So I apologize in advance to you my reader. Unfortunately, that's the nature of this aspect of this great debate. So if you want to skip this chapter and go to the next, you have my permission. You will not miss that much.

Annihilationism is the belief that only the souls and resurrected bodies of believers are given immortality by God in the afterlife. All others (unbelievers and the wicked) are mortal and at some point in the afterlife will be put out of existence all together and cease to exist in any form, manner, or shape. Consequently, this view is also known as Conditional Immortality—i.e., that people and their souls are not naturally immortal, per the Greek tradition. Rather, immortality is a conditional gift of God.

In recent years the annihilationist view has gained ground among conservative Christians as there has been a "steady flow of theologians away from the traditional notion of hell towards a variety of annihilationist positions."[2] Perhaps, the reason for this departure, as Christian Universalist Stetson suggests, is that they are "uncomfortable" with a "God who maintains an everlasting torture chamber."[3]

Interestingly once again, in what's termed "the debate over the nature of final punishment,[4] all sides have conceded "that certain biblical texts *seem* to teach the final destruction of the lost (whether that be understood in terms of eternal conscious torment or annihilation)."[5] And while both Annihilationists and traditionalists agree that the Bible teaches "eternal punishment" and "eternal life," they disagree "over what this punishment entails."[6]

Exclusivist Marshall attempts to place these disagreements in perspective by counseling that "the concept of a God who consigns some human beings to endless, conscious suffering is irreconcilable with what we know of the love of God. . . . [but] this understanding of hell as destruction [annihilation] rather than as eternal suffering removes one of the arguments for universalism, namely that the alternative makes out God to be a monster and also makes it hard for the saved to be happy in heaven while they know that other people are suffering in hell."[7]

Annihilationism . . .
"the dominant challenge in our day."

Thomas Johnson, on the other hand, is an Annihilationist who represents what some also referred to as "pseudo Universalism"—that is, "the salvation of all who should be permitted to be immortal."[8] He believes "the Bible teaches the universal saving and sovereign grace of God, who, out of love for all people and all creation, has provided ultimate reconciliation and restoration for all." But this universal reality only occurs after "unrepentant unbelievers will be destroyed after the last judgment. They will cease to exist, all the rest will be saved, and no one will be in hell forever. . . . [And] eternal life is a gift to believers."[9] Hence, "all will be saved *except* those who knowingly and willfully reject God and God's forgiving love. . . . Those who persist in rebellion will perish."[10]

Hanson provides this short historical perspective on Annihilationism. "Justin Martyr, A.D. 140, 162, taught *everlasting* suffering, and annihilation afterwards. The wicked 'are tormented as long as God wills that they should exist and be tormented. . . . Souls both suffer punishment and die.'" Hanson relates that Irenaeus also taught annihilation that "when it is necessary that the soul should no longer exist, the vital spirit leaves it, and the soul is no more, but returns thither whence it was taken."[11] Tertullian, on the other hand, "argued against the doctrine of their annihilation . . . that 'the wicked would be consumed, and not punished,' that is, endlessly."[12]

Thus, Annihilationists contend that all who are given immortality through Jesus Christ will be saved. But not all who have lived will be saved. Nor will they suffer eternal conscious punishment and torment. Again, the two major books on this topic are:

- *The Fire That Consumes: A Biblical and Historical Study of the Doctrine of Final Punishment* by Edward W. Fudge (Backinprint.com, Nov. 2000)
- *Two Views of Hell: A Biblical and Theological Dialogue* by Edward Fudge and Robert Peterson (IVP, 2000) – a side by side presentation and critique of each view.

In this latter book, Fudge unyieldingly writes:

The fact is that the Bible does not teach the traditional view of final punishment. Scripture nowhere suggests that God is an eternal torturer. It never says the damned will writhe in ceaseless torment or that the glories of heaven will forever be blighted by the screams from hell. The idea of conscious everlasting torment was a grievous mistake, a horrible error, a gross slander against the heavenly Father, whose character we truly see in the life of Jesus of Nazareth.[13]

Of course, Christian Universalists challenged Fudge's view. They contend to the contrary that "not one word . . . implies annihilation of those *individuals* for whom Christ suffered and died."[14] Furthermore, they chastise the exclusivist fear that "annihilation is a better afterlife scenario for the lost than never ending punishment" by claiming that "ultimate reconciliation is ever better since 'God was [is] reconciling the world unto himself in Christ and, not counting men's sins against them. And he has committed to us the [this] message of reconciliation.' (2 Cor. 5:19; Rom. 5:18)."[15]

So, once again, who's right, who's wrong?

Verses Supporting Annihilationism

A number of verses declare, in fact, that unbelievers will "perish." And again, the **bolds** are mine:

*"For God so loved the world that he gave his one and only Son, that whoever believes in him shall not **perish** but have eternal life"* (John 3:16).

*I give them eternal life, and they shall never **perish**; no one can snatch them out of my hand"* (John 10:28).

*"All who sin apart from the law will also **perish** apart from the law, and all who sin under the law will be judged by the law"* (Rom. 2:12).

*"For the message of the cross is foolishness to those who are **perishing**, but to us who are being saved it is the power of God"* (1 Cor. 1:18).

*"For we are to God the aroma of Christ among those who are being saved and those who are **perishing**"* (2 Cor. 2:15).

*"and in every sort of evil that deceives those who are **perishing**. They **perish** because they refused to love the truth and so be saved"* (2 Thess. 2:10).

*The Lord is not slow in keeping his promise, as some understand slowness. He is patient with you, not wanting anyone to **perish**, but everyone to come to repentance"* (2 Pet. 3:9).

*"For the LORD watches over the way of the righteous, but the way of the wicked will **perish**"* (Psa. 1:6).

Other passages speak of or imply "destruction:"

*"Do not be afraid of those who kill the body but cannot kill the soul. Rather, be afraid of the one who can **destroy both soul and body** in hell [Gehenna]"* (Matt. 10:28).

*"The man who loves his life will **lose** it, while the man who hates his life in this world will keep it for eternal life"* (John 12:25).

*"What if God, choosing to show his wrath and make his power known, bore with great patience the objects of his wrath – prepared for **destruction**"* (Rom. 9:22).

*"If anyone destroys God's temple, God will **destroy** him; for God's temple is sacred, and you are that temple"* (1 Cor. 3:17).

*"without being frightened in any way by those who oppose you. This is a sign to them that they will be **destroyed**, but that you will be saved – and that by God"* (Phil. 1:28).

*"Their destiny is **destruction**, their god is their stomach, and their glory is in their shame. Their mind is on earthly things"* (Phil. 3:19).

*"They will be punished with everlasting **destruction** and shut out from the presence of the Lord and from the majesty of his power"* (2 Thess. 1:9).

*"but only a fearful expectation of judgment and of raging fire that will **consume** the enemies of God"* (Heb. 10:27).

*"By the same word the present heavens and earth are reserved for fire, being kept for the day of judgment and **destruction** of ungodly men"* (2 Pet. 3:7).

Please notice that these verses say nothing about receiving Jesus Christ as your Savior or going to hell.

Another Great Disagreement over Words

Here, as elsewhere, we encounter another great disagreement that
centers on the meaning of words and what this fate for the wicked really
means. Not surprisingly, if "all" doesn't always or necessarily mean all,
all the time; and if "eternal" doesn't always or necessarily mean eternal
all the time; why must "perish," "destroy," or "destruction" always or
necessarily mean annihilation, extinction, or elimination?

Unfortunately, no New or Old Testament writer ever explained what
these terms meant. So opinions vary. Morris thinks perishing signifies
"eternal loss without defining that loss." In opposition to the
annihilationist view he adds that "we should not, of course, take
perishing as an exact description of the final state of the impenitent and
conclude that they simply cease to exist."[16] Ladd expresses his
understanding that destruction only means "exclusion from the joys and
pleasures of the presence of God in his Kingdom."[17]

Tellingly, the literal Greek for 2 Thessalonians 1:9 translated by
most translations as "They will be punished with everlasting destruction
and shut out from the presence of the Lord and from the majesty of this
power" actually reads, "who [the] penalty will pay destruction eternal
(*aionios*) *from* (*apo*) [the] face of the Lord and *from* the glory of the
strength of him" (*italics* mine). The latter is the better translation.
Moreover, the word *apo* could be translated "away from" or "coming
from." If the latter meanings are correct, then this would perfectly
harmonize with Revelation 14:10 concerning "anyone [who] worship the
beast and his image and receives his mark" that "he will be tormented
with burning sulfur in the presence of the holy angels and the Lamb."
Therefore, 2 Thessalonians 1:9 does not necessarily envision an eternal
separation from God for purpose of punishment or an annihilation-type
destruction.

Annihilationist John Stott advises that "I also believe that the
ultimate annihilation of the wicked should at least be accepted as a
legitimate, biblically founded alternative to their eternal conscious
torment."[18] Even Exclusivist Stevens seems to semi-support the evidence
that Stott and his co-author David L. Edwards brought forth while "weak
at best" is "not as far-fetch as many would think."[19]

But the modern-day reality is, Annihilationism is a small minority
view held only by a few conservative, evangelical interpreters who have

assumed that "perishing" and "destruction" mean annihilation, extinction, or elimination —i.e. "at some point [unsaved] human beings cease to exist at all"[20] They will simply be no more. It's the end of their personal existence in any form, manner, or fashion.

Once again, we encounter another great disagreement that centers on the meaning of words and what this fate for the wicked really means.

A typical annihilationist argument by analogy goes like this. If you burn a piece of paper, it is eternally destroyed. That is how we should view what will happen in hell. But this is not a good illustration because a burnt piece of paper is not utterly consumed and none of its elements are destroyed. Fire merely changes its form and nature—from paper to smoke and ashes. Fact is, combustion is a process by which chemicals combine to form new chemicals. Therefore, to burn means to change. And fire does not burn down. It burns up, seeking the highest level. That's why we say something burning "goes up in smoke" and then exists in a higher form and dimension.

Baker further explains what some Annihilationists believe about "those thrown into the lake's sulfur fire." They "suffer complete destruction or annihilation. They do not suffer eternal torment in hell but cease to exist completely. . . . God will burn them so that there is nothing left." She then announces that "that's just one way to interpret the meaning of the lake of fire" and offers to "give you one more that makes a lot of sense when we also consider the loving character of God and God's desire to reconcile with all people."[21]

But here's a scriptural reality check coupling this total extinction assumption with a few fiery incidences recorded in the Bible. Were Shadrach, Meshach and Abed-nego, who were thrown into a furnace of fire consumed and annihilated (Dan 3:19)? When Moses saw the burning bush, was it consumed by the fire and destroyed (Exod. 3:2)? Ironically, many Christians who believe the wicked will not be annihilated believe the heavens and earth will be annihilated or at least renovated by fire. Of course, I disagree with that view and maintain none of this will happen for reasons I have laid out in another book.[22]

What is obvious, however, is that opinions vary greatly. Some adherents believe annihilation may occur immediately at death. Others say it's upon entrance into hell. And others claim it's only after a time of punishment in hell. Whenever it occurs, if it does, then hell does not entail endless punishment. Thus, Holden portrays Annihilationism this way:

> In such a view hell is the condition of nonexistence; sinners are punished by being annihilated by God. . . . Indeed, in some ways annihilation . . . may be characterized as 'metaphysical capital punishment' as opposed to . . . life imprisonment."[23]

Conditional Immortality

This term originated from the belief "that immortality is inherent in God alone" and that "believers, now being mortal by nature, [will] receive immortality from Jesus Christ as a gift conferred at the resurrection of the last day"[24]—which according to most Christians has not yet happened.[25]

Conditionalists, as they are sometime called, contend that the human soul is not naturally immortal—i.e., capable of the eternal life that transcends death. But receiving immortality and living forever is what is meant by "in Christ all will be made alive" (1 Cor. 15:22: Rom. 5:18).

John L Bray, a Conditionalist/Annihilationist argues in a contrarian fashion that "an eternity in a fiery hell is neither death nor full destruction; it is immortality! But the Bible says that a mortal must 'put on' immortality (1 Cor. 15:53)—not that immortality is already a part of the human equation. The Word also says that only the King of Kings has immortality—not every human being as is commonly taught (1 Tim. 6:15)."[26]

On the other hand, Harris disagrees with Conditional Immortality's view that the wicked will be annihilated, "either at death, or after suffering divine punishment for a period." He argues that the opposite of eternal life given to those in Christ is not annihilation:

> This [eternal life] does *not* imply that existence beyond death is conditional or the unbelievers will be annihilated. Because, in the New Testament usage, immortality has positive content, being more than

mere survival beyond death, its opposite is not nonexistence, but the 'second death' (Rev 20:6, 14) which involves exclusion from God's presence (2Th 1:9). Forfeiture of immortality means the deprivation of eternal blessedness but not the destruction of personal existence. All human beings survive beyond death, but not all will become immortal in the Pauline sense.[27]

Another Argument over What 'Eternal' Means

The biggest textual problem Annihilationists face is the cluster of passages that speak of the "eternal" (i.e., unending) conscious punishment (Mark 9:47-48; Rev. 14:11; 20:10, 13-15). Some traditional Exclusivists, like Lutzer, believe that "unbelievers are granted eternal death" and, like Holden above, that "Hell is annihilation."[28]

According to traditional Exclusivist Peterson, Annihilationists "counter that this does not prove endless suffering but only suffering that lasts as long as the sufferers do."[29] They maintain that the word 'eternal' refers to the permanence of the results of judgment and not to the duration of the act of punishment. When confronted with Jesus' parable of the rich man and Lazarus in which conscious suffering is clearly portrayed, Annihilationists "correctly point out that Jesus' parable [in Luke 16:19-31] pertains to the intermediate state [of Hades] rather than the final state [of Gehenna]."[30] But at the least, Jesus' use of the parable of the rich man and Lazarus in Luke 16 shows that the wicked do face "conscious" negative consequences after death.

Is Destruction a Metaphor?

Peterson further discloses that "traditionalists also reject Conditionalists' equating the lake of fire with annihilation, arguing instead that death signifies not extermination but separation. The second death [the lake of fire is defined as 'the second death,' – Rev. 20:14] therefore stands for eternal separation from God." So Peterson contends that "destruction is a metaphor for terrible loss,"[31]—i.e., a condition of complete ruin.

And yet Peterson concedes that "if Scripture gave us no other teaching on the final destiny of the wicked than that provided by these and similar passages, Annihilationism would be a viable option." But he insists that "Annihilationism is an unlikely meaning for the words 'everlasting destruction.'"[32]

Oddly enough, notes Peoples, "everlasting destruction is precisely what the annihilationist believes will happen to the lost."[33] Also to be noted is the fact that "death and destruction are only one kind of 'picture' that the Bible uses to speak of final punishment . . . . Others are: 'darkness and separation, fire, 'weeping and gnashing of teeth,' punishment, and death and destruction."[34]

Further complicating this issue, involving the "terms of *destruction*," the Apostle Paul described the fate of the lost as both "death" (Rom. 6:23) and "destruction" (1 Cor. 3:17). Was he equating the two? He also wrote of the weak brother (i.e., a fellow believer) being "destroyed" by one's eating something offensive in front of him (Rom. 14:15). So what does this word "destroyed" mean in that context? Annihilationist, John Stott retorts with a bit of circular logic in reasoning that "it would seem strange, therefore, if people who are said to suffer destruction are in fact not destroyed."[35]

Another biblical fact is, the words "destruction/destroy" (disaster/desolate, etc.) are also commonly used for material ruin (Prov. 1:26-27; 21:7; Hos. 9:6 *KJV*) and for the destruction of a city or nation (Obad. 12-13; Isa. 47:11; Jer. 32:31; Ezek. 6:14; 14:16 KJV). Additionally, as Perriman notes, "Antiochus Epiphanes plotted the final destruction of the Jews, in this case by selling them into slavery (1 Macc. 3:42)."[36] This verse reads: "Now Judas and his brothers saw that misfortunes had increased and that the forces were encamped in their territory. They also learned what the king had commanded to do to the people to cause their final destruction."

The Greek word commonly used in the New Testament for "destruction" is *olethron* and can mean either "ruin" or "destruction" depending on context. Regarding its use in 2 Thessalonians 1:9, MacDonald admits that "nothing in the passage requires such an interpretation [of complete annihilation]" but he also thinks that "nothing precludes it either."[37]

Adding to this word's ambiguity is Paul's use of it in 1 Thessalonians 5:3 which reads, "While people are saying, 'Peace and safety,' destruction will come on them suddenly, as labor pains on a pregnant woman, and they will not escape." Equally ambiguous is its use in 1 Timothy 6:9 – "People who want to get rich fall into temptation and a trap and into many foolish and harmful desires that plunge men into ruin and destruction." Likewise, Paul's instructions in 1 Corinthians 5:5, "hand this man over to Satan, so that the sinful nature (body or flesh) may be destroyed and his spirit saved on the day of the Lord." This destruction only involves the annihilation of this man's sinful nature, and not his humanity or very existence. Moreover, this destruction was for his own good and salvation. Clearly here, Paul does not view this destruction as annihilation, but rather utter ruin.

The issue of variable meanings for the word "destroy" sets forth another and corresponding conundrum. The New Testament book of 1 John proclaims that "the reason the Son of God [Jesus] appeared was to **destroy** the devil's work" (1 John 3:8). Did Jesus fail? Then why do we still see the devil's work being manifested all about in our world today? Fact is, the word *destroy* occurs frequently in the New Testament with the sense of undo or pull to pieces, and not for the thing or person receiving it to cease from existing.

Paul writes in 1 Corinthians, "Then the end will come, when he [Jesus] hands over the kingdom to God the Father after he has destroyed all dominion, authority and power. For he must reign until he has put all his enemies under his feet" (1 Cor. 15:24-25). MacDonald makes these four prudent observations about this passage:

1) "No mention is made of the destruction of any humans.
2) The only enemies that are in view are the powers, sin, and death (vv. 24, 26).
3) The verb Paul uses in 15:24 is *katargeo* which literally means 'to nullify, to render powerless,' and the context determines what that means.
4) It certainly can mean 'to annihilate,' but such an interpretation is not required."

Next, let's notice the past tense usage when Paul writes in vs. 27: "For he 'has put everything under his feet." This is a quote from Psalm 8:6. Therefore, destroying and putting enemies under his feet could not possibly mean annihilation here. It means subjugation or, as MacDonald says to "render powerless" or "neutralize." He emphasizes, that this meaning "is *not* equivalent to annihilating them . . . . 'so that God may be all in all' (v. 28)."[38]

Strong's Exhaustive Concordance of the Bible gives this range of meanings for *katargeo*: "to be (render) entirely idle (useless), lit. or fig.:—abolish, cease, cumber, deliver, destroy, do away, become (make) of no (none, without) effect, fail, loose, bring (come) to nought, put away (down), vanish away, make void."[39]

Other Meanings of Perish (*apollumi*)

Another word used to support Annihilationism is the word "perish" or "perishing," which is also translated as "destroy" or "lost." It's the Greek word *apollumi* and means "to destroy fully." See again the perish scriptures at the start of this chapter. But there are different possible meanings here, too. Often this word is associated with someone physically dying or being killed, or something passing away. *Thayer's Greek-English Lexicon* defines destruction as "to be delivered up to eternal misery." Let's also take note of the different ways in which this word is used in these scriptures (**bolds** are mine):

> ". . . *Arise, and take the young child and his mother, and flee into Egypt, and be thou there until I bring thee word: for Herod will seek the young child to **destroy** him*" (Matt. 3:13 *KJV*).

Meaning to physically kill Jesus.

> "*Whoever finds his life will **lose** it, and whoever **loses** his life for my sake will find it*" (Matt. 10:39; also Matt. 16:25).

Meaning a prelude for salvation in dying to one's self.

> "*Then the Pharisees went out, and held a council against him, how they might **destroy** him*" (Matt. 12:14 *KJV*).

Meaning to physically kill Jesus.

*"The king was enraged. He sent his army and **destroyed** those murderers and burned their city"* (Matt. 22:7).

Meaning to physically kill people.

*"What do you want with us, Jesus of Nazareth? Have you come to **destroy** us? I know who you are—the Holy One of God!"* (Mark 1:24).

Who knows what this destroy might have entailed in these demons' minds?

*"and he was in the hinder part of the ship, asleep on a pillow; and they awake him, and say unto him, Master, carest thou not that we **perish**?"* (Mark 4:38 *KJV*).

The disciples were afraid that they would perish (*apollumi*) by drowning.

*"Then Jesus said to them, 'I ask you, which is lawful on the Sabbath; to do good or to do evil, to save life or to **destroy** it?"* (Luke 6:9).

Meaning, perhaps, to physically kill an animal or person.

*"What good is it for a man to gain the whole world, and yet **lose** or forfeit his very self?"* (Luke 9:25).

Meaning his salvation, not his existence.

*"When the disciples James and John saw this, they asked, 'Lord, do you want us to call fire down from heaven to **destroy** them?"* (Luke 9:54).

The disciples were asking about ruining or killing people in a Samaritan village who did not welcome them.

*"I tell you, no! But unless you repent, you too will all **perish**. Or those eighteen who died when the tower in Siloam fell on them— do you think they were more guilty than all the others living in Jerusalem? I tell you, no! But unless you repent, you too will all **perish**"* (Luke 13:3-5).

This perish is associated with being killed.

*"Suppose one of you has a hundred sheep and **loses** one of them. Does he not leave the ninety-nine in the open country and go after the **lost** sheep until he finds it?"* (Luke 15:4).

This sheep was lost (*apollumi*) by straying away.

*"But the day Lot left Sodom, fire and sulfur rained down from heaven and **destroyed** them all"* (Luke 17:29).

Meaning it physically killed them.

*"Every day he was teaching at the temple. But the chief priests, the teachers of the law and the leaders among the people were trying to **kill** him"* (Luke 19:47).

Meaning physically kill him.

*"When they were filled, he said unto his disciples, 'Gather up the fragments that remain, that nothing be **lost**'"* (John 6:12 KJV).

Translated as "wasted" in *NIV*.

*"Labour not for the meat which **perisheth**, but for the meat which endureth unto everlasting life, which the Son of man shall give unto you: for him hath God the Father sealed"* (John 6:27 KJV).

Meaning and translated as "spoils" in *NIV*.

*"And this is the will of him who sent me, that I shall **lose** none of all that he has given me, but raise them up at the last day"* (John 6:39).

Meaning those elect on the "last day" singular of the "last days" plural back in that 1st-century, end-times period.[40]

*"You do not realize that it is better for you that one man die for the people than the whole nation **perish**"* (John 11:50).

Nations pass away or perish in this world not in the afterlife.

*"So this weak brother, for whom Christ died, is **destroyed** by your knowledge"* (1 Cor. 8:11).

How may we destroy (*apollumi*) a weak brother by our knowledge?

*"For which cause we faint not; but though our outward man **perish** [**waste away** – NIV], yet the inward man is renewed day by day"* (2 Cor. 4:16 *KJV*).

Isn't this perish speaking of physical deterioration of our bodies as we age?

*"These are all destined to **perish** with use, because they are based on human commands and teachings"* (Col. 2:22).

This perish is dealing with "the basic principles of this world" (vs.21).

*"For the sun is no sooner risen with a burning heat, but it withereth the grass, and the flower thereof falleth, and the grace of the fashion of it **perisheth** [**fade away** – NIV]: so also shall the rich man fade away in his ways"* (Jas. 1:11 *KJV*).

This perish speaks of physical death.

*"These have come so that your faith—of greater worth than gold, which **perishes even though refined by fire**—may be proved genuine and may result in praise, glory and honor when Jesus Christ is revealed"* (1 Pet. 1:7).

This perish is something that happens to a believer's faith as it is refined by fire. But this faith does not go out of existence, thereafter.

*". . . I want to remind you that the Lord delivered his people out of Egypt, but later **destroyed** those who did not believe"* (Jude 5).

He brought them to ruin and physical death.

Regardless of how you understand the bold words above, which were all translated from the Greek word *apollumi*, they do contemplate something less than complete annihilation of the soul in the afterlife. In actuality, these destructions were physical death, a prelude to salvation, or maturing, and not extinction of a soul/spirit of a person.

Given this background of word usage, perhaps we should now revisit the possible meaning(s) of Jesus' 1st-century admonishment to "enter through the narrow gate. For wide is the gate and broad is the road that leads to destruction (*apollumi*), and many enter through it" (Matt. 7:13). Likewise, Paul's usage when he wrote about "God" who made "vessels/objects of his wrath – prepared for destruction (*apollumi*)" (Rom. 9:22). Do these verses now seem to support the Annihilationists' afterlife-cessation-of-existence-entirely position, or not?

Peter, on the other hand, certainly likens the destruction of the ungodly to the burning of Sodom and Gomorrah (2 Pet. 2:6). And these two cities were annihilated. But what of the "final destiny" of the wicked (see Psa. 73:17-19)?

Christian Universalist, Stetson, agrees "annihilationism seems compatible with some Bible verses about 'destruction' or 'perishing' . . . at least at first glance. However, other passages in the Bible refute the idea . . . ." He cites the "all" parallelism in 1 Corinthians 15:22 (see Chapter 9) and chides that "surely the power of sin is not greater than the power of Christ!" He concludes that this verse (and others like it) is "incompatible with both eternal hell and permanent annihilation of any soul."[41] He highlights two reasons "why annihilation of the wicked conflicts with the overall message of the Bible:"

First, "even the verses in the Bible that sound supportive of annihilationism actually only support the idea of temporary annihilation or a radical destruction and remaking of those who need such severe treatment, rather than a total and eternal expunging of unsaved souls from the universe."

Secondly, "no soul is 100% evil. Though 'all have sinned and fall short of the glory of God' (Rom. 3:23), we are nevertheless all created reflecting God's likeness . . . made 'in the image of God' (Gen. 1:27)." He reasons, "if something is not totally evil but contains good, then it cannot be totally destroyed. . . . Some parts of a personality might be destroyed in God's purging fires—maybe a large part—but it would not be the entire essence of any person that ceases to exist." He concludes that "total and permanent annihilation would mean God giving up on the small part of an evil person that can still be saved, that God wants to save as the Father of all people." Therefore, Stetson views annihilation as "not better than a halfway, feeble attempt to get out of the weighty philosophical problem of eternal hell by coming up with 'hell lite'— damnation without the endless pain."[42]

Robert A. Morey in his book, *Death and the Afterlife*, also does not believe annihilation will "survive careful analysis." He points out what we have seen above that "the word 'destroyed' as used in the Bible does not mean 'to annihilate.' The Greek word *apollumi* is used in passages such as . . . Luke 15:4, and John 6:12, 27. In none of those instances does it mean 'to pass out of existence . . . . There isn't a single instance in the New Testament where *apollumi* means annihilation in the strict sense of the word."[43]

D.A. Carson explains that the *apoleia* word-group "'has a range of meanings, depending on the context.' While it might literally refer to destruction, it need not always have this meaning in some contexts. He points to examples where this is the case: The 'lost' son and lost coin of Luke 15 [see vs. 4, 6, 9, 24, 32; also 19:10], the 'ruined' wineskins of Matt. 9:17 ("perish"), and similar examples. None of these things are simply 'destroyed,' so we might legitimately read the *apoleia* terms as referring to ruin or loss, and not complete destruction."[44]

Stevens believes that annihilationist logic, like that of John Stott's, "is purely deductive and not necessarily sound," regarding words translated as "destruction, perish, ruin" and other similar words. Nor do these words "imply utter annihilation of a subject." As an argument-by-analogy example, Stevens presents this illustration: *"The German army was destroyed in World War II and it was in ruin at the end of the war."* He emphasizes, "this phrase would not indicate that the German military ceased to exist at the end of the war, but that it was defeated by the allied forces, and it was in utter disarray." He concludes that Annihilationists have failed to prove that the biblical language supports their position and accuses Stott and others of "creating confusion for . . . readers."[45]

Lutzer cites Revelation 14:10 as part of his opposition to Annihilationism as he notices "that the fire does not annihilate the wicked but torments them."[46] Let's again take note that the location of this torment is also "in the presence of the holy angles and in the presence of the Lamb." That doesn't sound to me like the traditionally posited "hell" as a place of separation and exclusion from the presence of God and Jesus. How about to you?

Let's Vote

Annihilation is not an "open and shut" case. One Annihilationist even admits, "While we do not know all that is involved in someone being cast into the lake of fire at the last day, we know that it must be a horrible punishment."[47]

The primary fear traditionalists feel, however, regarding Annihilationism is that this belief lets the wicked off the hook, completely and eternally—i.e., for that which ceases to exist, ceases to suffer. It's assumed that most of these wicked probably wouldn't mind being blotted out of existence. Stevens outlined his similar and strong concerns regarding annihilationism in three insightful email messages to me:

> This would give the wicked much comfort and no motivation to look seriously at the claims of Christ, nor fear the consequences of unbelief. Just "eat, drink, and be merry, for one day we will cease to exist." Live it up now with no eternal consequences. There is no fear in annihilation. That is exactly what the wicked want. But eternal conscious punishment in the presence of the holy angels and in the

sight of God and His elect . . . then there is every reason to FEAR. It is supposed to be a terrifying thing to fall into the hands of the Lord.[48]

"Nonexistence" is NOT "just as fearful" as conscious punishment. " . . . It would have been better for him [Judas] if he had never been born." (Matt. 26:24). . . . If Judas Iscariot was annihilated, then he absolutely would have been in the same condition as if "he had never been born. . . . that makes Jesus' words totally ludicrous. Evidently Jesus envisioned some kind of conscious punishment awaiting Judas after death."[49]

The "fear of the Lord" is meaningless. It would really mitigate such passages as, "It is a terrifying thing to fall into the hands of the Lord." The atheist would scoff at this idea, right along with the Annihilationist. Annihilationists are a great comfort to the unbeliever. No motivation to change their ways.[50]

Ryken agrees that "they wouldn't mind being blotted out of existence. But that's not what the Bible teaches." Then he falls back into the traditional "hell" concept by elaborating that "the Bible describes hell as a place of darkness, misery, conscious anguish, and fire. To be in hell is to be separated from the presence, grace, and compassion of God."[51]

The primary fear traditionalists feel . . . is that this belief lets the wicked off the hook . . . for that which ceases to exist, ceases to suffer. It's assumed that most of these wicked probably wouldn't mind being blotted out of existence.

No matter how we feel or believe on this matter, many honest, sincere, conservative, and evangelical interpreters disagree, and their disagreement continues. But I believe both Grudem's and Peterson's assessments below merit worthwhile consideration. While Grudem acknowledges that he supports the traditional, eternal conscious punishment position, he also concedes that "the ultimate resolution of the depths of this question lies far beyond our ability to understand and remains hidden in the counsels of God."[52]

Peterson, in his article pertaining to the "evangelical debate over the nature and duration of hell" and in reference to a 1999 book titled, *The Nature of Hell: A Report by the Evangelical Alliance Commission of Unity and Truth Among Evangelicals*, summarized that this report was "a model of how evangelicals can agree to disagree."[53] In his opinion, however, "the conditionalist exegesis of the key texts falls short."[54]

In my opinion, neither side can claim a strength-of-argument advantage here. The viability of the annihilation option and arguments against it are just too vague, ambiguous, and inconclusive to give the advantage to either side.

Strength-of-argument advantage: a Draw

STRENGTH-OF-ARGUMENT ADVANTAGE
SCORECARD

	Christian Univ.	Excl.	Draw
Dispute over Universal Language?			✓
Power and Point of Parallelism?	✓		
One Way or Many Ways?		✓	
How Long Is 'Eternal' in Eternal Punishment?	✓		
The Annihilation Option?			✓
RUNNING TALLY	2	1	2

(How do you vote?)

Chapter 13

The Missions' Problem?

L et's face it; "our traditional focus . . . as an evangelistic tool" has been "on hell . . . to escape" its "eternal fires."[1]

Hell has been and still is the great negative incentive, prod, spur, hammer, and driving and motivating imperative for world missions and personal evangelistic efforts. Thus, hell is touted as "part and parcel of the good news!"[2] Throughout most of church history, it has also been credited with being a, if not *the*, major deterrent in trying to shape moral behavior for Christians and non-Christians alike. In other words, and as Baker puts it in question form, "Do we so passionately need a corporate scapegoat to prove our righteousness and goodness, to feel as though we have a handle on how to abolish and punish evil, to feel peace about our own eternal destination?"[3] Apparently, we do.

A concerned friend, while reading an early manuscript of this book, shared with me that he had spent thirty years of his life in one church where much of the time the only incentive and motivation taught for becoming and staying a Christian was the fear of hell.

Therefore, traditionally and axiomatically, it has been accepted that "to preach the good news, we must [also] preach the bad."[4] And "anything that reduces the urgency or motivation of missionary endeavor is a negative."[5] Even *Time* magazine recognizes that "to take away hell is to leave the church without its most powerful sanction."[6] Then, *Time* seriously asks this threatening question, "if [Rob] Bell is right about hell [in his recent book *Love Wins*] . . . . Why not close up the churches?"[7]

Consequently, both Annihilationism and any form of Universalism are viewed as extremely dangerous. Even the proponents of these two views admit that the necessity and sense of urgency for world missions and the motivation for risking one's life to go out into a 10/40-window country are lessened, or at least hindered, with just the entertainment, not to mention the allowance, of either of these two viewpoints.

Fact is, Exclusivists are greatly threatened by these two views. They fear not only what might happen to the zeal for missions and evangelism, but also the effect on churches and denominations if just a slight switch from eternal conscious punishment to Universalism or Annihilationism were to take place. Some have echoed *Time's* sentiment and declared that we'd have to "close all our churches and pull all our missionaries off the field since 'the world is saved; they just don't know it!'"[8]

Hell has been and still is the great negative incentive, prod, spur, hammer, and driving and motivating imperative for world missions and personal evangelistic efforts.

Others, on the other hand, contend that Calvin's view of predestination has had a similar negative effect. If certain people are elected by God for salvation and others are not, and if these final destinies have already been determined, why bother with missions or evangelism? If Christ did not die for everyone, why exhort the reprobate to "repent" and "believe?" Anti-evangelism is a major negative rap on Calvinism. Not surprisingly, weak evangelistic efforts characterize many Reformed congregations and denominations. On the other, other hand, Arminian groups espousing free will are generally recognized as the ones that historically have propelled people toward missions and evangelism. And many Christians like, if not love, the concept of free will. For one, it gets "God off the hook."

This is how Stetson, a Christian Universalist, explains one of the attractions of the freewill notion:

> Eternal hell . . . [then becomes] a matter of personal choice, not a decision by God to condemn anyone. Because God respects our free will, He will allow us to choose hell if that is our desire. . . . People like

the free will theory of hell because they don't have to think of God as a monster who holds people in the fire while they scream in agony for forgiveness, begging to have another chance that will never be given. . . . then we can write them off and stop worrying about them—they've got what they want.[9]

But I ask you, really and truly, how "free" is free will? It may not be as "free" or as absolute as we have been programmed to think. Let me challenge you, as Ludlow challenged her readers, "to consider whether there is ever such a thing as a totally free choice."[10] See for example John 6:44, 65; Romans 9:11-23 and 11:7-24—how much human free will is involved in those not drawn and enabled by God? Or in those unfortunate ones mentioned by Paul in Romans? Were or are any of them able to exercise their "free will" over and above and against God's sovereignty?

Most missiologists stridently support free will. They argue back, why would Christ have given the Great Commission if it were not necessary and human beings have the freedom of choice in this matter? And yet if a person could somehow be saved without hearing and believing the message here in this life, the Great Commission "would surely be superfluous."[11] "There would be no pressing reason to fulfill the Great Commission or to urge unbelievers to accept Christ in this life," they further contend.[12]

Is There Really No Second Chance in the Afterlife?

In one of his syndicated-newspaper columns, evangelist Billy Graham responded thusly to this question about people having a "second chance to turn to God after they are dead:"

The Bible does not teach that we will have a second chance after death to turn to Christ. Instead the Bible says, "man is destined to die once, and after that to face judgment" (Hebrews 9:27).[13]

With all due respect for Dr. Graham, while his cited verse does not teach a "second chance," it does not rule one out either. In another column he writes: "Nowhere does the Bible teach that we will have a second chance to be saved after we die . . ." (Hebrews 9:27).[14] Once again, this is true. But as we began to see in Chapter 10, nowhere does

the Bible teach that there will *not* be one either. Nor does it teach that
one's future and destiny after physical death is "irrevocably fixed and
eternally unchangeable."[15] I know of no verse that says any of this—even
the often cited 2 Corinthians 6:2 does not say or mean this: "today/now is
the day of salvation."

Ironically, Dr. Graham in a more recent column and in answer to the
direct question: "Does God ever give us a second chance?" answered in
the affirmative. He wrote: "God is the God of the second chance! The
Bible says that God 'is gracious and compassionate, slow to anger and
abounding in love, and he relents from sending calamity' (Joel 2:13)."[16]
Well, which is it, Dr. Graham? If God gives people a "second chance"
during this life, why not in the next life as well? What Bible verse would
you cite that precludes this from happening—i.e., that one's eternal
destiny is fixed at death (a pre-mortem finality of choice, termed in
theological circles as "restrictivism"[17])? Again, I know of *no verse* that
states that death brings an end to all opportunity for accepting Jesus, or
that anyone's final destiny is sealed at death.

MacDonald picks up on this theme and elaborates that "the
traditional view that there are no chances to repent after death is . . . very
hard to defend." He asks, "what possible reason would God have for
drawing a line at death and saying, 'Beyond this point I will show no
mercy to those who repent and turn to Christ?' . . . . There is no obvious
reason why God would draw the point of no return at death (or anywhere
at all). There is, however, a good reason for thinking that he would not—
namely, he is loving, gracious, and merciful and will accept all who turn
to him in repentance."[18]

Baker casts this issue into a comparative illustration. She brings up
the "deathbed confession" of someone receiving Jesus as Savior a minute
before he or she dies. She notes that "Christians aren't troubled by that
notion." Then why should they be troubled by the scenario of the same
thing happening a minute or more after someone dies, she queries? She
quips, "you see how wrapped up we are in the traditional sense of justice
as retributive?"[19] And yet Exclusivists are correct when they
dogmatically counter that "the idea that those who go there (hell) will
eventually be released and join the rest of humanity in heaven has not a
shred of biblical evidence."[20]

> **I know of *no verse* that states that death brings an end to all opportunity for accepting Jesus, or that anyone's final destiny is sealed at death.**

Likewise, where in the Bible does it state that there is an age of accountability? What is the age? Is a child headed for heaven one day and the next day after a birthday destined for hell? Does this make sense? Is this fair and just? Christian Universalist Amirault characterizes the existence of this theory in this manner: "it is just some people's way of trying to make God more humane than Hell teaching makes Him out to be."[21]

Dr. Graham's traditional call-upon-the-Lord-while-you-can conviction is simply an argument from silence. No where does the Bible state this. And of course, you can prove anything from silence. But as Grudem rightly admonishes, "Where Scripture is silent, it is unwise for us to make definite pronouncements."[22] Even the often-cited evangelistic verses in Romans 10:13-17 and 3:22 cannot be restricted to only trusting in or rejecting Jesus as Savior during one's earthly lifetime. Christian Universalist, Stetson, acknowledges our "natural human tendency to assume that death spells the end of our choices and our chance to grow and change. If a life was lived in sin and unbelief, we find it hard to imagine that something could change for the better in the afterlife—just like we cannot imagine a camel passing through the eye of a needle. But Jesus assures us that God has the power to make miracles a reality."[23]

Evidence for Postmortem Evangelism

While it's true, as I have conceded, that there is not abundant scriptural evidence for postmortem opportunities, it's not precluded, either. Marshall, however, is not correct when he argues that "there is no hint in the Gospels that he continues to seek out sinners in the next world until he is completely successful."[24] And Packer is just factually in error when he claims there "is no biblical support for any form of postmortem evangelism."[25] Fact is, in the Epistles there is more than a hint.

The Bible documents one major occurrence of what Erickson terms "postmortem evangelism," about which he states "has had a fairly long history, [but] only recently has it had any sort of popularity."[26] Sanders also points out that "this theory has some big names behind it" and "a key advantage of this position is that it allows for the evangelization of absolutely every single human being – every single person will come face to face with our risen Lord Jesus and will have to make a decision. Hence, this view affirms a totally universal evangelization." But he then disclaims that "the biblical evidence for it is highly questionable and it has a number of theological problems."[27]

As we have seen (see Chapter 5), "the earliest (patristic) fathers did not regard the grave as the dead-line which the love of God could not cross, but that the door of mercy is open hereafter as here."[28] The one major incident that Scripture records of postmortem evangelism was during the three days and three nights between his death and resurrection when Jesus descended into Hades and preached to the spirits of the dead (see 1 Pet. 3:18-20; 4:6; also Eph. 4:9).

Naturally, some scholars contest this interpretation and understanding. But as Hanson affirms, "one fact stands out very clearly from the pages of patristic literature, viz,: that all sects and divisions of the Christians in the second and third centuries united in the belief that Christ went down into Hades, or the Underworld, after his death on the cross, and remained there until his resurrection. . . . What did he do there? . . . he went down into Hades to preach the same glad tidings there, and show the way of salvation to those who had died before his advent."[29]

Christian Universalist, Stetson, who believes God in his sovereignty is free to do anything He desires as long as it does not conflict with his Word, sees Jesus' preaching to the spirits in that afterlife prison of Hades as "confirmation of Jesus' promise recorded in John 12:32 to draw all people to himself after leaving earth." He further sees this historical event as evidence that "even in death, in the spirit world, unbelievers and sinners can still have an opportunity to be saved by hearing the message of Jesus Christ delivered to them," which he terms "post-mortem salvation."[30]

But since many Exclusivists contest the meaning of these above verses and refuse to accept them as a postmortem precedent, they demand other "clear evidence that the process of 'final' judgement [sic] will lead to *all* who undergo it repenting and believing . . . but none has been provided. Otherwise, it makes better sense to interpret Romans 5 and similar passages in line with the very clear teaching of the rest of the New Testament,"[31] which is, of course, their view of Exclusivism. Hence, they conclude, "the church is left with the urgency of preaching the gospel to all the world both so that people may enjoy the blessings of salvation both here and hereafter and also so that people may not suffer the wrath of God and eternal separation from him."[32]

The Indictment of Lackluster Evangelism

But once again, the bottom line is, the Bible does not say that the un-evangelized will be lost unendingly if we do not go to them. The Bible just commands believers to "go" (Matt. 28:19-20).

So how are we Christians doing with our "Hell-to-be-shun-heaven-to-be-won-no-second-chance" oriented evangelism approach? Of course, the old saw is true—"there are three kinds of lies: lies, damn lies, and statistics." And the statistics do vary depending on whose statistics you look at. But take a look at these reports and statistics. As you do, the question that must be raised is: How representative are they—at least for us here in America?

First, as we saw in Chapter 1, pollster George Barna reports that "only 0.005 percent believe that they will be sent to the flames."

Secondly, "Southern Baptists evangelism statistics are grim . . . . That's the finding of a major new study . . . [that] demonstrates the Southern Baptist Convention is in an 'evangelistic crisis.'"[33]

Thirdly, "Americans are slowly becoming less Christian . . . 86% of American adults identified as Christians in 1990 and 76% in 2008."[34]

Fourthly . . .

> "95% of all Christians have never won a soul to Christ.
> 80% of all Christians do not consistently witness for Christ.
> Less than 2% are involved in the ministry of evangelism.
> 71% do not give toward the financing of the Great
>   Commission."[35]

Fifthly . . .

"One particular denomination did a survey on its leadership ministries (including deacons and elders). The results are as follows:

- 63% . . . have not led one stranger to Jesus in the last two years . . . ."
- 49% . . . spend zero time in an average week ministering outside of the church.
- 89% have zero time reserved on their list of weekly priorities for going out to evangelize.
- 99% . . . believe that every Christian, including leadership, has been commanded to preach the gospel to a lost world.
- 97% believe that if leadership had a greater conviction and involvement in evangelism, that it would be an example for the church to follow.
- 96% . . . believe their churches would have grown faster if they would have been more involved in evangelism.

Because of this, our results in evangelism have been mediocre, at best."[36]

But here's the additional rub. According to one missionary education group that agrees we Christians are not doing a good job in evangelism and have been the largest impediment to spreading the gospel, it also believes that Universalism would make things worse:

If God did have such an alternative plan, were He to reveal that to us, we who have proved so irresponsible and disobedient would no doubt cease altogether obedience to the Great Commission[37] . . . . Universalism . . . . may be the single most significant problem contributing to resistance to active missions even from within the body of Christ itself."[38]

This same missionary organization then compassionately asks, "Is it fair and just for God to condemn those who have not had an opportunity to respond to His offer of grace?" Perplexingly, it answers that "the Bible does not teach that God will judge a person for rejecting Christ if he has not heard of Christ . . . that God's judgment is based on a person's response to the truth he has received." In support they cite the scripture of "many blows . . . . few blows" in Luke 12:47-48[39] and "It would have been better for them not to have known the way of righteousness, than to have known it and then to turn their backs on the sacred commandment that was passed on to them" (2 Peter 2:21).

If this non-enlightenment theory is correct, does this mean people who have never heard the gospel could automatically go to heaven to hear and decide? Does this mean that the only condemning sin is rejecting Christ? If so, that brings up another major missions' problem. Erickson reckons that this realization would make "evangelism . . . not only unnecessary, but may even be improper."[40] He further delineates, "if indeed the only damnable offense against God were rejection of Christ, then we ought to leave the native alone. . . . because by informing him about Christ, we are placing his soul in eternal jeopardy."[41]

Complicating the task of world missionaries and personal evangelism even more, *Worldwide Perspectives* accurately recognizes the consequence of people being saved by the light they have through general revelation (Rom. 1:18-20), their consciences (Rom. 2:13-16), or with a second chance after death:

> A practical problem is that preaching the gospel seems almost criminal, for it brings with it greater condemnation for those who reject it, whereas they conceivably could have been saved through general revelation had they not heard the gospel. In any event, it certainly seems less urgent to proclaim the way of salvation to those who may well be saved without that knowledge. A mutation of this view is the idea that only those who reject the gospel will be lost. This viewpoint is not widespread because it makes bad news of the Good News! If people are lost only if they hear and reject, it is far better not to hear and be saved.[42]

Still, the words about hearing the gospel preached, in Romans 10:13-17 and Matthew 28:19-20 for example, are the most-cited passages employed by most churches and mission organizations to send people out to "save" those who will hear and receive.

In obedience, many Christian missionaries have gone out into mission fields. Many of them have suffered disfigurement, died, or been killed for the privilege of telling the lost about Jesus and his salvation.

Why did they sacrifice their lives for this cause? Is it because they believe that those who don't believe in Jesus, or won't believe, will be eternally damned to hell with no hope of escape and no second chance? One Exclusivist wonders "what these courageous saints (for example, The Voice of the Martyrs) would say to the teachers of the false doctrine of Universalism?"[43] Yet John Owen characterized this evangelical claim that the unrighteous dead are "irrevocably gone beyond the limits of redemption . . . [as] such a monstrous assertion."[44]

In obedience, many Christian missionaries have gone out into mission fields. Many of them have suffered disfigurement, died, or been killed for the privilege of telling the lost about Jesus and his salvation.

Seriously though, let's ask ourselves a hard question. Would God really entrust the eternal destiny of billions upon billions of the earth's inhabitants to only the less-than-enthusiastic evangelistic efforts of his Church—an institution that admits it falls far, far short of what it should be and is doing to spread the "Good News?"

Honestly, Let's Face Up to Our Deficiency

After church services are over on Sunday morning, few pastors or parishioners go out pounding on doors begging people to get right with God. Instead, we go to our favorite restaurant and eat with fellow Christians. Or, we go home and watch TV, do yard work, or play with the kids, etc. On our way home, we drive by or walk past thousands in our community. Seemingly, we appear indifferent to whether they will go to heaven or hell. Therefore, isn't it true that we really don't care? Or maybe we don't really believe they are going to hell, despite what our doctrine states? Honestly, what is our real attitude toward "the lost?"

Don Piper captured this all-too-common Christian reluctance and arguable hypocrisy like this:

We were sitting in a restaurant, and he paused to look around. "Yet here we are sitting in this place, surrounded by people, many of whom are probably lost and going to hell, and we won't say a word about how they can have eternal life. Something is wrong with us."[45]

One blogger discussing the "Age of Accountability" put the onus this way:

> If you really believe that all that are not born again by the time they die are going to be endlessly punished, then it HAS to be your responsibility to empty your bank account NOW! . . . . immediately! You must devote ALL of your resources and your every waking moment, your LIFE, to rescuing as many of earth's teeming billions as possible from this fate that you sincerely believe awaits them.

Perhaps, you consider this blogger's words offensive, over-the-top, or over-blown? But why? Doesn't he make a valid point? Maybe deep-down, as some have suggested, most Christians really don't believe this awful fate awaits non-believers? And given our less-than-enthusiastic or pathetic track record for witnessing, if you were God and desired that "none should perish" would you entrust the destiny of all people in the entire world (not to mention our neighborhood) to the "irresponsible and disobedient"[46] evangelistic efforts of most Christians? *Worldwide Perspectives* confirms these suspicions as it further laments:

> In a world in which nine out of every ten people is lost, three of four have never heard the way out, and one of every two cannot hear, the church sleeps on. "How come?" Could it be we think there must be some other way? Or perhaps we don't really care than much.[47]

Is it truly a mystery why those charged with sharing the Good News of salvation in Christ in our day and time spend most of our day and time doing other things, perhaps good things, but other thing, nonetheless? Stetson in the conclusion of his book, *Christian Universalism*, puts this damnation dilemma like this:

> Imagine if you really, *really* believed that most people are headed for hell, never to be released from an everlasting torment, because they have the wrong religious beliefs to obtain God's forgiveness for their sins. What would you do about it? How would you live your life?

Would you go about your ordinary business, working eight hours a day in a regular job and enjoying the recreational pleasures of a middle-class existence? Would you talk about sports and lawn care with your atheist or Buddhist neighbor, instead of the terrifying message of your religion? If so, you would be an uncaring hypocrite. Yes, that may sound harsh, but think about it.[48]

Amirault is even more critical and biting when he asks and asserts, "How can you not go crazy at just the thought of their fate? . . . If Hell is real and you have 'unsaved' family, friends, and business associates, when was the last time you went to them on your knees begging them to get saved? And if you haven't done this recently . . . don't you deserve to go to Hell yourself for being so callused and non-caring?"[49]

Fact is, Christians in droves are not only failing to take the gospel message across the seas, most of us refuse to take it across the street—to our neighbors. Hence, Stetson presses on chastising complacent Christians:

If the Ruler of the universe really is so merciless and unforgiving that he demands us to find the one and only true religion to escape a fiery doom, then it is everyone's responsibility as a compassionate human being to spend *every waking hour* warning people about the threat of eternal hell. . . . Getting in people's faces, disturbing the peace and shouting over and over again . . . [this] is tame in comparison to the actions that would be expected of us according to the basic principles of morality . . . . Saving even one individual from this fate would trump all other considerations.

He further charges that . . .

If eternal hell is the destiny of most people—or even a *possible* destiny for anyone—then it would be criminal to bring new children into this world. Who would be so callous as to risk creating a being that could someday end up being tortured for endless ages? . . . The birth of every new baby, instead of a cause of celebration, would be an event of sorrow and horror. . . .[50] (Remember Andrea Yates? See again Chapter 1, p-17.)

Fact is, most Christians have been hugely ineffective, if not totally missing-in-action, at sharing the so-called gospel message and in bringing people to salvation. Despite our poor record of spreading the exclusivist doctrine, however, most evangelicals firmly resist an annihilationist or universalist alternative. They insist instead that:

> The view that at least some of the unsaved receive a chance after death to believe in Christ is rejected by traditionalists and most conditionalists for the good reasons that "it is seriously lacking in exegetical foundation" and that it contradicts the solid biblical principle that "death represents a decisive and final step to final judgment."[51]

But Christian Universalists challenge these assertions and keep bringing up the problem of the souls of persons who lived before Christ, aborted babies, those dying in infancy, the mentally disabled, those who haven't reached the so-called "age of accountability," and those who have never heard the gospel. Exclusivists Peterson relents that the book *"The Nature of Hell* affirms a wider hope"[52] for them. Christian Universalists retort in kind, "well, if for them, why not for others as well?"

Fact is, Christians in droves are not only failing to take the gospel message across the seas, most of us refuse to take it across the street—to our neighbors.

But Traditionalists, inconsistently, balk at that idea. Why believe in God at all in this life, they complain, if we are going to have a second chance in the next life and be saved anyway? Belief, righteousness, and salvation in this life would be meaningless and pointless, they further contend. Cynically, they jibe; do whatever you want because there is no downside. There would be a great incentive to be wicked. Moreover, why would Christ have bothered to come to earth in this life and die on the cross if all are going to be saved anyway? He could have stayed in heaven and dealt with us there—after this life is over. Even worse (if that is possible) they hypothesize, moral and spiritual absolutes of right and wrong, saved and unsaved, and righteous and unrighteous lose all meaning and motivation without eternal consequences.

The bottom line is Exclusivists fear that Universalism of any type, and even Annihilationism to a major extent, would eliminate the

motivation for people to live a Christian life. In other words, it would
"totally annihilate ALL the moral and ethical force of the Bible's
teaching against ungodliness and wickedness." After all, if everyone is
going to heaven eventually, "why deny ourselves of the pleasures of this
life? . . . why bother being 'holy' and 'righteous' and 'godly' and 'pure'
in this life? Party Time! (if the Universalists are correct!) But it is
repentance time! (If Paul and the Biblical writers are correct!)"[53]

Additionally, why bother becoming a Christian before your die?
Why not just go out into the world and enjoy one's self? If we're all
going to be saved in the end anyway, what's the use of going through all
these things we have to endure to be righteous, many Exclusivists
charge? Anything goes! Everything is okay! Immature Christians could
easily be swayed by these teachings!

But Christian Universalists regard such talk as "ridiculous." It only
reveals someone "who has very little love for God and is serving Him
only out of fear of going to hell." If such a person had the fear of hell
removed, would he then "promptly tell God to go to hell" and immerse
himself in evil pleasures and fleshly pursuits? In other words, if the
wages of sin are removed, would multitudes immediately head out and
begin living it up? Christian Universalists, however, label such a person
"a hypocrite." He or she will always "find an excuse . . . . to relax and
live more carelessly."

**Why even bother becoming a Christian
before your die? Why not just go out into
the world and enjoy one's self? If we're
all going to be saved in the end anyway . . .**

So the answer to the bottom line question of "Why preach and teach
the Gospel and witness if all are to be saved ultimately?" for Christian
Universalists is: "the Christian life is so rich and beautiful and
worthwhile that it would be the only life to live, even if there were no
hereafter."[54]

Do We Have a (Methodology) Problem Here, Houston?

After all the pro and con rhetoric has been voiced about world missions, personal evangelism, and the potential negative effects of Christian Universalism and Annihilationism . . .

- "roughly 70 percent of today's world population is non-Christian,"[55]
- We are losing 6 to 7 out of every 10 children reared in the church by age 23.[56]
- In a 2003 poll among Americans, pollster George Barna found "only 4% of adults have a biblical worldview" and "only 9% of born again Christians have such a perspective on life."[57]

So given these grim statistics how can we not help but conclude that maybe, perhaps, possibly, our evangelistic methodology is off kilter? Surely, we can agree that Christian witnessing has fallen far, far short of our Father's revealed will and desire that none should perish but all should come to repentance and to the knowledge of the truth?

Once again, Amirault takes a hard stance. He charges that since "only one third of the world's languages have any written scriptures 2,000 years after the gospel was given to the Jews" and "if one MUST believe in the gospel to be saved, then God was very irresponsible in getting the good news to all mankind. . . . Furthermore, since most of the countries which presently don't have Bibles are non-white, doesn't that make God a racist."[58]

In the meantime, all sorts of salvation schemes have been devised to justify God in the face of dying infants, aborted babies, mentally disabled, the savages who have never heard, and even for those who died before Christ. Erickson introspectively speculates in this regard:

> Yet Abraham, Moses, David, and others did not know Jesus except as a "vague hope of the future which they proclaimed but only dimly understood." May it be that those who live after the time of Christ but never hear of him during their lifetime may be saved in a similar fashion to Old Testament believers?[59]

But Christian Universalists appropriately ask: How did those who died before Christ hear the gospel? And "why did God wait thousands of years and millions of souls after Adam's fall to provide the name and means of salvation? . . . Are all those before Jesus' birth damned forever because they never heard of the death, burial, and resurrection of Christ? Would that be just?"[60]

Once again, that is exactly why Jesus Christ Himself went to Hades and preached, most likely the gospel, to the spirits/souls of the righteous dead held captive in that afterlife prison (see again Chapter 4, p-83 – 1 Pet. 3:19-20; 4:6; Eph. 4:9)

Let's speculate here for a moment. Perhaps, there is a third view beyond Calvinism (predestination of elect and non-elect) and Arminianism (human free will). Is it possible that God's plan and methods may be far different, greater, and broader than we have realized? Perhaps his heaven is much bigger than we have envisioned? And perhaps the salvation of all those in our world today does not depend upon the hypocritical, lazy, and impotent evangelistic efforts of most of us in the church? Perhaps the realization of salvation is in much better hands than ours—in His? Perhaps we need to rethink and refashion the relationship between salvation, missions, and evangelism? Perhaps we need to re-address and reconsider the very notion of "what really is the gospel"?

Most notably, Jesus did not come into Galilee preaching Jesus. Nor was Jesus asking people the evangelistic question Evangelism Explosion has made so popular for several decades—"If you were to die tonight, do you know where you would go—heaven or hell?" Fact is, the gospel Jesus preached had absolutely nothing to do with his dying and going to heaven so that when we die we can escape hell and go to heaven—until approximately the three-year point in his 3 ½-year ministry.

For the first three years Jesus' gospel was all about the kingdom of God on earth, in this life, and as a there-and-then present reality (Mark 1:14-15). This gospel of the kingdom was also his central teaching, at the heart of his ministry, his worldview, and the very essence of New Testament Christianity. This gospel dealt with "the ethical question 'How then should we live?'"[61] Today, this gospel of the kingdom is no longer the central teaching of most of his church, at the heart of its ministry, its worldview, or its very essence. Red flag! What has happened? What has changed? Yes, we do have a problem here, Houston![62]

At approximately the three-year point in his earthly ministry, Jesus began teaching about his upcoming death and what that would mean—"From that time on Jesus began to explain to his disciples that he must go to Jerusalem and suffer many things at the hands of the elders, chief priests and teachers of the law, and that he must be killed and on the third day be raised to life" (Matt. 16:21).

Sadly, and for all practical purposes, most of Jesus' church today, basically and essentially, has abandoned Jesus' gospel of the kingdom (Mark 1:14-15). Instead, they have majored almost solely on this latter gospel of salvation. All of which has prompted some perceptive Christian writers to vocalize this methodological problem in how we moderns are presenting our faith to the world in these terms:

- Dallas Willard terms this kingdom deficiency, "the great omission" in his recent book by this title[63] and the primary reason "why . . . today's church [is] so weak." [Instead, the church is preaching the] "gospel of sin management"—in his classic, *The Divine Conspiracy.*[64]
- Darrell Guder calls it "reductionism of the gospel"—in his book, *The Continuing Conversion of the Church.*[65]
- Robert Lynn laments that "the gospel we proclaim has been shrunk"—in his article, "Far as the curse is found" in *Breakpoint Worldview* magazine.[66]
- Scot McKnight worries that "we have settled for a little gospel, a miniaturized version that cannot address the robust problems of our world"—in his article, "The 8 Marks of a Robust Gospel" in *Christianity Today* magazine.[67]
- Not surprisingly, therefore, George Barna's definition of a biblical worldview, mentioned earlier in this chapter, has no kingdom in it—i.e., he edited out the central teaching and worldview of our Lord Jesus Christ.

Question: why shouldn't this depreciation of the gospel be viewed in terms of the "other gospel" that Paul warned about in Galatians 1:8-9? Please keep in mind to be an "other gospel" it does not need to be totally different, only slightly.

In typical evangelical fashion, however, Jones maintains that his reductionistic, shrunken, and little gospel is *the* gospel by insisting that "Christianity is a religion meant to solve a sin problem. It is not a religion meant to solve all the problems of this world. . . . our ultimate mission is not to make this world a better place to live . . . . Our mission is to give every human being on earth the news that their relationship with God can be restored through Jesus' death on the cross."[68] But scripturally and factually, Jesus' presentation of the gospel was a both/and proposition and not an either/or. Later, and to his credit, Jones admits "it's never either/or in Scripture"[69] and asks a most pertinent question: "What business is Christianity in?"[70] My answer is: How about Jesus' nutshell admonition in Matthew 6:33 to put it most succinctly? And let's please note that the Greek word usually translated as "righteousness" in this verse is *dikaiosune* and can also and "easily mean *justice*. . . . Unfortunately, the translation *righteousness* has overtones of personal piety . . . . We need a stronger contrast between these works of piety and what constitutes the essence of the kingdom of God."[71]

Therefore and perhaps, it's our modern-day versions of Christianity and each of us—who "no longer feel the urgency to make evangelism their [our] top priority"[72]—who need re-challenged and stretched to re-think and change our approach to world missions and personal evangelism. Perhaps it is we who need to become fully consistent and compatible with Jesus' gospel as He presented it. And this was the presence of the redeeming reality of the kingdom of God—i.e., as God transforming this world and everything in it with our involvement in helping to make this happen. This gospel contrasts dramatically with the "miniaturized version" whose focus is only upon obtaining "fire insurance," securing a "get-out-of-hell-free card," and opening up an afterlife option or providing an election for a chosen few. Honestly and seriously, why don't we call this gospel reductionism and consequential evangelistic lukewarmness for what it is: "a dysfunctional version of Christianity that's ripe for reform?"

Perhaps it is we who need to become fully consistent and compatible with Jesus' gospel as He presented it . . . . the redeeming reality of the kingdom of God.

Let's Vote

This is a tough vote. Perhaps, it is the toughest to cast of the seven argumentative areas in PART III. Originally, I gave the nod to Christian Universalism because of the weakness of the exclusivist's "no-second-chance" argument, the deficiency of our defined-down gospel, and our well-recognized and poor performance record of evangelizing here in America. But my Bible study group convinced me otherwise. In the end I must agree with Erickson, the exclusivist's view is "the strongest motivation for evangelism."[73] Although it may be scripturally deficient, the strength of argument does favor the exclusivist view. Pragmatically speaking, re-thinking, re-gearing, and re-conceptualizing our approach to world missions and personal evangelism could prove difficult, if not overwhelming, for many. Why? Baker likely hits the proverbial nail on the head as she observes, "we hold tightly to our conveniently held beliefs, even if they don't make sense."[74]

In this regard, MacDonald cites a "more sophisticated version" of the exclusivist position on missions and evangelism:

> If we are honest, we should admit that there would probably be fewer Christians than there are now. This doesn't mean that all missionary activity and evangelism would cease. But it would surely be less common, since its urgency would be diminished. After all, what missionary would be willing to die in his or her own pool of blood at the hands of pagan tribes if the salvation of such tribes were in no way dependent on such risk?"

He acknowledges, of course, that:

> Universalists uniformly deny this connection, but common sense and study of denominational missionary activities clearly confirm a very high correlation between the teaching of universalism and a diluting or redefining of the Great Commission. Universalism does not logically entail a repudiation of a call to repentance and acceptance of Christ's Lordship, but these certainly seem to follow as a historical fact.[75]

Understandably, Christian Universalists are undaunted by this pragmatic criticism. They counter that their view "leaves the urgency of evangelism unimpaired."[76] And that "those who believe that Jesus is the

Savior of all mankind manifest more love towards their enemies than do serious Hell-fire types. . . . If we believe God loves all mankind and plans to save it, then we have no excuse but to do the same. However, if we believe God will cast away most of mankind, then we begin to manifest the very same spirit here on earth."[77]

Not all Christian Universalists agree, however, with the above assessment. For example, Thayer writes:

> We are told that the doctrine of unending punishment is the only safeguard of society, the great moral force of the world, without which it would speedily fall into irretrievable wreck and ruin. The truth is, this assumption is entirely barren of facts for its support. There is nothing in history to prove that believers in endless punishment are any better for their faith, or that those denying it are any worse for their want of faith. I do not say, now, that the belief of this doctrine makes people more vicious and wicked, though the last chapter shows that it would not be difficult to demonstrate that this *is* fact . . . so far as history speaks to this point, it gives unmistakable witness that the doctrine of endless torments makes people no more moral, and the absence of it makes them no less moral. . . . What a complete refutation of the assertion that the fear of hell is an effectual restraint on the wicked passions of men. . . . The belief of endless punishment does not tighten the bonds of morality, nor lead to a life of virtue; while, on the other hand, the disbelief of it does not loosen the bonds of morality, nor lead to a life of wickedness.[78]

And yet if the Christian Universalists' historical perspective is right, in that their position was the prevailing view during Christianity's first five hundred years, these years arguably were Christianity's most productive years (see again Chapter 5). Stetson admits that he understands "why Christians might worry that their faith . . . could be compromised or weakened by accepting universalism." But he contends "this problem originates from a lack of deeper understanding of what true Christianity is all about."[79]

Admittedly, and in my opinion, this area of argumentation is mostly a pragmatic and emotional argument that favors the exclusivist position. Fearfully and incessantly, they hammer on the possible negative ramifications Universalism of any kind has had or might have on world missions and personal evangelism—at least initially and given the way evangelism is currently structured. So, here's my vote . . .

Strength-of-argument advantage: Exclusivism

STRENGTH-OF-ARGUMENT ADVANTAGE
SCORECARD

	Christian Univ.	Excl.	Draw
Dispute over Universal Language?			✓
Power and Point of Parallelism?	✓		
One Way or Many Ways?		✓	
How Long Is 'Eternal' in Eternal Punishment?	✓		
The Annihilation Option?			✓
The Missions' Problem?		✓	
RUNNING TALLY	**2**	**2**	**2**

(How do you vote?)

Chapter 14

God's Revealed Character and Nature?

D oes anything about his [God's] nature give us insight into the number who will be saved?" It's a poignant and most appropriate question to kick off our last area of argumentation analysis. And this question is raised by an Exclusivist.[1]

Another exclusivist, J.I. Packer, calls "God's character . . . the true central battlefield" in this debate between Christian Universalists and Exclusivists.[2] Fact is, it's an argument that is broader and greater than the "broader-context-of-Scripture" argument appealed to by both sides. It's the *greatest context and contextual argument of all.*

Initially, this argument is a philosophical and emotional appeal, "How could God's love and justice possibly be made known in the everlasting conscious torment of human beings? . . . 'This question is also regularly cited by conditionalists as a starting point for their abandonment of the traditional position.' How is it just for God to punish for eternity sins committed in a finite lifetime?"[3] In defense, Peterson merely asserts that "traditionalists have affirmed that eternal conscious punishment will bring glory to God, the righteous Judge."[4]

Christian Universalists fire back that "the concept of hell paints a portrait of God as a vindictive despot incompatible with the loving Father revealed in Jesus. They further claim that the presence of people in hell throughout eternity contradicts the Christian truth that Christ has conquered every evil foe and God will reconcile all things in Christ"[5]

Even the Exclusivist Dr. Billy Graham supports this loving view of God when he writes: "that's who God is: our heavenly father, who gave us life and watches over us and loves us." He advises that "once you see God as your loving heavenly father, your prayers will never be the same."[6]

Christian Universalists bolster their fatherhood argument by pointing out that our all-powerful and all-loving God has not left us in the dark. He has emphatically revealed his character, nature, will, and desire on this matter. God the Father—"not wanting anyone to perish, but everyone to come to repentance" (2 Pet. 3:9). And God our Savior "who wants all men to be saved and to come to a knowledge of the truth" (1 Tim. 2:4).

But is this twice-stated will and desire of God only a wish and an empty one at that, as Exclusivists would have us believe? Is it possible that God might be disappointed and not get what He wants because rebellious human beings forever thwart his will and desire? Is God's will and desire not supreme over all human free will? If so, why would He create a world and set up a redemptive system in which his will and desire would not be met?

Exclusivists steadfastly maintain that God has not "decretively willed everyone to be saved." If He had, "*then* all would be saved." But "Christ's cross-work is intended for the elect only. . . . the doctrine of particular redemption!"[7] A few pages earlier, however, this Exclusivist author admitted that "Of course God is perfectly free to have a saving mercy on all if he so desires." Well, reply Christian Universalists, God has so stated that He so desires! But this Exclusivist refuses to budge. He persists to believe "there to be overwhelming Scriptural evidence to suggest that God does not have a saving mercy on all."[8]

Other Exclusivists posit that God has different types of wills. So Chan suggests that "it's helpful to consider what theologians have called God's *moral* will and His *decreed* will. Some things may be part of God's desire for the world, and yet these desires can be resisted. . . . His *moral* will—is resisted."[9] In a footnote, Chan cites "First Thessalonians 4:3—'For this is the will of God, your sanctification: that you abstain from sexual immorality.'" Wittmer also terms this difference as being "between God's hidden, sovereign will and his revealed, moral will." Then he elaborates that "God's sovereign will includes whatever happens in our world, whether good or bad." Next, however, he claims "we are responsible for God's revealed will, which, among other things, tells us that God wants all to be saved."[10] But the Bible never so qualifies, categorizes, or bifurcates God's will in this manner. So who are we to make this arbitrary distinction? Perhaps, indeed, God's moral will of "sexual morality" will be realized eventually in every individual along with their salvation in the afterlife?

Sanders, on the other hand, attempts to explain away these two desire verses by taking this freewill angle:

> Scripture presents us with a God who makes himself vulnerable to being hurt by creating beings who have the freedom to reject him. This God takes risks and leaves himself open to being despised, rejected and crucified. . . . making it possible that his every desire may not be fulfilled. . . . That is the price God was willing to accept in deciding to create this sort of world. . . . In other words, God is vulnerable and his will is defeated by human sin every day."[11]

Is Sanders right? Christian Universalist, Talbott, responds perceptively, "so the only insurmountable obstacle to the redemption of all, given his understanding, is God's own 'decretive will.'" He then cites Jesus' declaration, in response to his disciples question about "Who then can be saved?" "For mortals it is impossible, but for God all things are possible" (Matt. 19:26). Thus, as Parry & Partridge rightly deduce, "the debate about universalism is closely related to the debate about human freedom and divine sovereignty."[12]

So What Does God Have to Say about This?

Let's see, again, what God Himself has to say about his will and desires being accomplished.

> *"I say: **My purpose** will stand, and I will **do all that I please** . . . . What I have said, that will I **bring about**; what I have **planned**, that **will I do**"* (Isa. 46:10-11).

> *"who works out **everything** (all things) according to **the plan (purpose) of his will**"* (Eph. 1:11 *NIV-KJV*).

For more verses just like this, see again Chapter 6, pp-30-33 (Job
23:13; 42:2; Psa. 33:11; 115:3; 135:6; Isa. 14:24, 27; 55:11; Lam.
3:21-24; Dan. 4:35; Matt. 6:10; Gal. 1:4; Eph. 1:5, 9-11; Phil. 2:12-
13; also 2 Tim. 1:9).

Really and truly, how can we small specs of dust stuck on the surface
of planet Earth say it isn't so, it isn't going to happen, and come against
"the unchanging nature of his purpose" (Heb. 6:17)? Given the plethora
of affirming verses above, can there be any uncertainty or doubt here that
God will *not* accomplish what his heart desires? Furthermore, what about
"the secret things [that] belong to the LORD our God"? (Deut. 29:29)? Is
it possible that God's thoughts and ways are not ours and are higher—
perhaps much higher—than ours in this matter (Isa. 55:8-11)?

Seriously, shouldn't these scriptures and character-and-nature-of-
God revelations seal the deal? Shouldn't they confirm that all human
beings are going to be saved, eventually, somehow, someway? How can
we humans possibly underplay, twist, override, or trump these divine
revelations with any other scripture or stroke of human logic? Is it
possible we have misunderstood and misinterpreted God's will and
desire and purpose and plan, whether we like it or not? Or, does God just
desire to save all but can't? And if He can't, what do we do with verses
like Romans 11:32—"For God has bound all men over to disobedience
so that he may have mercy on them all." Perhaps we would be wiser to
just "let God be true and every man a liar" (Rom. 3:4). Remember, the
crux of this issue is not _can_ God save everyone. He can! The crux is: _will_
everyone be saved in accordance with his revealed will and desire?

Sincerely and honestly, let's stop and think about all this for a
moment. Shouldn't these scriptures and divine revelations at least give us
a cause for pause before advocating something that is contrary to them?
If, for example, some people go to hell who have never heard of Jesus
Christ during their lifetime, doesn't this go against God's revealed will
and desire, as well as against his character and nature?

Moreover, is God revengeful? Will He, for example, predestine four
generations of children to unending damnation in the afterlife because
some forefather ticked Him off (Exod. 20:5; 34:7; Num. 14:18; Duet.
5:9; Jer. 32:18)? Can people's freewill actions take God by surprise?
Does endless torment and punishment for finite transgressions serve any
remedial or glorification purpose? These are all serious questions relating

to the character and nature of God and his power. And they are answered differently by the opposing sides in this great debate.

So will God's ultimate intention, purpose, will, and desire be finally realized or thwarted? Will He just, therefore, be content with torturing forever or doing away entirely with his enemies? Baker believes that if "in the end God's will to save all people goes unfulfilled" this "puts God's power and goodness in doubt."[13]

Shouldn't these scriptures and divine revelations at least give us a cause for pause before advocating something that is contrary to them?

Let's also keep in mind one other revealed and prominent admonition in Scripture. God commands us to love our enemies (Matt. 5:44) and forgive them (Matt. 6:14-15). He has put his Spirit, power, and love in our hearts to enable us to do just that. However, if He condemns his enemies to an eternal destiny of punishment and suffering, or annihilates them for imputed sin and temporal sins, are we to love more than He does?

In this regard, Erickson asks these paradoxical questions. "Does God prescribe different standards for us than what he practices himself? . . . . Did not Jesus teach that we are to forgive those who wrong us, to love not only our friends but also our enemies? How then are we to understand a God who apparently does not love his enemies, who takes vengeance on them, and eternally so, who is never satisfied with the punishment of these people?"[14]

McLaren states this paradox this way. "Do you think God would require us to forgive and then be unwilling to do the same?" Or, if "God doesn't want people to go to hell" is He "forced to do so against his will . . .?"[15]

Following this kind of logic, Christian Universalist, Amirault, emotionally confronts Exclusivists by exhorting them, thusly:

- "How many loving parents do you know who would endlessly torture/punish any of their children because the children did not obey or love their parents?

- How many loving parents do you know who would annihilate
  their children because they did not do what they were told? . . .
- God is LOVE! That's His nature. . . . What is it about us that
  causes us to think the worst about our heavenly Father instead of
  the best? . . . .
- This God tells us to love our enemies while He endlessly tortures
  His?
- Satan, using traditional Christianity, has made us believe that our
  God is a hypocrite who tells us to do something that He is not
  willing to do Himself.
- This God's love is clearly VERY conditional, yet He demands
  we love Him unconditionally . . . . People are worshipping false
  images of God.
- As a result, they are under the power of the lie, not under the
  power of the Holy Spirit."[16]

Strong words, yes. But are they true or false? Hell yes? Hell no?

Traditionalists retort, in almost a knee-jerk fashion, that God doesn't send anyone to hell. They go on their own, by their own willful choice not to accept God's provision. But again, what about those who didn't have an opportunity to choose? Do we just write them off to predestination (Rom. 9:14-26)?

Exclusivists, like Lutzer, try to "ease" their minds about God's supposed punishment-demanding character and nature by suggesting "we should not be surprised that God allows multitudes to live in eternal misery. [Because] Think of the vast amount of suffering (preventable suffering, if you please) that God has allowed on this earth. . . . If God has allowed people to live in untold misery for thousands of years, why would it be inconsistent for Him to allow misery to continue forever?[17]

Let's Get Brutally Honest

*This is God's universe, and He is doing things His way. You may
think you have a better way, but you don't have a universe.*
—J. Vernon McGee[18]

Yes, our wills and desires may be different from God's on this matter. We want to be saved from something. Therefore, we require that some others not be. But isn't this the height of selfishness or religious pride? Wasn't a similar exclusivist mindset the problem with the 1st-century religious Jews who refused to accept Jesus as the Messiah and the type of kingdom He was bringing because He was including the Gentiles? Even more, doesn't Exclusivism go against God's revealed will, desire, purpose, character, and nature?

Billy Graham's wife may have it right as Dr. Graham shared in one of his recent columns: "My wife used to say that we're all going to be surprised when we get to heaven because we'll see people there whom we never expected to see! God's grace is far greater than our limited vision."[19]

Yes, I think many of us would agree that the extent of God's grace, mercy, love, justice and wrath may be far different and greater than our limited earthly view and our evolved church traditions. Surely God's loving offer of mercy cannot be limited, scripturally, to only our term of life on this earth.

When all is said and done, the bottom line is this. God is sovereign. He can do whatever He wants—as long as it does not contradict his revealed Word. And salvation is from and by Him. It is not from or by us humans. It's his gift and his work. And He has the right to do with his creation whatever He chooses, whether we agree or not—see Romans 9:19-21 for instance.

If He can impute sin through Adam, He can impute righteousness through Christ to whoever He desires, regardless of what we think or can grasp. Who now among us would deny that God is big enough to accomplish his revealed will, desire, and purpose? Who would contend with Him that He cannot give "life to all things" (1 Tim. 6:13), have "mercy on them all" (Rom. 11:32), "reconcile to himself all things" (Col. 1:20; 2 Cor. 5:19), and become "all in all" (1 Cor. 15:28; Eph. 1:9-11)? Who would contend with God by claiming his grace is not greater than the consequences of Adam and Eve's sin—a system God Himself set up, sustains, and allows to continue? Who would challenge God by claiming that the overwhelming power of his grace does not and will not far exceed the power of sin and death as God increasingly becomes "all in all?"

Johnson finds that "it is hard to see how the gospel can be good news if the vast majority of people who have ever lived are condemned to an eternal hell."[20] Guthrie in his textbook *New Testament Theology* contributes this additional advice regarding the attributes of God, his glory, and Romans 11:33 and Isaiah 40:13-14 about God's "unsearchable character . . . judgments and the inscrutable nature of his ways:"

> There is a whole area of knowledge of God which is beyond man's grasp. God is in a sense incomprehensible, although the Spirit's revelations of him are sufficient for man's understanding of his redemptive purposes . . . . What he (man) knows is at most no more than a glimpse at the whole reality. A massive area of mystery must remain.[21]

And this "massive area of mystery" is what we have been and are continuing to re-explore and deal with in this book! It's the "mystery that has been kept hidden for ages and generations, but is now disclosed to the saints . . . . which is Christ in you, the hope of glory. We proclaim him, admonishing and teaching everyone with all wisdom, so that we may present *everyone* perfect in Christ" (Col. 1:25-28, *italics* mine). Would the God whose character and nature has been revealed to us on this matter of the extent of his salvation settle for less than what this verse proclaims? Would He allow this eventual occurrence to be undermined by his predestination innovation or human free will? Furthermore, where in this passage, or anywhere else in the Bible, do we find this presentation of "everyone perfect in Christ" limited to only this earthly life?

When all is said and done, the bottom line is this. God is sovereign. He can do whatever He wants—as long as it does not contradict his revealed Word.

Talbott, in reference to Romans 11 and from his Christian universalist understanding, speculates that "the *very ones* whom God 'shuts up' to disobedience – whom he 'blinds', 'hardens', or 'cuts off' for a season – are those to whom he is merciful. His former act is but the first expression of the latter, and the latter is the goal and the *purpose* of the former. God hardens a heart in order to produce, in the end, a contrite spirit, blinds those who are unready for the truth in order to bring them ultimately to the truth, 'imprisons all in disobedience so that he may be merciful to all.'"[22]

If that is true, this means that God's election "as Paul understood it, was inclusive, not exclusive. The election of Isaac and Jacob, for example, carried no implication of rejection for Ishmael and Esau, nor did the election of Abraham imply the rejection of all others . . . ."[23]

Perhaps, once again, we are the ones who need to take God's revealed will, desire, purpose, and character and nature more honestly and seriously. After all, He has told us that He takes "no pleasure in the death of the wicked" (Ezek. 33:11). And the notion of a huge portion of humankind being predestined to everlasting torture in hell (or somewhere) by his pleasure and for his glory is inconsistent with and contradicts his revealed will, desire, purpose, and character and nature— does it not? Hell yes? Hell no?

Grudem, a reformed theologian, is partially correct and partially incorrect when he writes, ". . . in the presentation of Scripture the cause of election lies in God, and the cause of reprobation lies in the sinner."[24] The whole truth, according to Scripture, is—God is in control of and totally responsible for the beliefs of all his creation (Rom. 9:14-26; 11:5-10, 23, 32-36; Prov. 21:1). Hell yes? Hell no?

Perhaps . . . we are the ones who need to take God's revealed will, desire, purpose, and character and nature more honestly and seriously.

On the other hand, Grudem is totally accurate when he summarizes that "we have no claim on God's grace whatsoever. Our salvation is totally due to grace alone. Our only appropriate response is to give God eternal praise."[25] Grudem also and properly recognizes that "it would be perfectly fair for God not to save anyone."[26] Then why wouldn't the converse be true as well—that it would be perfectly fair for God to save . . . 1/4, 1/2, 3/4, or 9/10 of humankind, or everyone? Hell yes? Hell no?

Let's Vote

In concluding this last analysis area, let's recap the issue of salvation in this succinct manner:

- Calvinists say, Christ died for <u>some</u> (but only the elect) and all other people don't have a choice in the matter.
- Arminians say, Christ died for <u>all</u> and all have a choice in this matter—some will choose the way of salvation, most won't.
- Christian Universalists say, Christ died for <u>all</u> and all will eventually be saved in accordance with God's revealed character and nature, will, desire, and purpose and his stated ability to accomplish all his purposes and desires.
- Others, like Erickson, simply believe that we must leave the question of eternal destiny of all people "unanswered."[27]

Who is right? This is a significant question. Maybe we need to try and see the extent of salvation more from God's side than from our side. After all, and once again, are not God's thoughts and ways higher than our thoughts and ways (Isa. 55:8-11)? Perhaps, He sees things and thinks differently from us, don't you think? At least that is my understanding of his declarative statements in this Isaiah passage. Notably, in the pursuing, studying, teaching, and writing of this book, my constant prayer has been taken from this passage: "Lord, may your thoughts be my thoughts and your ways my ways."

In my opinion, this argument area on the revealed character and nature of God is a bigger, broader, and greater-context argument than the "broader-context-of-Scripture" appeal that is advocated, again, by both Exclusivists and Christian Universalists. It's the *greatest context and contextual argument of all*. And given the fact that God has not revealed everything to us, his sovereignty must trump everything. What else could be greater or higher? Why do we hesitate to bow in submission to this? Shouldn't our theologies and beliefs be subordinate to his divinely revealed will, desire, and purpose? Is it, perhaps, our pride that has prevented us from honestly bowing in submission? Or, is it God Who has deceived us? Heaven forbid!

Exclusivist, Lutzer, may have put his finger on the crux of this perplexity:

If our concept of justice differs from God's, we can be quite sure He will be unimpressed by our attempts to get Him to see things from our point of view. No one is God's counselor; no one instructs or corrects Him. He does not look to us for input on how to run His universe.[28]

Or perhaps, Christian Universalist, Clark H. Pinnock's position on this matter also summarizes this possible reality quite well:

I believe God wants everyone to be saved and come to a knowledge of the truth (1 Tim. 2:4), that Jesus was lifted up to draw everyone to himself (John 12:32), and that God is not willing that any should perish (2 Peter 3:9). God's grace abounds more than sin (Rom. 5:20) and God sent his Son as last Adam, signaling the desire to turn things around on a large scale. It is inconceivable to me to imagine that this God who seeks out one lost sheep would leave millions without hope of salvation.[29]

And remember about our great and almighty God, "He does as He pleases with the powers of heaven and the peoples of the earth. No one can hold back his hand or say to him: 'What have you done?'" (Dan. 4:35).

In sum, and before we vote, here's a simple syllogistic presentation on this "mysterious" topic for your consideration:

Premise #1: God's revealed will and desire is that no one should perish but rather that every person be saved and come to the knowledge of truth (2 Pet. 3:9; 1 Tim. 2:4).

Premise #2: God also has said, numerous times, "My purpose will stand, and I will do all that I please" (Isa. 46:10 etc.). He also "works out everything in conformity with the purpose of his will" (Eph. 1:11, 5; 2:7).

Conclusion: God's revealed will, desire, and purpose will not be thwarted but achieved.

Therefore, my vote goes to . . .

Strength-of-argument advantage: Christian Universalism

STRENGTH-OF-ARGUMENT ADVANTAGE
SCORECARD

	Christian Univ.	Excl.	Draw
Dispute over Universal Language?			✓
Power and Point of Parallelism?	✓		
One Way or Many Ways?		✓	
How Long Is 'Eternal' in Eternal Punishment?	✓		
The Annihilation Option?			✓
The Missions' Problem?		✓	
God's Revealed Character and Nature	✓		
FINAL TALLY	**3**	**2**	**2**

(How do you vote?)

Of course, you may disagree with some of my votes and this scoring recap. But essentially what I end up with is a statistical draw, a non-conclusive result. All of which brings us to the topic of our last section in PART IV—after these two short addendums that I thought would be appropriate amplifications at the end of this chapter.

Addendum #1 – The Hitler Conundrum

Critical Objection: *"Okay, I can accept that almost all people are saved, but what about Hitler?"*

Christian Universalist, Stetson, offers up some possible insights as he proposes that "some people are burdened with a more rebellious flesh than others here on earth" and "the spirit of each person may also be relatively weaker or stronger."

The bottom line for Stetson is this: "I do not believe God would ever create a soul with the intrinsic desire to be damned. That would be incompatible with love and justice. . . . under the right conditions . . . . in the afterlife all souls will desire to be redeemed, and will be willing to do whatever is necessary to be reconciled and reunited with their Creator. In other words . . . God has programmed us all with a will to return to Him in the end. . . . [And] God gets what He wants, and He has a plan to make it happen—for *everyone*."[30] Including Hitler?

The bottom line for me is: If total reconciliation is God's will, desire, and purpose, it will happen regardless of what you or I think, believe, say, or do. As we have seen, there are many scriptures that seem to support this happening. They cannot be written off as only a "wish." They are divine revelation and more substantive than our human speculations. God's sovereignty must trump all else. So if we are going to err, wouldn't it be wiser for us to err on God's side? And I've not seen any satisfactory explanation against the argumentation of the above syllogism.

A friend of mine, who is struggling with this whole question of the extent of God's grace . . . and wrath in the eternal afterlife destiny for all people, summarized his struggle this way:

> I haven't shared this with anyone yet, but I really do not see a purpose in this life if God isn't reconciling everyone back unto Himself through the finished work of our Lord Jesus Christ. If anyone is eternally left behind, what was the purpose in allowing all of these millions, billions of people to be born, just so that He could make or allow them to suffer in the afterlife? Whether the suffering in the afterlife is temporal (then annihilation) or never ending, it really doesn't seem like the better plan that our awesome and all powerful God could have come up with for our Lord Jesus to be the Savior of the world, who takes away the sin of the world.[31]

Addendum #2 – Application of the Parable of the Prodigal Son

Stetson presents a well-worth-considering argument for God's revealed character and nature by utilizing one of the best-known and most moving parables told by Jesus. You can read this parable of the Prodigal Son in Luke 15:11-32.

First, Stetson asks, "who does the unmerciful older brother represent?" He suggests there are some people "who are never satisfied with God's limited judgment but always demand more and more vindictive retribution, a never-ending wrath without hope of forgiveness." But in the parable, Stetson contends, "Jesus was making the point that God is like a loving, compassionate father, who is always willing to forgive us when we make a mistake and are willing to admit it and change direction. Unlike earthly, imperfect fathers who in some cases might disown their rebellious children and never be willing to reconcile with them, God 'our Father in heaven' (Matt. 6:9) is better than that." He concludes that "the possibility of reconciliation is always available—never to be withdrawn."[32]

Secondly, Stetson extrapolates this parable further and cites Jesus' admonishments about repeatedly forgiving others (see Luke 17:3-4; Matt. 18:22). He declares "Surely, God, who is infinitely superior to us, could not do any less Himself! . . . . The door will always be open. Whenever we are ready to exit the hell of sin and return to our Father's house, we will find Him standing there waiting for us, with arms wide open, ready to embrace us in joyful reconciliation. Unlike the older brother in the parable of the Prodigal Son . . . the real God is infinitely more loving and compassionate and would not leave any of us outside His door in the hell of permanent judgment."[33]

"Who does the unmerciful older brother represent?"

Rob Bell, in his popular book *Love Wins*, also applies this parable to the extent-of-salvation debate. He compares the older brother to many Christians and Christian leaders "who are barely hanging on," who have been "slaving all these years," who have believed "the right things and so they're 'saved,' but it hasn't delivered the full life that it was supposed to, and so they're bitter." Hence, he cautions that "a quiet resentment can creep in that comes from believing that they're sacrificing so much *for God*, while others get off easy. Hell can easily become a way to explain all of this: . . . . but someday we'll go to heaven, where *we won't have to do anything*, and they'll go to hell, where *they'll get theirs.*"[34]

"The Lord is good to all; he has compassion on all he has made" (Psa. 145:9).

Critical Objection: But what about human sin and wickedness?

Stetson believes, "that human sinfulness is all part of a larger divine purpose, which we cannot fully comprehend while we are living on earth. 'For God has bound all men over to disobedience so that He may have mercy on them all. . . . For from Him and through Him and to Him are all things.' (Rom. 11:32, 36). . . . God is in control. Human beings are currently sinners because this is part of God's plan." He then and controversially adds, "Mysteriously, even Hitler was part of the plan."[35]

MacDonald utilizes another of Jesus' parables to convey the same character and nature of God issue with a twist: "This Father is a shepherd who, as Jesus taught, does not give up seeking his beloved, wayward sheep, but looks for it *until he finds it* (Luke 15:4)." But "the Lord is [ALSO] just" (2 Chron. 12:6b). Sin still has consequences, severe consequences. And justice is also part of God's plan of redemption. So as MacDonald also recognizes and as we shall see, "the love of God . . . is perfectly compatible with divine wrath and punishment (Heb. 12:7-11)."[36]

> *"For men are not cast off by the Lord forever. Though he brings grief, he will show compassion, so great is his **unfailing love**. For he does not willingly bring affliction or grief to the children of men"* (Lam. 3:31-33 *NIV*).

> *"For the Lord will not cast off for ever: But though he cause grief, yet will he have compassion according to the **multitude of his mercies**. For he doth not afflict willingly nor grieve the children of men"* (Lam. 3:31-33 *KJV*)

Baker makes an interesting observation about this passage. The Hebrew word translated as "mercies" in the *KJV* is *raham* "and comes from the Hebrew word for 'womb' or 'uterus,' and evokes for us a beautiful image of God's deeply felt compassion and tender love, just as the love between a mother and the child she carries in her womb . . . . God has the same kind of compassion for all God's children, the compassion that a mother has for her babies."[37] Thus, she advises, "I cannot emphasize strongly enough the importance of how we conceive of God, the image we hold dearest."[38]

Consequently, and as Christian Universalist, Talbott concludes, "All these texts [2 Pet. 3:9; 1 Tim. 2:4; Ezek. 33:11 and Lam. 3:31-33] seem to suggest that God sincerely wants to achieve the reconciliation of all sinners, and other texts, such as 1 John 2:2, further suggest that Jesus Christ suffered and died precisely in an effort to achieve that end."[39]

Johnson lends support to the topic of this chapter when he emphasizes that "the nature or character of God is an important consideration in assessing the outcome of salvation. . . . Whatever God does must be in accord with his character. It was out of love that God sent the Son to save the world."[40]

And "will not the Judge of all the earth do right?" (Gen. 18:25).

Fact is, throughout the Scriptures the cry of God's heart is restoration. It always has been (see for example Ezek. 33 and 37).

What's more, if God "makes known the end from the beginning," and we couple this revelation with his many assertions that "I will do all that I please" (Isa. 46:10), how can the final destiny of all humankind be contrary to his will, desire, and purpose? Seriously, and as the Apostle Paul rhetorically asks, "For who resists his will?" (Rom. 9:19b). Or, will everything eventually turn out like Rob Bell sarcastically writes, "this is the God for whom 'all things are possible'. . . . [But] Will all people be saved, or will God not get what God wants? . . . . Will God shrug God-size shoulders and say, 'You can't always get what you want'?"[41]

And "will not the Judge of all the earth do right?" (Gen. 18:25)

In our next PART IV, we will speculate on "how" God may get everything He wants as He brings all people to repentance, to be saved, and to the knowledge of the truth (2 Pet. 3:9; I Tim. 2:4). How might all this be effectuated in accordance with his will, desire, and Word?

PART IV: A SOLUTION OF SYNTHESIS

Chapter 15

Thinking outside the Box—
Like God

Yes, the battle lines are drawn. The sides are fixed. And the arguments are essentially exhausted. From the time of prominent early church fathers, nothing has been resolved or scripturally reconciled—until now.

In this great debate and stalemated stand-off between Christian Exclusivists and Christian Universalists over the eternal afterlife destiny of the lost and damned, we have tried to stress sound biblical hermeneutics in analysis of their competing and conflicting positions and pro-and-con arguments. And, yes, the stakes are high. But something is lacking.

When questions of the ultimate and eternal destiny of billions upon billions of un-evangelized and Christ-rejecting nonbelievers hang in the balance, more is demanded than human opinions, rote repetition of traditionally held beliefs, or the continuance of theological debates. After all, if we have received, accepted, and are now passing along erroneous answers, we may be misleading people, resulting in tragic and eternal consequences. Moreover, you and I will *now* be held accountable for how we respond to the information contained in this book.

So as we continue to re-explore the possibility that God's grace, mercy, love, justice, and wrath may be far different and more extensive than our limited earthly view(s), let's re-address how we might be able to honor all the demands of Scripture bearing on this issue and harmonize and reconcile them via a solution of synthesis into one consistent, coherent, Christ-honoring, Scripture-authenticating, and faith-validating view.

To get us started, I have identified and boiled down from all sides in this great debate what I am calling "The Twelve Demands of Scripture for Salvation and Eternal Life." I believe they are clear, emphatic, and inescapable. I also think they are exhaustive. See if you agree with them. Also can you think of any I have missed and that we must also satisfy? As an aside and while proofreading the manuscript for this book, my wife tellingly commented, "I can't wait to see how you synthesize all this."

Yes, the stakes are high. But something is lacking.

Admittedly, synthesizing the seven argumentative areas of PART III is a somewhat daunting task. As Christian Universalist MacDonald observes, "here, then, is a problem for all evangelicals; for, when taken at face value, the Bible *seems* to teach three things which *cannot* all be true." He cites these "three propositions:"

1. "It is God's redemptive purpose for the world (and therefore his will) to reconcile all sinners to himself.
2. It is within God's power to achieve his redemptive purpose for the world.
3. Some sinners will never be reconciled to God, and God will therefore either consign them to a place of eternal punishment, from which there will be no hope of escape, or put them out of existence all together."[1]

Another Christian Universalist, Talbott, echoes these same sentiments and terms these three propositions an "inconsistent set . . . . because at least one of these propositions is false."[2] And yet he admits that "the Bible teaches all three propositions."[3]

So are we locked into a hopelessly deadlocked stalemate that is not just difficult but impossible to harmonize or reconcile, as many would contend? Let's begin the process and see.

The Twelve Demands of Scripture for Salvation and Eternal Life

1. God's numerous statements that He will do all He pleases (Isa. 46:10-11; 14:24, 27; 55:11; Psa. 33:11; 115:3; 135:6; Dan. 4:35; Job 23:13; 42:2; Heb. 6:17) and "work(s) out everything in conformity with the purpose of his will" (Eph. 1:11; 2 Tim. 1:9). This includes God's "not wanting anyone to perish, but everyone to come to repentance" (2 Pet. 3:9) and "all men to be saved and to come to the knowledge of the truth" (1 Tim. 2:4), so that "all" who die "in Adam" will eventually "all" be saved "in Christ." (Rom. 3:23-24; 5:12, 15, 18-19; 1 Cor. 15:22-23).

2. Grace abounding much more than sin (Rom. 5:15, 20).

3. Jesus being God's only provision for and the means of salvation and eternal life as "the Savior of all men, and especially of those who believe" (1 Tim. 4:10).

4. A special-ness and incentives for those who believe, are saved, and obedient in this life.

5. Salvation only coming to a person after hearing about it (Rom. 10:13-14, 17).

6. Salvation only coming to a person after the Father having "mercy on them all" (Rom. 11:32), "drawing" (John 6:44), "enabling" (John 6:65), "un-hardening" (Rom. 9:18; 11:7-10), and/or "re-grafting" them in again (Rom. 11:23).

7. Salvation only coming to a person after a "willing" and conscious profession of faith and belief, and placing one's trust in Christ and his work on the cross and resurrection from the dead—all people must do this to be saved (Rom. 10:4, John 1:12; 3:15, 36; 6:47; 8:24). Those who do not so "believe" (per #5, #6, #7), are not saved, do not enter heaven, nor have eternal life. Instead, they are "condemned" (Mark 16:16; John 5:28-29;

Jude 4) and "God's wrath remains" on them (John3:36).

8. Given the paucity, if not total non-existence, of scriptural
    support for the orthodox, traditional, and modern-day doctrine
    and understanding of "hell," we must reconsider this mainstay of
    Christianity as *not* being part of God's plan of afterlife
    punishment and/or redemption.

9. But "eternal" judgment, punishment, loss of rewards, and fire are
    certainly real and part of God's justice and wrath in the
    afterlife—for both unbelievers and believers. For as the
    Scriptures state: "The law of the LORD is perfect . . . . the
    judgments of the LORD true and righteous . . . . By them is your
    servant warned; in keeping them there is great reward" (Psa.
    19:7-11). These must be retained as clear consequences not only
    of unbelief but also for disobedience. The question is, are these
    to be understood in retributive terms, in restorative terms, or
    both?

10. The individual reality frequently spoken of as both "perishing"
    and "destruction" must also be worked into this synthesis.

11. The fate of the "un-evangelized" (those who never heard about
    Christ or the gospel of salvation) must be better explained than
    has been done to date. These include those who died as: unborns,
    infants, young children, mentally disabled, pre-Christ heathen,
    and post-Christ heathen.

12. If all the above demands are true and reconcilable in a proposed
    synthesis fashion, then several other major concepts in modern-
    day Christianity will have to be readdressed and redefined in
    better agreement with what the Scriptures actually present and
    with more accuracy than what is currently being taught and
    preached today. These include: evangelism, missions, eternal
    security, the Great Commission, and even the question of what is
    the gospel.

My reflections on these twelve demands have led me to conclude that they all can be met, and a conservative, Bible-honoring, and reconciliatory synthesis achieved. Yes, I'm aware that this synthesis may arouse fierce opposition from Exclusivists. And I do find both perplexing and disturbing the idea that just entertaining this possibility (even from a conservative evangelical standpoint) might cause some to accuse me of forfeiting any claim to being an "evangelical" or even being a Christian. Hopefully, however, this synthesis exercise might give us a better, broader, and greater insight into how God's loving forgiveness and reconciliation *may* be consummated along and in harmony with his revealed will, desire, purposes, grace, mercy, and love, as well as with his righteous judgment, justice, and wrath.

If all the above demands are true and reconcilable in a proposed synthesis fashion, then several other major concepts in modern-day Christianity will have to be readdressed and redefined . . . .

DISCLAIMER: Just because these demands *may* be reconcilable and synthesizable, does not mean this synthesis is right. Nor that I am right. I know I don't have all the answers, not even all the questions. I am simply seeking truth in the midst of tumult. I am also aware that I may now be entering into territory no one else that I'm aware of has trodden or mapped. Yet I confess that I am compelled to see if all these demands of Scripture can be reconciled in a practical and Christ-honoring manner. I hope you are, too.

No doubt, what J. Barton Payne said about the field of biblical prophecy also applies to this arena of the afterlife destiny of all people, "no truly comprehensive study has as yet been undertaken. . . . There has been little attempt to synthesize the whole field . . . and there is a great need for a synthetic study and presentation . . . ."[4]

Nevertheless, let's now see if all this *can* be reconciled—via a solution of synthesis. In other words, how might it be possible for God to save everyone, eventually and in harmony with all the demands revealed in his Word?

"And, if it is hard for the righteous to be saved,
what will become of the ungodly and the sinner?"
(1 Pet. 4:18; quoted from Prov. 11:31).

Getting outside the Box

Unfortunately, we humans tend to box ourselves into narrow mindsets. Nowhere may this be truer than in the topic we've been re-exploring in this book—the eternal afterlife destiny of all people. In my opinion, we would do well to humble ourselves and keep this godly tidbit of "un-boxing" reality in the forefront of our hearts and minds as we seek to wrap up our journey of re-discovery—"'For my thoughts are not your thoughts, neither are your ways my ways,' declares the Lord" (Isa. 55:8).

Let's also remember we are delving into a mystery! (see again, Rom. 11:33-36). In reference to this passage, Johnson wisely perceives that "there is a wideness in God's mercy that is far beyond human understanding. His wisdom, knowledge, judgments, and understanding are unfathomable (11:33). How God will apply this universal saving benefit to all is not stated . . . ."[5]

Consequently, our problem-solving attempt and this synthesis approach may be more than some can grasp or handle. But for all of us, it surely is more than any human being can totally explain! And yet this verse must encourage us, "With God nothing is impossible" (Luke 1:37).

Let's also recall that the gospel of Jesus Christ is a message of reconciliation. Hence, our words and actions need to be consistent with that message as well as sensitive to its potential appeal to others. It has been well documented that many un-churched people are turned off by anything that smacks of exclusiveness and the arrogance that an "ins-vs.-outs" or "us-vs.-them" mentality projects.

In this last section, as we attempt to un-box our thinking and expand our imagining regarding the scope and extent of God's grace, mercy, love, justice, wrath in his offer of salvation and eternal life, let's again emphasize that Scripture does not limit when this can happen—now, in the future, in this life, or in the next life. As Erickson perceptively notes, "it may require an opportunity for faith after death."[6] Thus, we must not confine or limit ourselves to a traditional, boxed-in way of thinking and believing.

Thinking "outside the box," so to speak, means that we think outside the limit of this earthly life and into the unlimited realm of the afterlife. Who of us would doubt that this is how God thinks and acts? Perhaps, God's will, desire, and purposes extend beyond this life as well. After all, isn't this what the expressions "in heaven" and "under the earth" are all about (see again Phil 2:10-11; Rev. 5:3, 13)?

And yet Exclusivists, like Erickson, astutely warn us about the downside of trying to think this way, especially in regards to the "exclusiveness paradigm" (a box?), thusly, ". . . it is very easy to . . . think of one's own way as the right way, and indeed, as the only way. When something different was [is] encountered, it was [is] immediately thought wrong by virtue of being different."[7]

One relevant example of this type of negative reaction is the *Worldwide Perspectives* missions course. It teaches with great confidence and little, if any, support that "Universalism cannot be reconciled with biblical data."[8] It also adamantly admonishes that "we should refrain from such theorizing."[9] But as we shall see, their opinion may not be valid if we are willing to think "outside the box."

On the other hand, Galli in a somewhat knee-jerk fashion warns that "the problem with speculation is that it knows no bounds." If we allow "the universalist idea for solving the problem of unbelief is to speculate that God will eventually win people over after they suffer enough judgment. Why would we not then postulate reincarnation," or "suppose that all language of judgment is culturally conditioned, that in the end God doesn't judge anyone for anything? And so on."[10]

Thinking "outside the box," so to speak, means that we think outside the limit of this earthly life and into the unlimited realm of the afterlife.

But in this book, we do have "bounds." They are "The Twelve Demands of Scripture for Salvation and Eternal Life." Therefore, as we proceed together through this last section, let's do so with a sizeable degree of humility. After all, we are departing rather significantly from the mainstream of Christian tradition (at least after its first five hundred years – see again Chapter 5) as we . . .

- Seek a scripturally viable solution of synthesis to help us break out of our mental mindsets (box) in this two-millennia-long debate.
- Search for a resolution of how God may, indeed, extend salvation beyond those elected or those who choose it in this life.
- Hunt for a better, more biblically accurate, consistent, and reasonable way of understanding God's plan for dealing with the problem of sin and reconciliation.

MacDonald is most astute when he acknowledges the fact that, "the debate needs to move into a new arena."[11] And this "new arena" is exactly where we are headed. As we seek a resolution, a reconciliation, a synthesis to the tensions inherent in this debate, keep asking yourself these questions:

- If Universal Salvation is, indeed, God's plan, his will, desire, and purpose—why cannot He accomplish it?
- Will He fail?
- Can He be thwarted by human free will?
- Or, are we the ones who possibly have failed to properly understand and appreciate his revealed character, nature, thoughts, and ways?

Exclusivists Parry and Partridge, likewise, caution us about going this direction:

> This poses a problem for the universalist because it is not immediately clear how God could ensure all people will *freely* embrace salvation if he does not determine their choices. This has been a major reason for many contemporary theologians rejecting universalism."[12]

Obviously, such a harmony and reconciliation is clearly desirable, if it can be done without twisting or distorting God's revealed Word, and by staying faithful to its texts. And yet "many have resisted the urge to harmonise [sic] biblical teaching and have felt that the tension between texts must be maintained." All of which has led others into compromise and to equivocate that "the Bible hopelessly contradicts itself and so we must chose the texts which seem to us to be either more numerous, closer to the theological heart of the Bible or, slightly cynically, the ones we like best. Other texts must be pushed to the periphery."[13]

Still others have argued that eternal damnation and universal salvation are "an irreconcilable paradox" that "remains a mystery known to God alone"[14] and "two irreconcilable visions of the fate of humanity . . . . The damnation texts set out very clearly the fate sinful humans *deserve* whilst the universal salvation texts set out the fate that, by God's grace and through the atoning work of Christ, sinful humans will *actually* receive. Both damnation and salvation texts are important and both are 'true.'"[15]

Perhaps, the most appropriate way to end this chapter and set the tone for our transition into our final two chapters are these words from annihilationist Thomas Johnson:

> Our theology is continually being revised, modified, and deepened as we submit ourselves to God's word. It is not helpful, therefore, to come to the study of 'universalism' with our minds already made up, as is often the case. . . . it is best that we be both generous and wary in our reading of each other's interpretations of Scripture, especially on controversial issues. We should not too readily say that a particular view is unbiblical or without Scriptural warrant, especially if it is a view that is contrary to or challenges what we already believe.[16]

Onto a Synthesis

In our next chapter, we'll further boil down these twelve demands of Scripture into seven points of synthesis for addressing and documenting how all this *might, could, and may* happen without God violating, undermining, compromising, or conflicting with any scripture in his revealed Word, and as we "test and approve what God's will is – his good, pleasing and perfect will" in this matter (Rom. 12:2b).

Does Scripture, in fact, teach a wider, broader, greater and different view of God's grace, mercy, love, justice, and wrath than we've been led to believe? Does it provide a wider, broader, greater, deeper, and different theological grid that will allow us to make better sense of a wide range of seemingly conflicting and confusing themes and texts whose interpretations have been long debated and disputed?

**Obviously, such a harmony and reconciliation
is clearly desirable, if it can be done without
twisting or distorting God's revealed Word,
and by staying faithful to its texts.**

Clearly, the burden of proof rests mostly, if not squarely, on the minority view of Christian Universal Salvationism. It is, therefore, to this seemingly daunting task of resolution, reconciliation, and synthesis of "The Twelve Demands of Scripture for Salvation and Eternal Life" and how God *might, could, and may* just work everything out in both this world and in the afterlife that we next turn.

Chapter 16

Seven Points of Synthesis

*The great Christian revolutions come not by the discovery
of something that was not known before. They happen when
somebody takes radically something that was always there.*
—H. Richard Niebuhr[1]

Is God the Father of all, Christ the Savior of all, and heaven the final
home of all, or not? In this chapter, we will boil down "The Twelve
Demands of Scripture for Salvation and Eternal Life" from our last
chapter into "Seven Points of Synthesis." Once again, please do not
misunderstand or jump too quickly into an inappropriate conclusion. Just
because these twelve demands can be synthesized does not mean this
synthesis is right, or that I'm right. Never forget that we are dealing with
a mystery. But I do maintain that this synthesis contains no
contradictions or violations of Scripture. Once again, you be the judge.

Seven Points of Synthesis

1. **God's revealed will, desire, and purpose are supreme,
   knowable, and will be achieved.**

2. **Jesus Christ alone is the sole and sufficient Savior.**

3. **The 'elect' are saved in this life and have special advantages and incentives.**

4. **Sin cannot be overlooked; God's wrath, justice, and punishment cannot be jettisoned—for both the unsaved and saved.**

5. **Postmortem evangelism and redemption are not only possible but likely.**

6. **Annihilation, most likely, will not play a part in God's redemptive plan.**

7. **The gospel must be redefined for us to do a better job of evangelizing.**

Synthesis Point #1 – God's revealed will, desire, and purposes are supreme, knowable, and will be achieved. – On numerous occasions, God has stated in a clear and straightforward fashion that "My purpose will stand, and I will do all that I please . . . What I have said, that will I bring about; what I have planned that will I do." (Isa. 46:10-11; also Isa. 14:24, 27; 55:11; Psa. 33:11; 115:3; 135:6; Dan. 4:35; Job 23:13; 42:2). Also, the Apostle Paul confirmed that God "works out everything in conformity with the purpose of his will" (Eph. 1:11, 5; also see Phil. 2:13 and Heb. 6:17). Part of this achievement of God's revealed will, desire, and purpose is that none should perish but every person be saved and come to the knowledge of truth and to repentance (1 Tim. 2:4; 2 Pet. 3:9). Hence, this revealed truth cannot be ignored or lightly brushed aside as an empty wish or as unattainable. It must be honored and affirmed.

In my opinion, God's sovereignty and this revelation of divine providence is broader and greater than the appeal to the "broader-context-of-Scripture" argument used by both Exclusivists and Christian Universalists. It is the *greatest context* and *contextual argument* of all. When coupled with the known and agreed-to facts that not everything has been revealed to us by Scripture and God knows infinitely more than any of us, it must be held as supreme.

Still, much mystery remains (Rom. 11:33-36). And God is under no obligation to further explain Himself or his ways to any of us. We are accountable to Him, and not Him to us. Therefore, we must accept our limited knowledge in this area of the extent of his grace, mercy, love, justice, and wrath in the salvation of all people.

Perhaps the two major reasons for views to the contrary here are, as Amirault suggests, our: "failure to hold onto clear statements of God's sovereignty, foreknowledge, power, omniscience, purpose of creation, and unconditional love" and our "failure to believe direct statements of scripture declaring the ultimate salvation of all through the saving work of Jesus Christ."[2]

Consequently, this first synthesis point is a strong, if not the strongest, perspective and most convincing argument for Christian Universalism. Not only must it be honored, it must also be considered the overarching revelation to which all other passages of Scripture must be subordinated. This is true whether or not we desire this end result or can or cannot conceive of how salvation and eternal life might be made effectual for everyone, as Jesus Christ reconciles "all things" (Col. 1:20) to Himself, draws "all men to myself" (John 12:32), and keeps fulfilling his mission of doing his Father's will (Gal. 1:4).

Nonetheless, J.I. Packer correctly notes that the controversial issue here "is whether God has a universal saving purpose that he guarantees, by hook or by crook as we would say, to fulfill in every respect in every case . . ."[3] In answer to Packer, let's look more deeply into Jesus' parable of the lost sheep in Matthew 18:10-14 and highlight not only what Jesus proclaims, but also how He proclaims it.

In this parable, Jesus concludes by saying, "Even so it is not the will of your Father which is in heaven, that one of these little ones should perish" (Matt. 18:14). The phrase "not the will of your Father" is the proper rendering of the literal Greek (see *KJV* version). In literary style, this phrase is called a contrapositive. A contrapositive is used to make the meaning more emphatic, like John F. Kennedy's famous phrase, "ask not what your country can do for you . . . ." Biblical statements, too, are sometimes made more powerful by using a negative. Are they not? Instead of strengthening a point by using a superlative, the statement is emphasized by using a negative. "I am not ashamed of the gospel of Christ" (Rom. 1:16 *KJV*) is an example. What it really means is, I am exulting in it, I am proud of it.

Hence, the contrapositive phrase "not the will of your Father" makes the latter part of this declaration even more emphatic—"that one of these little ones should perish." And regardless of who or what we may think the hundred sheep represent (all people or only a chosen few), let's also note that this full statement is in complete harmony with the two statements of God's will, purpose, and desire cited at the first of this synthesis point (1 Tim. 2:4; 2 Pet. 3:9). So, if this is a correct understanding of this parable, we now have the strength and confirmation of a threefold witness (see Matt. 18:16 from Duet. 19:15; 17:6; also 2 Cor. 13:1; 1 Tim. 5:19; Heb. 10:28).

This revealed truth cannot be ignored or lightly brushed aside as an empty wish or as unattainable. It must be honored and affirmed.

Before going to our next synthesis point, let us note, once again, that some at this point, no doubt, will object and reject my whole synthesis approach out of hand. The authors of *Sense & Nonsense About Heaven & Hell,* for example, would argue that "we can speculate all day long as to whether God might have chosen to save people in another way, but the fact is that we have no reliable way of knowing, and in fact Scripture says he has chosen this one way and no other."[4] But let's see if this exclusivist argument still holds up as we continue assembling a reliable way of "knowing" that provides a possible biblical basis and explanation for how God *might, could, and may* save everyone, eventually—i.e., those who have never heard of Jesus and the gospel in this life as well as those who heard and rejected.

Synthesis Point #2 – Jesus Christ alone is the sole and sufficient Savior. – Jesus Christ's name is the only name and He is the only Person and only way of salvation and eternal life with the Father (John 14:6; Acts 4:12; 1 Tim. 2:5). The Scriptures on this are far too many, too clear, and too emphatic to side-step or deny. He is the only One Who died a saving death for all. And God in his sovereignty is free to bestow this salvation through his Son as a gift and as He desires.

Hence, salvation cannot be placed in the wider hope of pluralism or in the universality of general revelation. Neither of these avenues is sufficient. Both must be ruled out and in spite of Universalist Clark Pinnock's view to the contrary:

> God is always reaching out to sinners by the Spirit. There is no general revelation or natural knowledge of God that is not at the same time gracious revelation and a potentially saving knowledge. All revealing and reaching out are rooted in God's grace and are aimed at bringing sinners home.[5]

Hence, the incomparable uniqueness and centrality of Jesus Christ as the sole source of salvation is maintained in this synthesis. Please do not misconstrue the shortness of exposition or amount of space devoted to this point of synthesis as indicative of its significance. Quite to the contrary, the saying "less is more" is certainly applicable here.

Synthesis Point #3 – The 'elect' are saved in this life and have special advantages and incentives. – Those who believe in Christ and are saved during this life are, most likely, those whom the Bible calls "the elect" (Col. 3:12 *KJV*; Matt. 24:22), the "firstfruits" (Rom. 8:23; 1 Cor. 15:23; Jas. 1:18), "the firstborn among many brothers" (Rom. 8:29), the "remnant" (Rom. 11:5), "his sheep" (John 10:26-29), and possibly even "the many" (Rom. 5:19) and "the church of the firstborn" (Heb. 12:23). Whether this happens by predestination or by freewill choice is not pertinent here and is beyond the scope of this discussion. Upon physical death, they immediately go to heaven to face the judgment and a possible time of going through some fire (Heb. 9:27; 1 Cor. 3:12-15).

But special advantages and incentives are available for this group. That is what the word "especially" means in the Apostle Paul's statement in 1 Timothy 4:10 about "the living God, who is the Savior of all men, *especially* of those who believe. "The others, however, (the rest of the harvest) may be brought in later (John 10:16).- *Talking about Gentiles*

At this point, some may still be wondering why anyone should become a Christian in this life, live a righteous life, and serve God now if all are eventually going to be saved. Of course, it is true that some people receive Christ and become Christians for fear of going to "hell" and being "eternal" punished if they don't. Perhaps if they thought there were no prospects of punishment in the afterlife many of them might promptly tell God to go to hell and they would go live for the devil. But the question of why become a Christian now in this life is a valid question.

Below is a bullet point list of reasons. I believe you will find plenty of motivation and wonderful reasons for being a Christian in this life as well as for evangelism and missions apart from saving people from a so-called hell. Perhaps, you can think of more?

A Wrath to Avoid

- To be saved from God's wrath in both this life and in the afterlife.
- There is still a punishment (not "hell") to shun and a heaven to be won (as the saying goes), even if this punishment is not unending but only age-ly or age-enduring (*aionios*).
- Those who believe in this life and whose names are "found written in the book of life" have already passed through the "second death" (when born again) and will not be thrown into the "lake of fire" in the afterlife (Rev. 20:14-15).
- Most likely, this lake of fire is God Who is "a consuming fire" (see Chapter 4, p-91f). And even if all will eventually be saved, it is still a "dreadful thing to fall into the hands of the living God" (Heb.10:31). But unless people repent and believe here in this life, they will continue to go through varying amounts and durations of this punishment, purification, refinement, etc. in the lake of fire in the afterlife before entering heaven itself.
- Hence, sparing people from this fate of punishment would still be motivation for missions and evangelism. These life and afterlife degrees of punishment and suffering are well worth avoiding or, at least, minimizing. Therefore, this destiny of postmortem punishment still needs to be made known to both non-believers and believers alike.
- Divine punishment could be quite long and painful. And lest anyone should think otherwise, I am not encouraging immorality with this synthesis approach.
- But the Good News of salvation should not be thought of in mostly negative terms or just as a deliverance from punishment. Its positive aspects must be equally, if not more, proclaimed.

Life More Abundantly

- Jesus proclaimed, "I am come that they might have life, and that they might have it more abundantly" (Matt. 10:10 *KJV*).
- We who believe in his life have the privilege of entering his kingdom and experiencing God's love, grace, mercy, forgiveness, blessings, power, and more, here and now.
- True followers of Christ in this life have the privilege and joy of already walking with God and being brought into a closer relationship with Him.
- They have the opportunity to lead a "blessed life" – "Now that you know these things, you will be blessed if you do them" (John 13:17).
- Evangelistically, we should not deny others the opportunity for joy, peace, and power that the knowledge of Christ and fellowship with God in this life offers by not telling them about it and not modeling it and witnessing about it.
- But there is more, much more!

Rewards

- As Origen taught, in heaven there are and will be "differing degrees of blessedness . . . . 'a different glory will be given to every one according to the merits of his actions; and every one will be in that order which the merits of his work have procured for him.'"[6]
- As God's ambassadors on this earth (2 Cor. 5:20), we will be rewarded and/or suffer loss in heaven depending upon our faithfulness in witnessing (Acts 1:8; 2 Cor. 5:10; Col. 3:23-24; 1 Cor. 3:12-13). All believers will be held accountable.
- There is a "fire" and "loss" from this fire of some magnitude for believers to which they will be subjected—"suffer loss; but he himself will be saved yet so as through fire" (1 Cor. 3:14, 15). This loss may be a loss of rewards, blessings, privileges, opportunities in heaven for all eternity.
- But everyone, including believers, will go through God's "fire" and possibly suffer "loss" of some sort before being "saved yet

so as through fire" (1 Cor. 3:14, 15). This loss may be unpleasant if not painful. Most likely, this fire is one of purification and refinement. But it could also be one of punishment as well (Luke 12:47-48).

Store Up Treasures in Heaven

- Believers in Christ in this life have the special opportunity and advantage to store up rewards, blessings, and special privileges in heaven that they will be able to enjoy for all eternity.
- That's why Jesus commands his followers to "store up for yourselves treasures in heaven," (Matt. 6:20a).
- This is quite an incentive (when you really think about it) and part of the motivation for all believers in this life to go and be a blessing and make *disciples*, not just converts saved from "hell," of all nations, regardless of the eventual outcome of God's saving work (Gen. 12:3; Matt. 28:18-20).
- Your time spent on earth storing up rewards or wasting your time and efforts on things that will result in loss will determine how you spend eternity. If you find this difficult to believe or appreciate now, perhaps you won't after you have been there "ten thousand years" as one of the lines in John Newton's (1725-1807) famous hymn, "Amazing Grace" proclaims.
- So regarding the storing up treasures in heaven and avoiding losses—would you like to know about this now while you can still do something about it? Or, would you rather wait until later in the afterlife when you can't?
- But how do we do this?

Being a Fellow Worker in the Kingdom

- When we are saved in this life, we have the opportunity to become "fellow workers for the kingdom of God" (Col. 4:11).
- Baker amplifies how this works. Our salvation "makes us God's partners in the work of transforming the world into a better place for all to live . . . . makes us God's agents, God's ministers of reconciliation—not so that we can work to keep people out of

hell, but so we can transform the world through reconciliation. . . . It's not about fire insurance. It's about transformed life, kingdom-of-God growth, binding up the brokenhearted, proclaiming liberty to the captives and freedom to prisoners. . . . so that God may be glorified."[7]

- This is how we can have life and have it more abundantly, store up treasures in heaven for all eternity. We send it on ahead by our "good works" (Eph. 2:10 – more on this in Chapter 17).
- Thus, as MacDonald recognizes, we are: "playing a part in God's glorious purpose of reconciling the whole creation (Col. 1:20). . . . Working with the Spirit . . . ."[8]
- So Christians in this life have been "especially" called by God. Therefore, we have the opportunity to be "fellow workers" with Christ in this age and in his kingdom for the purpose of presenting and advancing the gospel of the kingdom and of salvation to our family, friends, neighbors, and to the ends of the world.
- All Christians in this life need to be actively involved in this purpose. It involves the alleviating or eliminating of evil, injustice, oppression, etc. in our world, here and now—for which we will be rewarded (or suffer loss) later in the afterlife (see again Eph. 1:11-14).

What about non-believers in this life who become postmortem believers? Will they sharing in the heavenly rewards, blessings, and special privileges with pre-mortem believers? My guess is: they may not, or at least not nearly as much, since they were not able through their "good works" during their earthly lives to "store up for yourselves treasures in heaven" (see Eph. 2:10; Matt. 6:19-20). But I'm content to leave this up to God as well.

When we are saved in this life, we have the opportunity to become "fellow workers for the kingdom of God" (Col. 4:11).

Synthesis Point #4 – Sin cannot be overlooked; God's wrath, justice, and punishment cannot be jettisoned—for both the unsaved and saved. – Some may fear and ask, does salvation of all people negate God's wrath, justice, and punishment? Commonly, Universalism of any sort is criticized for undervaluing the power and severity of sin. But in this synthesis, sin cannot be overlooked or undervalued.

Not only does sin corrupt, it is harmful and destroys much in this life. It is also utterly offensive to God. Hence, divine punishment for sin and sins is a just and fitting response from God. This traditional concept is totally scriptural and has a prominent place and role in the afterlife—with one major, scriptural, and applicational caveat—"but where sin abounded, grace did much more abound" (Rom. 5:20). We cannot put an earthly limit on God's grace, mercy, and love.

Furthermore, a strong scriptural case can be made that some sins are worse than others, even in God's eyes (as opposed to a traditionally posited notion and retributive model of hell that all sin/sins are equally bad and must be punished, equally and infinitely). Be assured that salvation is not automatic for everyone and heaven may not be initially open to the un-evangelized—those who never heard of Jesus or the gospel and died as unborns, infants, young children, mentally disabled, pre-Christ heathen, and post-Christ heathen. Certainly, it won't be open to those unbelieving, profane, and condemned persons who heard the gospel message during their earthly lives and rejected Christ. And yet all in both groups died and still die in their sin state and sins.

Long before He created human beings and gave us some sort of free agency, God in all his power and foreknowledge knew that we would sin. He could have prevented it. But He didn't. Instead, He placed Adam and Eve into a world that He created and that would allow sin to happen. It did. Scripture testifies to God's foreknowledge in all this. That's why we are told that Christ was "slain from the creation/foundation of the world" (Rev. 13:8b; 1 Pet. 1:20).

Yes, sin came into the world through us human beings. But the evil to produce that sin was place here by God Himself in the form of a tree (Gen. 2:9, 16-17). This tree was part of his "very good" creation (Gen. 1:31). Regarding God's purpose for doing this, some theologians have suggested what "may sound ghastly to many readers" and that is "God specifically wants . . . the evils in the world . . . to exist." They advocate what's called a "'soul making theodicy.' According to this theory, God wanted suffering and evil in order to 'build' our characters, make us more mature."[9] In other words, evil helps us grow into the likeness and character of Christ. Hence, "our light and momentary troubles are achieving for us an eternal glory that far outweighs them all" (2 Cor. 4:17; see all of Paul's exposition in 2 Cor. 4).

Whether you can subscribe to this theory or not, the historical fact is, ever since Adam and Eve's sin, Scripture clearly affirms that all people have been, will, or are being raised (depending on your eschatological view) some "to live" but others "to be condemned" (John 5:29). The question next becomes, can those "condemned" later be reconciled to God, redeemed, and saved? After all, this whole, "very good" world, as well as heaven and the afterlife, is of God's making and under Christ's control.

Be assured that salvation is not automatic for everyone and heaven may not be initially open to the un-evangelized . . .

Consequently, Baker asks three most astute questions, "Does the defeat of sin within a person take place only in the temporal realm, within time itself, while we live in this body? Why should it? If we are beings who live on after death, like the Bible seems to say, what makes us think that God limits the bestowing of eternal grace to one time period?" She answers with a fourth question, "Why can't God extend the offer of grace, forgiveness, and reconciliation through Jesus even at judgment—when all will be laid bare, when all persons will see the extent of their sin and the extravagance of God's love? If the effectiveness of Jesus' work on our behalf extends even beyond the grave, that means that no one is ever beyond grace."[10]

On the other side of the coin, Baker affirms that all people "have to answer for the terrible things they've done. . . . God will hold the guilty accountable . . . . the victims need to know that God looks out for them too, right?"[11] Therefore, I contend that God's justice is not just remedial, it is also "retributive." Although Baker does not agree with this form of divine justice, she defines "retributive justice" as "any form of justice that puts things right through punishment or payback, an eye for an eye."

And yet she assures us that "victims need justice." But Baker questions, "must that justice necessitate eternal punishment?"

Another form of justice she calls "restorative justice. It is justice served by reconciling with the guilty and restoring relationship. This form of justice requires forgiveness."[12] In her opinion, "there's nothing redemptive or restorative about [our modern-day notions of] hell."[13] To counter this, she references Proverb 21:3: "To do what is right and just is more acceptable to the LORD than sacrifice." Then Baker reminds us that "we are called to imitate this God, to 'be perfect' as God 'is perfect' (Eph. 5:1; Matt. 5:48)."[14] And "God is just" (2 Thess. 1:6a) and will "Judge . . . right" (Gen. 18:25). He has commanded us to forgive and love our enemies (Matt. 18:21-35; 5:44). He says He won't forgive us if we don't forgive others of their sin (Matt. 6:14-15).

In the end, however, Baker is "not sure we can harmonize the retributive form of justice . . . with the restorative nature of God's love."[15] I, however, see no problem synthesizing both forms into a harmony.

Hanson leans support to my both/and position as he assures his readers back in the 1800s that God "hates sin with unlimited hatred, but loves the sinner with illimitable love. His omnipotence is directed by omniscience and can and will overcome all evil and transform it to good. His threats and punishments have but one purpose, and that the good of the punished. Hereafter those who have here remained obdurate will be chastened until converted. Man's freedom will never be lost, and ultimately it will be converted in the last and wickedest sinner."[16]

Admittedly, however, we know very little about the exact conditions in the place, state, or dimension of the afterlife where the un-evangelized and evangelized-but-reject -Christ reside, at least initially. But given the paucity, if not total non-existence, of biblical support for the orthodox and traditional doctrine of "hell," that view needs to be jettisoned for the reasons we cited in chapters 1-4. And as McLaren aptly and succinctly puts it, "the fact that Christianity thinks it needs the doctrine doesn't make it true."[17]

Nevertheless, judgment, punishment, and God's fury and wrath are stressed in Scripture, remain compelling doctrines of the faith, and are still things to be feared as we all will "face judgment" (Heb. 9:27). For some it may be fire and wailing and gnashing of teeth (Matt. 5:22; 13:50; Mark 9:44-48). For others it may be darkness (Matt. 8:12; 22:13; 25:30).

We also know there could be varying degrees of judgment, penalty, correction, and punishment imposed, in both severity and duration depending upon the amount of "wrath against yourself" one has stored up (Rom. 2:5; 3:19). But for the unborn, infants,[18] mentally disabled, and all the un-evangelized it may only be a temporary place of finally hearing, being spiritually awakened and educated, believing, repenting, growing, maturing, and receiving. Whether this process takes place in a blink of any eye or over a long time, we cannot know now.

The bottom line here is this. The salvation of all people does not negate this interim and varied administration of God's wrath, justice, and punishment being poured out—even for some "firstfruits" believers as they suffer loss and/or punishment, and possibly receive "many" or "few blows" (Luke 12:47-48; ; Jas. 3:1; 2 Pet. 2:21; Matt. 5:22; 8:12; 25:14-30). Most Christians have never heard much, if anything, at their church about this doctrine of loss and punishment for believers in the afterlife (more on this in our next chapter and Appendix A). But immediately following physical death, believers are also judged and receive rewards or suffer losses and/or punishment (Heb. 9:27; 2 Cor. 5:10; Rom. 14:10-12; 1 Cor. 3:8, 13-15). Where this punishment is administered (now or some time in the future) might be in heaven itself, or, temporarily, in the unrighteous side of Hades, or in the lake of fire—which is the surviving reality (Rev. 20:14-15), but it's not in Gehenna or "hell." Or, it could be somewhere else.

Furthermore, and as we have seen, the lake of fire may not be a place of separation from God at all. But, as we let Scripture interpret Scripture, is actually God Himself (Heb. 12:29; Exod. 24:17; Deut. 4:24; Isa. 30:27; 33:14; Lev. 10:1-2; Hos. 6:5; Luke 12:49, and many more). Yes, all these scriptural possibilities set up a totally different afterlife scenario than we've been accustomed to hearing. If true, and as McLaren hypothesizes, "everyone—in this life and beyond it—lives related to God. So people shouldn't think of their destiny in relation to heaven or hell . . . but in relation to God . . . ."[19] and yet being in "God's presence . . . is a place some people would find intolerable."[20]

So, biblically, there is a place of afterlife punishment and also possible redemption, purification, and refinement, and more. Accordingly, MacDonald claims that "this is not too difficult to see if universalism is true, but it is very hard to see . . . if traditional doctrines of hell are correct."[21]

Synthesis Point #5 – Postmortem evangelism and redemption are not only possible but likely. – Undoubtedly, the biggest problem Exclusivists face is what happens to the un-evangelized: those who never heard of Jesus or the gospel and died as unborns, infants, young children, mentally disabled, pre-Christ heathen, and post-Christ heathen.

The exclusivist authors of *Sense & Nonsense About Heaven & Hell* try to explain away this problem by merely asserting that "God can save such persons apart from any conscious, explicit knowledge and affirmation of the gospel or of any truth about God at all." They rhetorically ask, "doesn't the salvation of these people prove that some people are in fact saved apart from knowing and affirming any revelation of God's redemptive purpose in Christ?"[22] But as we have seen, God's Word says otherwise.

They conditionally add that "the issue is not whether God must save the heathen . . . The issue is whether God *might* save *some* of the heathen even if they never receive a human witness to the gospel during their mortal lifetimes. If he can regenerate infants and the mentally incapable apart from knowledge of the gospel, might he not be able to do so for some of the heathen?" Once again, and as we have seen, the scriptural answer is "no."

But these authors persist in their unscriptural assumption by claiming that "God can and will save many people through Jesus Christ as their Savior even though they have never heard of him or of his sacrificial death on the cross for their salvation." They cite "the billions of children who die before birth or in infancy" and a "sizable number of people whose mental capacities are so limited that they are incapable of doing good or evil," as well as "believers in the Old Testament [who] had varying degrees of understanding of his redemptive purposes and plan . . ."[23] And they appropriately ask, were "people in the Old Testament saved, then, without knowing about Jesus or his redemptive death?"[24] They conclude that "we don't have enough information to be sure."[25] But as we shall see, we do have enough information. It's in the form of postmortem evidence.

Not so, says J.I. Packer. He insists "there is no scriptural support for any form of this postmortem evangelism, probation, or conversion theorizing,"[26] Wittmer adamantly advises that "we can readily avoid this danger by following a simple rule: speak when the Bible speaks and remain quiet when the Bible is silent." He then utilizes his rule to his advantage in correctly claiming that "the Bible never promises postmortem salvation" but he totally ignores the fact that the Bible does not rule it out, either.[27] Instead, he pejoratively snips, "those who assert there is a chance for postmortem salvation inadvertently claim to know better than God what God should have included in his Word."[28]

Other conservative theologians disagree with Packer's and Wittmer's "silence" opposition. Donald G. Bloesch opts "for postmortem evangelism as a solution."[29] Millard J. Erickson in his book, *How Shall They Be Saved?*, devotes a whole chapter to "postmortem evangelism."[30] And Hilborn and Horrocks report that "one of the more intriguing trends in current evangelical theology is the growing number of evangelical theologians since the 1960s who have either endorsed or seriously entertained the concept of 'second chance' or 'post-mortem' evangelism. This group now includes, at least, George Beasely Murray, Charles Cranfield, Donald Bloesch, Clark Pinnock, Gabriel Fackre and Nigel Wright. With Milliard Erickson, we suspect that the group will grow."[31]

Packer, however and to his credit, does acknowledge the simple yet profound fact that universalism "requires successful postmortem evangelism for some and heart-changing corrective discipline for others. . . ."[32] So, once again, the lines are drawn over this point as well.

But in this fifth synthesis point let's re-think the biblical possibility of postmortem evangelism and redemption. Admittedly, nothing in Scripture says this happens. But nothing says it cannot happen, either. Nor is there any biblical obstacle preventing this from happening—i.e., for dead people receiving knowledge of the gospel and motivation to receive Christ in the afterlife. Yes, this is mostly, but not totally, an argument from silence. But postmortem evangelism has happened before, as we have seen (see again Chapter 4, p-83). This double silence, however, does leave God free to do this again (and perhaps again and again) without violating, compromising, or contradicting his revealed Word in any way. Here are four reasons why this is so.

First and foremost, the Scriptures are clear that faith comes by hearing the Word of God (Rom. 10:13-14, 17). Therefore, to be saved all persons must be told (preached to and taught) and given "ears to hear" to believe in Christ, to confess Him with their mouths, and receive Him as their Lord and Savior to the glory of God (Acts 16:31; Rom. 10:9, 13; but not to believe like the demons do – Mark 3:11; Matt. 8:29). These are God's divinely determined requirements for saving faith. These requirements cannot be discarded or overridden, even by Him. They must be met.

Universalism "requires successful postmortem evangelism for some and heart-changing corrective discipline for others."

Secondly, we have biblical evidence that postmortem evangelism and redemption most likely has happened before. Although this is contested by some scholars and numerous explanations have been given,[33] the apostle Peter writes that Jesus descended into Hades during the three days and three nights between his death and resurrection. There, He preached to the spirits of the dead held captive there in that prison (1 Pet. 3:19-20; 4:6; Eph. 4:9).[34] That's postmortem evangelism, is it not? Thereby, these departed souls were then able to "call on the one they have not believed in" and "in the one of whom they have not heard" (Rom. 10:14). This occurred back then in the hadean realm, which was also the place termed "under the earth" (Phil. 2:10; Rev. 5:3, 13; also see Psa. 22:27-29; 66:3-4).

So if Jesus did this once in the afterlife, why can't He, an angel, a resurrected saint like Paul, or somebody else do it, again and again, with other individuals or groups of postmortem un-evangelized or condemned nonbelievers? Erickson concurs that "they may still be treated in the same way as those who lived before the completed plan of salvation and the revelation?"[35]

Thirdly, if it is true as Paul writes in Romans around A.D. 55-57 that God is capable of grafting back in branches He previously broke off—and this could go back as far as Abraham's day (Gen. 12) or even to Adam and Eve's day (Gen. 3)—then this would require postmortem evangelism and redemption. Why? Because some of these "branches" are people who had been dead for several thousand years prior to the death and resurrection of Jesus (see Rom. 11:5-11, 17-23, 33-36). Let's also not forget that Christ is called "Lord of both the dead and the living" (Rom. 14:9), is He not?

Fourthly, all persons consigned and/or condemned to this place of punishment, evangelizing, education, maturing, and/or perfecting (again, not "hell") must spend some time there before entering heaven. Or, this might occur somewhere in heaven itself. That time period is an *aionios* (age of) time appropriate to each person's situation. During that *aionios* time, God the Father, Christ Himself, and/or God's Spirit will cause them to turn away from wickedness (2 Tim. 1:9), repent, and come to saving faith (Eph. 2:8-9; Rom. 1:17). In other words, what God has done for the elect in this life—giving them his grace and faith and drawing (John 6:44) and enabling (John 6:65)—He could do for the rest in the afterlife. (More on this in our next chapter.)

Erickson speculates that an opportunity to hear after death might be "more convincing than that which an ordinary human evangelist could make."[36] In the same vein, Bloesch sees this area of the afterlife (which he still refers to as "hell") as part of God's loving plan, and as exclusion from communion with Him, but not from his presence. He depicts it as "a sanatorium of sick souls presided over by Jesus Christ."[37] And since God is omnipresent, (Psa. 139:7f), Erickson may be right in asking, "What, then, is the correct understanding of hell (sic)? It must be seen, not as eternal punishment, but as reclamatory, as an instrument of love, for the sake of the sinner . . . . Just like the Good Shepherd who insists on finding the hundredth sheep, God cannot be sovereign love without salvation 'unto the last'. . . . his ability to accomplish his ends fully, is a vital part of the salvation of all persons. . . . The will of God extends beyond this life.'"[38]

Pinnock, on the other hand, is rather tenuous as he contends that the opportunity for postmortem evangelism and repentance "rests on the insight that God, since he loves humanity, would not send anyone to hell without first ascertaining what their response would have been to his grace. Since everyone eventually dies and comes face to face with the risen Lord, that would be the obvious time to discover their answer to God's call."[39]

However this postmortem scenario might work out; when the time comes for each person's punishment, education, and/or purification to be over and he or she has trusted in Christ as God's merciful provision for sin, he or she will be saved, released from this holding place (not hell), and transferred to heaven—or, perhaps, freed up and release to enjoy a heavenly existence.

Once again, and I cannot emphasize this enough: the possibility of postmortem evangelism and redemption does not contradict any scripture, compromise Jesus Christ or his redemptive work, or go against

God's revealed will, desire, and purpose in any way. And just because Scripture is silent about this possibility does not mean it cannot happen. God is sovereign. And He is sovereign in the exercise of his mercy, grace, love, justice, and wrath. He calls the shots. We don't. This aspect of his sovereignty could very well be a big part of his "secret things" (Deut. 29:29). And Jesus in the heavenly realm is still able to do what He came to earth to do as "the Savior of all men, especially of those who believe" (1 Tim. 4:10)—would you agree or not?

Synthesis Point #6 – Annihilation, most likely, will not play a part in God's redemptive plan. – It is possible that not every single person will believe, eventually. Some may stubbornly refuse to accept God's grace, mercy, and love and receive Jesus as their Savior. If this is true, then, at some point, might they be annihilated or choose annihilation—i.e., perish, be totally destroyed, and go out of existence altogether?

McLaren posits this termination possibility this way, "God always acts in the most loving way possible in regard to the person who rejects God . . . offering the disintegrating being the postmortem possibility of using its freedom to end its existence."[40]

Others take a hard line and contend that if only one person does not believe, then universal salvation does not hold true. But this statement is assumptive. It may or may not be true. If some people at some point in time no longer exist in any form or fashion, it may be that God would no longer consider them part of the "all things," which He is in process of reconciling to and in Christ.

But in my opinion, this is not likely. Such an "out" would be akin to God, on the one hand, revealing though many scriptures (as He has done) that all will eventually be saved and with the other hand attaching an asterisk (*) to each scripture explaining—"expect for those annihilated, eventually, whom I will no longer consider among humankind."

In my opinion, this is not likely.

More likely, in my opinion, the meaning of the biblical terms "perish," "destroy," and "destruction" are in keeping with other uses and ranges of meaning depending upon the context. As we've seen in

Chapter 12, that would be something less than total extinction in the strictest sense. Such as:

- "material ruin."
- "loss"
- "exclusion from the joys and pleasures"
- "exclusion from God's presence"
- "deprivation of eternal blessedness"
- "a metaphor for terrible loss"
- "eternal misery / torment"

And even though we certainly do not want to be dogmatic here, let's again point out that all of God's postmortem "fury" and "wrath" takes place "in the presence of the holy angles and in the presence of the lamb" (Rev. 14:10). That, most likely, is not a place of separation or elimination.

Synthesis Point #7 – The gospel must be redefined for us to do a better job of evangelizing. – If Erickson is right in concluding that the exclusivist's view is "the strongest motivation for evangelism,"[41] then why do most Christians today admit that we do such a shameful job? Perhaps the problem is the product or proposition we have been taught to present?

The traditional approach is based primarily on the assumption that the gospel and the motivation for proclaiming it is to save people from going to hell after they die. Likewise, the main meaning of life on this earth is in sorting out where one is going to spend eternity.

But when we read the Gospels, we find that Jesus did not come preaching Jesus, or hell, or people dying and going to heaven. Rather, during his 3 ½-year earthly ministry, He focused primarily on this life. And his gospel was centered on the kingdom of God on this earth, there and then. Thus, for Jesus the gospel was much more than just the promise that someday in the future some people would be saved from their sins and go to heaven.

If we sincerely desire to see present-day Christians do a better job of evangelism and missions, the gospel itself will need to be re-aligned in harmony with Jesus' presentations in the Gospels. That means we will need to develop a better understanding of God's kingdom, his justice, and our roles in advancing that kingdom "on earth as it is in heaven" (Matt. 6:10b). That means we must rediscover the whole, full, and true gospel that Jesus as well as Paul presented (see Acts 28:31; 20:25-27; 19:8).

McLaren helps us to readjust our understanding of this gospel this way: It's "not just how individual souls will be saved but instead how the world will be saved . . . from human sin and all that goes with it—human greed, human lust, human pride, human oppression, human hypocrisy and dishonesty, human violence and racism, human chauvinism, human injustice."[42]

If . . . the exclusivist's view is "the strongest motivation for evangelism," then why do most Christians today admit that we do such a shameful job?

So what difference do you think a kingdom-oriented gospel such as Jesus was presenting, modeling, and conferring would make in how people in our world today respond to the Christian faith? What difference do you think this would make in how interested and willing Christians might be to share this redefined gospel with others? What difference do you think this reconstituted gospel that exhorts us to live out Jesus' full teaching of the kingdom of God—especially in the area of compassion for the weak, needy, vulnerable, and oppressed—would actually have in how most Christians live their earthly lives? Would the results be about the same, lower, or greater than the current response to the reductionist, shrunken-down, and dying-go-to-heaven-and-avoid-hell gospel we are supposed to be presenting now?

McLaren answers these questions through this fictional dialogue in his book, *The Last Word and the Word after That.* See if you agree with him. "We have to tell people the good news . . . that God is even better than we thought, that the gospel is better than we realized. That their thoughts of God have been too small, too unworthy . . . that the truly good news is bigger and better and more powerful than the conventional news they've been believing and preaching."[43]

Baker concurs that "if we receive Jesus as Savior because we want to escape the eternal fires of hell, we miss the entire point of the good news." That point is: "salvation has almost everything to do with transforming the world for God's glory and little to do with eternal destination for our personal comfort."[44] But I'd recommend we amend Baker's view here to be a both/and, and not an either/or proposition. Why? Because a person cannot even "see" or "enter" the kingdom until he or she is "born again" (John 3:3-5). That is why the two great works of the Messiah were the establishment of the final form of the kingdom of God on earth and salvation. According to Jesus and the whole New Testament, that's the whole gospel, is it not?

Regarding the inclusion of Christian Universalism into a redefined gospel, Exclusivist Marshall thinks this change would be a wash—i.e., neither harmful nor helpful. He reasons, "it also recognizes that there is no salvation outside of Christ and faith in him . . . . [and] leaves the urgency of evangelism unimpaired."[45] But he balks at the notion that "'You would do better to repent and believe the gospel now because otherwise you will be subjected to intense pain inflicted by the wrath of God until you respond to his love and freely accept salvation.'" Instead, he claims, from the traditional viewpoint, that "this is not what the New Testament preaches or teaches. . . . It teaches the reality of final judgement [sic] on the impenitent and sadly it states that some will be lost. This is why there is such an urgency to proclaim the gospel to all the world."[46]

A quick fact-check of the Bible, however, reveals that not one scripture ever uses the expression "final judgment" or "last judgment"— after which there will be no more judgment, and for a good reason. We live in a world "without end" (Eph. 3:31 *KJV*) and have been given a kingdom whose "increase" has "no end" (Isa. 9:7; Luke 1:33).[47] Also, and unfortunately as we noted in this book's opening chapter, and as Ludlow confirms, there has been and still is "a deep-rooted ambivalence" about hell and its "public discussion."[48]

MacDonald, in my opinion, makes more sense when he counsels that "even though it is not mainstream within Christianity, universalism [Christian Universalism] is no threat to orthodox Christianity." He cites these foundational reasons. It has "not sidestepped the centrality of God's work in Christ, so the cross and resurrection remain at the heart of the gospel." It also does not reduce "the importance of faith in Christ nor the missionary calling of the church." It does not "undermine the authority of the Bible." Nor has it "'gone soft' on God's wrath." In sum, it has "not tinkered with any of the key doctrines of orthodox Christianity."[49]

So what are we to do? Stetson advises "we must relearn the Gospel."[50] How do we do this? Bob Ekblad in his book, *A New Christian Manifesto*, knows how when he writes, "There is an urgent need today . . . to proclaim the good news gospel of God's kingdom on earth as in heaven."[51] And this would be "incredibly good news!"[52] Evangelistically, we would then be re-calling all believers into "the whole ministry of Jesus." This would be the ministry and whole gospel "having the power to save, heal, liberate, deliver, and transform" everything, here and now.[53] Yes, this would be in contrast to the reductionist, shrunken-down gospel of only dying and going to heaven. In my opinion, this is the redefined and reformed gospel we should be pledging allegiance to—the kingdom of God.[54]

"If we receive Jesus as Savior because we want to escape the eternal fires of hell, we miss the entire point of the good news."

In sum, we moderns desperately need to shift our emphasis from the dominant   "Jesus-died-so-that-when-you-die-you-can-go-to-heaven" gospel and more toward the "kingdom-of-God" gospel as Jesus presented, taught, modeled, and conferred it. According to Ekblad this is "a movement with unlimited potential."[55] This reintegration would also be a return to the radical faith of Christianity's 1st century that was accused of having "turned the world upside down" (Acts 17:6 *KJV*). This same kingdom should be the centerpiece of a reformed gospel and evangelism approach.

Will this reformed gospel and evangelism approach work better than what we are currently presenting and doing, or rather not presenting or doing, or not presenting or doing very well? Ekblad believes that "young people throughout the world are desperate for a legitimate and sustainable way to live out their lives" and "they are willing to give their lives to something worth dying for, but it is not being offered to them." And yet this whole gospel and faith is exactly what propelled the 1st-century Christians (see again Acts 17:6 *KJV*). Today, on the other hand, we "find people idle,"[56] yes, God's people idle. Instead of being "recruiters for a growing movement to advance the kingdom God throughout the world,"[57] most are longing and waiting around for Jesus to return and take them out of this world and fix all wrongs in their absence.

Proclaiming and demonstrating the way to embody God's will on earth as it is in heaven and combating, defeating, and transforming evil, overcoming oppression, and seeking justice—this is "the good fight of faith" (1 Tim. 6:12). *This is the gospel of the kingdom and of salvation. It's the whole gospel.* Isn't it time for a change back to and in conformity with the central teaching of Jesus Christ—the kingdom?

Onward and Upward

If this seven-point synthesis is right, then let us take this redefined and reformed good news of "the unsearchable riches of Christ" to the world and ". . . make plain to everyone the administration of this mystery, which for ages past was kept hidden in God, who created all things" (Eph. 3:8-9). Who are we to deny, devalue, diminish, or depreciate this divine and ultimate reality? Remember, each of us will be held accountable, forever!

Baker is right on target about how we should change our approach "from one of stagnating doom and gloom in the fires of hell, to one of transforming faith and hope and love in the kingdom of God." She confidently concludes and asks that "only a transformed world can stanch the flow of evil, stop the vicious cycles of violence, and propagate peace on earth through goodwill toward all people. This is good news, is it not?"[58]

Yes, for many this redefined and reformed gospel will be a dramatically enhanced or, at least, a different view of what Christianity is all about compared to the lesser tradition that has been handed down to us. But this gospel of the kingdom and of salvation that Jesus presented and the 1st-century church demonstrated to the world of their day, turning it "upside down" (Acts 17:6 *KJV*), must take primacy. We today could do the same with this message, if we recovered and restored the same faith—the faith that was "once for all delivered unto the saints" (Jude 3). Would you agree or disagree?

Let's close this chapter with MacDonald's synopsis of the "pastoral benefits" for the Christian Universalism view. He claims that they are "significant" and provide the foundational basis for the gospel and evangelism. But you be the judge. Christian Universalism . . .

> Yields a theology of hope, of divine love, and presents a vision of the victory of God that has significant advantages over the tradition, with its eternal hell. It also yields an inspiring ecclesiology and missiological motivation. Indeed, it accentuates the love and grace of God without diminishing his severity and wrath. It lifts the saving work of Christ to new heights without losing sight of judgment. . . . it inspires a new understanding of worship and provides the inspiration for heartfelt devotion to our great God—Father, Son and Holy Spirit.[59]

This gospel of the kingdom and of salvation that Jesus presented and the 1st-century church demonstrated to the world of their day, turning it "upside down" (Acts 17:6 *KJV*), must take primacy.

Originally, I planned to end this book with this chapter and the conclusion. But after writing both of these and in the interest of thoroughness, I feel an additional and amplifying chapter is required. See if you agree.

Chapter 17

The Postmortem Experience

"And it is appointed unto men once to die, but after this the judgment."
(Heb. 9:27, *KJV*)

Someday, each and every one of us—believers and unbelievers—
will face, go through, and dwell forever in the postmortem
experience. It's the afterlife destiny of every person who has ever
lived, is now living, or will live on planet Earth. Individually, you and I
will "stand before God's judgment seat . . . . [and] give an account of
himself to God" (Rom. 14:10b, 12b). There and then, we will "receive
what is due him for the things done while in the body, whether good or
bad" (2 Cor. 5:10). Jesus amplified about this experience like this: "But I
tell you that men will have to give account on the day of judgment for
every careless word they have spoken. For by your words you will be
acquitted, and by your words you will be condemned" (Matt. 12:36-37).
No one is exempt, despite this use of masculine language, not even
females.[1]

Twice, and on the positive side, this encouraging tidbit also has been
revealed. "However, as it is written: 'No eye has seen, no ear has heard,
no mind has conceived what God has prepared for those who love him' –
but God has revealed it to us by his Spirit" (1 Cor. 2:9-10; from Isa.
64:4).

On the negative side, this judgment event will not only involve
blessings and reward, but also loss and possible punishment:

"If any man builds on this foundation using gold, silver, costly stones, wood, hay or straw, this work will be shown for what it is, because the Day will bring it to light. It will be revealed with fire, and the fire will test the quality of each man's work. If what he has built survives, he will receive his reward. If it is burned up, he will suffer loss; he himself will be saved, but only as one escaping through the flames." (1 Cor. 3:11-15)

How all this transpires for each person—saved and unsaved—has not been revealed. But this universal reality and the administration of this process has been the subject of many debates over the centuries.

Nevertheless, this postmortem experience is both the challenge and theme of our final chapter. In keeping with the result of our synthesis in the previous chapter, we are going to re-explore how God might, could, and may possibly save all people as they go through this afterlife experience. After all, emphatically and on numerous times, God has stated that He will carry out his plan and accomplish all He wills, desires, and purposes that none should perish but every person be saved and come to the knowledge of truth and to repentance (1 Tim. 2:4; 2 Pet. 3:9). The culmination of this process is the Godhead being "all in all" (1 Cor. 15:28).

Even more challenging, if possible, we are going to re-explore how our omnipotent, omniscient, and omnibenevolent God might, could and may *cause* all people who haven't done so to accept Christ and be saved, willingly and freely, in the afterlife without violating anyone's so-called "free will." As Talbott confidently affirms, God is "wise and resourceful enough to accomplish *all* of his loving purposes in the end."[2] And Erickson reminds us of the reason why all this might, could, and may be possible: "The omnipotence of God, his ability to accomplish his ends fully, is a vital part of the salvation of all persons. . . .[because] The will of God extends beyond this life."[3]

So how might, could, and may God soften all the hearts He has previously hardened long ago in history, today, and in the future (Rom. 11:7)? How might, could, and may God draw and enable all in the afterlife whom in this life He did not draw and enable, or those who never heard, or those who heard and refused to believe and receive (John 6:45, 65)? How might, could, and may He graft back in all those He previously broke off (Rom. 11:17-23)? How might, could, and may He un-bind all those He has "bound . . . over to disobedience so that he may have mercy on them all" (Rom. 11:32)? How might, could, and may He punish and/or treat the wicked—even Judas and Hitler—so that they would longingly and sincerely desire to be righteous and saved?

There is one more sticky little issue, or not-so-little depending on your perspective. Many, if not most, believers who have confessed Christ as their Savior in this life have been told, taught, and think they will completely avoid God's wrath and punishments and upon physical death go instantly into the blissful paradise of heaven. Maybe some will.

But biblically, it has been revealed that the souls of many, if not all, believers may not be ready to receive and enjoy the blessings of heaven immediately after they die. Plenty of scriptures warn that we all will be held accountable for what we have done and/or not done in this life and some unpleasant afterlife consequences are possible after we face and undergo "the judgment" (Heb. 9:27; Rom. 14:10-12; 2 Cor. 5:10). Below are several additional verses from the New Testament that many ignore or lightly brush aside, which seem to teach this truth:

"Everyone will be salted with fire" (Mark 9:49).

"That servant who knows his master's will and does not get ready or does not do what his master wants will be beaten with many blows. But the one who does not know and does things deserving punishment will be beaten with few blows. . . . (Luke 12:47-48a).

"Then he will say to those on his left, 'Depart from me, you who are cursed, into the eternal fire prepared for the devil and his angels. For I was hungry and you gave me nothing to eat, I was thirsty and you gave me nothing to drink, I was a stranger and you did not invite me in, I needed clothes and you did not clothe me, I was sick and in prison and you did not look after me.' They also will answer, 'Lord, when did we see you hungry or thirsty or a stranger or needing clothes or sick or in prison, and did not help you?' He will reply, 'I tell you the truth, whatever you did not do for one of the least of these, you did not do for me'" (Matt. 25:41-45).

And arguably one of the most troubling and "scariest passages . .
. in the entire Bible:"[4] *"Many will say to me on that day, 'Lord,
Lord, did we not prophesy in your name, and in your name drive
out demons and perform many miracles?' Then I will tell them
plainly, 'I never knew you. Away from me, you evildoers!'"*
(Matt. 7:22-23).

"for our God is a consuming fire" (Heb. 12:29; Deut. 4:24; Isa.
33:14).

So, really, is a believer in Christ in this life immune from all, some,
or none of these negative consequences in the afterlife, or not? Baker
certainly recognizes this possibility or reality that everyone may "stand
in the fiery presence of God and suffer the purifying flames of God's
love. This burning love might feel like burning wrath to the one who
experiences it." And since everyone is a sinner, even those of us already
saved by grace, this fire may just be God's "love that burns away the sin,
purifying the sinner so that true reconciliation and restoration can take
place."[5]

But I also think we believers can rest assured that this divine use of
fire is good for us because everything God does is good, right, and just.
And this postmortem experience, whatever it might entail, will likewise
be good, right, and just for each of us because He is the loving Father of
all and we are all made in his image and likeness. We can also rest
assured that God in his omniscience knows what will work best in each
case to bring about his desired result.

So how might, could, and may all this positive and negative stuff
happen in the postmortem experience and everybody eventually be
saved? To us, this outcome surely seems impossible. But never forget,
"nothing is impossible with God (Luke 1:37; also 18:27; Matt. 19:26;
Mark 10:27). And according to many scriptures—He works *both* in this
world, in this life, and in the afterlife.

Stetson, of course, has no problem believing God can do all this.
That's why he is so sure that "some people will be saved during their
earthly life, while others will not be saved until after physical death."[6]
After all, and once again, this full reconciliation of "all things" is
"according to the plan of him who works out everything in conformity
with the purpose of his will" (Eph. 1:11b).

My Cautious Disclaimer

Granted, the content of this final chapter is speculative. But it is not pure speculation. What's more, I'm not the first person in church history to speculate about these possible afterlife scenarios and experiences. As Stetson historically observes, "early Christians held a great diversity of views about the nature of the afterlife, so this was a subject of much debate."[7] Therefore, and in addition to prominent early church fathers, Clement of Alexandria and Origen particularly, we will look at some writings from the late 1800s and from recent Christian writers.

Notwithstanding, I make no pretense that the contents of this chapter are either right or exhaustive—only that they are all scripturally possible. This I also can assure you. Nothing we will be re-exploring herein violates or contradicts any text or demand of Scripture I'm aware of. Nor does it compromise God's character and nature. If anything, the material contained herein only enhances our perception of God's divine attributes. Hence, the bottom line is and must remain: God is fully free to use these or any other methodologies He so chooses to achieve his revealed will, desire, and purpose that none should perish but every person be saved and come to the knowledge of truth and to repentance (1 Tim. 2:4; 2 Pet. 3:9), provided, once again, they do not conflict with his revealed Word.

Surprisingly, Sinclair B. Ferguson agrees and also offers some wise caution in this regard that "we must recognize that what God may do is not limited to what he has revealed to us that he will do. But by the same token we may not presume that he will do what he has not specifically revealed that he will do."[8]

Consequently, the purpose of this final chapter is to offer insights, explanations, and methodologies as to how God might, could, and may bring about the salvation of all human beings, eventually. No, this will not be a cogent or systematic account. Remember we are dealing with a mystery. The three major areas we will re-explore are: the un-hardening and re-grafting process, the functions of fire, and God's incentive plan.

As you will see, these possible postmortem experiences are not an end in themselves, but a means to an end. As we proceed, please keep in the forefront of your mind this question: Why would God create a person in his image and likeness (Gen. 1:26-27) and yet with a soul that would never seek Him? Of course, on earth, some are deluded and seduced by sin, selfish, and/or evil temptations. But after physical death, many, if not all, of those fleshly things that kept us away from God will have been removed, and it could be a whole new ball game, so to speak. There in the postmortem afterlife the human spirit/soul is liberated from the earthly flesh. Perhaps it already is or will someday be contained in a new spiritual body (1 Cor. 15:44). Either way, as MacDonald suggests: "the post-mortem state" may be "vastly better suited for the conversion of the unregenerate."[9] For believers, this experience also may be quite overwhelming.

Before we jump in, Stetson offers this final bit of wisdom:

> Regardless of one's beliefs about how the afterlife works, what really matters is that God knows what's best for each and every soul He has created. I believe that God will put us wherever we need to be at any particular time—whether on earth or in hell or somewhere else unknown—until we have reached the full stature of divinity that we were created to reflect and manifest in our lives.[10]

If you are ready for a possible preview of the ultimate adventure, let's now see how all this might, could, and may be worked out by the Godhead in the successful achievement of God's stated will, desire, and purpose in every single case.

The Un-hardening and Re-grafting Process

Scripture teaches that "at the present time," in circa A.D. 57 as the Apostle Paul wrote, "there is a remnant chosen by grace" and "only the remnant will be saved" (Rom 11:5; 9:27b). This passage also teaches that for many thousands of years prior God had "hardened" some people (also see John 12:38-40). It further reveals that He did this, and perhaps still does, by giving them "a spirit of stupor, eyes so that they could not see and ears so that they could not hear, to this very day" (Rom. 11:7-8; Deut. 29:4; Isa. 29:10; 2 Cor. 4:4). Furthermore, He had "broken off" some "branches" (people) in "unbelief" so that other branches (people) "could be grafted in" (Rom. 11:17-19). Likewise, He had made some into vessels of "honour" but others into vessels of "dishonour" (Rom. 9:21 *KJV*). Therefore, He had elected some like Jacob but not others like Esau (Rom. 9:10-13). This passage further relates that God "loved" Jacob but "hated" Esau (Rom. 9:13; Mal. 1:2, 3).

None of these unfortunate people "at the [that] present time" were part of God's "remnant chosen by grace" (Rom. 11:5). Seriously, consider this for a moment. If God had done this to you, do you think your human "free will" could have overridden his sovereign dis-election and supernatural disenabling powers? Keep in mind that many of these unfortunate people would have been long-dead for several thousand years before the coming, death, resurrection, and ascension of Jesus Christ, the Messiah.

So how might, could, and may God soften all the hearts He has previously hardened long ago in history, today, and in the future (Rom. 11:7)?

But here is the good news that is also revealed in this passage, "God is able to graft them in again." How after thousands of years? Probably by reversing what He had done to them in the first place so that they would no longer "persist in unbelief" (Rom. 11:23). Where and when might, could, or may this happen? The only feasible answer is: in the postmortem afterlife and in the lake of fire. How would this be effectuated? Simply but profoundly, by God supernaturally reversing what He caused previously—i.e., by un-hardening them, by removing that spirit of stupor, by giving them eyes to see and ears to hear, and by remaking them into vessels of honor. Seriously, if God can harden hearts, minds, feelings, inclinations, etc. and break people off, why can't He un-harden and re-graft them back in as well?

Most likely, this un-hardening process will not be merely a "second chance" or another opportunity to repent and believe. Much more will likely be involved, especially if we view this process as the means by which God disperses his mercy, grace and love, as well as justice and wrath, and with the end-goal being conversion.

For the un-evangelized, those who never heard about Jesus and salvation during their earthly life—unborns, infants, children, mentally disabled, and heathens, this process may simply and positively be one of bringing them into his light and love in kindly ways; of departing information, education, and enlightenment; of drawing, enabling, and leading them up and into a state of righteousness and maturity. Once again, just because somebody is physically dead that does mean he or she cannot hear the gospel and be saved (see again 1 Pet. 4:6).

On the other hand, for the perverse and Christ-rejecting group this might be a totally different experience. It may be dreadful, and even "hell-like," so to speak. Perhaps, this process will start with varying degrees and durations of judgment, correction, punishment, isolation, loss, discipline, purification, and rehabilitation (in "the lake of fire" and described as the "second death" – Rev. 20:15; 21:8) to bring them to their senses before they enter into the information, education, enlightenment, drawing and enabling phase that takes them into a state of righteousness and maturity.

But somehow within all of God's omni power, knowledge, love, and control all non-believers might, could, and may be brought into the faith this very way. And yet God probably would not do this by overriding or violating what we think of as a person's free will. In other words, this conversion and salvation process would not be forced upon a person against their will. It eventually would be *freely* chosen, so to speak. But Scripture also plainly tells us that "no man can say Jesus is Lord, but by the Holy Spirit" (1 Cor. 12:3). Well, God can send and provide the Holy Spirit in the afterlife as well as in this life, can He not?

Admittedly, this postmortem change-of-heart experience may not be pleasant for some as God inflicts as much pain mixed with love over different periods of time as is necessary to bring about justice and repentance. And this process might, could, and may be applied, again and again, as more and more individuals die and come into it.

So if this afterlife scenario is correct, this means that the vast majority of people will be converted to faith in Christ after death. And since faith is a gift of God given only to some in this life as God predestines his chosen, his elect, and somehow puts faith in their hearts, He can simply and profoundly give the dis-elected this same gift of faith and graft them back in postmortem-wise as well, can He not? Thus, by loving, drawing, enabling, awakening, educating, persuading and/or inflicting pain, purification, disciplining, and remaking in a number of dramatic ways, God can "cause" people in the afterlife to want to be saved, to be willing to confess their belief in Christ, and to freely trust Him for their salvation *the same as He has done for some in this life, can He not?*

Critical Objection: But what about "the beast" and the "false prophet" (Rev. 19:20) and "the devil" (Rev. 20:10) who are also cast into this lake of fire? Will they be saved, eventually, as well? My answer is: probably not because God's Word only reveals that Christ died for those who died in Adam (see again 1 Cor. 15:22 and other parallelism in Chapter 9). As far as I know, these other entities did not die in Adam.

Admittedly, this postmortem change-of-heart experience may not be pleasant for some as God inflicts as much pain mixed with love over different periods of time as is necessary to bring about justice and repentance.

Graduation Day

When each person's time of postmortem experience has been completed and the time is right (I have no idea how long or short of a time this might take), He "makes all things new" by finally "drawing" and "enabling" them to believe (John 6:44, 65). If they had been in the lake of fire (again, which most likely is God), they are transferred out and into heaven. This might, could, and may be an overview of how God's grace, mercy, and love, and justice and wrath ultimately prevail as Christ eventually becomes the "choice" of everyone as "every eye" encounters and sees Him (Rev. 1:7) and "every knee bows and every tongue confesses"—either by their own free will and/or after God bestows faith on them (depending upon whether one is an Arminian or a Calvinist), or all of the above and more.

Thereby and in so doing, their postmortem "choice" of salvation is made in *exactly the same way* as pre-mortem believers made their decisions during their lives on earth—by responding in saving faith. If this above scenario is correct, this could be how the redemption of all is made effectual in the three realms of "in heaven, "on the earth" and "under the earth" (Phil. 2:10; also Rev. 5:3, 13). Obviously, this process of bringing non-believers and even believers into unity with the Godhead would be different for different people. And there's no single innocent or guilty sentence that fits everyone.

Clement and Origen were the first to teach and write (as far as I know) that sinners could be rehabilitated and ultimately find their way to heaven. Of course, their Christian Universalism view was rejected by some church leaders. But nothing I know of in Scripture precludes the scenario we've just covered from being a possible means God might, could, and may use, or is currently using, to accomplish his revealed will, desire, and purpose that "not . . . anyone should perish, but everyone to come to repentance" (2 Pet. 3:9) and "all men to be saved and to come to a knowledge of the truth" (1 Tim. 2:4).

Daley quotes Origen in support of our above afterlife scenario for both non-believers and believers in that "all the torments of a good God are designed for the benefit of those who endure them" and "all souls need to be purified by 'fire' from the 'lead' intermingled with their natural 'gold,' in order to be saved . . . . the degrees and durations of suffering for those confined in it will vary, depending on their guilt."

Daley concludes that "this process of purification seems to include, for Origen, not only the negative experience of detachment from the passions and the effects of sin, but also a positive growth in knowledge and wisdom as a preparation for the eternal vision of God." Origen terms this place of preparation a "'school for souls' situated somewhere 'in the heavenly regions.'"[11]

Commenting further, N.T. Wright draws references from John Hick's book, *Evil and the God of Love*, and phrases this possibility like this. It is "a universalism in which God will endlessly offer to the unrepentant the choice of faith until at last all succumb to the wooing of divine love."[12] Or, as Wright also puts it in his explanation of the Christian universalist position that "God will continue, after death, to offer all people the chance of repentance until they finally give in to the offer of his love."[13]

Perhaps, however, the best explanation of this afterlife scenario is found in the fictional bestseller, *The Shack*, when Papa (God the Father) explains to Mack, concerning the "millions of reasons to allow pain and hurt and suffering rather than to eradicate them . . . ."

If you could only see how all of this ends and what we will achieve without the violation of one human will—then you would understand.

One day you will. . . . You really don't understand yet. You try to make sense of the world in which you live based on a very small and incomplete picture of reality. . . . The real underlying flaw in your life, Mackenzie, is that you don't think that I am good . . . .[14]

So does any one of us think the Godhead is too small or too ill-equipped to break through the hard and calloused shells some people have built around their hearts, minds, and bodies by repeatedly turning their backs on Christ during this life and refusing to hear God's voice calling them to repentance? Once again, in the afterlife lake of fire, this may be a totally different story. What kept that person away from God during this life may no longer be present or at least not possess the same level of importance or attachment.

Another insight from Scripture may also shed light on this postmortem scenario. It says, "because of the LORD's great love we are not consumed, for his compassions never fail. They are new every morning . . . . though he brings grief, he will show compassion, so great is his unfailing love." (Lam. 3:22-23a, 32). And because both God's compassion and "the will of God extends beyond this life,"[15] Rob Bell feels "that no one can resist God's pursuit forever, because God's love will eventually melt even the hardest of hearts."[16] This likelihood causes Amirault to exclaim "the Bible FINALLY made perfect sense! Scriptures like 'Mercy shall triumph over judgment!' (James 2:13b) all of a sudden fit."[17]

The reason God's mercies might, could, and may never fail and triumph over sin and judgment is because they extend beyond physical/biological death into postmortem evangelism, purification, education, remediation and redemption. Hence, all are saved by his grace in like manner, whether in this life or the next. Hanson offers this explanation for this potential reality "for nothing can resist to the last, the Almighty power of divine love, which works not by constraint . . . but by persuasion."[18]

Also spot on, at least partially, may be these additional thoughts and insights from Rob Bell's recent blockbuster book, *Love Wins*:

- "If at any point God overrides, co-opts, or hijacks the human heart, robbing us of our freedom to choose, then God has violated the fundamental essence of what love even is."[19]

- "if you get another chance after you die, why limit that chance to a one-off immediately after death? . . . . there will be endless opportunities in an endless amount of time for people to say yes to God. . . . The love of God will melt every hard heart, and even the most 'depraved sinners' will eventually give up their resistance and turn to God."[20]
- "Restoration brings God glory; endless torment doesn't. Reconciliation brings God glory; endless anguish doesn't. Renewal and return cause God's greatness to shine through the universe; never-ending punishment doesn't."[21]
- All this may take place as Bell further speculates "in the blink of an eye . . . But our heart, our character, our desires, our longings—those things take time."[22]

As we saw in Chapter 5, a long tradition of Christians, beginning with the early church fathers—including Clement of Alexandria, Origen, the two Gregories, and Eusebius—believed and taught this way. In contrast, Baker laments that our evolved traditional view "causes significant theological difficulties" and "creates an artificial tension between love and justice." It makes God out to be "like Dr. Jekyll and Mr. Hyde. Such a view of God's love, mercy, justice, and wrath leads to the conclusion that to love is to punish eternally and, therefore, to punish eternally is just. We believe that this form of retributive justice sets all things right and justifies the accompanying violence of punishment."[23]

"As an example of the harmony between justice and love," Baker relates, "by way of illustration, an event in the life of Peter the Great (died 1725). In an attempt to squelch the Streltsy revolt, many men and women who betrayed the Tsar were imprisoned and tortured in order to exact a confession of guilt and bring forth repentance." One prisoner resisted all torture and "seemed to harden his resolve to keep silent. Having heard of the prisoner's cold determination, Peter released him from torture, embraced the man, kissed him, and promised that he would not only pardon him, but would also make him a colonel in the Tsar's army. . . . 'this unorthodox approach so unnerved and moved the prisoner that he took the Tsar in his arms and said, 'For me, this is the greatest torture of all. There is no other way you could have made me speak.' The prisoner confessed all and repented."

Baker applies this rather left-leaning illustration to what possibly may be part of what occurs in the postmortem experience when determined unbelievers are "brought face-to-face with unexpected love and grace" and realize "the full extent of his [their] betrayal." She sympathizes that "when confronted with the extravagance of love (not punishment), the prisoner saw the depth of his wrongdoing against the Tsar and repented. Justice in harmony with love brought about redemption and restoration where punishment could not." She then suggests that "Peter's act of mercy . . . may have something in common with God's form of justice."[24] In support, Baker cites another "beautiful example of forgiveness freely given, without payment or punishment, in the story of Jesus and the woman caught in adultery (John 8:1-11)."[25] And Baker may have a good point here. "When a person is brought face-to-face with his or her sins and experiences the unexpected grace of forgiveness rather than the expected retributive punishment, real repentance may occur."[26] But I think Scripture speaks of both God's grace and wrath operating in the postmortem experience for hardened Christ-rejecters and some believers as well.

Thus, it may be true, as Talbott believes, "in the afterlife every single person will respond positively to the suffering they experienced" and that "God will use irresistible grace, grant us full knowledge, wisdom and moral purity so that we all make free and rational decisions to improve our characters."[27] For some, this experience may involve no infliction of punishment but be a waiver by his grace. For others, God may need to inflict differing degrees and durations of pain before they eventually cry out for mercy and believe.

The reason God's mercies might, could, and may never fail and triumph over sin and judgment is because they extend beyond physical/biological death into postmortem evangelism, purification, education, remediation and redemption.

We are not told how all this may happen. But we do know that "with God all things are possible" (Matt. 19:26b). And this certainly is a big part of "all things." Many of us, on the other hand, do recognize as

Talbott relates, "the more I separate myself from God, the more miserable I become . . . . Alternatively, the more closely I am drawn to God, the closer I come to compelling evidence concerning the ultimate source of joy."[28] And as the writer of Proverbs noted long ago, "the way of the unfaithful is hard" (Prov. 13:15b). Likewise, Billy Graham warns that "once you leave God out of your life, it can be miserable. . . . We weren't only made by God, we were made for God – and life's greatest joy comes from knowing him."[29] Therefore, part of what we are re-exploring in this chapter is the possibility that both misery and joy can happen in the afterlife in heaven as they do in this earthly life. And if both can happen, can and may they be more real and impacting in the afterlife?

The question, nevertheless, that remains for many of us is whether what Talbott further believes is true or not: "No one can finally defeat God's redemptive love or resist it forever, God will triumph in the end and successfully accomplish the redemption of everyone whose redemption he sincerely wills or desires."[30]

Interestingly, military interrogators now claim to know enough about human behavior to also claim they can win anybody over without the use of torture techniques, given enough time. So why do we humans have a problem believing that the Godhead (Father, Son, and Holy Spirit) can win everybody over in the afterlife—in which the Godhead and the departed have unlimited time?

Functions of Fire

In the physical realm, fire has many different uses and functions. In the postmortem spirit realm this variability may also be true.

In the physical realm, fire produces heat, light, smoke and gases, cooks food, refines, purifies, and separates metals from their ores, is used in forging and shaping metals, destroys waste and kills harmful bacteria, changes clay into pottery, changes the chemical compositions of materials, drives machines, generates electricity, and more. It also burns things up and cause great pain if you get too close. Controlled fire is useful. Uncontrolled fire kills and destroys. And not all substances burn in the same manner nor produce the same by-products.

And since God is just and cannot allow sin into heaven, He probably uses this fire of his to burn away whatever impurities remain in the lives of those after their deaths before they can enter heaven. Thus and eventually, this fire functions in a purifying manner. Once again, where this fire blazes—in heaven, in the lake of fire, in both, or wherever—we are not told.

Likewise, whether this fire is a literal/physical fire, a spiritual fire, or something else entirely has not been revealed. Nor can we know how much fire is enough for each individual's need. This fire might also be how postmortem unbelievers "work out their own salvation with fear and trembling" (Phil. 2:12) as it causes them pain to repent, to respond positively, and to eventually receive God's grace, mercy, and love.

Wherever this fire is located and however it functions in the afterlife, Stetson claims that "fire is an apt metaphor for this transformative process that causes matter to change its form and become something else." In his opinion, this is how "sinners will experience the presence of God and His work in their life as a raging fire that will burn much, while saints will experience God's fire as a light that cannot harm them, because the saintly soul has already been changed in the fires of judgment and no longer 'burns' (suffers judgment) when touched by the divine."[31] But opinions about this do vary, as we shall further see.

Stetson adds that this is why "the Bible uses the metaphor of refining valuable metals in fire to get rid of the impurities within, as a description of how the fire of God transforms people and perfects them"[32] (see for instance Mal. 3:2-3). Of course, this fire can burn in this life (see 1 Pet. 1:7) and/or in the afterlife's lake of fire (Rev. 20:15). Scripture places no restrictions on this fire. And fire in the lake of fire could be multi-purposeful as well—especially, as I've previously suggested, if it is a symbol for God Himself as "a consuming fire" (Heb. 12:29; Deut. 4:24; Isa. 33:14).

"Fire is an apt metaphor for this transformative process that causes matter to change its form and become something else."

If all that is so, then there is no place of separation from this fire and from God Himself in this life or in the afterlife. McLaren aptly terms the work of this fire as "God's wrath is God's justice in action."[33] Hence, we become un-inclined or, perhaps in the afterlife, even unable to sin. After this fire does its work in us, we have a changed heart, mind, feelings, and inclinations. Freely and consistently, we now choose God and godly thoughts and things. If this sounds predestinarian, perhaps a better word for it might be "postmortem-destinarian" as we fully respond to his irresistible grace, love, mercy, justice, and wrath in the afterlife. By the way and deep down, isn't this exactly what we all desire in our hearts as creatures made in the image and likeness of our Creator?

Different Amplifying Insights

Unapologetically, in this section we will only be looking at different views and insights into the possible postmortem-reclamation function of God's fire that are offered by a few Christian Universalist writers. Throughout church history, Christian Universalists have been the primary, if not the sole, scribes who have written extensively about this possibility. Exclusivist writers, not surprisingly, have had little to say. For them, unbelievers either suffer in the fires of "hell" forever or are totally annihilated by it.

John Wesley Hanson in 1899 commenting on and quoting Origen:

- As we examine the "nature of the fire which tries everyman's work . . . . The sinner's life lies before him as an open scroll, and he looks on it with shame and anguish unspeakable . . . . the great school of souls, and their upward and onward progress depends on their purity and love of truth. He who is saved is saved as by fire, that if he has in him any mixture of lead the fire may melt it out, so that all may be made as the pure gold. The more lead the greater will be the burning, so that even if there be but little gold, that little will be purified." This fire is both "a punishment and a remedy, burning up the wood, hay, stubble, according to each man's merits, yet all working to the destined end of restoring man to the image of God, though, as yet, men must be treated as children, and the terrors of the judgment rather than the final restoration have to be brought before those who can be converted only by fears and threats." Origen saw all this happening on "the last day." But in opposition to the annihilationist view of his day Origen assures his readers that while "God is indeed a consuming fire . . . that which he consumes is the evil that is in the souls of men, not the souls themselves."[34]

- This fire may not be material fire, but, as Hanson citing Origen again suggests, it produces "spiritual remorse ending in reformation" and possessing "a disciplinary, purifying quality that will consume in the sinner whatever evil material it can find to consume."[35]

- Hanson insists with Origen that "'everyone shall be subjected to punishment for his sins; a time which God alone knows, when he will bestow on each one what he deserves.' . . . in the sense of limited duration; and fire, as an emblem of purification. . . . the purpose of all punishment, by a good God, must be medicinal."[36] Thereafter, "one by one we shall enter into rest never to stray again." This is how "God shall be all in all."[37] It "is a purifying fire, which all must pass through, though it will impart no pain to the good." Next, citing Origen's writings on God as a "Consuming Fire," "Origen thinks, because he 'does indeed consume and utterly destroy; that he consumes evil thoughts, wicked actions, and sinful desires when they find their way into the minds of believers.'" And Origen taught that "'God's consuming fire works with the good as with the evil, annihilating that which harms his children. This fire is one that each one kindles; the fuel and food is each one's sins'. . . . 'the evil has to be burned out by fire . . . that God our Physician, desiring to remove the defects of our souls, should apply the punishment of fire.' . . . no evil is so strong that it may not be overcome . . . ."[38]

- Thus, Hanson summarizes, "Origen interprets 'fire' in the Bible not only as a symbol of the sinner's suffering but of his purification. The 'consuming fire' is a 'refiner's fire.' It consumes the sins, and refines and purifies the sinner. It burns the sinner's works, 'hay, wood, and stubble,' that result from wickedness. The torture is real, the purifications sure; fire is a symbol of God's severe, certain, but salutary discipline. . . .

What we call wrath is another name for his disciplinary processes. . . . The 'eternal fire' is curative."[39]

- But also according to Hanson, "Origen declares that sinners who are 'incurable' are converted by the threat of punishment . . . 'these will come upon them after they have refused all remedies . . . . Such is our doctrine of punishment; and the inculcation of this doctrine turns many away from their sins.'" Origen admits that these uses are a "painful mode of cure." But as Hanson further reports, Origen "always makes salvation depend on the consenting will; hence he [Origen] says, (De Prin. II, i:2), 'God the Father of all things, in order to ensure the salvation of all his creatures through the ineffable plan of his Word and wisdom, so arranged each of these, that every spirit, whether soul or rational existence, however called, should not be compelled by force, against the liberty of his own will, to any other course than that to which the motives of his own mind led him.'"[40]

John Wesley Hanson in 1899 commenting on and quoting Clement:

- Hanson states that "fire is an emblem of divine punishments which purify the bad." Then he cites Clement, whose "works . . . abound with passages referring to the love and mercy of God." He continues, "'Punishment is, in its operation, like medicine; it dissolves the hard heart, purges away the filth of uncleanness, and reduces the swellings of pride and haughtiness; thus restoring its subject to a sound and healthful state. . . . therefore he [the Lord] truly saves all, converting some by punishments, and others by gaining their free will, so that he has the high honor that unto him every knee should bow . . . .'"[41]
- "Clement insists that punishment in Hades is remedial and restorative and that punished souls are cleansed by fire. The fire is spiritual, purifying the soul. 'God's punishments are saving, disciplinary, and lead to conversion . . . . especially since souls, although darkened by passions, when released from their bodies, are able to perceive more clearly because of their being no longer obstructed by the paltry flesh.'"[42]
- Hanson quotes Clement, "'If in this life there are so many ways for purification and repentance, how much more should there be

after death! The purification of souls, when separated from the body, will be easier. We can set no limits to the agency of the Redeemer; to redeem, to rescue, to discipline, is his work, and so will he continue to operate after this life.'"[43] "This extension of the day of grace . . . . 'the never ending day of God, extends over eternity.'"[44]

- "Clement would not tolerate the thought that any soul would continue forever to resist the force of redeeming love. Somehow and somewhere in the long run of ages, that love must prove weightier than sin and death, and vindicate its power in one universal triumph." Thus, "Clement's view of man's destiny is called restorationism."[45]

- Hanson further points out that "Clemens [sic] was of the same opinion as his scholar Origen, who everywhere teaches that all the punishments of those in hell are purgatorial, that they are not endless, but will at length cease when the damned are sufficiently purified by the fire."[46] And all "these souls" are "purified beyond the grave."[47]

John Wesley Hanson writing in 1899:

- Thus, for Hanson, it is "by this means" that everyone "shall have been brought to fear God, and to regard him with good will" and "they shall obtain the enjoyment of his grace" as opposed to "continuing in sin" and "in misery. . . . Where . . . would be the benefit of a resurrection to such persons, if they were raised only to be punished without end?"[48] Importantly, he stresses, once again, "it is the sins which are consumed, not the very persons to whom the sins have befallen."[49]

- And in this "furnace of purifying fire . . . everything that had its origin from God shall be restored to its pristine state of purity." He calls it "the end of our hope, that nothing shall be left contrary to the good, but that the divine life, penetrating all things . . . . so that he [God] may be 'all in all'"[50]

- Hanson does acknowledge, however, that there may be some "who have not at all needed purification" and "punishment will be administered in proportion to each one's corruptness."[51] (i.e., the time, intensity, and type of punishment and purification thereof.)

- Hanson in quoting others affirms: "the purifying effects of all future punishment, and the separation thereby of the evil from the good in man . . . . the perfect obliteration of wickedness, for if God shall be in all things that are, obviously wickedness shall not be in them" and "the process of healing shall be proportioned to the measure of evil in each of us, and when the evil is purged and blotted out, there shall come in each place to each immortality and life and honor."[52]

- Hanson believes that for "unbelievers" this punishment and purification postmortem process is called the "second death." But he staunchly maintains that "God does not give up on them, for they are his property, spiritual natures allied to him." Therefore, "his love, which draws pure souls easily and without pain to itself, becomes purifying fire to all who cleave to the earthly, till the impure element is driven off. As all comes forth from God, so must all return into him at last. . . . So not even a trace of the evil which now abounds in us shall remain, etc." Consequently, "if sin be not cured here [in this life on Earth] its cure will be effected hereafter. . . . consumed by the *aionion* fire."[53]

- Thus for Hanson, "the punishments are holy, as they are remedial and salutary in their effect on transgressors; for they are inflicted, not to preserve them in their wickedness, but to make them cease from their wickedness. . . . that it might cure them" and be "changed for the better" and "not annihilated." What "remains . . .is pure and clean."[54]

- Next, Hanson brings up an additional possible insight, "God gave death, not as a penalty, but as a remedy; death was given for a remedy as the end of evils." According to his view, this is the only way all things can and will be subject to Christ and God the Father, Christ the Son, and God the Holy Spirit will "be all in all."[55] Therefore, he summarizes, "Death is not bitter; but to the sinner it is bitter, and yet life is more bitter, for it is a deadlier thing to live in sin than to die in sin, because the sinner as long as he lives increases in sin, but if he dies he ceases to sin. . . .

whatever that punishment be, it is a state distinctly preferable to a sinful life."[56]

- Hence, Hanson notes that some are only "punished for a brief period according to the amount of malice in their works . . . . the penalties to be inflicted for their many and grave sins are very far surpassed by the magnitude of the mercy to be showed them. The resurrection, therefore, is regarded as a blessing not only to the good, but also to the evil."[57]

- Hanson concludes that "the purpose of the judgment, as of all the divine penalties, is always remedial . . . a constructive factor." Hanson believes this is true in both this life as well as in the afterlife and "a necessary element of the educational process."[58]

Eric Stetson writing in 2008:

- Stetson claims "no soul is 100% evil. Though 'all have sinned and fall short of the glory of God; (Rom. 3:23), we are nevertheless all created reflecting God's likeness . . . 'in the image of God' (Gen. 1:27)."[59]

- For him the bottom line is: "some people get more fire than others, because some people require more attention from God in order to be changed. Some people only need to be 'salted' with fire, while others will need a whole 'lake' of fire to find salvation."[60]

- No doubt this afterlife-reclamation process will be "a radical destruction and remaking of those who need such severe treatment, rather than a total and eternal expunging of unsaved souls from the universe."[61] Until the unbeliever gets to "the point where being in the presence of God no longer is painful, but joyful." At that point, "instead of experiencing God as a tormenting lake of fire," the sinner may repent and attain salvation and begin experiencing God in his "essence of holiness." Stetson terms this "the hard way by experiencing the full-blown judgment of God" and "certainly not the most pleasant way to be saved." But he assures his readers that "God doesn't give up on anyone—even those who require severe trials and penalties before they can be set free of their sins."[62]

- Stetson further elaborates that "fire is difficult and unpleasant to go through, as long as there is something for it to burn. If one's soul is still sinful . . . we will suffer pain and loss when God's fire touches us."[63] This is true in the afterlife as well, where "some parts of a personality might be destroyed in God's purging fire—maybe even a large part—but it would not be the entire essence of any person that ceases to exist."[64]

Thomas Talbott writing in 2003:

- God's consuming fire "destroys . . . all that is false within us, so our perspective is bound to change."[65]
- For Talbott "there are no obstacles to salvation in anyone, not even in the most recalcitrant will or the hardest of hearts, that God cannot eventually overcome."[66]
- He explains his Christian Universalist position this way: "all paths have the same destination, the end of reconciliation, but some are longer and windier (not to mention more painful) than others. Because our choice of paths in the present is genuinely free, we are morally responsible for that choice; but . . . the end is foreordained. . . . Because God has truth and reality on his side, he can permit his loved ones to choose freely."[67]
- He compares this conversion with what God "did for Paul on the road to Damascus and exactly what he did for [C.S.] Lewis when this self-described prodigal was 'brought in kicking, struggling, resentful, and darting his eyes in every direction for a chance of escape.'"[68]

Sharon L. Baker writing in 2010:

- Baker presents a fictional account of a man going through the postmortem "purifying process in the fiery furnace of God" and characterizes it as "no picnic in the park." It could involve what seems to be "unending agony," "teeth gnash together . . . as sin and the damage he has caused others confronts him face-to-face and heart-to-heart. The severity of his grief serves as a sort of punishment for sure!" As "God's incomprehensible love faces off with . . . [his] incomprehensible sin . . . . He is not let off the hook. Instead, his confrontation with God's love forces him to face the gravity of his own sin. He sees his sin as God sees it and feels the pain of his testing and purification by fire. Although his experience is brief, relatively speaking, he goes through hell."[69] She also allows that this "whole process might happen in an instant . . . although it may seem much longer to those standing in the flames of God's presence."[70]

- Referring to God saying, "Never will I leave you; never will I forsake you (Heb. 13:5; from Deut. 31:6) and especially "God was reconciling the world to himself in Christ, not counting men's sins against them" (2 Cor. 5:19), Baker surmises that "the very character of the Christian faith is forgiveness."[71] And since Jesus did pray from the cross, "Father, forgive them, for they do not know what they are doing" (Luke 23:34), Baker believes these words of Jesus "provide a clue to the importance of forgiveness."[72]

- So Baker theorizes that "to do justice is to love; to do justice is to forgive; to do justice is to reconcile; this is a chain reaction in which love forgives, forgiveness reconciles, and reconciliation restores—all characteristics of divine justice, God's reconciling justice."[73]

- Baker further counsels that "rather than eternal punishment that finally satisfies an offended God, the gospel message speaks of mercy, reconciliation, and restoration as God's justice . . . . rather than forms of retribution that require suffering for all eternity, without hope of redemption."[74] She warns that this tradition only serves "to cheapen the extravagant grace of God" and "contradicts God's overflowing grace, desire, and ability to save all people. It diminishes the extent and effectiveness of Jesus—his life, death, and resurrection—to reconcile all people to God."[75] What we need, she exhorts is "a significantly different image of God than one of an angry, vengeful divinity determined to punish the world for every last shred of sin." And "instead . . . see a God who lovingly pours forth compassion . . . ."[76]

Final Consuming Fiery Thoughts

When God called Isaiah to serve as a prophet, an angel placed a fiery coal on his mouth to purify this new prophet and said, "See, this has touched your lips; your guilt is taken away and your sin atoned for" (Isa. 6:7). This fire made Isaiah holy in his life. Also in this life there is the baptism "with fire" (Matt. 3:11). Then why can not this fire of God function in the afterlife, where it may be severe or mild. And as we've seen in Chapter 12, the adjective *aionios* when used to modify the noun punishment does not set a time parameter but allows for both an extended time and/or a short time. Yet the more determined we are to cling to our fleshly desires and sins in both this life and the next life, the longer and more painful this process may be. Nonetheless, it's highly unlikely that anyone will be left in God's fire after it has served its cleansing and purification purpose. For surely "the Judge of all the earth" shall "do right" (Gen. 18:25) in achieving his will, desire, and purpose for all his creatures.

And despite Christian claims to the contrary that in the afterlife "your future will be irrevocably fixed and eternally unchangeable"[77] and "it will be too late,"[78] we, once again, must remember and emphasize that there is no biblical obstacle preventing a transfer from "the lake of fire" into heaven itself after a period of time (assuming for the moment that the lake of fire is not part of heaven, *per se*, which it may be).

There is no biblical obstacle preventing a transfer from "the lake of fire" into heaven itself after a period of time.

Furthermore, the biblical fact is, the whole human race, past, present, and future (believers and non-believers alike), are subject to postmortem fire. But since God wills, desires, and purposes to save all, this may be the means by which He accomplishes it—through both a pre-mortem and postmortem, age-enduring process (not an event) of loving, witnessing, speaking, exhorting, entreating, educating, preaching, correcting, proclaiming, persuading and/or inflicting pain, purification, disciplining, remaking, showing his power, and even punishing and tormenting, etc., etc. until his "drawing" and "enabling" conquerors the will of all men and women and they, willingly and freely, come, turn to, and believe in the Lord Jesus Christ (Acts 16:30-31), and truly trust in and receive Him as their Lord and Savior (Heb. 11:6). Amen?

Therefore, in the afterlife, this great fire may be used by God in multiple ways like fire in our world and life to cleanse, purify, purge, temper, and produce change from a lower into a higher form. No doubt, when God turns on this heat, things will begin to melt and be transformed, but not to destroy the person. Hereby, the purpose of God's postmortem punishment or correction for inaccurate beliefs and/or wrongs committed in this finite earthly life becomes more redemptive and less revengeful and retributive. As a consequence of these postmortem possibilities, these scriptures may be totally fulfilled only in the afterlife:

> *"through the greatness of your power your enemies shall submit themselves to you. All the earth shall worship You and sing praises to you"* (Psa. 66:3, 4).

> *"All the ends of the world shall remember and turn to the Lord, and all the families of the nations shall worship before you. All those who go down to the dust shall bow before you"* (Psa. 22:27, 29).

> *"I revealed myself to those who did not ask for me; I was found by those who did not seek me"* (Isa. 65:1).

Even the exclusivist authors of *Sense & Nonsense About Heaven & Hell* admit that this postmortem scenario and divine methodology is a possibility, ". . . we should assume that people who have never heard the gospel need it in order to be saved, while also acknowledging that God may very well have found a way to save some people apart from the human preaching of the gospel."[79]

Yes, the postmortem evangelism by Jesus, an angel, the Apostle Paul, or some other postmortem saint is biblically possible in God's lake of fire (which likely is God), in heaven, in Hades or wherever—if we are willing to think outside the box but also in harmony with Scripture. Would you now agree or disagree? Hell yes? Hell no?

God's Incentive Plan—a Hierarchical View of Heaven

Service rendered in the kingdom of God while on earth is not in vain. It does not go unrewarded. Not only do a believer's righteous acts (see Rev. 19: 8), here and now, bring rewards in this life, but perhaps even more and greater rewards in the afterlife and for all eternity. It's termed "The Doctrine of Eternal Rewards and Punishment for Believers." Sadly, this doctrine is rarely, if ever, taught in most churches. But please be assured, it is a legitimate incentive plan that culminates in heaven.

WARNING: This may or may not be a message some believers in Christ want to hear.

When the word "heaven" is mentioned, what do you immediately think of or see in your mind's eye (your mental picture)? Or, how do you ponder the reality of the afterlife in eternity ahead? Some Christians think heaven sounds boring—like floating around on clouds with a bunch of angels playing harps or a never-ending church service. Others dream of it as a fantasy land—like a Christian Disneyland or theme park—or as some gigantic galactic space craft (the "Mothership")/city gliding through space. Or maybe you picture it like C.S. Lewis' depiction of Narnia, either the book and/or the movie version. Some gravitate to the expansive and heavenly images portrayed in the book of Revelation (chapters 4, 5, 6, not 21 & 22) with weird animals roaming all around.

But let's think about heaven this way. Heaven is another world created and inhabited by the same God who created this world, the Earth, and the cosmos. And just look at how magnificent, spectacular, and drawing this world is, especially for the adventurers among us. I, for one, love to travel and God has given me many opportunities for adventure travel around this world—for instance, to climb great mountains and write about my experiences.[80]

Of course, God has not revealed much about what heaven is like. Yet He has "peaked" the interest of many of us with statements like: "No eye has seen, no ear has heard, no mind has conceived what God has prepared for those who love him" (1 Cor. 2:9 from Isa. 64:4; also see Heb. 11:13-16). Yes, this verse may apply to both this life and the afterlife in heaven.

So, what will heaven be like? Apart from God's few revelations, no one really knows for sure. But He created the Garden of Eden in a "very good" Earth. How about heaven being at least as good as that original garden or as Earth, if not "gooder?" I know that's not good English, but it might be great theology. Then, how about heaven not being a totally foreign experience? In other words, it could have things in it with which we are familiar. Like what? Like: a sea, land, mountains, valleys, fields, rivers, streams, trees, plants, flowers, vistas, and dwelling places and cities, etc—but all more beautiful, spectacular, wondrous, and exciting than what God has provided for our temporary existence here on planet Earth.

After all, Jesus did say that He was going there to "prepare" that real place for us (John 14:2). As long as we are speculating, how about this? We may no longer be land-fastened. That's right! We may be able to fly! Seem far out? We'll have new spiritual bodies (1 Cor. 15:44). And, reportedly, one of the most frequent dreams we humans have is that of flying. Throughout the Bible God gave people dreams (also see Acts 2:17). This dream of flying might just be a preview of coming attractions.

But most Christians I've talked to over the years about this topic say something condescending like, "I'll just be happy getting in (and avoiding "hell"). And if all I am is a pauper in a little cabin in the corner of glory land, that will be okay with me." I find those comments a little strange, however, since I know some of them would not have been happy being a pauper for their short stay on earth. So why would they think they'd be happy with only getting into heaven and being a pauper there for all eternity? When they actually get there, they may care, a lot.

In this perfect and more glorious environment they may find out how much they could have had to enjoy and be blessed with, verses how much they will be missing out on for all eternity. But then it will be too late to do anything about it. Does this seem far out? Contrary to popular thinking that there will be no pain or sorrow in heaven, Tony Evans doesn't agree. He believes quite a bit of remorse may be part of heaven because "God is going to say to many believers in heaven, 'Let Me show you what I had stored up for you as an inheritance that you never credited to your account by being faithful.'"[81]

The Bible also clearly teaches we will not all be the same in heaven. There will not be equality. Billy Graham writes about this future reality in one of this recent newspaper columns. He knows that:

If we know Christ, however, our salvation is already assured. We'll still stand before God – but not to be judged for our salvation. We will stand before God to be rewarded for our good deeds. We are accountable to God for the way we live as believers.[82]

Dr. Graham is right, of course. Our salvation does not depend upon our good works. But our position and blessings in heaven for all eternity do. As Grudem writes in his *Systematic Theology* textbook, the judgment for believers will be "to evaluate and bestow various degrees of reward. . . . there will be those with greater rewards, or who have higher status and authority . . . . those nearest the throne of God."[83] For believers alive today he characterizes this judgment as "an incentive to faithfulness and good works, not as a means of earning forgiveness of sins, but as a means of gaining greater eternal reward. This is a healthy and good motive for us—Jesus tells us, 'Lay up for yourselves treasures in heaven' (Matt. 6:20)."[84]

The Bible clearly teaches we will not all be the same in heaven.

Grudem further and rightly advises, "it would be morally and spiritually beneficial for us to have a greater consciousness of the clear New Testament teaching on degrees of heavenly reward. Rather than making us competitive with one another, it would cause us to help and encourage one another that we all may increase our heavenly reward . . . ." He then cites, and emphasizes with italics, portions of this verse to support his stance, "*Let us consider how to stir up one another to love and good deeds,* not neglecting to meet together, as is the habit of some, but *encouraging one another,* and all the more as you see the Day drawing near" (Heb. 10:24-25).

He concludes that "a heartfelt seeking of future heavenly reward would motivate us to work wholeheartedly for the Lord at whatever task he calls us to, whether great or small, paid or unpaid. It would make us long for his approval rather than for wealth or success. It would motivate us to work at building up the church on the one foundation, Jesus Christ (1 Cor. 3:10-15)."[85]

In his section on "Questions for Personal Application," Grudem asks these two challenging questions: "Have you previously thought very much about laying up treasures in heaven, or about earning greater heavenly reward? If you really believe this doctrine, what kind of effect do you think it should have on your life?"[86]

Scriptures for Heavenly Rewards and Punishment

Certainly, the Bible does not teach salvation by works. Salvation is a gift and comes by faith alone (Eph. 2:8-9). But once you are saved, and if this happens in this life, you then have the opportunity to do "good works" (Eph. 2:10). Those "good works" are the basis for storing up heavenly rewards (Matt.6:19-21). It is also true that we are not saved *without* works (Phil. 2:12-13; Jas. 2:17-20), that rewards and punishments for believers are based on works for or against God, and works are also the basis of punishment for both believers and non-believers.

Let's look at some scriptures for rewards:

"God 'will give to each person according to what he has done'" (Rom. 2:6; Psa. 62:12; Prov. 24:12).

"For we must all appear before the judgment seat of Christ, that each one may receive what is due him for the things done while in the body, whether good or bad" (2 Cor. 5:10).

"So do not throw away your confidence; it will be richly rewarded. You need to persevere so that when you have done the will of God, you will receive what he has promised" (Heb. 10:35-36).

"And without faith it is impossible to please God, because anyone who comes to him must believe that he exists and that he rewards those who earnestly seek him" (Heb. 11:6).

"Then all the churches will know that I am he who searches hearts and minds, and I will repay each of you according to your deeds (Rev. 2:23b).

"'Blessed are the dead who die in the Lord from now on.' 'Yes,' says the Spirit, 'they will rest from their labor, for their deeds will follow them'" (Rev. 14:13b).

"The dead were judged according to what they had done as recorded in the books" (Rev. 20:12b).

"My reward is with me, and I will give to everyone according to what he has done" (Rev. 22:12b).

As we can see from these scriptures and as Randy Alcorn writes, "Works do *not* affect our redemption. Works *do* affect our reward. Just as there are eternal consequences to our faith, so there are eternal consequences to our works." He defines our "reward-earning works" as those works that "are empowered by the Holy Spirit (Colossians 1:29)." Next, he adds this interesting insight that *"Eternal* rewards are guaranteed; *temporal* rewards are not. . . . Scripture does not guarantee I will always receive rewards on earth." But "in the end, our righteous God promises to make all things right.[87]

But Alcorn also warns his readers and confesses that "when it comes to my bad works and my failure to do good works, it gets tricky. . . . Once lost or squandered, opportunity doesn't reappear. . . . many times as I've failed him . . . . The question is, will you seek to do more rewardable works for him now, while you still can? Anticipating this future joy should fuel our present ministry efforts. . . . God is watching. He's keeping track. In heaven he'll reward us for our acts of faithfulness to him. . . ."[88]

Likewise and in this light of future heavenly rewards, Tony Evans makes some poignant points:

God paid a high price for you and me. We cost Him the life of His Son. Not only that, but He has entrusted us with the stewardship of His kingdom. He has given us the privilege of ruling with Him in His kingdom. Are we going to turn around and give God sloppy work, our left-over time, talents, and treasure? . . . the fundamental question that Christ will ask every believer at His judgment seat is this: 'Did you finish? Did you complete the task of living for Me that I gave you when I saved you? Were you faithful to Me?[89]

How each of us fares on that day of judgment when this evaluation is made will determine how we spend eternity. And yet, what this overall distribution of heavenly rewards, blessings and/or losses looks like in our hierarchical view of heaven—whether it's portrayed as a triangle, a pyramid, a bell-shaped curve, or something else—is impossible to know. Most likely, they will range from the highest level, to the next highest level, to middle levels, to lower levels, to a minimal level, to a pauper level, and perhaps down to nothing more than entry.

George Eldon Ladd expounds on 1 Cor. 3:12-15's afterlife testing of each individual's works by fire that "some Christians will live worthless lives; their works, like wood, hay, and stubble, will be consumed in the flames of judgment so that nothing remains as a result of their life on earth. This does not mean the loss of salvation: 'he himself will be saved,' but will suffer loss of the 'well done, good and faithful servant.' Those who have built faithfully and effectively will be rewarded for their love and devotion." Ladd also notes that "Paul does not indicate what the reward will be." Nevertheless "Christians are left in no doubt that they are regarded by God as fully answerable for the quality of their present lives in the body."[90]

How each of us fares on that day of judgment when this evaluation is made will determine how we spend eternity.

Admittedly, we've just scratched the surface of this study of "The Doctrine of Eternal Rewards and Punishment for Believers." It is a fascinating and rewarding study, but one largely neglected or denied in most churches today. But why wouldn't you want to know about this *now* while you can do something about it, rather than *later* when you won't be able to do anything about it?

Remember, Jesus taught his followers and us today:

*"Do not store up for yourselves treasure on earth, where moth
and rust destroy, and where thieves break in and steal. But store
up for yourselves treasure in heaven, where moth and rust do not
destroy, and where thieves do not break in and steal. For where
your treasure is, there your heart will be also"* (Matt. 6:19-21).

For more, see Appendix A. It provides a more extensive scriptural
recap of God's Incentive Plan, a Hierarchical View of Heaven, and "The
Doctrine of Eternal Rewards and Punishment for Believers."

Life in Heaven?

The following is a sad but true story. It's an excerpt from an article I
wrote titled, "Why Are Christians Losing America?" This article was
published in *MovieGuide* magazine, September 2007 issue:

What is eternal life in heaven really going to be like?

Rarely, if ever, is the doctrine of eternal rewards, loss, and
punishments for believers taught or preached. Therefore, "there are
countless 'Christians' who believe they have a ticket to heaven, and
nothing else really matters." (*Whistleblower* magazine, April, 2005, 22.)

So, why is this biblical teaching rarely if ever taught? Here's a short,
recent, and true story that might shed some light on this omission.

The senior pastor's sermon that Sunday was on the topic of
"Universal Judgment." Confidently, he assured the large congregation
that if they are believers in Jesus Christ, they have nothing to fear,
nothing to worry about, concerning judgment, because Christ has taken
care of it for us.

In a follow-up conversation, I asked this pastor if he was familiar
with the doctrine of eternal rewards, loss, and even punishment for
believers in heaven. He said he wasn't interested. I mentioned that there
are many verses that speak of this and I'd be happy to send them to him.
He responded that there are many more verses that speak of God's grace
and love and of setting people free. He would focus on these and not the
others, thank you.

No doubt, this pastor is both a victim as well as a perpetrator of a
dumbed-down version of Christianity.

These comments from Brian McLaren speak frankly and directly to this area of dumbed-downedness:

> What could be more serious than standing in front of your Creator—the Creator of the universe—and finding out that you had wasted your life, squandered your inheritance, caused others pain and sorrow, worked against the good plans and desires of God? What could be more serious than that? To have to face the real, eternal, unavoidable, absolute, naked truth about yourself, what you've done, what you've become? . . . . Nothing could be more serious than that . . . . We cannot select out comfortable passages and ignore those that make us uneasy. (McLaren, *The Last Word*, 79, 80, 96.)

Yet McLaren reminds his readers that he is "not denying salvation by grace . . . . I'm just advocating judgment by works," and that "being judged isn't the same as being condemned and that being saved means a lot more than not being judged." (Ibid., 138.)

What do you think?

In sum, a hierarchical heaven is where some, many, most, or all will spend eternity. And heaven is gift, not a reward. But how we spend eternity there will be determined by our good works on this earth during this life. These works earn rewards. Hence, how we live this life determines our next life—our status, privileges, provisions, levels of reward, treasure, glory, authority, joy, enjoyment, and also "rewards lost due to disobedience on earth."[91]

And contrary to what most Christians have been told and taught, "all men [and women] are *not* equal before God; the facts of heaven and hell (sic), election and reprobation, make clear that they are not equal."[92] Hence, these differing degrees of reward will be determined according to:

1. The knowledge, time, talents and resources given us.
    (Matt. 25:14-30; Luke 19:11-27)
2. How we use them for God's glory to expand his kingdom.
    (2 Thess. 1:4-5; 1 Pet. 4:13; Phil. 3:10-11).

Yes, we have a great and unlimited heavenly future awaiting us. But since there will be different rewards, different positions, and different experiences in heaven that are currently being determined in *this* life, doesn't this future destiny give this life even greater meaning? You might be wondering how could someone in heaven be happy with a "lesser" amount than they could have received or with less than someone else receives? The answer is, I don't know. And, yes, this is a threatening, controversial, and surprising message for some people. But once again, would you rather hear it now while you can do something about it? Or would you rather wait until later when you can't and have it come as a complete surprise?

So what's going to be your degree of glory, level of blessings, rewards, station, position, responsibilities, joy, and/or punishment in this eternal afterlife in God's hierarchical heaven?

Closing Quotes

"No wonder Scripture makes clear that the one central business of this life is to prepare for the next. . . . Your life on earth is a dot. From that dot extends a line that goes on for all eternity. Right now you're living *in* the dot. But what are you living *for*? Are you living for the dot or for the line? Are you living for earth or for heaven? Are you living for the short today or the long tomorrow?"[93]

—Randy Alcorn, *In Light of Eternity*

"There is a long list of martyrs . . . . The famous Lutheran martyr Dietrich Bonhoeffer . . . In his last letters from prison, Bonhoeffer reveals how his Christian faith gave him the resources to give up everything for the sake of others. . . . had a joy and hope in God that made it possible for him to do what he did."[94]

—Timothy Keller, *The Reason for God.*

"Let me tell you, if you are too busy to serve Christ, you are too busy to be great in His kingdom. If you are too busy to serve now, you are too busy to be recognized then."[95]

—Tony Evans, *What a Way to Live!*

"Not that I have already obtained all this, or have already been made perfect, but I press on to take hold of that for which Christ Jesus took hold of me. Brothers, I do not consider myself yet to have taken hold of it. But one thing I do: Forgetting what is behind and straining toward what is ahead, I press on toward the goal to win the prize for which God has called me heavenward in Christ Jesus."

(Philippians 3:12-14)

"I have fought the good fight, I have finished the race, I have kept the faith. Now there is in store for me the crown of righteousness, which the Lord, the righteous judge, will award to me on that day – not only to me, but also to all who have longed for his appearing."

(2 Timothy 4:7)

"Therefore, since we are surrounded by such a great cloud of witnesses, let us throw off everything that hinders and the sin that so easily entangles, and let us run with perseverance the race marked out for us."

(Hebrews 12:1)

Dear reader, let's you and I do this! Let's get our eyes on this prize, fight the good fight of faith, and finish the race . . . unto our "crowning day" when hopefully we will hear these words, "Well done, good and faithful servant! You have been faithful with a few things; I will put you in charge of many things. Come and share your master's happiness!" (Matt. 25:21, 23). So, what do you say now? Hell yes? Hell no?

Let's now conclude this book.

Conclusion

My Current Official Position

"Hell yes," each of us has the responsibility to question and test our assumptions and beliefs about our faith against what the Bible actually says. But, "hell no," God doesn't fall off his throne because someone asks questions, even tough questions.[1] In this book, that is exactly what we have done.

We have also stood on the shoulders of many other writers, past and present. Some I quoted extensively as we drew on their wisdom, were blessed by their insights, and even gained from their disagreements. For them I, and now you, should be most thankful (see the Dedication, p-*iii*).

As a result, we have seen the paucity of biblical and historical evidence to support our modern notions of hell, as it traditionally has been conceived. We have seen that the prevailing doctrine of the early church for its first five hundred years, most likely but arguably, was that of Christian Universalism. And we have re-explored the greater issue of the extent of God's grace . . . and wrath for the eternal afterlife destiny of all people.

We have also seen that competing views are both riddled with problems and filled with compelling arguments. And yet neither side can be proven conclusively right or totally wrong. In fact, no resolution was possible until we went beyond the proof-text debates and brush-off tactics to return to Scripture and think outside the box—like God. Consequently, I suggest, the great advantage of the "both/and" synthesis approach I have proposed and presented in Chapter 16 has been to offer a way to ferret all this out. No doubt, this synthesis produces a somewhat different view of Christianity than what traditionally has been handed down to us today.

Today, however, many Christians are lukewarm, or cold, about sharing our current version of the gospel and our faith. In my opinion, this is a huge red flag that something is clearly wrong. Frankly, I must ask you, how open are you to the possibility that we have misread some important parts of the Bible? In my opinion, it is time for all Christians— biblical scholars, theologians, pastors, teachers, and all of us who value Scripture—to re-address these three questions: What is our faith? What is the gospel? What is and should be the message of evangelism?

Competing views are both riddled with problems and filled with compelling arguments.

So how many will be saved—some, many, most, or all? The scriptures seem divided. What each side regards as the clear teaching of Scripture, others explain away or reject. Most likely, none of us have a corner on God's truth and postmortem reality in these matters. Other possibilities may lie beyond what we have discussed or even imagined. Perhaps, *Time* magazine puts it rather well and most succinctly: "It is a case for living with a mystery rather than demanding certitude."[2]

My Closing Advice

After openly, honestly, and seriously re-exploring the issues covered in this book, reviewing the Scriptures and the biblical arguments from all sides in this great debate, and attempting to re-think their implications and unravel their considerable difficulties, my closing advice is this. Regardless of where we stand or what we may now think and believe about the extent of God's plan of salvation, we should take on a much more humble attitude, be extra cautious, and drop the "heretical" label— if for no other reason than knowing that the traditions of men can "nullify the word of God" and make it of little or "none effect" (Mark 7:13; Matt. 15:6 *KJV*). We may be in danger of having done that in this most significant area of our faith.

Dogmatism, arrogance, and fighting over argument points are clearly out of place. And, yes, I am aware that critics from the majority view may charge me with being "soft," or worse. But in the end, the decision is God's alone. It lies in the mystery of his sovereignty to extend his mercy to some, many, most, or all, or to withhold it entirely.

Moreover, we creatures have no business calling our Creator to account (Rom. 9:20-21) or criticizing Him (Rom. 11:33-36). Nor can we put limitations on his love, mercy, and grace, or what He can or cannot do, or what He must or must not do in this matter. Naturally, more questions and other issues remain to be addressed and reconsidered. But surely we can now agree that God is within his sovereignty, mercy, power, and love to save no one, anyone, or everyone. Can we not? *Hell yes? Hell no?*

Can we at least concede that we don't fully know how God thinks, works, or functions in a postmortem *modus operandi*? *Hell yes? Hell no?*

Throughout this book, we have utilized much exegetical and historical evidence. We have also avoided resorting to emotional appeals, which are all-to-common. At the end, if my solution of synthesis at first seems far-fetched, maybe that is because we have been so deeply and for so long indoctrinated with the exclusivist position. But I submit that absolutely everything I have suggested can be harmonized with all "The Twelve Demands of Scripture for Salvation and Eternal Life" presented in Chapter 15. I further submit that this solution is a Christ-honoring, Scripture-authenticating, and faith-validating solution. On the other hand, I also agree with McLaren that I and we "need to keep listening and learning in openness to the Spirit and the world for the sake of the gospel . . . to keep conversations going and not to end them."[3]

Likewise, we'd be well advised to respect McLaren's declaration about Christian Universalists, that "they have the highest opinion possible about the efficacy and scope of the saving work of Jesus!"[4] In his sovereignty and without violating, contradicting, or compromising his revealed Word—in any way—can we now see how God might, could, and may save some, many, most, or all, regardless of what we have been taught, believe, or want Him to do. Do you agree? *Hell yes? Hell no?*

So let's let God be God and "God be true, and every man a liar" (Rom. 3:4)—including me if I'm in error in any way on anything or everything we've been re-exploring in this book. God alone will determine what is just and fair. And Scripture assures us that we can rest in the fact that God's "works are perfect, and all his ways are just. A faithful God who does no wrong, upright and just is he." (Deut. 32:4).

In the end, and in my opinion, we must put aside the sin of certainty and the arrogance of pretending we know more than we do. May we soften our views and simply trust in the goodness of God. He will do what is good, right, just, and loving for every person. And He will accomplish what He wants. Amen? *Hell yes? Hell no?*

My Current Official Position

Lest I be misunderstood or misrepresented, my current and official position regarding the eternal afterlife destiny of the all people is this:

I'm not so sure we can be so sure, anymore.

Yes, I'm still struggling with some of this and my position may change in the future. Perhaps, I've overlooked something and one or more of my critics can straighten me out. For now, I am hanging onto the mystery of Romans 11:33-36. And if the Apostle Paul left this hanging up in the air and could only bow before this mystery, why can't I?

But if I'm leaning, I'm leaning toward God's revealed will, desire, and purpose being supreme and achievable. In my opinion, the scriptural case for this eventual outcome is stronger than the case against it. Furthermore, the competing and conflicting positions we have re-explored in this book are reconcilable in the form of the synthesis I've proposed and presented.

But, make no mistake; I do not want to place myself in opposition to God and his sovereignty being supreme in this matter and end up in "heck, by gosh," as some of my critics, no doubt, will say I shall—a little hellacious humor to end this book as we began it.

Parting Wisdom

Still, the vast majority is like Sanders, "I remain unpersuaded that universalism is true."[5]

Chan perhaps nails the real reason why so many are unpersuaded when he surmises, "maybe we don't want to admit that we believe in a God who is *so* free to do whatever He wants."[6] He historically elaborates, "the fact is, Scripture is filled with divine actions that don't fit our human standards of logic or morality. But they don't need to, because we are the clay and He is the Potter." He humbly and appropriately concludes by stating the obvious, "we serve a God whose ways are incomprehensible, whose thoughts are not like our thoughts."[7]

Galli, in his concluding his book, spotlights a growing hope: "some conservative theologians today hope for universal salvation. . . . of course, this is hardly inappropriate. If God wishes all to be saved, surely we who love God and want what he wants should hope for the salvation of all as well." Then he adds his exclusivist caveat, "But we cannot confuse a pious hope with the biblical teaching we are called to proclaim to all."[8] This book, the one you hold in your hand, may have provided a possible way, or model, by which all this might, could, and may happen—if, as Galli further advises, we are willing "to listen patiently and wrestle with difficulties afresh . . . . step back, listen hard to the doubts and concerns, and take time to engage charitably."[9]

Lastly, he shares these sentiments, which I also wholeheartedly embrace, as he longs "for an authoritative body to pronounce a final verdict" and for the Holy Spirit to "guide us into all truth, that through discussion and debate a sifting process will allow the truth of God in Christ to deepen and broaden."[10]

Most notably, in this regard and as Erickson documents, the Church has never formally addressed this issue:

> Elements of the doctrine of salvation were certainly treated, especially by councils such as Trent, but the question of how many will be saved and the ultimate destiny of the lost, or the duration of punishment for unbelievers, did not receive such attention. . . . This means there is a back-load of unresolved issues . . . ."[11]

Perhaps, Grudem's previously cited comment concerning Annihilationism bears repeating and applying to the whole realm of salvation and redemption. "The ultimate resolution of the depths of this question lies far beyond our ability to understand, and remains hidden in the counsels of God."[12]

Lest I be misunderstood or misrepresented, my current and official position regarding the eternal afterlife destiny of the all people is this:

I'm not so sure we can be so sure, anymore.

So, what do you now think? *Hell yes? Hell no?* Or, are you like me—not so sure you are so sure, anymore?

Appendix A

A Scriptural Recap of God's Incentive Plan

—A Hierarchical View of Heaven—

—'The Doctrine of Eternal Rewards and Punishment for Believers'—

I have found this order of scriptures and associated content cues that are presented below works well in small-group discussions of these above topics. However, this list is not exhaustive. You may want to add to it and/or rearrange the order.

General Concept:

1 Cor. 2:9 (Isa. 64:4) – "what God has prepared"
2 Cor. 4:17 – "our light and momentary troubles are achieving for us"
Heb. 11:13-16 – "a better country – a heavenly one"
Eph. 2:8-10; Phil. 2:12-13; Jas. 1:17-20 – "to do good works"
1 Cor. 15:58 – "not in vain"
2 Tim. 2:12 – "if . . . ."
Luke 16:10-12 – "if . . . ."

Rewards:

Rom. 2:5-6; 14:10-12 – "what done"
Rev. 14:13 – "their deeds follow them"
Rev. 20:11-15 – "according to what he had done"
Rev. 2:23 – "according to your deeds"
Rev. 22:12 – "My reward is with me"
2 Cor. 5:10 – "whether good or bad"
Heb. 10:35-36; 11:6, 39-40 (This was not previously the case.)
Matt. 5:11-12, 46 (also Luke 6:22-23, 35) – "great is your reward in heaven"
Matt. 10:41-42 – "a prophet's reward"

Matt. 13:8, 23 – "a hundred, sixty or thirty times what was sown"

Matt. 19:29-30 – "a hundred times as much"

Matt. 25:14-30 (the parable of the talents – according to our God-given time, abilities, and resources – God has expectations of you/us.)

Luke 19:11-27 (the parable of the ten minas – a "mina" is an amount of money, about three month's wages for a laborer. How literally should we take this promise of cities? The point is there will be a difference in rewards.)

Mark 12:41-44 (the widow's offering – the point is, the value of the gift is not measured by its size but by its sacrifice.)

Matt. 6:19-21 – "store up . . . treasures in heaven" (Also: Luke 12:32-34; Mark 10:21; 1 Tim. 6:18-19)

John 4:35-36; 14:2 – "the fields! They are ripe for harvest"

1 Cor. 3:8; 4:5 – "rewarded according . . ."

Eph. 6:7-8 – "Serve wholeheartedly . . . the Lord will reward"

Col. 3:23-24 – "an inheritance from the Lord as a reward"

1 Pet. 1:7 – "greater worth than gold . . . refined by fire"

2 Pet. 1:10-11 – "receive a rich welcome"

Rev. 2-3 – (These promises of heavenly reward will be given us accordingly.)

Punishment/Loss (of privileges, position, etc.):

Matt. 12:36-37, (also Luke 20:47) – "give an account . . . every careless word"

Matt. 18:23-35 – (the parable of the unmerciful servant.)

Rom. 2:5-6 – "storing up wrath"

Col. 3:25, 5-6 – "repaid for his wrong . . . no favoritism"

2 Thess. 1:6 – "pay back trouble"

Heb. 10:30-31 – "a dreadful thing"

1 Pet. 4:3-5 – "to give an account"

Rev. 11:18 – "rewarding . . . destroying"

Eccl. 12:14 – "God will bring every deed to judgment"

2 Cor. 5:10 – (loss due to bad works.)

1 Cor. 9:27; Col. 2:18 – (Don't get "disqualified.")

2 John 8 – (Don't "lose what you have worked for.")

1 Cor. 3:10-15 – (Don't "suffer loss.")

1 Cor. 6:2-3 – "judge the world . . . . judge angels"

Matt. 5:19; 6:1-5, 16-18 – "called least . . . called great"
Matt. 25:31-46 (Note the criteria here – how we treated the poor, hungry, imprisoned, naked masses – the "least of these." Will there be a goat group in heaven?)
Jas. 3:1 – "judged more strictly"
2 Pet. 2:21 – "better not to have known the way or righteousness"
Luke 12:47-48 – (Note the degrees of punishment.)
Heb. 10:29 – "more severely"
Matt. 8:12; 22:8-14; 5:22 – "the subjects of the kingdom . . . thrown out"

What Our Motivation Should Be:

There is a wrong way of thinking of rewards (i.e., as an ulterior motive).

- If we are only serving for what we get, we are no more than hirelings.
- Still, there is a right way to think about rewards.
- And this motive is open, front, and center in God's Word.
- For one, it can strengthen our perseverance (see Heb. 11:26).

Bottom line is: If we obey God, He *may* reward us in this life but definitely will in the next.

If we don't, He won't. He'll discipline and/or perhaps punish us, here and there.

The realization of these facts should be a present motivating force and factor in our lives, here and now, to avoid laziness and disobedience.

Heb. 11:26 – "looking ahead to his reward"
Phil. 2:12-14 – "continue to work out . . ."
2 Tim. 4:7 – "the good fight . . . finished the race"
Heb. 12:1 – "throw off . . . run with perseverance"
2 Thess. 1:4-5 – "be counted worthy"
1 Pet. 4:13 – "you may be overjoyed"
Phil. 3:10-11 – "know Christ and the power"
John 15:2 – "bear fruit . . . more fruitful"
Rev. 5:9-10 – "serve our God . . . reign on the earth."

**<u>Five Crowns—as Reward and "lasting reminders of our work on
earth and Christ's faithfulness in empowering us to do that work:"</u>**[1]

The crown of life (Jas. 1:12; Rev. 2:10; 3:11)
The incorruptible crown that lasts forever (1 Cor. 9:24-25)
The crown of glory (1 Pet. 5:1-4)
The crown of righteousness (2 Tim. 4:6-8)
The crown of rejoicing in his presence (1 Thess. 2:19; may be related to
    Dan. 12:3)

Are these trophies, all-access passes, or what? Who knows?

Once again, these possible, heavenly, and eternal rewards or losses
depend on what you and I do, or don't do, here and now, on this earth,
during this short life.

MORE BOOKS FROM JOHN NOE

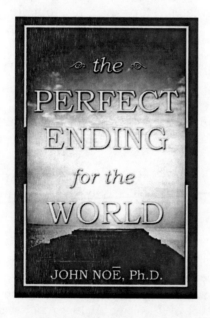

Why All 'End-of-the-World' Prophets Will <u>Always</u> Be Wrong!

The perennial prophets of doom have failed to recognize that our world is without end and "the end" the Bible consistently proclaims *for* the world is behind us and not ahead of us; is past and not future. This is the perfect ending! It's also the climax of the rest of the greatest story ever foretold. In this book you'll discover:

~ WHY THE WORLD WILL NEVER END.
~ HOW THE PERFECT ENDING FOR THE
  WORLD CAME RIGHT ON TIME.
~ DIVINE PERFECTION IN GOD'S END-TIME PLAN.
~ A NEW & GREATER PARADIGM OF THOUGHT AND
  FAITH.
~ OUR GREATER RESPONSIBILITIES HEREIN.
~ WHY THE FUTURE IS BRIGHT AND PROMISING.
~ THE BASIS FOR THE NEXT REFORMATION OF
  CHRISTIANITY.

"Noē's book just could be the spark that ignites the next reformation of Christianity." – Dr. James Earl Massey, Former Sr. Editor, *Christianity Today* Dean Emeritus, School of Theology, Anderson University & Distinguished Professor-at-Large

"Your treatment of the 'end of the world' is the best treatment of this idea . . . . Your book could really open the eyes of a lot of people." – Walter C. Hibbard, Former Chairman, Great Christian Books

"Noē . . . argues, with no little energy, against traditional views . . . [it] does have an internal logic that makes for exegetically interesting reading." – Mark Galli, Book Review Editor, *Christianity Today*

Revised edition – PEAK PERFORMANCE PRINICIPLES FOR HIGH ACHIEVERS *is a dynamic story of how one man transformed himself, sedentary and out-of-shape in his mid-thirties, into a dynamic leader – and how you can too.*

John R. Noē is using his mountain-climbing adventures as an allegory for the challenge of goal setting and the thrill of high achievement. He shows you how to choose accurate goals, how to reach them, how to remain committed to the accomplishment of a goal whether earthly or spiritual, and—in short—how to become a high achiever. To help you succeed, Noē offers a unique philosophy of reaching "beyond self-motivation" to the spiritual motivation that comes from God.

In this revised edition, Noē adds further insights and updates his reader on how these principles have fared in his life since the book's original writing in 1984—which was named one of Amway Corporation's "top ten recommended books."

Noē shows you how to learn the six essential attitudes of a high achiever:

1. High Achievers make no small plans.
2. Are willing to do what they fear.
3. Are willing to prepare.
4. To risk failure.
5. To be taught.
6. And must have heart.

"After reading this marvelous book I realized how little I have accomplished with my life . . . compared to what I could have done. But, it's not too late."

Og Mandino, Author of:
The Greatest Salesman in the World

"So many Christians are going through life settling for mediocre, settling for second best, and choosing the path of least resistance. Not Dr. John R. Noē, author of this old (1984) and new (2006) book, *Peak Performance Principles for High Achievers – Revised Edition*. He reminds us that the first mountain we need to conquer is that of ourselves and that God wants us to accomplish great things for His glory."

Dr. D. James Kennedy, Ph.D.
Senior Minister
Coral Ridge Presbyterian Church

What's Next?

Eleven more pioneering and next-reformation titles are in development and coming from John Noē and East2West Press. Tentatively titles and subtitles are (but not necessarily in this order):

NO THAT'S NOT JESUS
Unearthing the contemporary Christ—a much greater Jesus than we've been led to believe

UNRAVELING THE END
A balanced scholarly synthesis of four competing and conflicting end-time views—Unifying 'One of the most divisive elements in recent Christian history'

KINGDOM CHRISTIANITY
In search of a once-mighty faith

THE ISRAEL ILLUSION
15 popular misconceptions about this modern-day nation and its role in Bible prophecy

'WARRIORS OF THE LAST TEMPLE'
The story, theology, and script behind the movie

THE ORIGIN AND PURPOSE OF EVIL
Solving the problem of the presence of evil

GOD THE ULTIMATE COMPETITIVE EDGE
Why settle for anything less?
Transcending the limits of self-motivation, self-esteem & self-empowerment in a tough competitive world

YOUR LAST & GREATEST ADVENTURE
What really happens today immediately after you die?—you may be surprised!

THE SCENE BEHIND THE SEEN
A Preterist-Idealist commentary of the book of Revelation—unveiling its fulfillment and ongoing relevance—past, present & future

AN EXEGETICAL BASIS FOR A PRETERIST-IDEALIST UNDERSTANDING OF THE BOOK OF REVELATION
A reprint of John Noē's article published in the Journal of the Evangelical Theological Society

THE SUPERIORITY OF PRETERISM
A publication of John Noē's Ph.D. dissertation

Books Out-of-Print

BEYOND THE END TIMES

SHATTERING THE 'LEFT BEHIND' DELUSION

DEAD IN THEIR TRACKS

TOP TEN MISCONCEPTIONS ABOUT JESUS' SECOND COMING AND THE END TIMES

PEOPLE POWER

Scripture Index

ENDNOTES

Introduction

[1] Sharon L. Baker, *Razing Hell* (Louisville, KY.: Westminster John Knox Press, 2010), 5.

[2] Ibid., 148.

[3] Ibid., 8.

[4] Ibid., 66.

[5] *The World Book Encyclopedia*, H Volume 9, (World Book—Childcraft International, Inc., 1982), 168.

[6] ibid. For a good overview of many religious traditions and beliefs on hell, go online to www.en.wikipedia.org. Click on "hell."

[7] Dante Alighieri, translated by John Ciardi, *The Divine Comedy: The Inferno, The Purgatorio, and the Paradiso* (New York, NY.: New American Library, 1954-1970), *xi*.

[8] Ibid., *xii*.

[9] Ibid., Virgil in Dante's *The Inferno*, Canto 1, 20.

[10] Ibid., Dante in Canto 3, 31.

[11] *The Doré Illustrations for Dante's Divine Comedy* (New York, NY.: Dover Publications, 1974), back cover.

[12] Michael E. Wittmer, *Christ Alone: An Evangelical Response to Rob Bell's Love Wins* (Grand Rapids, MI.: Edenridge Press, 2011), *vii*.

[13] Timothy Keller, *The Reason for God* (New York, NY.: Dutton, 2008), 69.

[14] Christopher W. Morgan and Robert A. Peterson, general editors, *Hell Under Fire* (Grand Rapids, MI.: Zondervan, 2004), 97 – in presenting the Universalism view.

[15] Mentioned in: Kenneth D. Boa and Robert M. Bowman Jr., *Sense & Nonsense About Heaven & Hell* (Grand Rapids, MI.: Zondervan, 2007), 91.

[16] Edwin W. Lutzer, *One Minute After You Die* (Chicago, IL.: Moody Publishers, 1997), 101.

[17] Ibid., 103.

[18] In a private email to me, 6/11/11.

[19] Jeffery L. Sheler, "Hell Hath No Fury," *U.S. News & World Report Magazine*, 31 January 2000, 45-46.

[20] R. Albert Mohler, Jr., in Christopher W. Morgan and Robert A. Peterson, *Is Hell for Real or Does Everyone Go to Heaven?* (Grand Rapids, MI.: Zondervan, 2011), 11.

[21] Brian D. McLaren, *The Last Word and the Word After That*, (San Francisco, CA.: Jossey-Bass, 2005), *xiii*.

[22] *The World Book Encyclopedia*, H Volume 9, 168.

[23] Randy Alcorn in the Foreword to Mark Galli, *God Wins: Heaven, Hell, and Why the Good News Is Better than Love Wins* (Carol Stream, IL.: Tyndale House, 2011), *xi*.

[24] Wittmer, *Christ Alone*, 3, 155.

[25] Francis Chan and Preston Sprinkle, *Erasing Hell: What God said about eternity, and the things we've made up* (Colorado Springs, CO.: David C. Cook, 2011), 72.

[26] For more see the author's recent book: John Noē, *The Perfect Ending for the World* (Indianapolis, IN.: East2West Press, 2011). Also the author's 13-week podcast teaching series "Unraveling the End: A Biblical Synthesis of Competing Views" – go to www.prophecyrefi.org.

Chapter 1

[1] Dinesh D'Souza, *What's So Great about Christianity* (Washington, D.C.: Regnery Publishing, 2007), 267.

[2] For a fuller account see: Andrea Yates, *Wikipedia.org*, 12/5/2009.

[3] Galli, *God Wins*, ix.

[4] Chan and Sprinkle, *Erasing Hell*, 149.

[5] Results of these two surveys were quoted from McLaren, *The Last Word*, 104.

[6] Baker, *Razing Hell*, 186. "You can read the article online at http://pewforum.org/news/display.php?NewsIE=16260)."

[7] Wayne Grudem, *Systematic Theology: An Introduction to Biblical Doctrine* (Grand Rapids, MI.: Zondervan, 1994), 1152.

[8] Lutzer, *One Minute After You Die*, 94-95.

[9] Brian Jones, *Hell Is Real (But I Hate to Admit It)* (Colorado Springs, CO.: David C. Cook, 2011), 35.

[10] Ibid., 37.

[11] Billy Graham, "My Answer," (*The Indianapolis Star*, 4 December 2009), C5.

[12] *Strong's Exhaustive Concordance of the Bible*, Reference Library Edition (Iowa Falls, IA.: World Bible Publishers, n.d.), 474-475.

[13] Morgan and Peterson, *Hell Under Fire*, 226.

[14] Gary Amirault, "The Hell Test," www.tentmaker.org/articles/hell_test. html, 12/1/10, p-13.

[15] Jones, *Hell Is Real (But I Hate to Admit It)*, 74.

[16] N.T. Wright, *Surprised by Hope* (New York, NY.: HarperOne, 2008), 19.

[17] Keller, *The Reason for God*, 68-83.

[18] Quoted by Paul E. Engle in Morgan and Peterson, *Is Hell for Real or Does Everyone Go to Heaven?*, 9.

[19] Timothy Keller in Morgan and Peterson, *Is Hell for Real or Does Everyone Go to Heaven?*, 74.

[20] McLaren, *The Last Word*, xiii.

[21] Baker, *Razing Hell*, xiii.

[22] Ibid., xiv.

[23] Ibid., 81.

[24] Ibid., 98.

[25] Ibid., 102.

[26] Ibid., 145.

[27] Ibid., 149.

[28] Ibid., 164.

[29] Justin Taylor, "Rob Bell: Universalist?" blog, http://thegospelcoalition.org/blogs;justintaylor/2011/02/26/reb-bell-universalist/

[30] Rob Bell, *Love Wins: A Book About Heaven, Hell, and the Fate of Every Person Who Ever Lived* (New York, NY.: HarperOne, 2011), x.

[31] jeff@passingthebaton.org., "Is Rob Bell On the Right Track?" 4/21/11, 3.

[32] Janice Shaw Crouse, "Beware: Hell exists," April 19, 2011, on www.washingtontimes.com.

[33] Mark Galli, "Heaven, Hell, and Rob Bell: Putting the Pastor in Context," www.christianitytoday.com/ct/article_print.html?id=91120, 3/8/2011.

[34] Timothy Dalrymple, "Liberal 'love,'" *World*, April, 9, 2011, 65-66.

[35] Jon Meacham, "Is Hell Dead?" *Time*, April, 25, 2001, 38-43.

[36] Jon Meacham, "Rob Bell: Rethinking heaven and hell—and everything in between," May 2, 2011, 75.

[37] As of July 25, 2011, *Love Wins* has been on *Publishers Weekly's* Hardcover Bestseller/Nonfiction list for eighteen weeks.

[38] Hank Hanegraff, Christian Research Institute, mass email, 4/5/11.

[39] Morgan and Peterson, *Hell Under Fire*, back cover.

[40] Ibid., 11.

[41] Ibid., 102.

[42] Boa and Bowman Jr., *Sense and Nonsense*, 121.

[43] Ibid., 91.

[44] Ibid., 122.

[45] Lutzer, *One Minute After You Die*, 101-102.

[46] Ibid., 103.

[47] Randy Alcorn's Foreword in Galli, *God Wins*, vii.

[48] Ibid., *viii.*

[49] Ibid., *xiii.*

[50] Ibid., *xvi.*

[51] Ibid., *xvii.*

[52] Ibid., *xviii.*

[53] Galli, *God Wins*, 57.

[54] Ibid., 94.

[55] Ibid., 101.

[56] Ibid., 114.

[57] Ibid., 136.

[58] Chan and Sprinkle, *Erasing Hell*, *ii-iii.*

[59] Ibid., 25.

[60] Ibid., 29.

[61] Ibid., 34.

[62] Ibid., 36.

[63] Ibid., 40.

[64] Ibid., 108.

[65] Wittmer, *Christ Alone*, *i.*

[66] Michael S. Horton's Preface in Wittmer, *Christ Alone*, *viii.*

[67] Ibid., *ix.*

[68] Wittmer, *Christ Alone*, 1.

[69] Ibid., 2.

[70] Ibid., 3.

[71] Ibid., 21.

[72] Ibid., 22.

[73] Ibid., 25.

[74] Ibid., 56.

[75] Ibid., 59.

[76] Ibid., 61.

[77] Ibid., 69.

[78] Ibid., 71.

[79] Ibid., 121.

[80] Jones, *Hell Is Real (But I Hate to Admit It)*, 34.

[81] Ibid., 185.

[82] Ibid., 2.

⁸³ Ibid., 25.
⁸⁴ Ibid., 28.
⁸⁵ Ibid., 29.
⁸⁶ Ibid., 39.
⁸⁷ Engle in Morgan and Peterson, *Is Hell for Real or Does Everyone Go to Heaven?*, 8.
⁸⁸ Morgan and Peterson, Ibid., 81.
⁸⁹ Engle in Ibid., 8.
⁹⁰ J. I. Packer in Ibid., 71-2.
⁹¹ Morgan and Peterson in Ibid., 83.
⁹² Eric Stetson, *Christian Universalism* (n.l.: Sparkling Bay Books, 2008), 74-75.
⁹³ Keller, *The Reason for God*, 69.
⁹⁴ Meacham, "Rob Bell," 75.
⁹⁵ Jones, *Hell Is Real (But I Hate to Admit It)*, 108.
⁹⁶ Wittmer, *Christ Alone*, 127.

Chapter 2

¹ McLaren, *The Last Word*, 45.
² J. Lee Grady, "Don't Get Brainwashed," *Charisma*, March 2009, 6.
³ Meacham, "Is Hell Dead," 40.
⁴ *The World Book Encyclopedia*, H Volume 9, 168.
⁵ "Valley of Haunted History," *The Holy Land Magazine, Christian Tourism to Israel* (Israel, Lishar Publications, Ltd., 2008). 26-27.
⁶ Boa and Bowman, *Sense & Nonsense*, 91.
⁷ W.E. Vine, *An Expository Dictionary of Biblical Words* (Nashville, TN.: Thomas Nelson, 1984), 542-543.
⁸ This history, like most everything else in this book and arena of theology, is contested. According to Chan and Sprinkle, the "'gehenna is a garbage dump' theory is both misleading and inaccurate. . . . there is no evidence for hundreds and hundreds of years after Jesus that there ever was a garbage dump in the Hinnom Valley in the first century. Nor is there any archaeological evidence that this valley was ever a dump. . . . the first reference . . . is made by a rabbi named David Kimhi in a commentary, which was written in AD 1200." (*Erasing Hell*, 59-60). But numerous Bible dictionaries and encyclopedias contain discussions about *Gehenna* being a garbage dump throughout Old and New Testament history. Here are some examples:

- After "being defiled by Josiah (2 K 23), for the purpose of preventing these rites. Thereafter it became the place for the burning of the refuse of the city, along with dead animals and the bodies of criminals. It was natural, therefore, that the name should become a synonym of hell." (*Hastings' Dictionary of the Bible,* 1909, 1994, p-285).

- "When Josiah overthrew this idolatry he defiled the valley by casting into it the bones of the dead, the greatest of all pollutions among the Hebrews; and from that time it became the common jakes [*British Dialect.* for privy or toilet] of Jerusalem, into which all refuse of the city was cast, and where the combustible portions of that refuse were consumed by fire. Hence it came to be regarded as a sort of type of hell, the Gehenna of the New Testament being no other than the name of this valley of Hinnom (Ge-Hinnom);" (*The Popular and Critical Bible Encyclopaedia and Scriptural Dictionary,* 1908, p-813).
- "The fact, also that the city's offal was collected there may have helped to render the name synonymous with extreme defilement." (*The International Standard Bible Encyclopaedia,* 1937, p-1183).
- "The valley also served for the incineration of the city's refuse and for dumping of animal carcasses and the bodies of criminals." (*The Oxford Dictionary of the Jewish Religion,* 1997, p-266).
- But no references are made to this valley being a garbage dump in the *Encyclopaedia Judaica,* 2007, or in *The Jewish Encyclopedia,* MDCCCCIII.

[9] Also see: 2 Chron. 28:3; 33:6 – God terms this practice "evil." 2 Ki. 23:10 – Josiah put a stop to it. For other mentions of this valley location in the Old Testament, see: Josh. 15:8; 18:16; 2 Chron. 33:6; Neh. 11:30.

[10] Some today feel that Molech is still around, but is known by a different name—Pro-choice—and is still deceiving people into sacrificing their children to him. But instead of these children being burned in Molech's stomach, they burn and cry out in the womb.

[11] Bernhard W. Anderson, *Understanding the Old Testament,* Third Ed., (Englewood Cliffs, NJ.: Prentice-Hall, 1975), 377-378.

[12] Noē, *The Perfect Ending for the World* – available only on Amazon.com.

Chapter 3

[1] Philip Graham Ryken, *My Father's World* (Phillipsburg, NJ.: P&R Publishing, 2002), 252.
[2] Billy Graham, "My Answer," *The Indianapolis Star,* April 5, 2011, E4.
[3] Galli, *God Wins, ix.*
[4] Ibid., *x.*

⁵ Ibid., 95.
⁶ Ibid., 102.
⁷ Chan and Sprinkle, *Erasing Hell*, 48-49.
⁸ Robert W. Yarbrough in Morgan and Peterson, *Is Hell for Real or Does Everyone Go to Heaven?*, 23.
⁹ For more, see John Noē, *The Perfect Ending for the World*, 149-202.
¹⁰ The immediate historical setting for this fulfillment was the destruction of Jerusalem by the Babylonians in the 6th century B.C.
¹¹ Josephus, *Wars*, 7, 1,1 – 3, 4, in William Whiston, translator, *The Works of Josephus* (Peabody, MA.: Hendrickson Publishers, 1987), 750-751.
¹² Ibid., *Wars*, 5, xii, 4; 5, xiii, 7, 724, 726.
¹³ Yarbrough in *Is Hell for Real or Does Everyone Go to Heaven?*, 25.
¹⁴ Josephus, *Wars*, 6, ix, 3. – 420, 749.
¹⁵ See again footnote #12 above.
¹⁶ See Noē, *The Perfect Ending for the World*, 149-202.
¹⁷ Yarbrough in Morgan and Peterson, *Is Hell for Real or Does Everyone Go to Heaven?*, 29.
¹⁸ Morgan and Peterson, *Hell Under Fire*, 227.
¹⁹ Baker, *Razing Hell*, 129-130, 136.
²⁰ Yarbrough in Morgan and Peterson, *Is Hell for Real or Does Everyone Go to Heaven?*, 35.
²¹ Ibid., 36.
²² Packer in Morgan and Peterson, *Is Hell for Real or Does Everyone Go to Heaven?*, 67.
²³ Mohler in Ibid., 14.

Chapter 4

¹ *The New Encyclopedia Britannica*, Vol. 5, 15ᵗʰ edition (Chicago, IL.: Encyclopedia Britannica, Inc.), 813.
² See "Hell" in *Webster's New Collegiate Dictionary* 1980 by G. & C. Merriam Co., Springfield, MS. It further elaborates that hell's origin is from middle English, old English, and old high German by using these initials: "ME fr. OE; akin to OE *helan* to conceal, OHG *helan* . . . ." Also, see www.wikipedia.org/wiki/Hell, p-2.
³ "Hell" in *Webster's New Collegiate Dictionary* – "[MF, dim of *helme* helmet, of Gmc origin; akin to OE *helm* helmet, OHG *helan* to conceal."
⁴ N.T. Wright, *Surprised by Hope,* 176-177.
⁵ Lutzer, *One Minute After You Die,* 31.
⁶ *Collier's Encyclopedia* (1986, Vol. 12), 28.

[7] *The Encyclopedia Americana* (1956, Vol. XIV), 81.

[8] Also see *The Aeneid* (Book VI) by Virgil (written during the time of Augustus Caesar) and in which Virgil describes a descent to Hades by Aeneas. Here we get a view of Greco-Roman notions of Hades.

[9] *Vine's An Expository Dictionary of Biblical Words*, 517-518.

[10] According to Wikipedia.org, "Josephus's Discourse to the Greeks concerning Hades," 11/20/2007 – "Erroneously attributed to the Jewish historian since at least the 9th century, it is now believed to be (at least in its original form) the work of Hippolytus of Rome."

[11] Josephus, *An Extract out of Josephus' Discourse to the Greek Concerning Hades*, in William Whiston, translator, *The Works of Josephus* , 813.

[12] Lutzer, *One Minute After You Die*, 40-41.

[13] Ibid., 120.

[14] Ibid., 41.

[15] For more on this, see the author's self-published book, *Shattering the 'Left Behind' Delusion*. It is not my purpose in this book to engage in eschatological (end-times) arguments. Therefore, I will occasionally use "was/will be" language because the focus of this book is the final and surviving reality, regardless of when that happened or is yet to happen.

[16] See Wayne Grudem, *Systematic Theology*, 586-594.

[17] For instance, Chan calls 1 Peter 3:19-20 "a rather strange passage, but it almost certainly doesn't mean that Jesus was preaching the gospel to unbelievers who had died." He claims "the word *spirits*, when used without any qualifications . . . refers to supernatural beings, whether good or bad" and "Jesus went to that angelic prison and proclaimed victory in light of the cross over these disobedient demons (see Col. 2:15)" – in Chan and Sprinkle, *Erasing Hell*, 161. But he doesn't mention 1 Pet. 4:6 or Eph. 4:9, which, in my opinion, refute his understanding. Re: Eph. 4:9, Charles C. Ryrie, recognizes that "some understand this to mean that our Lord descended into hades between His death and resurrection to take those in the 'saved compartment' of hades into heaven." But he also states that "the phrase 'of the earth' may be an appositional phrase, meaning that Christ descended (at His Incarnation) into the lower parts (of the universe), namely the earth." (Charles C. Ryrie, *Basic Theology* (Wheaton, IL.: Victor Books, 1986), 519.)

[18] The Preterist view (meaning past in fulfillment) believes this happened in the 1st century. Futurist views (premillennial, amillennial, and postmillennial) claim this has not yet happened, but will someday. Your author subscribes to the former view. Again, see my self-published book on this topic mentioned in footnote #15 above.

[19] W.E. Vine, *An Expository Dictionary of Biblical Words*, 268.

[20] John McRay, *Paul: His Life and Teaching* (Grand Rapids, MI.: Baker Academic, 2003), 425.

[21] McLaren, *The Last Word*, 102.

[22] Ibid., 78.

[23] Morgan and Peterson, *Hell Under Fire*, 226.

[24] Ibid., 227.

[25] Keller, *The Reason for God*, in footnote #10, 259.

[26] Galli, *God Wins*, 111.

[27] For more, see: David Chilton, *The Days of Vengeance* (Ft. Worth, TX.: Dominion Press, 1987), 244.

[28] Ibid.

[29] Chan and Sprinkle, *Erasing Hell*, 153.

[30] Glenn Peoples, "Fallacies in the Annihilation Debate: a Critique of Robert Peterson and Other Traditionalist Scholarship," *Journal of the Evangelical Theological Society* (June 2007, Vol. 50, No. 2), 333.

[31] William Hendriksen, *More Than Conquerors* (Grand Rapids, MI.: Baker Book House, 1940, 1982), 120.

[32] Baker, *Razing Hell*, 113.

[33] One universalist author believes that this "apocalyptic description of the historic destruction of the nations" may have "little or no bearing on the issue of post-mortem punishment." Gregory MacDonald, *The Evangelical Universalist* (Great Britain, SPCK, 2008), 126.

[34] Chan and Sprinkle, *Erasing Hell*, 56.

[35] Ibid., 51.

[36] Ibid., 78.

[37] Ibid., 89.

[38] Ibid., 97.

[39] James Hastings, Ed., *Hastings' Dictionary of the Bible* (n.l. Hendrickson Publishers, 1994), 285.

[40] Chan and Sprinkle, *Erasing Hell*, 52. In the Latin version 4 Ezra 2:29 also mentions Gehenna.

[41] David Noel Freedman, *The Anchor Bible Dictionary*, Vol. 3 (New York, NY.: Doubleday, 1992), 14.

[42] Ibid., Vol. 2, 927.

[43] Geoffery W. Bromiley, *Theological Dictionary of the New Testament* (Grand Rapids., MI.: Eerdmans, 1985), 113. Also Freedman, *The Anchor Bible Dictionary*, Vol. 2, 926-927.

[44] McLaren, *The Last Word*, 93.

[45] Ibid., 94.

[46] N.T. Wright, *Following Jesus: Biblical Reflections on Discipleship* (Grand Rapids, MI.: Eerdmans, 1995), 92-93.

[47] Condensed from Wm. Paul Young, *The Shack* (Los Angeles, CA.: Windblown Media, 2007), 162-163.
[48] Wittmer, *Christ Alone*, 145.

Chapter 5

[1] Robert Van Kampen and Charles Cooper, "Understanding Scripture at Face Value," *Zion's Fire Magazine*, Nov.-Dec. 1999, 6.
[2] Robert A. Peterson, "Undying Worm Unquenchable Fire," *Christianity Today Magazine*, 23 October 2000, 33. In citation of a report, *The Nature of Hell*, by the Alliance Commission of Unity and Truth Among Evangelicals.
[3] John Wesley Hanson, *Universalism: The Prevailing Doctrine of the Christian Church During Its First Five Hundred Years (1899)*, (Boston and Chicago: Universalist Publishing House, 1899), reprinted by Kessinger Publishing, LLC, n.d., subtitle.
[4] Some have argued that claiming to be an evangelical and holding to a universalist view of salvation are theologically incompatible.
[5] Ty Conley, "Salvation sans Jesus," *Christianity Today,* October 2005, 88.
[6] John Wilson, "A Distorted Predestination," *Christianity Today*, September 2003, 73.
[7] Hanson, *Universalism*, subtitle.
[8] Philip Schaff, *History of the Christian Church*, Vol. 1 & 2 (Grand Rapids, MI.: Eerdmans, 1910 [3rd revision]).
[9] Bruce L. Shelley, *Church History in Plain Language* (Dallas, TX.: Word Publishing, 1982), 96.
[10] Hanson, *Universalism*, 132.
[11] Ibid., 173.
[12] Stetson, *Christian Universalism*, 108.
[13] Schaff, *History of the Christian Church*, Vol. 3, 415.
[14] Brian E. Daley, *The Hope of the Early Church* (Peabody, MA.: Hendrickson Publishers, 2003, 1991), 47.
[15] Shelley, *Church History in Plain Language*, 99.
[16] Howard Clark Kee, *Understanding the New Testament* (Englewood Cliffs, NJ.: Prentice-Hall, 1983, 1973, 1965, 1957), 364.
[17] Henry H. Halley, *Halley's Bible Handbook*, Twenty-Fourth Edition (Grand Rapids, MI.: Regency Reference Library – Zondervan, 1965), 744, 764.
[18] Millard J. Erickson, *How Shall They Be Save?* (Grand Rapids, MI.: Baker Books, 1996), 69.
[19] Schaff, *History of the Christian Church*, Vol. 3, 537.
[20] Hanson, *Universalism*, 235.

[21] Ibid., 288.
[22] Schaff, *History of the Christian Church*, Vol. 2, 380.
[23] Schaff, *History of the Christian Church*, Vol. 3, 536.
[24] Hanson, *Universalism*, 224.
[25] Shelley, *Church History in Plain Language*, 95. Catechetical means "teaching by questions and answers; like or according to a catechism." (*The World Book Dictionary*, 1982).
[26] Ibid., 47.
[27] Ibid., 287-288.
[28] Stetson, *Christian Universalism*, 106.
[29] Hanson, *Universalism*, 305.
[30] Ibid., 231.
[31] Ibid., 306.
[32] Ibid., 19.
[33] Ibid., 33.
[34] Ibid., 193.
[35] Ibid., 191-192.
[36] Ibid., 260.
[37] Schaff, *History of the Christian Church*, Vol. 3, 8.
[38] Hanson, *Universalism*, 271.
[39] ibid.
[40] Ibid., 274-275.
[41] Ibid., 175.
[42] Ibid., 278.
[43] Ibid., 273-274.
[44] Ibid., 273.
[45] Stetson, *Christian Universalism*, 111-112.
[46] Hanson, *Universalism*, 280-281.
[47] Ibid., 295.
[48] Ibid., 306.
[49] ibid.
[50] Ibid., 243.
[51] Ibid., 307.
[52] Ibid., 270.
[53] Ibid., 233.
[54] Ibid., 305.
[55] Ibid., 167.
[56] Ibid., 173.
[57] Ibid., 282.
[58] Ibid., 282, 284-285.
[59] Ibid., 294.

[60] Stetson, *Christian Universalism*, 113.
[61] Hanson, *Universalism*, 279.
[62] Ibid., 173.
[63] Ibid., 279.
[64] Ibid., 279-280.
[65] Ibid., 288.
[66] Ibid., 181.
[67] Ibid., 184.
[68] Ibid., 185.
[69] ibid.
[70] Ibid., 181.
[71] Ibid., 175.
[72] Ibid., 307.
[73] ibid.
[74] Ibid., 225.
[75] Ibid., 272.
[76] Ibid., 296.
[77] Ibid., 302.
[78] Ibid., 224-225.
[79] Gary Amirault, "The Early Christian View of the Savior,"
www.tentmaker.org/books/Early Christian view.html, 2/8/11.
[80] Schaff, *History of the Christian Church*, Vol. 3, 57.
[81] Mark Galli, "What's Up with Hell?" *Christianity Today, April 2011, 63.*
[82] Mark Galli, "Heaven, Hell, and Rob Bell," 1-2.
[83] Ibid., 2.
[84] ibid.
[85] Galli, *God Wins*, 119.
[86] Ibid., 120.
[87] Chan and Sprinkle, *Erasing Hell*, 23.
[88] Ibid., 3 – in quotation of Richard Bauckham, in a survey of the history of universal salvation in the theological journal, *Themelios, 1978.*
[89] Erickson, *How Shall They Be Saved?*, 159.
[90] Meg Crossman, ed., *Worldwide Perspectives* (Pasadena, CA.: William Carey Library, 1996), 1-19.
[91] Ibid., 2-20.
[92] J. Lee Grady, "Don't Get Brainwashed," *Charisma*, March 2009, 6.
[93] David Shibley, "24 Reasons Why I Believe in Hell," *Charisma*, April 2003, 72.
[94] C.S. Lewis, *Mere Christianity* (New York: MacMillan, 1952), 65.
[95] Christine A. Scheller, "A Divine Conspirator," *Christianity Today*, Sept. 2006, 46.

[96] Shelley, *Church History in Plain Language*, 51.

[97] Kee, *Understanding the New Testament*, 334.

[98] Daley, *The Hope of the Early Church*, 222.

[99] Billy Graham, "My Answer" column (The Indianapolis Star, 3 June 1997).

[100] Erickson, *How Shall They Be Save?*, 27.

[101] Ibid., 9 and 14.

[102] Daniel B. Clendenin, "The Only Way," *Christianity Today Magazine*, 12 January 1998, 39.

[103] Heresy is defined as "a belief different from the accepted belief of a church, school, profession, or other group" (*World Book Dictionary*, 1982 ed.). By this definition, Jesus was a heretic. So were the New Testament writers.

[104] Rev. C.H. Spurgeon, "The Sons of God," Sermon No. 339, delivered October 7, 1860, www.spurgeon.org/sermons/0339.htm, 12/20/08.

[105] Judith Cebula, "Grace Under Fire," *The Indianapolis Star*, January 26, 2002, F1, 3.

Chapter 6

[1] Thomas Talbott, "Reply to my Critics," in Robin A. Parry & Christopher H. Partridge, Editors, *Universal Salvation? The Current Debate* (Grand Rapids, MI.: Eerdmans, 2003), 251.

[2] Wittmer, *Christ Alone*, 64.

[3] Gregory MacDonald, *The Evangelical Universalist* (SPCK, 2006, 2008), 36.

[4] Engle discussing J.I. Packer's contribution in Morgan and Peterson, *Is Hell for Real or Does Everyone Go to Heaven?*, 9.

[5] Packer in Morgan and Peterson, *Is Hell for Real or Does Everyone Go to Heaven?*, 58.

[6] Thomas Talbott, "Toward a Better Understanding of Universalism," in Robin A. Parry & Christopher H. Partridge, Editors, *Universal Salvation? The Current Debate* (Grand Rapids, MI.: Eerdmans, 2003), 19.

[7] David Hilborn & Don Horrocks, "Universalistic Trends in the Evangelical Tradition: An Historical Perspective," in Robin A. Parry & Christopher H. Partridge, Editors, *Universal Salvation? The Current Debate* (Grand Rapids, MI.: Eerdmans, 2003), 236.

[8] Talbott, "Toward a Better Understanding of Universalism," 20.

[9] Amirault, "The Hell Test," 7.

[10] Robin A. Parry & Christopher H. Partridge, Editors, *Universal Salvation? The Current Debate* (Grand Rapids, MI.: Eerdmans, 2003), *xix*.

[11] Airmault, "The Hell Test, 10.

[12] Ibid., 7.

[13] Hannah Whitall Smith, *The Unselfishness of God and How I Discovered it* (New York, NY.: Revell, 1903), chap. 22 (1st ed. only); www.godstruthfortoday.org/Library/smith/hwsmith9.html.

[14] I. Howard Marshall, "The New Testament Does Not Teach Universal Salvation," in Robin A. Parry & Christopher H. Partridge, Editors, *Universal Salvation? The Current Debate* (Grand Rapids, MI.: Eerdmans, 2003), 70.

[15] Thomas Johnson, "A Wideness in God' Mercy: Universalism in the Bible," in Robin A. Parry & Christopher H. Partridge, Editors, *Universal Salvation? The Current Debate* (Grand Rapids, MI.: Eerdmans, 2003), 78.

[16] Ibid., 89.

[17] Talbott, "Toward a Better Understanding of Universalism," 48.

[18] ibid.

[19] Airmault, "The Hell Test," 7.

[20] MacDonald, *The Evangelical Universalist*, 39.

[21] Armirault, "The Hell Test," 25.

[22] Marshall, "The New Testament Does Not Teach Universal Salvation," 68-69.

[23] Ibid., 69.

[24] Ibid., 90.

[25] MacDonald, *The Evangelical Universalist*, 99, 100.

[26] Talbott, "Toward a Better Understanding of Universalism," 23.

[27] Ibid., 24.

[28] Baker, *Razing Hell*, 12, 149.

[29] Stetson, *Christian Universalism*, 132.

[30] Amirault, "The Hell Test," 20.

[31] MacDonald, *The Evangelical Universalist*, 112-113.

[32] Marshall, "The New Testament Does *Not* . . .," 55.

[33] Talbott, "Toward a Better Understanding of Universalism," 22, 23.

[34] Wittmer, *Christ Alone*, 24-25.

[35] MacDonald, *The Evangelical Universalist*, 43, 44, 45.

[36] Ibid., 44.

[37] Schaff, *History of the Christian Church*, Vol. 1, 322.

[38] Kevin DeYoung, "God Is Still Holy and What You Learned in Sunday School Is Still True: A Review of *Love Wins* by Rob Bell, Senior Pastor, University Reformed Church, East Lansing, Michigan, thegospelcoalition.org/blogs/kevindeyoung, 2011, 11.

[39] Amirault, "The Hell Test," 9.

[40] A personal email, 5/19/2010.

[41] G.K. Baele, quoted in MacDonald, *The Evangelical Universalist*, 112.

[42] MacDonald, *The Evangelical Universalist*, 72-73.

[43] Johnson, "A Wideness in God' Mercy: Universalism in the Bible," 79-80.

[44] Parry & Partridge, *Universal Salvation?*, xix

[45] Galli, *God Wins*, 117-118,

[46] MacDonald, *The Evangelical Universalist*, 46.

[47] Parry and Partridge, *Universal Salvation?*, *xxii*.

[48] MacDonald, *The Evangelical Universalist*, 5.

[49] Ibid., 47.

[50] Amirault, "The Hell Test," 12.

[51] Ibid., 19.

[52] John Sanders, "A Freewill Theist's Response to Talbott's Universalism," in Robin A. Parry & Christopher H. Partridge, Editors, *Universal Salvation? The Current Debate* (Grand Rapids, MI.: Eerdmans, 2003), 169.

[53] Peterson, "Undying Worm Unquenchable Fire," *Christianity Today*, 33.

[54] Parry and Partridge, *Universal Salvation?*, *xxii*.

[55] Evelyn Uyemura, www.amazon.com/Inescapable-Love-God-Thomas-Talbott/dp/158112831/ref=sr_1_, 5/4/2010.

[56] Johnson, "A Wideness in God' Mercy: Universalism in the Bible," 97.

[57] S. Kierkegaard, *Soren Kierkegaard's Journals and Paper*, trans. And ed. H. V. Hong and E. H. Hong (Bloomington, IN.: Indiana University Press, 1978), 6:557.

[58] Morwenna Ludlow, "Universalism in the History of Christianity," in Robin A. Parry & Christopher H. Partridge, Editors, *Universal Salvation? The Current Debate* (Grand Rapids, MI.: Eerdmans, 2003), 208.

[59] Hilborn & Horrocks, "Universalistic Trends in the Evangelical Tradition: An Historical Perspective," 236.

[60] www.thetruegospel.net/main_page.htm, 1/21/2011.

[61] Lutzer, *One Minute after You Die*, 106.

Chapter 7

[1] Marshall, "The New Testament Does *Not . . .*," 56.

[2] Boa and Bowman, *Sense & Nonsense*, 85-86, 84.

[3] Stetson, *Christian Universalism*, 58, 60..

[4] For more, see author's book, *The Perfect Ending for the World*.

[5] Stetson, *Christian Universalism*, 33.

[6] Amirault, "The Hell Test," 2.

[7] Ibid., 9.

[8] From a personal email to me from a person with universalist sympathies.

[9] Stetson, *Christian Universalism*, 53.

[10] Jones, *Hell Is Real (But I Hate to Admit It*, 148.

[11] Amirault, "The Hell Test", 2.

[12] Ibid., 12.

[13] Stetson, *Christian Universalism*, 131.
[14] Ibid., 116-117.
[15] Amirault, "The Hell Test," 2.
[16] Ibid., 4.
[17] Ibid., 11.
[18] Talbott, "Towards a Better . . .," 4.
[19] Baker, *Razing Hell*, 51.
[20] Amirault, "The Hell Test," 12.
[21] Baker, *Razing Hell*, 20.
[22] Ibid., 17.
[23] Marshall, "The New Testament Does *Not* . . .," 56.
[24] Amirault, "The Hell Test," 2.
[25] Ibid., 9.
[26] Baker, *Razing Hell*, 37-38.
[27] Galli, *God Wins*, 129.
[28] Wittmer, *Christ Alone*, 7.
[29] Amirault, "The Hell Test," 2.
[30] Ibid., 11.
[31] Ibid., 8.
[32] Ibid., 9.
[33] Ibid., 20.
[34] Ibid., 16.
[35] Ibid., 21.
[36] Ibid., 23.
[37] Baker, *Razing Hell*, 63, 148.
[38] Wittmer, *Christ Alone*, 120.
[39] Marshall, "The New Testament Does *Not* . . . ," 55.
[40] Amirault, "The Hell Test," 11.
[41] Ibid., 12.
[42] Hanson, *Universalism*, 250.
[43] Hilborn & Horrocks, "Universalist Trends . . . ," 233.
[44] Amirault, "The Hell Test," 14.
[45] Ibid., 11.
[46] Ibid, 9.
[47] Ibid., 13.
[48] In a private email to me.
[49] Thomas Baldwin Thayer, *The Origin and History of the Doctrine of Endless Punishment* (n.l., BiblioBaaar, n.d.) 247 – reprint, original (Boston, MA.: James M. Usher, 1856).
[50] Ibid., 250-251.

[51] From: Preterist1@aol.com, "More about Universalism," 23 Feb 2005, p-4 of 13.

[52] Wittmer, *Christ Alone*, 62.

[53] McLaren, *The Last Word and the Word After That*, 103, in quotation of Berton and Chase, p, 72.

[54] In a private email to me.

[55] Stetson, *Christian Universalism*, 137.

[56] Schaff, *History of the Christian Church*, Vol. VIII, 347-348

Chapter 8

[1] Boa and Bowman, *Sense & Nonsense*, 83.

[2] Grudem, *Systematic Theology*, 596-597.

[3] MacDonald, *The Evangelical Universalist*, 82.

[4] Marshall, "The New Testament Does *Not* . . .," 73.

[5] Johnson, "A Wideness in God's Mercy . . .," 77.

[6] John Owen, *The Death of Death* (Carlisle, PA.: The Banner of Truth Trust, reprinted 1995, pub. 1852), 190.

[7] Ibid., 260.

[8] *Strong's Exhaustive Concordance of the Bible – Reference Library Ed.* (Iowa Falls, IA.: World Bible Publishers, no date), 56.

[9] W.E. Vine, *An Expository Dictionary of Biblical Words*, OT-3; NT-38.

[10] Walter Bauer, William Arndt, Felix Gingrich, Frederick Danker, *A Greek-English Lexicon of the New Testament and Other Early Christian Literature* (Chicago and London: University of Chicago Press, 2nd ed., 1958), 631-632.

[11] John Owen, *The Death of Death*, 258.

[12] Douglas J. Moo, *Hell Under Fire*, 100.

[13] *Strong's Concordance*, #3625.

[14] Also see, Noē, *The Perfect Ending for the World*, 198-201.

[15] Four different Greek words are translated as "world" in the New Testament. Owen also points out five different ways this word may be taken (pp. 192-3). An additional argument by analogy can be made regarding Christ being "the Savior of all men" (1Tim. 4:10). Does this literally mean that no women are saved? Of course, not. The word "men" is used inclusively in the Bible to represent both male and females. They why should "all" be an exclusive term?

[16] *Worldwide Perspectives*, 2-13.

[17] John Murray, *The Epistle to the Romans* (Grand Rapids, MI.: Eerdmans, 1996), Vol. 2, 103.

[18] Leon Morris, *The Epistle to the Romans* (Grand Rapids, MI.: Eerdmans, 1988), 239.

[19] Grudem, *Systematic Theology*, 599.
[20] Ibid., 601.
[21] ibid.
[22] John Owen, *The Death of Death*, 231.
[23] Gary North, "Aren't There Two Kinds of Salvation?", Question 75 in North, *75 Bible Questions Your Instructors Pray You Won't Ask* (Tyler, Texas: Spurgeon Press, 1984).
[24] Moo, *Hell Under Fire*, 102.
[25] Amirault, "The Hell Test," 19.
[26] Erickson, *How Shall They Be Saved*, 174-175.
[27] Grudem, *Systematic Theology*, 603.

Chapter 9

[1] MacDonald, *The Evangelical Universalist*, 35.
[2] Henry A. Virkler, *Hermeneutics* (Grand Rapids, MI.: Baker Books, 1981), 106.
[3] Ibid., 107.
[4] *The Anchor Bible Dictionary*, Vol. 5 (New York: Doubleday, 1992), 155.
[5] Adele Berlin, *The Dynamics of Biblical Parallelism* (Bloomington, IN.: Indiana University Press, 1985), 2.
[6] *The Anchor Bible Dictionary*, Vol. 5, 157.
[7] Ibid., 158.
[8] John Murray, *The Epistle to the Romans*, 1:202.
[9] *The World Book Dictionary.*
[10] Murray, *The Epistle to the Romans*, 1:203.
[11] Guthrie, *New Testament Theology*, 834.
[12] Boa and Bowman, *Sense & Nonsense*, 84.
[13] Ibid., 85.
[14] Guthrie, *New Testament Theology*, 834.
[15] Sam Frost, "Universalism and Preterism: Bedfellows or Bedlam?" www.planetpreterist.com/news-2590. html, 9/4/05.
[16] Morris, *The Epistle to the Romans*, 235.
[17] Talbott, "Reply to my Critics," 253.
[18] See Noē, *The Perfect Ending for the World*, 151-169.
[19] Douglas J. Moo in Morgan and Peterson, *Hell Under Fire*, 98.
[20] Ibid., 102.
[21] Some have claimed that the focus of Paul's universalism of "all" and "all men" references only applied to the Jew/Gentile remnant under the law compared that same group being in Christ (Rom. 3:19; Gal. 3:22).
[22] Amirault, "The Hell Test," 19.

²³ Ibid., 7.
²⁴ Stetson, *Christian Universalism*, 52.
²⁵ Talbott, "Reply to my Critics," 254.
²⁶ MacDonald, *The Evangelical Universalist*, 79-80.
²⁷ Talbott, "Christ Victorious," 25.
²⁸ All quotes and thoughts above from "The First Adam and the Last Adam—What Is God Telling Us? www.willard-oh.com/emmenar/lastadam.htm, 2/9/01.
²⁹ Paul Rowntree Clifford, *The Reality of the Kingdom* (Grand Rapids, MI.: Eerdmans, 1996), 39-40.
³⁰ Schaff, *History of the Christian Church*, Vol. I, 323.
³¹ Marshall, "The New Testament Does *Not . . .*," 71.

Chapter 10

¹ MacDonald, *The Evangelical Universalist*, 47.
² Reported by Judith Cebula, "Grace under fire," *The Indianapolis Star*, January 26, 2002, F-1, 3.
³ ibid.
⁴ Cited by David Shibley, "Is Jesus Really the Only Way, *Charisma*, October 2009, 28
⁵ Galli, *God Wins*, 119.
⁶ Ibid., 120.
⁷ Jones, *Hell Is Real (But I Hate to Admit It)*, 35.
⁸ On the other hand, if one argues that all children are saved up to some age of awareness or point of accountability, this, too, lends credence to Universalism.
⁹ Boa and Bowman, *Sense & Nonsense*, 130-131.
¹⁰ This discussion is beyond the scope of this book. For more, see Noē, *The Perfect Ending for the World*, Chapter 13.
¹¹ Daniel B. Clendenin, "The Only Way," 39.
¹² Moo in Morgan and Peterson, *Hell Under Fire*, 98.
¹³ Stetson, *Christian Universalism*, 49.
¹⁴ Ibid., 50.
¹⁵ Ibid., 51.
¹⁶ Ibid., 52.
¹⁷ Ibid., 54.
¹⁸ Ibid., 55.
¹⁹ Ibid., 56.
²⁰ Ibid., 57-58.

Chapter 11

[1] Gary North, "Aren't There Two Kinds of Salvation?", Question 75 in North, *75 Bible Questions Your Instructors Pray You Won't Ask* (Tyler, Texas: Spurgeon Press, 1984).

[2] Yarbrough in Morgan and Peterson, *Is Hell for Real or Does Everyone Go to Heaven?*, 29.

[3] Marshall, "The New Testament Does *Not. . .,*" 71.

[4] J.I.Packer in Morgan and Peterson, *Is Hell for Real or Does Everyone Go to Heaven?*, 67.

[5] Ibid., 69.

[6] Boa and Bowman, *Sense & Nonsense*, 80-81.

[7] Talbott, "A Pauline Interpretation of Divine Judgment," in Parry & Partridge, *Universal Salvation?*, 45.

[8] Stetson, *Christian Universalism*, 38.

[9] *Strong's Concordance*, 9.

[10] W.E. Vine, *An Expository Dictionary of Biblical Words*, 33.

[11] Bauer, Arndt, Gingrich, Danker, *A Greek-English Lexicon*, 27-28.

[12] Leon Morris, *New Testament Theology*, 267.

[13] George Eldon Ladd, *A Theology of the New Testament* (Grand Rapids, MI.: Eerdmans, 1974, 2000, 339.

[14] John MacArthur, *The Second Coming*, 188.

[15] Ed Stevens, Preterist1@aol.com, "More about Universalism," 2/23/05.

[16] Murray J. Harris, *From Grave to Glory* (Grand Rapids, MI.: Academi Books, Zondervan, 1990), 243.

[17] Gary Amirault, "The Power of Life and Death in a Four Letter Greek Word . . . (Aion)," (Hermann, MO.: Tentmaker, no date), 1-2.

[18] Hanson, *Aion-Aionios*, 17.

[19] Ibid., 34.

[20] Ibid., 36.

[21] Ibid., 35.

[22] The Greek word *aion* is used for the Hebrew word *olam* in the Septuagint.

[23] Compare with similar idiomatic uses in Heb. 1:8, Rev. 11:15, and Isa. 45:17. A few scholars feel this double use in the idiom does not speak of eternity or endlessness, but of aggregated or compounding periods of time—until all ages have run their course. Most, however, do agree with the explanation given here.

[24] Noē, *The Perfect Ending for the World*, 84.

[25] Hanson, *Aion-Aionios*, 35.

[26] Ibid., 45.

[27] Ibid., 18.

[28] Ibid., 25.

[29] Ibid., 27.

[30] ibid.

[31] Ibid., 38-39.

[32] Ibid., 39.

[33] Ibid., 40-41.

[34] Ibid., 41.

[35] W.E. Vine: An Expository Dictionary of Biblical Words, 117-118.

[36] Ralph L. Smith, *Old Testament Theology* (Nashville, TN.: Broadman & Holman, 1993), 162.

[37] Baker, *Razing Hell*, 137.

[38] Hanson, *Universalism*, 115.

[39] Ibid., 134.

[40] Hanson, *Aion-Aionios*, 48.

[41] Ibid., 49.

[42] Thayer, *The Origin and History* . . ., 204-205.

[43] Ibid., 206.

[44] ibid.

[45] Ibid., 207.

[46] Murray J. Harris, *From Grave to Glory*, 243.

[47] Stetson, *Christian Universalism*, 40.

[48] Ibid., 131.

[49] Hanson, *Universalism*, 9.

[50] Ibid., 11.

[51] Ibid., 23.

[52] Amirault, "The Hell Test," 12.

[53] Ibid., 22.

[54] Hanson, *Universalism*, 36-37f

[55] Ibid., 41.

[56] Ibid., 39.

[57] Stetson, *Christian Universalism*, 40-41

[58] Ibid., 43.

[59] Talbott, "A Pauline Interpretation. . . , 46-47.

[60] Chan and Sprinkle, *Erasing Hell*, 83. In a footnote he relates that "New Testament scholar William Barclay also says that *kolasis* 'originally meant the pruning of trees to make them grow better." (p-90).

[61] *BAGD* does not, p-440. *Vine's* does – "punishment . . . describes a process . . . where God's love is being perfected in us, it gives no room for the fear of meeting with His reprobation," 903. *Strong's* does not.

[62] Hanson, *Aion-Aionios*, 54-55.

[63] Ibid., 55.

[64] Ibid., 56.

[65] Ibid., 56-58.

[66] Stetson, *Christian Universalism*, 41.

[67] Hanson, *Universalism*, 45-46

[68] Ibid., 46.

[69] Ibid., 49.

[70] Ibid., 51-52.

[71] Ibid. 53.

[72] Ibid., 55.

[73] Ibid., 57.

[74] Ibid. 58.

[75] Marshall, "The New Testament Does *Not* . . .," 72.

[76] Johnson, "A Wideness in God's Mercy . . .," 83.

[77] Hanson, *Aion-Aionios*, 52.

[78] Quoted in Daley, *The Hope of the Early Church*, 56-57.

[79] Hanson, *Universalism*, 117.

[80] Ibid., 118.

[81] Kenneth L. Gentry, Jr., *He Shall Have Dominion* (Tyler, TX.: Institute for Christian Economics, 1992), 298.

[82] Hanson, *Aion-Aionios*, 62.

[83] Erickson, *How Shall They Be Saved?*, 73.

[84] Origen, *De Principiis,* ii, X: 3, 4. I, i. *Against Celsus*, iv, 13. Quoted in Hanson, *Universalism*, 150-151.

[85] George Eldon Ladd, *A Theology of the New Testament*, 416.

[86] Hanson, *Universalism*, 65-67.

[87] Email from Ed Stevens, "Problem of Universalism," Oct. 31, 2003.

[88] Chan and Sprinkle, *Erasing Hell*, 85.

[89] Ibid., 86.

[90] Hanson, *Aion-Aionios*, 72-73.

[91] Ibid., 75.

[92] L. Ray Smith, "Letter to John Hagee," forwarded emailed, 3/19/2010, 19.

Chapter 12

[1] Morgan and Peterson, *Hell Under Fire*, 102.

[2] Parry & Partridge, *Universal Salvation?*, xxiii.

[3] Stetson, *Christian Universalism*, 75.

[4] Peoples, "Fallacies in the Annihilation Debate: *Journal of the ETS,* 329.

[5] Parry & Partridge, *Universal Salvation?*, xix.

[6] Peoples, "Fallacies", ETS art. 346.

[7] Marshall, "The New Testament Does *Not . . .*," 60.

[8] Hanson, *Universalism*, 79.

[9] Johnson, "A Wideness in God's Mercy. . .," 77-78.

[10] Ibid., 98.

[11] Hanson, *Aion-Aionios*, 69.

[12] Thayer, *The Origin and History of . . .*," 199.

[13] Edward W. Fudge and Robert A. Peterson, *Two Views of Hell* (Downers Grove, IL.: InterVarsity Press, 2000), 20, 82.

[14] Talbott, "Reply to my Critics," 254.

[15] In a private email to me, 2/5/2011.

[16] Morris, *The Epistle to the Romans,* 122.

[17] George Eldon Ladd, *The Presence of the Future* (Grand Rapids, MI.: Eerdmans, 1974), 209.

[18] David L. Edwards and John Stott, *Evangelical Essentials* (Downers Grove, IL.: Intervarsity Press, 1989), 320.

[19] Edward E. Stevens, "A short analysis of John Stott's position on Hell," posted on Planet Preterist, January 20, 2003, 2.

[20] Erickson, *How Shall They Be Saved,* 217.

[21] Baker, *Razing Hell,* 142-143.

[22] Noē, *The Perfect Ending for the World*, Chapter 13.

[23] Michael D. Holden, Book review of *The Problem of Hell*. By Jonathan L. Kvanvig. Oxford University Press, 1993. *Journal of the American Academy of Religion*, Winter 1996, 890.

[24] Robert L. Whitelaw, ed., editorial masthead, *Resurrection Magazine,* 3/ 1996, 2.

[25] For more, see again, Noē, *The Perfect Ending for the World*, Introduction and chapters #8-12.

[26] John L. Bray, "Two Views of Hell," in *Biblical Perspectives* newsletter, 2 October, 2006, 2.

[27] Harris, *From Grave to Glory*, 268-9.

[28] Lutzer, *One Minute After You Die*, 106.

[29] Peterson, "Undying Worm Unquenchable Fire," 34.

[30] Ibid., 34.

[31] Ibid., 35.

[32] Peterson, "A Traditional Response to Stott" 554 – quoted in Peoples ETS art., 336.

[33] Peoples, "Fallacies," ETS art. 336.

[34] Ibid., 338.

[35] David L. Edwards and John R. Stott, *Evangelical Essentials: A Liberal-Evangelical Dialogue* (London: Hodder and Stoughton, 1988), 312-20 – quoted in Peoples' *ETS* art.

[36] Perriman, *The Coming of the Son of Man*, 88.
[37] MacDonald, *The Evangelical Universalist*, 154.
[38] Ibid., 88-89.
[39] *Strong's* #2673.
[40] For more, see Noē, *The Perfect Ending for the World*, Introduction and chapters #8-12.
[41] Stetson, *Christian Universalism*, 75.
[42] Ibid., 76-77
[43] Robert Morey, *Death and the Afterlife* (Minneapolis: Bethany, 1984), 90.
[44] Carson, *Gaggin of God* 519 – quoted in Peoples ETS art. 340.
[45] Stevens, "A short analysis . . .," 3.
[46] Lutzer, *One Minute After You Die*, 108.
[47] John L. Bray, *Biblical Perspectives*, (Lakeland, FL.: Aug. 18, 2003 newsletter), 3.
[48] Edward E.Stevens, email, 3 Dec. 2000.
[49] Edward E. Stevens, email, 17 Sept. 2000.
[50] Edward E. Stevens, email, 31 Oct. 2003.
[51] Ryken, *My Father's World*, 251.
[52] Grudem, *Systematic Theology,* 1151.
[53] Peterson, "Undying Worm Unquenchable Fire," 30.
[54] Ibid., 37.

Chapter 13

[1] Baker, *Razing Hell, xiv.*
[2] Ibid., 66.
[3] Ibid., 67.
[4] Sheler, "Hell Hath No Fury," 50.
[5] Erickson, *How Shall They Be Saved*, 255.
[6] Meacham, "Is Hell Dead," *Time*, 40.
[7] Ibid., 43.
[8] Edward Jordan, "Letters," *Charisma*, January 2003, 8.
[9] Stetson, *Christian Universalism*, 70-71.
[10] Ludlow, "Universalism in the History of Christianity," 211.
[11] Erickson, *How Shall They Be Saved*, 52.
[12] Lutzer, *One Minute After You Die*, 106.
[13] Billy Graham, "My Answer," *The Indianapolis Star*, 19 June 1998.
[14] Billy Graham, "My Answer," *The Indianapolis Star*, 20 May 2008.
[15] Lutzer, *One Minute After You Die*, 9.
[16] Billy Graham, "My Answer," *The Indianapolis Star*, 4 October 2010.

[17] Sanders, "A Freewill Theist's Response . . ., 170.
[18] MacDonald, *The Evangelical Universalist*, 32.
[19] Baker, *Razing Hell*, 117.
[20] Boa and Bowman, *Sense & Nonsense*, 86., in quotation of John Blanchard.
[21] Amirault, "The Hell Test," 8.
[22] Grudem, *Systematic Theology*, 500.
[23] Stetson, *Christian Universalism*, 60.
[24] Marshall, "The New Testament Does *Not* . . .," 57.
[25] Packer in Morgan and Peterson, *Is Hell Real for Real or Does Everyone Go to Heaven?*, 69.
[26] Erickson, *How Shall They Be Saved?*, 159f.
[27] Sanders, "A Freewill Theist's Response . . .," 170.
[28] Hanson, *Universalism*, 61.
[29] Ibid., 65.
[30] Stetson, *Christian Universalism*, 45.
[31] Marshall, "The New Testament Does *Not* . . .," 73.
[32] ibid.
[33] "SBC in 'evangelistic crisis,' but would be worse off without resurgence, study says," www.bpnews.net/bpnews.asp?id=20723, 6/26/11, 1.
[34] "Evangelism Statistics showing cultural trends," www.evangelismcoach.org/2009/highlights-from-aris-survey, 6/26/11. 1.
[35] "Evangelism Statistics," www.bible.org/illustration/evangelism-statistics, 6/26/11, 1.—from "Street Level Evangelism, Where is the Space for the Local Evangelist, by Michael Parrott, *Acts Evangelism*, Spokane, WA, 1993, pp-9-11.
[36] ibid.
[37] *Worldwide Perspectives*, 2-25.
[38] Ibid., 2-20.
[39] Ibid., 2-24.
[40] Erickson, *How Shall They Be Saved*, 24.
[41] Ibid., 57.
[42] *Worldwide Perspectives*, 2-23.
[43] Arthur Melanson, "Is Universalism Biblical?" on www.planetpreterist.com/news-2544.html , 8/2/05.
[44] Owen, *The Death of Death*, 242.
[45] Don Piper, *90 Minutes in Heaven* (Grand Rapids, MI.: Revell, 2004), 130-131.
[46] *Worldwide Perspectives*, 2-25.
[47] Ibid., 2-26.
[48] Stetson, *Christian Universalism*, 124.
[49] Amirault, "The Hell Test," 11.
[50] Ibid., 124-125.

[51] Peterson, "Undying Worm Unquenchable Fire," 35.

[52] ibid.

[53] Edward E. Stevens, email, "More about Universalism," 2/23/05.

[54] J. Preston Eby, "Why Teach Salvation For All?"
www.planetpreterist.com/news-2550.html, 8/8/05.

[55] Clendenin, "The Only Way," *Christianity Today*, 37.

[56] Leslie Leyland Fields, "The Myth of the Perfect Parent," *Christianity Today,*
January 2010, 24.

[57] Barna Research Online, "A Biblical Worldview Has a Radical Effect on a
Person's Life" (www.barna.org/cgi-bin/PagePressRelease.asp., 1 December
2003), 1-2.

[58] Amirault, "The Hell Test," 8.

[59] Erickson, *How Shall They Be Saved*, 60.

[60] Amirault, "The Hell Test," 9.

[61] Baker, *Razing Hell*, *xvi*.

[62] For more on this, listen to the "Kingdom Christianity" podcast series on
www.prophecyrefi.org. This series will be the basis for a future book by the
same title.

[63] Dallas Willard, *The Great Omission* (San Francisco, CA.:
HarperSanFrancisco, 2006).

[64] Dallas Willard, *The Divine Conspiracy* (San Francisco, CA.:
HarperSanFrancisco, 1997), 40-41.

[65] Darrell L. Guder, *The Continuing Conversion of the Church* (Grand Rapids,
MI.: Eerdmans, 2000), *xiii*.

[66] Robert Lynn, "Far as the curse is found," *Breakpoint Worldview* magazine,
October 2006, 14.

[67] Scot McKnight, "The 8 Marks of a Robust Gospel," *Christianity Today*
magazine, March 2008, 36.

[68] Jones, *Hell Is Real (But I Hate to Admit It)*, 106.

[69] ibid.

[70] Ibid., 107.

[71] David Neff, "Signs of the End Times," *Christianity Today*, August 2001, 48.

[72] Ibid., 108.

[73] Erickson, *How Shall They Be Saved*, 268.

[74] Baker, *Razing Hell*, 13.

[75] Quoting Jay Wesley Richards in MacDonald, *The Evangelical Universalist*,
170.

[76] Marshall, "The New Testament Does *Not* . . .," 72.

[77] Amirault, "The Hell Test," 8.

[78] Thayer, *The Origin and History*. . ., 229-230, 232, 238.

[79] Stetson, *Christian Universalism*, 79.

Chapter 14

[1] Erickson, *How Shall They Be Saved?*, 198.
[2] Packer in Morgan and Peterson, *Is Hell for Real or Does Everyone Go to Heaven?*, 69.
[3] Peterson, "Undying Worm Unquenchable Fire," 35.
[4] ibid.
[5] Quoted in Stanley J. Grenz, "Is Hell Forever?," *Christianity Today Magazine*, 5 October 1998, 92.
[6] Billy Graham, "My Answer," *The Indianapolis Star*, 1/17/11, E-4.
[7] Strange, "A Calvinists Response to Talbott's Universalism,"160-161.
[8] Ibid., 157-158.
[9] Chan and Sprinkle, *Erasing Hell*, 31.
[10] Wittmer, *Christ Alone*, 73-74.
[11] Sanders, "A Freewill Theist's Response . . .," 174-175
[12] Parry & Partridge, "Introduction," xxii.
[13] Baker, *Razing Hell*, 12.
[14] Erickson, *How Shall They Be Saved*, 24-25.
[15] McLaren, *The Last Word*, 40.
[16] Gary Amirault, "God 'Might' Save the World?" www.planetpreterist.com/news-2521.html, 7/19/05.
[17] Lutzer, *One Minute After Your Die*, 114.
[18] J. Vernon McGee, *Ephesians* (Nashville, TN.: Thomas Nelson, 1991), 76.
[19] Billy Graham, "My Answer," *The Indianapolis Star*, 9/16/09, C-12.
[20] Johnson, "A wideness in God's Mercy . . .," 86.
[21] Donald Guthrie, *New Testament Theology*, 93-94.
[22] Talbott, "A Pauline Interpretation . . .," 34.
[23] Ibid., 37.
[24] Grudem, *Systematic Theology*, 686.
[25] Ibid., 687.
[26] Ibid., 682.
[27] Erickson, *How Shall They Be Saved*, 124.
[28] Lutzer, *One Minute After You Die*, 114.
[29] Clark H. Pinnock, "Toward a More Inclusive Eschatology," in David W. Baker, Ed., *Looking into the Future: Evangelical Studies in Eschatology* (Grand Rapids, MI.: Baker Academic, 2001) 254.
[30] Stetson, *Christian Universalism*, 71-72.
[31] Private email to me, 2/5/11.

[32] Stetson, *Christian Universalism*, 30-31.
[33] Ibid., 31-32.
[34] Bell, *Love Wins*, 180.
[35] Stetson, *Christian Universalism*, 79.
[36] MacDonald, *The Evangelical Universalist*, 103.
[37] Baker, *Razing Hell*, 74.
[38] Ibid., 83.
[39] Talbott, "Towards a Better Understanding of Universalism, 9.
[40] Johnson, "A Wideness in God's Mercy . . .," 84
[41] Bell, *Love Wins*, 97-98, 103.

Chapter 15

[1] MacDonald, *The Evangelical Universalist*, 38.
[2] Talbott, "Reply to my Critics," 248.
[3] Talbott, "Toward a Better Understanding of Universalism,"10.
[4] J. Barton Payne, *Encyclopedia of Biblical Prophecy* (Grand Rapids, MI.: Baker Books, 1973), v-vi.
[5] Johnson, "A Wideness in God's Mercy . . .", 86.
[6] Erickson, *How Shall they Be Saved*, 65-66.
[7] Erickson, *How Shall They Be Saved*, 18 and 21.
[8] *Worldwide Perspectives*, 2-22.
[9] *Worldwide Perspectives* believes, p-2:25.
[10] Mark Galli, "God Wins," in Bits & Pieces, *Christianity Today*, August 2011, 72. Also in Galli, *God Wins*, 148.
[11] MacDonald, *The Evangelical Universalist*, 36.
[12] Parry & Partridge, "Introduction," in Parry & Partridge, *Universal Salvation?*, xxii.
[13] Ibid., xx.
[14] Galli, "Heaven, Hell, and Rob Bell," *Christianity Today*, 3.
[15] Parry & Partridge, "Introduction" in Parry & Partridge, *Universal Salvation?*, *xx*.
[16] Johnson, "A Wideness in God's Mercy . . .," 78.

Chapter 16

[1] H. Richard Niebuhr, quoted in Philip Yancey, *What's So Amazing About Grace?* (Grand Rapids, MI.: Zondervan, 1997), 13-14.
[2] Amirault, "The Hell Test," 23.

[3] J.I. Packer, *Hell Under Fire*, 190.

[4] *Sense & Nonsense about Heaven & Hell*, 124.

[5] Clark Pinnock, *Flame of Love* (Downers Grove: InterVarsity Press, 1996), 187.

[6] Hanson, *Universalism*, 154-155

[7] Baker, *Razing Hell*, 176-177.

[8] MacDonald, *The Evangelical Universalist*, 168.

[9] Sanders, "A Freewill Theist's Response . . . ," 182.

[10] Baker, *Razing Hell*, 107.

[11] Ibid., 80.

[12] Ibid., 81.

[13] Ibid., 84.

[14] Ibid., 16.

[15] Ibid., 90.

[16] Hanson, *Universalism*, 120.

[17] McLaren, *The Last Word*, 187.

[18] John the Baptist was filled with the Holy Spirit before he was born (Luke 1:15)—i.e., born again before he was born? Does this not demonstrate another way that God can save apart from hearing, understanding, and receiving the gospel?

[19] McLaren, *The Last Word*, 164.

[20] Ibid., 172.

[21] MacDonald, *The Evangelical Universalists*, 164.

[22] Boa and Bowman, *Sense & Nonsense*, 138.

[23] Ibid., 147.

[24] Ibid., 134.

[25] Ibid., 135

[26] J.I. Packer, *Hell Under Fire*, 188.

[27] Wittmer, *Christ Alone*, 30.

[28] Ibid., 31.

[29] David W. Baker, *Looking into the Future*, 251.

[30] Erickson, *How Shall They Be Saved?*, 159-175.

[31] Hilborn and Horrocks, "Universalistic Trends . . ." 229.

[32] J.I. Packer, "Salvation sans Jesus" *Christianity Today*, Oct. 2005, 88.

[33] See Boa and Bowman, *Sense & Nonsense*, 144-146.

[34] See Grudem, *Systematic Theology*, 586-594.

[35] Erickson, *How Shall They Be Saved*, 194.

[36] Ibid., 28.

[37] Donald G. Bloesch, *Essentials of Evangelical Theology* (San Francisco: Harper and Row, 1978), 2:225.

[38] Erickson, *How Shall They Be Saved?*, 73.

[39] Clark H. Pinnock, *A Wilderness in God's Mercy: The Finality of Jesus Christ in a World of Religions* (Grand Rapids, MI.: Zondervan, 1992), 171.
[40] McLaren in quoting Kvanvig, *The Last Word*, 188.
[41] Erickson, *How Shall They Be Saved?*, 268.
[42] McLaren, *The Last Word*, 69.
[43] Ibid., 68.
[44] Baker, *Razing Hell*, xiv.
[45] Marshall, "The New Testament Does Not . . .", 72
[46] Ibid., 73-74.
[47] For more, see Noē, *The Perfect Ending for the World*.
[48] Ludlow, "Universalism in the History of Christianity," 207.
[49] MacDonald, *the Evangelical Universalist*, 176.
[50] Stetson, *Christian Universalism*, 133-134.
[51] Bob Ekblad, *A New Christian Manifesto* (Louisville, KY.: Westminster John Knox Press, 2008), 3, 12.
[52] Ibid., 5.
[53] Ibid., 6.
[54] Ibid., 9. This topic will be the subject of a future book from your author and tentatively titled, *Kingdom Christianity: In search of a once-mighty faith*.
[55] Ibid., 134.
[56] Ibid., 138.
[57] Ibid., 139.
[58] Baker, *Razing Hell*, 177.
[59] MacDonald, *The Evangelical Universalist*, 8.

Chapter 17

[1] Whether this is happening currently every day as people die (I think so) or is a future event yet to happen will not be addressed. In this regard, the reader is encouraged and referred, once again, to the author's book, *The Perfect Ending for the World*.
[2] Talbott, "Towards a Better Understanding of Universalism," 5.
[3] Erickson, *How Shall They Be Saved?*, 73.
[4] Chan and Sprinkle, *Erasing Hell*, 118.
[5] Baker, *Razing Hell*, 122.
[6] Stetson, *Christian Universalism*, 104.
[7] Ibid., 100.
[8] Ferguson, *Hell Under Fire*, 236.
[9] MacDonald, *The Evangelical Universalist*, 161.
[10] Stetson, *Christian Universalism*, 101.

[11] (*Hom I* in Ezek 3), quoted in Daley, *The Hope of the Early Church*, 57.

[12] N.T. Wright, *Surprised by Hope*, 20.

[13] Ibid., 181.

[14] Wm. Paul Young, *The Shack*, 125-126.

[15] Erickson, *How Shall They Be Saved?*, 73.

[16] Bell, *Love Wins*, 108.

[17] Amirault, "The Hell Test," 4.

[18] Hanson, *Universalism*, 86.

[19] Bell, *Love Wins*, 104.

[20] Ibid., 106-107.

[21] Ibid., 108.

[22] Ibid., 51.

[23] Baker, *Razing Hell*, 15.

[24] Ibid., 92-93.

[25] Ibid., 96.

[26] Ibid., 98.

[27] Sanders, "A Freewill Theist's Response . . .," in quoting Talbott, 184.

[28] Talbott, "Reply to my Critics," 262.

[29] Billy Graham, "My Answer," *The Indianapolis Star*, July 7, 2011, E-4.

[30] Talbott, "Towards a Better Understanding of Universalism," 7.

[31] Stetson, *Christian Universalism*, 36.

[32] Ibid., 36

[33] McLaren, *The Last Word*, 70.

[34] Hanson, *Universalism*, 157-158. (from the "Dictionary of Christian Biography").

[35] Ibid., 134.

[36] Ibid., 146, 148. (De Prin. I, vi: 1, 2; Selecta in Exodum; also De Prin. I, vi, 3.)

[37] Ibid., 149. (De Prin. II, iii: 5.)

[38] Ibid., 150-151. (De. Prin. II, x : 3, 4. I, i. Ag. Cels. Lv, 13.)

[39] Ibid., 152.

[40] Ibid., 154. (Ag. Cels. VIII. xxix. xi.; Com. II, pp.194, 195.)

[41] Ibid., 120-121. (from "Christian Dot. Period I, Sec. 39.")

[42] Ibid., 117. (Strom. Vii, vi; VI, vi; VII, xiv; VII, ii.)

[43] Ibid., 118. ("Quoted by Neander.")

[44] Ibid., 119.

[45] Ibid., 123.

[46] Ibid., 126.

[47] Ibid., 127.

[48] Ibid., 216-217.

[49] Ibid., 233.

[50] Ibid., 236-237.

[51] Ibid., 238.

[52] Ibid., 228-229.

[53] Ibid., 240-241.

[54] Ibid., 245.

[55] Ibid., 246.

[56] Ibid., 247.

[57] Ibid., 256.

[58] Ibid., 122.

[59] Stetson, *Christian Universalism*, 76.

[60] Ibid., 38.

[61] Ibid., 76.

[62] Ibid., 38.

[63] Ibid., 35.

[64] Ibid., 76.

[65] Talbott, " A Pauline Interpretation . . .," 39.

[66] Talbott, "Reply to my Critics," 249-250.

[67] Ibid., 264.

[68] Ibid., 265.

[69] Baker, *Razing Hell*, 140.

[70] ibid.

[71] Ibid., 102.

[72] Ibid., 98.

[73] Ibid., 103.

[74] Ibid., 17.

[75] Ibid., 20.

[76] Ibid., 76.

[77] Lutzer, *One Minute After You Die*, 9.

[78] Boa and Bowman, *Sense & Nonsense*, 90.

[79] Ibid., 149.

[80] See John Noē, *Peak Performance Principles for High Achievers* (Hollywood, FL.: Frederick Fell Publishers, 2006).

[81] Tony Evans, *What a Way to Live!* (Nashville, TN.: Word Publishing, 1997), 180.

[82] Billy Graham, "My Answer, *The Indianapolis Star*, 6/8/09, C-5.

[83] Grudem, *Systematic Theology*, 1143, 1145.

[84] Ibid., 1148.

[85] Ibid., 1145.

[86] Ibid., 1153.

[87] Randy Alcorn, *In the Light of Eternity* (Colorado Springs, CO.: Waterbrook Press, 1999), 117-118. Alcorn also believes that the eternal destiny of believers in Christ is not in heaven, which is a temporary abode, but in "a New Earth, a

resurrected universe inhabited by resurrected people living with the resurrected Jesus (Revelation 21:1-4)." – Randy Alcorn, *Heaven* (Wheaton, IL.: Tyndale House Publishers, 2004), *xx*. But I disagree. See Noē, *The Perfect Ending for the World*, Chapter 14.

[88] Ibid., 118-120, 122.

[89] Evans, *What a Way to Live!,* 169, 182.

[90] Ladd, *A Theology of the New Testament*, 612.

[91] Alcorn, *In Light of Eternity*, 123.

[92] Rousa John Rushdoony, *The Institutes of Biblical Law* (n.l.: The Presbyterian and Reformed Publishing Company, 1973), 509-510.

[93] Alcorn, *In Light of Eternity*, 142-143.

[94] Keller, *The Reason for God*, 66.

[95] Evans, *What a Way to Live!*, 192.

Conclusion

[1] As my late friend, John Anderson, host of the radio program "The Voice of Reason" was found of saying.

[2] Meacham, "Is Hell Dead?" *Time*, 40.

[3] Brian D. McLaren, *A Generous Orthodoxy* (Grand Rapids, MI.: Zondervan, 2004), 13.

[4] Ibid., 114.

[5] Sanders, "A Freewill Theist's Response to Talbott's Universalism," 185.

[6] Chan and Sprinkle, *Erasing Hell*, 129.

[7] Ibid., 135.

[8] Galli, *God Wins*, 123.

[9] Ibid., 192.

[10] Ibid., 192-193.

[11] Erickson, *How Shall They Be Saved?*, 26.

[12] Grudem, *Systematic Theology*, 1151.

Appendix A

[1] Alcorn, *In Light of Eternity*, 125.

CPSIA information can be obtained at www.ICGtesting.com
Printed in the USA
LVOW051926180812

294901LV00002B/317/P